Augmented Reality - Situated Spatial Synergy

Edited by Michael Cohen

Published in London, United Kingdom

Augmented Reality - Situated Spatial Synergy
http://dx.doi.org/10.5772/intechopen.1005700
Edited by Michael Cohen

Contributors
Ahmed Azough, Alaeddin Nassani, Chi-Ruei Li, Chih-Wei Huang, Chiu-Chun Chen, Delsa Silva Amino Cufuna, Enes Yaşa, Erdem Köymen, Fatima-Zahra Kaghat, Frederico Pereira, Gerardo-M. Sarria-M., Ghina-Alexandra Garcés-Rojas, Gizeh Rangel-de Lazaro, Hsi-Kai Tsou, Jean-Marc Jot, Jens Herder, Josep M. Duart, Khalid Alaoui Zidani, Louis Rosenberg, Maja Michaelis, Mao-Shih Lin, Michael Cohen, Michael Frishkopf, Mihrimah Şenalp, Mohammed Kadri, Scott Smallwood, William L. Martens

First published in London, United Kingdom, 2026 by IntechOpen
IntechOpen is the global imprint of INTECHOPEN LIMITED, registered in England and Wales, registration number: 11086078, 167-169 Great Portland Street, London, W1W 5PF, United Kingdom

For EU product safety concerns: IN TECH d.o.o., Prolaz Marije Krucifikse Kozulić 3, 51000 Rijeka, Croatia, info@intechopen.com or visit our website at intechopen.com.

British Library Cataloguing-in-Publication Data
A catalogue record for this book is available from the British Library

Augmented Reality - Situated Spatial Synergy
Edited by Michael Cohen
p. cm.
Print ISBN 978-1-83634-623-4
Online ISBN 978-1-83634-622-7
eBook (PDF) ISBN 978-1-83634-624-1

If disposing of this product, please recycle the paper responsibly.

Meet the editor

Michael Cohen is Professor Emeritus at the University of Aizu and Adjunct Professor at Higashi Nippon International University, both in Fukushima, Japan. He received his Sc. B. in Electrical Engineering from Brown University (1980), M. S. in Computer Science from the University of Washington (1988), and Ph.D. in Electrical Engineering and Computer Science from Northwestern University (1991). With more than three decades of experience across academia and industry, Cohen was an early pioneer in applying augmented reality to telecommunication and multisensory interaction. His research spans interactive multimedia, mobile and ubiquitous computing, audio windowing and stereotelephony, computer music, digital typography and hypermedia, extended reality (VR/AR/MR), mechatronic and cyberphysical systems, and spectral clustering of recurrence relations. Cohen has authored or co-authored over 200 publications, including 15 book chapters. He serves on the Scientific Committee of the *Journal of Virtual Reality and Broadcasting* and is an Associate Editor of *Presence: Virtual and Augmented Reality*. His professional memberships include ACM, the Audio Engineering Society, and the Virtual Reality Society of Japan. He is also a Senior Member of the IEEE Computer Society.

Contents

Preface

Augmented reality (AR) has emerged as a versatile medium for enhancing human experience across education, design, medicine, architecture, sound, and beyond. This volume brings together diverse perspectives on AR, grouped into four thematic Parts that move from foundational questions to technical advances, practical applications, and critical reflections. Together, these chapters illustrate the breadth of AR research today and suggest directions for its future development.

Section I: Foundations and Frameworks: Education and Learning

1. *Immersive Technologies vs. Traditional Methods in Medical Education: Enhancing Spatial Understanding and Interactivity through AR and VR:* Mohammed Kadri, Fatima-Zahra Kaghat, Ahmed Azough and Khalid Alaoui Zidani provide a comparative framework for assessing immersive tools against conventional pedagogical practices, highlighting their ability to enhance spatial reasoning in medical contexts.

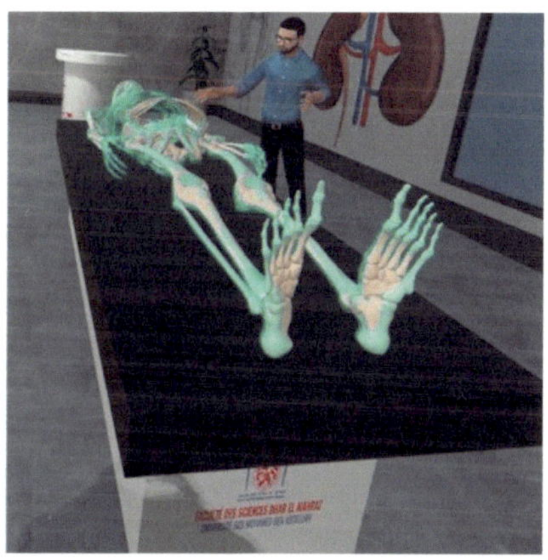

2. *Effects of AR on a Mixed-Media Math Teaching Environment for Primary School Students:* Ghina-Alexandra Garcés-Rojas and Gerardo-M. Sarria-M examine how augmented overlays can enrich primary mathematics education, encouraging engagement and conceptual understanding.

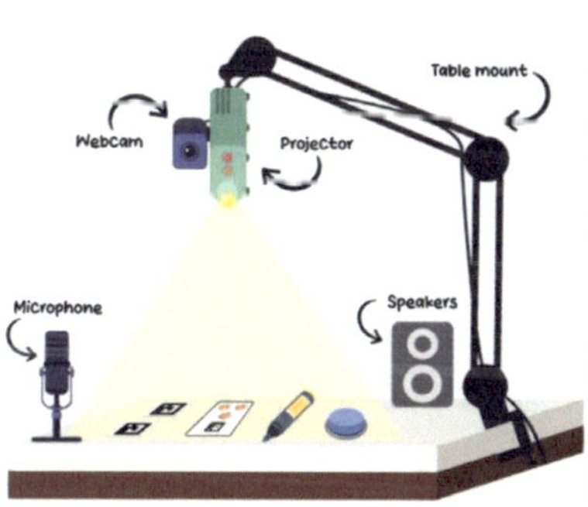

3. *Learning in Informal Educational Spaces: Augmented Reality and Merge Edu in Natural Science Museums:* Delsa Silva Amino Cufuna, Gizeh Rangel-de Lazaro and Josep M. Duart shift focus to informal settings, showing how museum-based AR applications can spark curiosity and deepen science learning outside the classroom.

Section II: Technical Approaches: Sensory Modalities, Perception, and Interaction

4. *Auditory Augmented Reality for Well-Being:* Michael Frishkopf and Scott Smallwood investigate how soundscapes and auditory overlays can foster well-being and immersive affective experience.

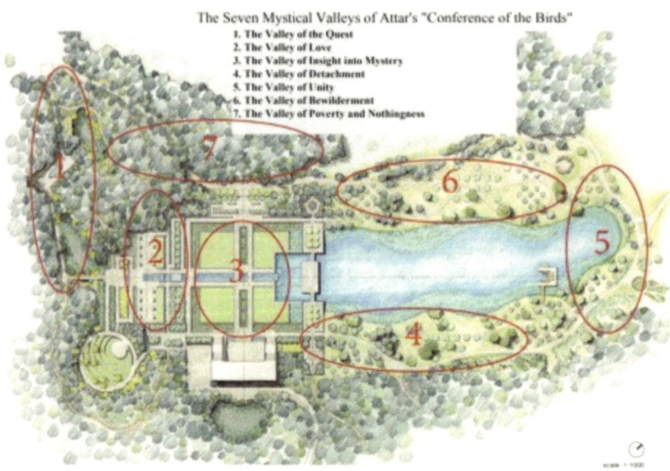

5. *Spatial Sound Rendering for Audio Augmented Reality:* Jean-Marc Jot and Michael Cohen *in*troduce technical strategies for rendering and positioning sound sources in three-dimensional augmented space, enabling more convincing and spatially accurate audio-AR environments.

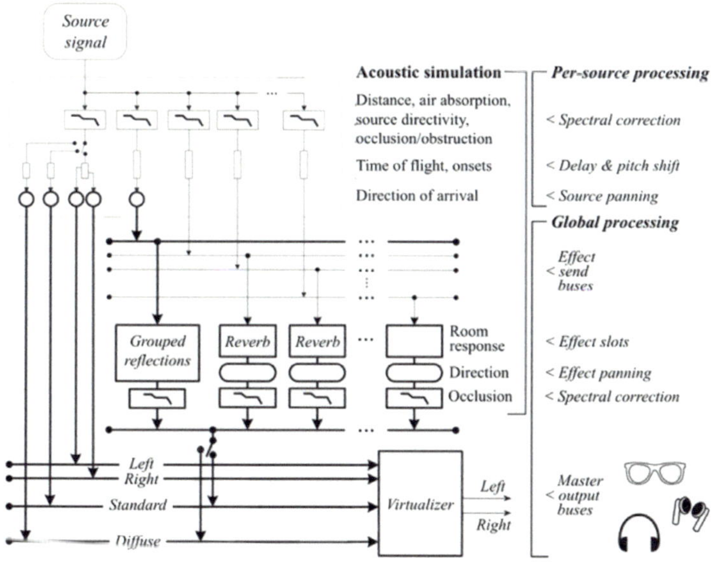

6. *AR Applications That Fail to Support Proper Sensorimotor Coupling Can Result in User Disorientation and Disappointment*: William L. Martens and Frederico Pereira analyze the risks of mismatched sensory cues and warn of disorientation when design principles are neglected.

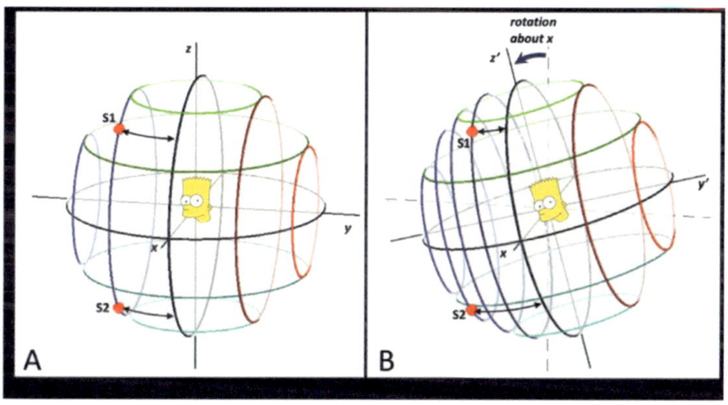

7. *Redirected Seating (RDS) in Helical Space*: Michael Cohen and Alaeddin Nassani explore novel redirected interaction techniques, demonstrating how subtle manipulations of perception can create entirely new spatial and bodily experiences in AR.

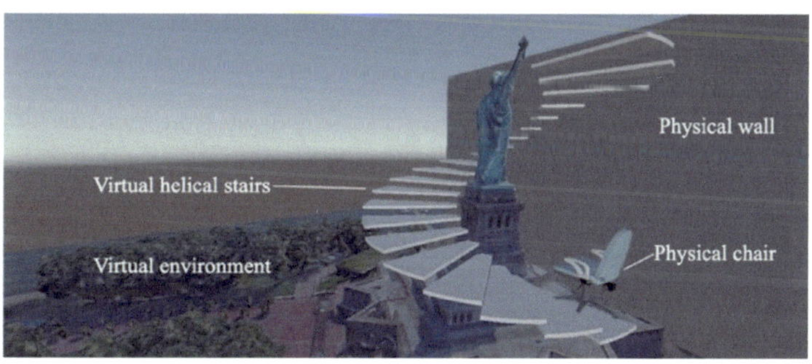

Section III: Applications: Professional and Design Practice

8. *Transforming Neurosurgery with Augmented Reality*: Chih-Wei Huang, Chi-Ruei Li, Mao-Shih Lin, Chiu-Chun Chen and Hsi-Kai Tsou illustrate the high-stakes application of AR in surgical planning and intraoperative guidance, showing its potential to improve precision and safety in neurosurgery.

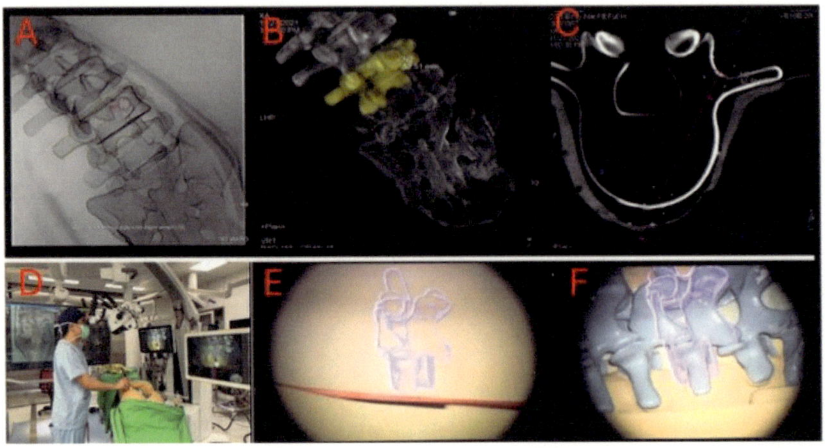

9. *Augmented Reality as a Tool for Improving Energy Efficiency in the Conservation of Heritage Buildings*: Mihrimah Şenalp, Erdem Köymen and Enes Yaşa address the intersection of technology and sustainability, revealing how AR can support conservation practices while promoting energy efficiency in historical architecture.

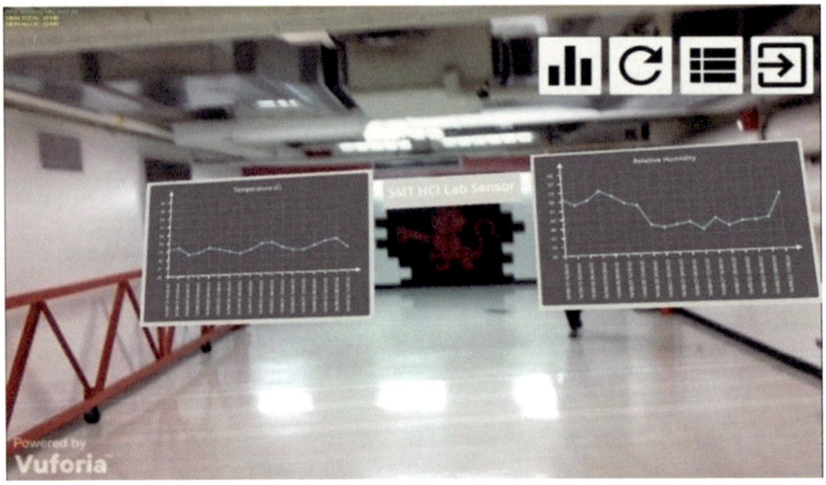

10. *Augmented Reality for Lighting Adjustment in a Virtual Studio*: Maja Michaelis and Jens Herder demonstrate AR's role in the creative industries, where designers use immersive tools to refine lighting and staging in virtual studios, bridging technical rigor with artistic expression.

Section IV: Critical and Societal Perspectives: Ethics and Futures

11. *AI-Powered Augmented Reality as a Threat Vector for Human Manipulation:* Louis Rosenberg issues a timely caution about the capacity of AR, when combined with artificial intelligence, to manipulate perception and behavior, and calls for ethical frameworks to guide future deployment.

Taken together, the chapters in this volume illustrate the dual character of augmented reality: at once a tool for learning, a medium for sensory exploration, a professional instrument, and a site of ethical concern. The diversity of perspectives here, from classroom to operating room, from sound rendering to redirected motion, from heritage preservation to critical warnings, shows both the promise and the complexity of AR as it becomes integrated into human life.

As Academic Editor, I am grateful to all contributors for their insights, and to Process Manager Mia Vulovic for making everything run smoothly. I have been inspired in my career by many great scientists, including Michitaka Hirose, Susumu Tachi, Hiroo Iwata, Yasushi Ikei, Masahiko Inami, Steve Feiner, Mark Billinghurst, and Kouta Minamikawa. I thank former members of the Spatial Media Group at the University of Aizu for gratifying enthusiasm, and professional mentors William Chase, Andries van Dam, Gary Kendall, Woodrow Barfield, Tom Furness, Nobuo Koizumi, Michio Tohyama, Tak Kamae, Tosiyasu Lawrence Kunii, Yôichi Suzuki, and Jens Blauert for their guidance and encouragement.

We hope this anthology will serve as a resource not only for specialists in AR, but also for the broader readership seeking to understand how immersive technologies are reshaping knowledge, practice, and society.

Academic Editor

Michael Cohen
University of Aizu,
Fukushima, Japan

Higashi Nippon International University,
Fukushima, Japan

Section 1

Foundations and Frameworks: Education and Learning

Chapter 1

Immersive Technologies vs. Traditional Methods in Medical Education: Enhancing Spatial Understanding and Interactivity through AR and VR

Mohammed Kadri, Fatima-Zahra Kaghat, Ahmed Azough and Khalid Alaoui Zidani

Abstract

Medical education is increasingly in need of assessing how well emerging immersive technologies stack up against traditional teaching methods. This chapter offers a comparative look at spatial understanding in anatomy education across three approaches: traditional learning (TL), augmented reality (AR), and virtual reality (VR). We examined these teaching methods through a two-phase assessment: pre-test baselines and immediate post-test results. Students were divided into three distinct groups: one following traditional learning methods, another working with an AR anatomy mobile app, and a third using our Immersive Virtual Anatomy Laboratory (IVAL) virtual reality system. This structured evaluation lets us track initial learning gains across all three methods. Our findings show that while both AR and VR outperform TL in immediate knowledge acquisition, VR demonstrates greater effectiveness in our context of spatial learning; however, AR may be better suited for particular use cases requiring portability or layered visualization. These insights offer evidence-based advice for effectively incorporating immersive technologies into medical curricula, taking into account resource limitations and educational goals.

Keywords: virtual reality, augmented reality, immersive technologies, spatial understanding, medical education

1. Introduction

In recent years, medical education has faced the growing challenge of developing pedagogical approaches to anatomy that not only convey factual knowledge but also foster spatial understanding and support long-term retention [1]. Traditional methods often rely on textbooks and 2D images, leading to a superficial understanding of the material, especially when it comes to visualizing complex 3D relationships between anatomical structures [2, 3]. Medical students must have a good understanding of how each part of the human body functions and how each relates to the others. Many studies emphasize the role that spatial understanding plays in knowledge retention [4–6]. However, most universities still teach traditionally, increasing medical students' distress, especially when trying to project flat images into real three-dimensional concepts [7]. The importance of this task is clearly emphasized in clinical practice, where in-depth 3D knowledge is naturally required [8].

In response to these limitations, immersive technologies such as virtual reality (VR) and augmented reality (AR) have emerged as promising tools to revolutionize how anatomy is taught and learned [9, 10]. AR and VR offer unique advantages that directly address the shortcomings of conventional teaching methods. VR employs stereoscopic displays to create a fully immersive environment where students can perceive depth and spatial relationships in a lifelike manner [11]. This immersive quality enhances the sense of presence—the feeling of "being there"—which has been shown to improve both engagement and comprehension. In contrast, AR overlays digital information onto the real world, thereby enriching traditional learning by adding interactive, contextually relevant layers to standard anatomical images [12]. Such real-world integration helps bridge the gap between theoretical knowledge and practical application, making abstract concepts more tangible.

At the heart of these technologies lies a robust theoretical framework based on three key constructs: immersion, presence, and interaction. Immersion refers to the degree to which a VR system can envelop the user in a realistic digital environment, thereby facilitating deep cognitive engagement with the subject matter [13]. Presence captures the user's subjective experience of actually "being" in that virtual space, which enhances the learning experience by making it more memorable [14]. Interaction is the mechanism by which learners actively manipulate virtual models—whether by rotating, zooming, or dissecting them—thus reinforcing spatial and procedural understanding [15]. For example, VR's stereoscopic imaging allows students to perceive subtle depth cues that are critical for accurate anatomical interpretation, while AR's capability to overlay digital content onto real-world views directly supports the identification and contextualization of anatomical structures.

This chapter integrates these theoretical principles into a comprehensive study comparing TL, AR, and VR in anatomical education. By linking the theoretical framework with practical, hands-on experiences, the introduction sets the stage for the experimental study, which is detailed later in the chapter. The subsequent sections describe our methodology, present empirical findings, and discuss the implications of these immersive technologies for modern medical education. In doing so, we aim to demonstrate not only the technical capabilities of AR and VR but also their profound potential to enhance learning outcomes by transforming the way students interact with and understand complex anatomical information.

2. Background: Immersive technologies in medical education

2.1 Augmented reality (AR) in medical education: Definition and key features

AR, in the context of medical education, involves the seamless integration of digital information – including visuals, and potentially auditory or haptic feedback – into the learner's real-world environment in real-time [16]. This augmentation enhances the perception of reality and offers a powerful tool for visualizing abstract anatomical concepts. Unlike VR, which creates a fully immersive digital environment, AR strategically overlays virtual elements onto the physical world, allowing students to interact with both simultaneously [16]. This positions AR within the Extended Reality (XR) spectrum, offering a balance between real-world context and digital enhancement, particularly valuable for anatomy learning.

2.1.1 Defining AR for anatomy education

Building on broader definitions, AR in medical anatomy education can be defined as any interactive system that combines computer-generated virtual anatomical entities with real-world physical elements in real time [16]. Following Azuma's foundational work [17], AR "allows the user to see the real world with virtual objects superimposed, composed, or overlaid," crucially complementing rather than replacing the real environment. In anatomy, this means students can visualize 3D anatomical models overlaid on textbooks, physical models, or even their own bodies, enhancing their understanding of spatial relationships in situations.

2.1.2 Core characteristics of AR systems for anatomical learning

For effective application in anatomy education, AR systems should possess key characteristics [17]:

- *Combination of real scenes and virtual objects*: AR should seamlessly integrate three-dimensional virtual anatomical entities into the real world, providing contextually relevant visualizations. For example, visualizing the skeletal system overlaid on a patient or an anatomical model.

- *Real-time interaction for active learning*: AR systems must enable dynamic, real-time interaction with virtual anatomical content. This interactivity moves beyond passive observation, fostering active exploration and manipulation of anatomical structures, crucial for spatial understanding. This excludes pre-rendered media, such as films, emphasizing live engagement.

- *3D registration for spatial congruence*: Accurate 3D registration is essential. Virtual anatomical objects must be precisely aligned with the real-world environment, ensuring spatial congruence and believable augmentation. Misalignment would hinder spatial understanding rather than enhance it.

2.1.3 Display technologies relevant to medical AR applications

Several display technologies are utilized to implement AR in practical medical applications:

- *Video see-through AR*: In this approach, virtual content is overlaid onto a real-time video feed of the physical environment captured by outward-facing cameras. Users do not see the real world directly through the AR device; instead, they view a combined video stream of the real and virtual elements presented on opaque internal displays. Common examples initially included smartphones and tablets. More recently, sophisticated mixed reality headsets such as the Apple Vision Pro, Meta Quest 3, and HTC Vive XR Elite utilize high-resolution video passthrough technology, effectively operating as advanced video see-through systems for their AR/MR capabilities.

- *Optical see-through AR*: This method uses transparent display surfaces (such as waveguides or specialized lenses) to project virtual content into the user's line of sight while allowing them to see the real world directly through the display. This aims to blend virtual elements more directly into the user's natural field of view. Current devices utilizing this technology include high-end mixed reality headsets like the Microsoft HoloLens 2 and Magic Leap 2, specialized industrial solutions (e.g., Orion), and some consumer-focused smart glasses (e.g., Ray-Ban Meta Smart Glasses). These devices demonstrate various approaches to superimposing virtual visuals onto the real world.

- *Projection-based AR*: In projection-based AR (also known as Spatial AR), projectors are used to cast light, images, or information directly onto real-world surfaces, effectively turning physical objects or spaces into display screens. This method creates an augmented experience without requiring users to wear or hold any personal devices. Examples include location-based entertainment (LBE) projection-mapping experiences, such as those offered by TeamLab and Meow Wolf attractions, as well as industrial applications like projecting assembly instructions onto a workpiece.

2.2 VR in medical education: Definition and key features

2.2.1 VR's impact on anatomy education

VR transcends being merely advanced hardware and software; it is a transformative medium capable of creating a compelling sensory illusion of presence within a digitally constructed environment [18]. For medical education, particularly anatomy, VR offers the potential for deeply immersive and interactive learning experiences. This capability is primarily achieved through three fundamental characteristics: immersion, presence, and interactivity.

2.2.2 Core characteristics of VR systems for anatomy education

- *Immersion for enhanced spatial visualization*: In VR, immersion refers to a VR system's capacity to create a vivid and encompassing illusion of reality. This is achieved through technological capabilities such as high-resolution displays, high refresh rates, high-quality spatial audio, and, in advanced systems, haptic feedback. Immersion bridges the gap between technology and psychological experience, making users feel "inside" a virtual anatomical world [13]. High levels of immersion, especially with stereoscopic 3D and haptic elements, are crucial for effectively conveying the three-dimensional complexity of anatomical structures and spatial relationships. When immersed, learners become less aware of their physical surroundings and more deeply engaged with the simulated anatomical environment.

- *Presence for enhanced engagement and retention*: Closely linked to immersion is presence, the subjective sensation of "being there" in the virtual environment, even while physically located elsewhere [14]. Presence depends on the realism and coherence of the virtual environment. High levels of presence are achieved when sensory inputs and interactions are seamlessly aligned, creating a convincing illusion of spatial and temporal existence within the VR anatomical space. This sense of presence can significantly enhance engagement and potentially improve knowledge retention in anatomy learning.

- *Interactivity for active anatomical exploration*: Interactivity in XR defines the extent to which users can actively engage with and manipulate the virtual world in real time [15]. Realistic interactivity is predicated on intuitive controls (such as hand controllers), precise tracking of movements, and immediate feedback. This enables users to perform natural movements within the virtual anatomy lab, such as virtually grasping, rotating, and examining anatomical structures from any angle. The spatial degrees of freedom (DoF) in VR systems are crucial for enabling natural and intuitive interaction. 6-DoF systems, allowing both translational and rotational tracking, are particularly beneficial for anatomy exploration, mimicking real-world manipulation of physical objects. Combined with interactive tools and haptic feedback, interactivity in VR empowers users to navigate and influence the virtual anatomical environment dynamically, fostering a deeper understanding of spatial relationships through active exploration.

3. Immersive technologies in medical education

The integration of immersive technologies has transformed medical education, particularly in anatomy learning, where spatial understanding is crucial. Recent research demonstrates substantial improvements in learning outcomes, with 63.6% of investigations focusing on practical skills reporting significant performance enhancements [12]. AR and VR have emerged as complementary approaches to enhancing medical education, each offering unique advantages for anatomical learning. Studies show that both technologies significantly improve knowledge retention through experiential learning opportunities, with VR excelling in simulating real-world scenarios [13] and AR making abstract concepts more tangible through interactive visualization [14, 15].

3.1 AR in medical education

AR technology enhances learning by overlaying digital content onto real-world-environments, facilitating immediate understanding and practical application of anatomical knowledge [19]. A comprehensive meta-analysis found that AR significantly improves learning effectiveness, motivation, critical thinking, and practical skills [4]. In a study assessing AR's impact on anatomical education, a validated survey achieved an 85.4% response rate, with participants reporting enhanced spatial relationship comprehension [20]. However, while AR enhances practical skills and overall learning experience, its impact on theoretical knowledge acquisition appears less pronounced compared to traditional methods [12].

3.2 VR in medical education

VR creates fully immersive environments where students can explore and manipulate three-dimensional anatomical structures without real-world distractions [8]. This technology has proven particularly effective in surgical skills development and emergency medicine training [16, 17], addressing resource limitations, especially in low- and middle-income countries (LMIC) [18]. VR's immersive nature facilitates deeper engagement with learning materials, leading to improved retention and understanding of complex anatomical concepts [17, 18].

3.3 Key differences between AR and VR in educational contexts

AR and VR offer distinct advantages in medical education, each catering to different learning objectives. For a detailed comparison of their learning environments and interaction capabilities, see **Table 1**. AR enhances spatial understanding by inserting 3D models into real-world environments, providing contextualized views that bridge theoretical and practical knowledge. It supports situational awareness and real-time collaboration in physical spaces, making it ideal for anatomy visualization and hands-on applications.

In contrast, VR immerses learners in fully virtual environments, enabling in-depth exploration of complex spatial relationships without physical constraints. Its high level of immersion fosters critical thinking and problem-solving in risk-free simulated scenarios, such as virtual labs. While AR is more accessible and cost-effective, VR delivers unparalleled engagement through complete isolation from the physical world. Together, these technologies address diverse educational needs, offering complementary tools for accessibility, skill development, and overcoming challenges in educational contexts. For a comparison of their accessibility, applications, and challenges, see **Table 2**.

Aspect	Augmented reality (AR)	Virtual reality (VR)
Learning environment	Combines real-world settings with virtual overlays for enhanced understanding.	Creates a fully immersive, simulated environment for experiential learning.
Interaction with content	Enables interaction with virtual objects in real-world settings for contextual learning.	Facilitates interaction with entirely virtual objects and environments for active learning.
Immersion level	Medium: learners stay connected to the physical world while interacting with virtual elements.	High: learners are fully immersed in a virtual environment.
Spatial understanding	Overlays 3D models onto physical structures, offering contextualized views.	Offers a fully virtual space to explore and manipulate spatial relationships.
Engagement	Blends physical and digital worlds, enabling real-time collaboration.	Provides total immersion, focusing students on the virtual experience.

Table 1.
Comparison of learning environments and interaction in AR and VR.

Aspect	Augmented reality (AR)	Virtual reality (VR)
Accessibility	Requires smartphones, tablets, or AR glasses; more accessible in classrooms.	Requires specialized hardware such as VR headsets, limiting accessibility.
Applications in education	Ideal for topics needing real-world context, for example, architecture or anatomy.	Suitable for subjects needing full immersion, such as virtual labs or medical training.
Skill development	Enhances situational awareness and hands-on skills in real-world settings.	Builds critical thinking and problem-solving in risk-free environments.
Challenges	Limited immersion may reduce effectiveness in complex simulations.	High costs and technical requirements are barriers to implementation.
Best use cases	Enhancing real-world understanding and linking theory to practice.	Ideal for simulations, virtual labs, and inaccessible environments.

Table 2.
Accessibility, applications, and challenges in AR and VR in education.

4. Methodology: Bridging theory and experimental design

Having established the theoretical foundations for the potential of immersive technologies, particularly AR and VR, to enhance spatial understanding in medical education, this section details the experimental methodology employed to empirically investigate these claims. The study was designed to directly compare the effectiveness of traditional learning and AR/VR methods in improving spatial anatomy knowledge among medical students. This rigorous experimental approach allows us to move beyond theoretical discussions and assess the practical impact of these technologies on learning outcomes. The following subsections outline the specifics of the study, including participant demographics, the learning modalities implemented, the research design, and the experimental procedure.

4.1 Participants

The study included 75 participants, evenly divided into three groups: TL (n = 25), AR (n = 25), and VR (n = 25). The participants in this study were biological and medical students from Sidi Mohamed Ben Abdellah University in Fez, Morocco, with an age range of 18 to 23 years (Means: TL = 19.76, AR = 19.68, VR = 19.72; SDs ≈ 1.1–1.18). The distribution of academic years was consistent across groups, with the majority of participants enrolling in their first or second year (TL: 48% first-year, 44% second-year; AR: 56% first-year, 36% second-year; VR: 44% first-year, 48% second-year). The chi-square test did not reveal a significant difference in AR/VR proficiency levels between the groups ($\chi^2 = 1.332$, df = 3, $p > 0.05$). The majority of participants in both the AR and VR groups indicated high or very high proficiency. The provision of informed consent and the preservation of participant anonymity bolstered the study's ethical and methodological rigor.

4.2 Learning modalities

This study employed three distinct learning modalities, ordered by increasing level of immersion, to evaluate their effectiveness in enhancing spatial understanding and knowledge retention in anatomy education: traditional learning (TL), augmented reality (AR anatomy), and virtual reality (IVAL). TL and AR were selected for comparison as established methods in anatomy education, while IVAL was custom-designed. This progression, from TL to AR to IVAL, follows the reality-virtuality continuum, moving from purely physical learning environments (TL) through augmented reality (AR) to fully immersive virtual experiences (IVAL). Each modality was then carefully structured to deliver the same core anatomical content but through fundamentally different instructional approaches, allowing for a comprehensive and comparative analysis of their effectiveness in fostering spatial learning. The specific platforms and procedures for each learning modality are detailed below, presented in order from the least to the most immersive learning experience.

4.2.1 Traditional learning (TL)

The TL approach, representing the least immersive modality and positioned at the "real environment" end of the reality-virtuality continuum, was the control condition, employing conventional methods widely used in anatomy education (**Figure 1**). This modality provided a baseline for comparison against the immersive technologies. The TL procedure included:

1. *Visualization and identification from 2D resources*: Students begin by visualizing anatomical structures through 2D diagrams and illustrations in standard anatomy textbooks. Using these static visual resources, they identify key anatomical structures and their nomenclature as presented in the textbooks. This step relies on interpreting two-dimensional representations to build an initial understanding of anatomical forms and components.

2. *Conceptual exploration of spatial relationships (Non-interactive)*: Learners then engage in conceptual exploration of spatial relationships based on the 2D information provided. Through careful study of textbook diagrams and written descriptions, they attempt to mentally construct three-dimensional relationships between anatomical structures. This step involves a non-interactive, cognitive effort to infer spatial arrangements from limited visual and textual cues, relying on their spatial reasoning abilities to build a conceptual model.

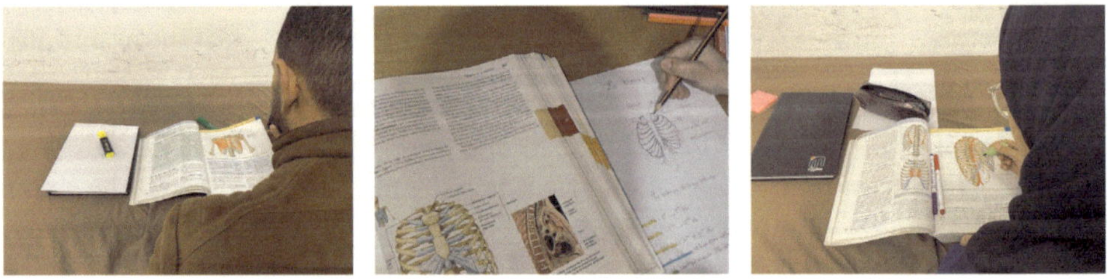

(a) (b) (c)

Figure 1.
Traditional learning (TL) modality: Textbook study. (a) Visualization and identification from 2D resources, (b) Conceptual exploration of spatial relationships, and (c) Knowledge consolidation and self-assessment through review.

3. *Knowledge consolidation and self-assessment through review*: In the final step, students focus on knowledge consolidation and self-assessment. They are encouraged to review the textbook material independently, along with lecture notes and other resources. This self-directed review process serves as the primary method for reinforcing learned material and for students to self-assess their understanding of anatomical concepts and terminology, preparing for later assessments. This step represents the TL equivalent of "practice" by consolidating knowledge through repetition and self-testing.

4.2.2 Augmented reality (AR anatomy)

To represent the AR-based approach, the AR anatomy platform, offering a medium level of immersion and positioned within the "mixed reality" range of the reality-virtuality continuum, was implemented using the "AR anatomy" mobile application [21], accessed on students' personal devices (**Figure 2**). This readily accessible AR application was selected to represent a practical and scalable example of mixed-reality technology currently available for medical education. The AR anatomy app provided a semi-immersive experience by overlaying 3D anatomical models into the user's real-world environment, visually integrating them with the scene, although advanced realism features like dynamic shadow casting were not a primary focus of this particular application. The learning process within the AR anatomy modality involved the following steps:

1. *Visualization and contextualization*: Students begin by visualizing anatomical structures overlaid onto their real-world surroundings using their device's camera. They can contextualize anatomical models within their physical space, resizing, rotating, and examining them from various viewpoints using multitouch controls. This step aims to establish an initial visual understanding within a real-world context, bridging abstract representations with the tangible environment.

2. *Exploration and identification through interactive features*: Learners then engage in interactive exploration of specific anatomical details. Through multitouch controls, they can isolate structures, view cross-sections, and explore anatomical relationships in detail. The application provides labeled structures and descriptions, supporting identification and terminology acquisition through interactive visual exploration

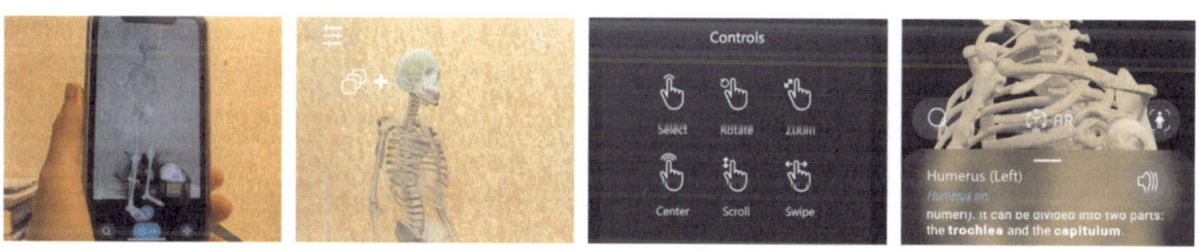

(a) (b) (c) (d)

Figure 2.
Augmented reality (AR anatomy) modality: Mobile application. (a) Visualization and contextualization (b) Exploration and identification (c) Interactive manipulation (d) Knowledge application through quizzes.

3. *Interactive manipulation for enhanced understanding*: This step emphasizes interactive manipulation of the 3D anatomical models. Using multitouch gestures, students can rotate and manipulate the virtual structures directly on their devices. This interactive manipulation, despite being on a 2D screen, still provides a degree of hands-on engagement to enhance understanding of 3D forms and spatial arrangements.

4. *Knowledge application through quizzes and self-assessment*: The final step focuses on knowledge application and self-assessment. Students utilize built-in quizzes and self-assessment tools to test their anatomical knowledge. Immediate feedback on their responses serves to reinforce learning and identify areas for further practice and review. This step emphasizes knowledge consolidation through practice and self-evaluation.

4.2.3 Virtual reality (IVAL)

The immersive virtual anatomy laboratory (IVAL) platform, representing the highest level of immersion in this study's VR condition and positioned at the "virtual environment" end of the reality-virtuality continuum, is a custom-developed VR-based educational tool [22, 23], accessed *via* Meta Quest 2 headsets. IVAL was specifically designed to offer a highly controlled, fully immersive VR learning environment tailored for anatomy education (**Figure 3**). This platform was selected to explore the potential of high-immersion VR for spatial anatomy learning. The IVAL platform facilitated a highly interactive and completely immersive learning environment structured around a four-step learning process designed to maximize spatial understanding:

1. *Visualization and navigation*: Students begin by visualizing anatomical structures within the immersive VR environment. Using intuitive controls such as gaze-based navigation and hand gestures, they navigate freely within the virtual space, examining structures from multiple perspectives. This step is crucial for developing an initial holistic spatial understanding of anatomical arrangements in a 3D context.

2. *Interactive exploration and identification*: Learners then engage in active exploration of specific anatomical structures. Utilizing interactive tools such as a virtual laser pointer and receiving audio feedback, students identify and examine

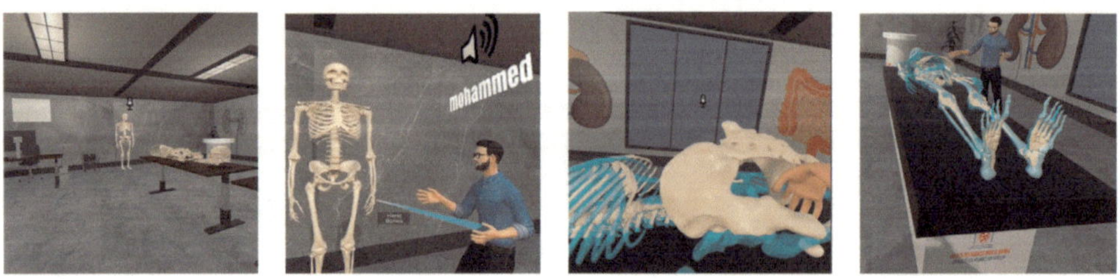

(a) (b) (c) (d)

Figure 3.
Immersive virtual anatomy laboratory (IVAL) modality: VR environment. (a) Visualization and navigation, (b) Interactive exploration and identification, (c) Manipulation and interaction for spatial reasoning, and (d) Knowledge application through placement and practice.

individual bones and their nomenclature. This step combines visual and auditory sensory inputs to reinforce memorization of anatomical components and their names within a spatial context.

3. *Manipulation and interaction for spatial reasoning*: This step focuses on hands-on interaction with virtual anatomical structures. Using bimanual Meta Quest Touch controllers, students can grasp, rotate, and manipulate individual bones, mimicking real-world handling. This direct manipulation is designed to enhance spatial reasoning skills by allowing learners to actively explore the three-dimensional form and spatial relationships of anatomical parts.

4. *Knowledge application through placement and practice*: In the final step, students apply their acquired spatial knowledge through a practical task. They must position virtual bones correctly onto a virtual skeleton model. Immediate feedback is provided to validate their understanding and reinforce accurate spatial placement, solidifying learning through application and practice.

While all three modalities deliver identical core anatomical content, their instructional processes differ in structure and emphasis. Traditional learning consists of a linear, three-step process that emphasizes the visual nature of the material, an introduction to exploratory concepts or processes and assessment. We added an interactive phase to the AR anatomy method, introducing a fourth step: learners are able to touch and therefore augment their learning through touch as well as seeing and exploring. Virtual Reality (IVAL) can take these steps further by offering highly immersive, hands-on interaction in a unified experience that combines exploration and manipulation seamlessly. This comparative framework highlights how different levels of immersion—ranging from simpler TL to more complex AR to our equivalent IVAL—provides increasingly rich environments for developing spatial understanding for these modalities while noting that each modality's approach is specific to its own adopted technological and pedagogical affordances.

4.3 Research design and data collection

This study employed a between-subjects experimental design to compare the impact of traditional learning (TL), augmented reality (AR), and virtual reality (VR) on spatial understanding in anatomy education. Participants were randomly assigned to one of three groups: TL, AR, or VR. The independent variable was the learning modality (TL, AR, and VR), while the dependent variable was spatial understanding, assessed through pre-test and post-test evaluations.

To measure learning outcomes, we designed an anatomical vocabulary test focused on spatial understanding. This test included six multiple-choice questions (see the Appendixes), with three administered before the learning session (pre-test) and three after (post-test). The questions, carefully selected by medical experts, required participants to identify anatomical structures from images. Different questions were used in the pre-test and post-test to minimize recall bias and ensure a more accurate measurement of learning progression.

4.4 Procedure

The study commenced with obtaining ethical approval and informed consent from all participants. Initially, participants underwent a pre-test spatial understanding quiz to establish their baseline knowledge. After that, we randomly assigned participants to one of three groups: TL, AR, and VR. The traditional methods group studied using textbooks and 2D diagrams, the AR group interacted with anatomical structures using an AR platform, and the VR group experienced an immersive learning environment through IVAL. As illustrated in **Figure 4**, the procedure included a structured flow from pre-test to assigned learning modality and post-test, ensuring systematic approach to data collection and analysis. Post-intervention, participants completed a post-test quiz to evaluate improvements in spatial understanding. We conducted the study in a controlled laboratory setting to ensure consistency across all groups.

5. Results and discussion

5.1 Findings

Table 3 presents the descriptive statistics for the pre-test and post-test scores of the three groups: TL, AR, and VR. The TL group did not show a significant improvement from pre-test ($M = 2.44$, $SD = 0.69$) to post-test ($M = 2.84$, $SD = 0.92$), with ANOVA results ($F(1.48) = 2.86$, $p = 0.097$) and pairwise t-test ($t(24) = -4.00$, $p = 0.0005$, $d = 0.48$). The AR group demonstrated a significant improvement from pre-test ($M = 2.68$, $SD = 0.88$) to post-test ($M = 3.52$, $SD = 0.57$), with ANOVA results ($F(1.48) = 15.295$, $p = 0.0003$) and pairwise t-test ($t(24) = -8.89$, $p < 0.001$, $d = 1.11$). The VR group showed a significant improvement from pre-test ($M = 2.52$, $SD = 0.70$) to post-test ($M = 3.88$, $SD = 0.32$), as indicated by the ANOVA results ($F(1,48) = 74.58$, $p < 0.001$) and pairwise t-test ($t(24) = -10.66$, $p < 0.001$, $d = 2.44$).

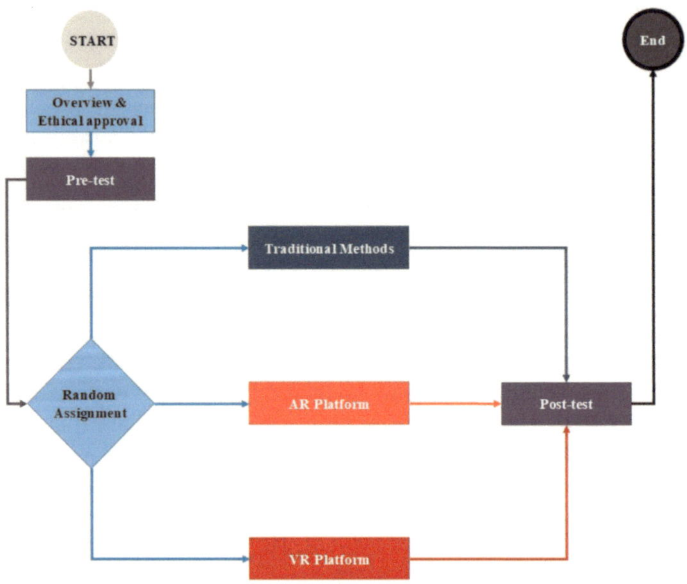

Figure 4.
Overview of the study procedure.

	Pre-test		Post-test		N
Group	**Mean**	**SD**	**Mean**	**SD**	
TL	2.44	0.69	2.84	0.92	25
AR	2.68	0.88	3.52	0.57	25
VR	2.52	0.70	3.88	0.32	25

Table 3.
Descriptive statistics for pre-test and post-test scores.

5.2 Discussion

The findings of this study provide robust evidence supporting the value of immersive technologies in enhancing spatial understanding when compared to traditional learning (TL) methods. While all three conditions led to learning gains, the traditional group showed the lowest post-test performance, as detailed in **Table 3** (descriptive statistics) and **Table 4** (comprehensive T-test analysis). Furthermore, retention rates for the TL group, illustrated in **Figure 5**, were notably lower (10.39%) compared to the other conditions, suggesting that traditional methods may be less effective for long-term knowledge retention in this context. The AR group demonstrated higher post-test scores and improved retention than TL, indicating the benefits of spatial overlays and interactive content in supporting learners' spatial cognition. However, the AR condition still lagged slightly behind VR in terms of engagement and performance. Among the three modalities, the VR group (IVAL) exhibited the strongest performance, both in immediate post-test results and long-term retention. This may be attributed to the immersive, hands-on experience offered by VR, which supports deeper cognitive processing. Nevertheless, it is important to note that these findings are context-specific and that alternative tasks, tools, or participant populations may yield different results.

5.2.1 TL shows limited improvement

TL group showed only modest improvement, with a mean increase of 0.40 points from pre-test (M = 2.44, SD = 0.69) to post-test (M = 2.84, SD = 0.92), as shown in **Table 3**. The effect size was small (**Table 5**) Cohen's d = 0.48, and the improvement

Phase	Comparison	t-statistic	p-value	Cohen's d	Effect size
Pre-test	VR vs. AR	−0.6963	0.4896	0.1969	Small
	VR vs. TL	0.3967	0.6933	−0.1122	Small
	AR vs. TL	1.0458	0.3009	−0.2958	Small
	VR vs. AR	2.673	0.010	−0.756	Medium
Post-test	VR vs. TL	5.2000	0.0000	−1.4708	Large
	AR vs. TL	3.062	0.004	−0.866	Large

Table 4.
Comprehensive T-test analysis.

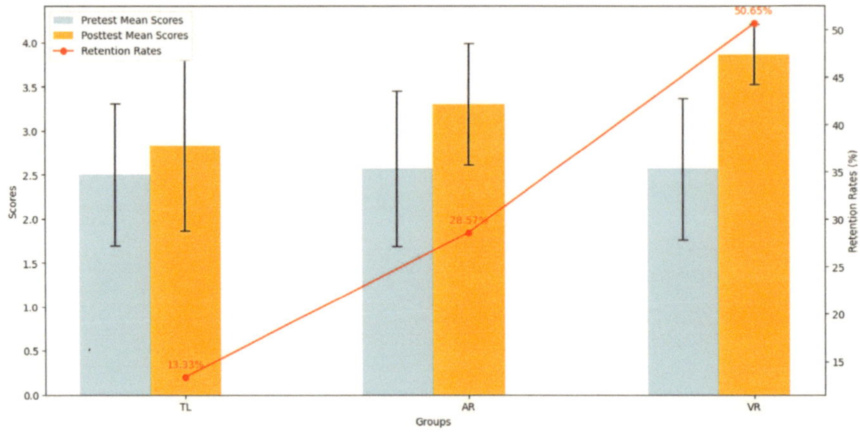

Figure 5.
Pre- vs. post-test scores and retention rates by group.

Group	t-statistic	p-value	Cohen's d	Effect size
TL	−4.000	0.0005	0.479	Small
AR	−8.887	0.0000	1.106	Large
VR	−10.663	0.0000	2.443	Large

Table 5.
Pre- and post-test pairwise comparison.

was not statistically significant ($p = 0.097$). This highlights the limitations of traditional teaching methods in fostering spatial understanding, as they often rely on passive learning and lack the interactive and immersive elements that AR and VR provide.

5.2.2 AR outperforms TL with a large effect size

The AR group also demonstrated significant improvement, with a mean increase of 0.84 points from pre-test ($M = 2.68$, $SD = 0.88$) to post-test ($M = 3.52$, $SD = 0.57$), as shown in **Table 3**. This improvement was supported by a large effect size (**Table 5**) Cohen's $d = 1.11$. As highlighted in **Table 4**, the post-test comparison between AR and TL revealed a large effect size ($t = 3.06$, $p = 0.004$, $d = -0.87$), indicating that AR significantly outperformed TL. The effectiveness of AR can be attributed to its ability to overlay spatially relevant information onto the real world, providing learners with dynamic visual cues and interactive elements that enhance spatial reasoning. This suggests that AR, while less immersive than VR, still offers a significant advantage over traditional methods by making abstract spatial concepts more tangible and accessible.

5.2.3 VR outperforms TL with a large effect size

As shown in **Table 4**, the VR group significantly outperformed the TL group, with a large effect size ($t = 5.20$, $p < 0.001$, $d = -1.47$). The mean post-test score for the

VR group (M = 3.88, SD = 0.32), as presented in **Table 3**, was significantly higher than that of the TL group (M = 2.84, SD = 0.92). This large effect size underscores the transformative potential of VR in enhancing spatial understanding compared to traditional methods. Immersive and interactive nature of VR allows learners to engage with spatial concepts in ways that are not possible with static, traditional teaching approaches.

5.2.4 VR outperforms AR with a medium effect size

The VR group showed the largest improvement, with a mean increase of 1.36 points from pre-test (M = 2.52, SD = 0.70) to post-test (M = 3.88, SD = 0.32), as shown in **Table 3**. This improvement was supported by a large effect size of Cohen's d = 2.44 (**Table 5**). As seen in **Table 4**, the post-test comparison between AR and VR revealed a medium effect size (t = 2.67, p = 0.010, d = −0.76), indicating that VR significantly outperformed AR. This superiority can be attributed to the immersive nature of VR, which provides a fully interactive and engaging environment. The high level of immersion in VR likely enhances spatial understanding by allowing learners to manipulate and explore spatial concepts in a more intuitive and hands-on manner.

6. Conclusion

6.1 Summary of key findings and implications for medical education

This study compared TL, AR, and VR conditions for enhancing spatial understanding in anatomy education among medical students. The key findings, supported by ANOVA and t-test analyses, demonstrate the superior effectiveness of both AR- and VR-based pedagogies over traditional learning for immediate knowledge acquisition. Specifically:

- Traditional learning (TL) resulted in the smallest learning gains, with only a modest improvement and a small to medium effect size (Cohen's d = 0.48), significantly lower than both AR and VR.

- Augmented reality (AR anatomy) also demonstrated a substantial and statistically significant improvement over traditional learning, with a large effect size (Cohen's d = 1.11), although to a lesser extent than VR.

- Virtual reality (IVAL) significantly outperformed all other modalities, showing the largest learning gains with a large effect size (Cohen's d = 2.44) and achieving the highest post-test scores.

These statistically significant results have potential implications for consideration in medical education. Recognizing that effective anatomy instruction is crucial and that traditional methods may have limitations in conveying certain spatial aspects, the AR and VR applications used in this study present evidence-based options. The findings highlight that such immersive technologies can contribute to anatomy learning, specifically by facilitating the transition from 2D resources to 3D spatial understanding important for healthcare professionals. However, these results pertain to the specific implementations studied, and the optimal integration of such tools likely depends on various contextual factors.

6.2 Limitations

While the statistically significant findings of this study are promising, several limitations warrant consideration. Firstly, the modest sample size, drawn from a single university in Morocco, limits the generalizability of the results to diverse student populations, varying cultural contexts, or different levels of technological access. Future research should address this by including larger and more diverse samples. Secondly, the study's conclusions are specific to the AR (AR anatomy) and VR (IVAL) platforms evaluated. Given the platform-dependent nature of immersive technology outcomes, these findings cannot be generalized to all AR or VR applications; further research should compare a broader range of platforms. Thirdly, this study only assessed immediate post-intervention learning gains, and thus, the long-term retention of spatial understanding remains unexamined. Longitudinal studies with delayed post-tests are necessary to evaluate the durability of learning. Finally, although statistically addressed, the use of self-reported AR/VR proficiency introduces a potential for selection bias, as subtle pre-existing differences in attitudes or aptitudes for technology cannot be entirely excluded. Despite these limitations, this study provides valuable initial insights into the comparative effectiveness of AR and VR for enhancing spatial understanding in anatomy education within the studied context, strongly suggesting the pedagogical promise of immersive technologies for this learning outcome.

6.3 Future directions

Future research should consider longitudinal studies to track retention of spatial understanding over extended periods. Additionally, correlational studies that explore the relationship between learning outcomes and subjective experiences with the technologies could provide valuable insights. It would also be beneficial to investigate the practical implementation of AR and VR in educational settings, including cost-effectiveness and the role of instructor training in maximizing the potential of these technologies. Exploring how these technologies can be integrated into existing curricula and examining their impact on different learner types are also important areas for future exploration.

In conclusion, this study's findings give evidence of the effectiveness of both AR and VR in anatomy education, enhancing spatial understanding. Although VR generally performed better overall—the quickest learning gains in our experimental conditions—different modalities have unique benefits. In environments where technology resources are limited or self-paced, low-cost study is desired, traditional learning (TL) is still an attractive option. In general, these findings suggest that the successful adoption (uptake) of a modality depends on a selection process that balances performance metrics with crucial contextual factors, such as resource availability and learning preferences. In essence, AR's situated, real-world overlay may be not only more accessible but also more appropriate in contexts where portability, ease of integration, or contextually based interactions are of utmost importance. While the findings are promising, further research is needed to fully understand the long-term benefits and practical applications of these technologies in education.

Author details

Mohammed Kadri[1]*, Fatima-Zahra Kaghat[2], Ahmed Azough[2] and Khalid Alaoui Zidani[1]

1 Faculty of Sciences Dhar El Mahraz, Sidi Mohamed Ben Abdellah University, Fez, Morocco

2 Research Center, Léonard de Vinci Pôle Universitaire, Paris La Défense, France

*Address all correspondence to: mohammed.kadri1@usmba.ac.ma

References

[1] Mantovani F, Castelnuovo G, Gaggioli A, Riva G. Virtual reality training for health-care professionals. Cyber Psychology and Behavior. 2003; **6**(4):389-395. DOI: 10.1089/109493103322278772

[2] Freer F, Ail G, Chan T, Jones M, Broad J, Canale GP, et al. Out With the Old, in With the New? Virtual Reality vs. Cadaveric Based Teaching Materials for Anatomy Education. British Journal of Surgery. 2024;**111**(6). DOI: 10.1093/bjs/znae163.315

[3] Veeraraghavan VP. Comparing the benefits and drawbacks of traditional and online anatomy learning in medical education. Medical Science Educator. 2024;**34**(2):501-501. DOI: 10.1007/s40670-024-01986-1

[4] Yammine K, Violato C. A meta-analysis of the educational effectiveness of three-dimensional visualization technologies in teaching anatomy. Anatomical Sciences Education. 2014; **8**(6):525-538. DOI: 10.1002/ase.1510

[5] Langlois J, Bellemare C, Toulouse J, Wells GA. Spatial abilities and anatomy knowledge assessment: A systematic review. Anatomical Sciences Education. 2016;**10**(3):235-241. DOI: 10.1002/ase.1655

[6] Pambudi PS, Setyaningrum W, Retnawati H, Sugiman. Augmented Reality to Improve Self-Regulated Learning and Spatial Ability. Volume 2575. Melville, New York, USA: AIP Publishing; 2022. p. 050022. DOI: 10.1063/5.0111057

[7] Koney NK-K, Ansah AO, Asaku BNA, Ahenkorah J, Hottor BA, Adutwum-Ofosu K, et al. Anatomage virtual dissection versus traditional human body dissection in anatomy pedagogy: Insights from ghanaian medical students. BMC Medical Education. 2024;**24**(1):ISSN 1472-6920. DOI: 10.1186/s12909-024-06029-2

[8] Liu Y-Q. Virtual reality: The bridge between medical education and clinical practice. World Journal of Clinical Cases. 2024;**12**(32):6575-6579. DOI: 10.12998/wjcc.v12.i32.6575

[9] Tene T, López DFV, Aguirre PEV, Puente LMO, Gomez CV. Virtual reality and augmented reality in medical education: An umbrella review. Frontiers in Digital Health. 2024;**6**. Article no: 1365345. DOI: 10.3389/fdgth.2024.1365345

[10] Li X, Elnagar D, Song G, Ghannam R. Advancing medical education using virtual and augmented reality in low- and middle-income countries: A systematic and critical review. Virtual Worlds. 2024;**3**(3): 384-403. DOI: 10.3390/virtualworlds3030021

[11] Neyem A, Cadile M, Burgos-Martínez SA, Cabello EF, Inzunza O, Alvarado MS, et al. Enhancing medical anatomy education with the integration of virtual reality into traditional lab settings. Clinical Anatomy. 2024;**38**:249-268. DOI: 10.1002/ca.24213

[12] Korre D, Sherlock A. Augmented Reality in Higher Education: A Case Study in Medical Education. iLRN2023. Montana, USA: The Immersive Learning Research Network; 2023. pp. 95-98. DOI: 10.56198/itig293lt

[13] Slater M, Steed A, McCarthy J, Maringelli F. The influence of body movement on subjective presence in virtual environments. Human Factors:

The Journal of the Human Factors and Ergonomics Society. 1998;**40**(3): 469-477. DOI: 10.1518/001872098779591368

[14] Witmer BG, Singer MJ. Measuring presence in virtual environments: A presence questionnaire. Presence Teleoperators and Virtual Environments. 1998;**7**(3):225-240. DOI: 10.1162/105474698565686

[15] Steuer J. Defining virtual reality: Dimensions determining telepresence. Journal of Communication. 1992;**42**(4): 73-93. DOI: 10.1111/j.1460-2466.1992.tb00812.x

[16] Azuma RT. A survey of augmented reality. Presence Teleoperators and Virtual Environments. 1997;**6**(4): 355-385. DOI: 10.1162/pres.1997.6.4.355

[17] Azuma R, Baillot Y, Behringer R, Feiner S, Julier S, Mac Intyre B. Recent advances in augmented reality. IEEE Computer Graphics and Applications. 2001;**21**(6):34-47. DOI: 10.1109/38.963459

[18] Biocca F, Levy MR, editors. Communication in the Age of Virtual Reality. London, England: Routledge; 2013. DOI: 10.4324/9781410603128

[19] Tamam B, Corebima AD. Implementing augmented reality to improve students' biology learning outcomes: Gender-based effect. International Journal of Evaluation and Research in Education (IJERE). 2023; **12**(4):2157. DOI: 10.11591/ijere.v12i4.25645

[20] Tavanti M, Lind M. 2d vs 3d, implications on spatial memory. In: IEEE Symposium on Information Visualization. Piscataway, New Jersey, USA: IEEE; 2001. INFOVIS 2001. pp. 139-145. DOI: 10.1109/infvis.2001.963291

[21] Virtual Medicine. Virtual Medicine: AR Anatomy - 3d Atlas of Human Body; 2024. Available from: https://play.google.com/store/apps/details?id=com.virtualmedicine.aranatomy

[22] Kadri M, Boubakri F-E, Kaghat F-Z, Azough A, Zidani KA. Ival: Immersive virtual anatomy laboratory for enhancing medical education based on virtual reality and serious games, design, implementation, and evaluation. Entertainment Computing. 2024;**49**: 100624. DOI: 10.1016/j.entcom.2023.100624

[23] Kadri M, Boubakri F-E, Teo T, Kaghat F-Z, Azough A, Zidani KA. Virtual reality in medical education: Effectiveness of immersive virtual anatomy laboratory (ival) compared to traditional learning approaches. Displays. 2024;**85**:102870. DOI: 10.1016/j.displa.2024.102870

Chapter 2

Effects of AR on a Mixed-Media Math Teaching Environment for Primary School Students

Ghina-Alexandra Garcés-Rojas and Gerardo-M. Sarria-M.

Abstract

This chapter serves as a proof-of-concept (PoC) for an AR-based mixed-media system in early mathematics education. It explores the impact of an interactive system that incorporates Augmented Reality (AR) to teach foundational mathematical concepts to bilingual children aged 6–10. The target audience consisted of students who had previously participated in an intensive mathematics program due to persistent difficulties in understanding the concept of number. Observations and initial assessments using their school's digital learning platform revealed significant challenges in completing basic numerical exercises. An exploratory implementation was conducted to evaluate the effectiveness of the proposed system, comparing student performance with and without the mixed-device approach. The results indicate notable improvements in task efficiency and accuracy when using the interactive system. Although this exploration does not constitute a controlled experiment with randomized trials, the observed benefits align with prior research on the role of interactive and embodied learning in mathematics education. AR-based learning environments have been shown to enhance engagement, reduce cognitive load, and support conceptual understanding by providing dynamic, hands-on interaction with abstract ideas. The findings suggest that the integration of AR and mixed-media tools into early mathematics education can positively influence learning outcomes, warranting further investigation through larger-scale studies.

Keywords: numeracy, learning environment, mixed media, digital learning tools, physical manipulatives, educational technology

1. Introduction

Integration of technology in contemporary education has been instrumental in promoting equity and inclusion by democratizing access to diverse information sources and enabling flexible, student-centered learning experiences. This advancement represents a pivotal shift in teaching and learning paradigms. However, despite these benefits, the incorporation of technology often fails to adequately address the unique needs of young learners. Most of the educational applications used in classrooms focus on digitizing mathematical concepts, relying heavily on screen-based interactions to make education portable. While these methods are convenient, they often fail to engage students deeply or foster meaningful understanding. This is particularly evident in mathematics, where abstract concepts demand a more tangible and interactive approach to learning.

Traditional screen-based educational tools have significant limitations. Research indicates that students retain less information and engage in shallower cognitive processing when interacting with screens compared to physical media. This phenomenon, known as "screen inferiority," is exacerbated by the repetitive and unisensory nature of most digital learning tools. The problem with a lot of these applications is that they do not take into account the way the human brain has been learning for millennia, which is a process that includes the entire variety of physical stimuli. These tools typically engage only vision and, occasionally, the auditory senses, neglecting the potential of tactile and kinesthetic interactions to create deeper neural connections and enhance memory retention.

1.1 Augmented reality and pedagogy

This PoC explores the potential of Augmented Reality (AR) technology in overcoming these limitations by integrating interactive and tangible elements into mathematical learning environments.

1.2 PoC: AR-based mathematical learning system

An exploratory implementation is presented to illustrate the application of AR in early mathematics education. The investigated learning system utilized AR technology to transform abstract mathematical concepts into interactive physical media. Through this system, learners engaged with mathematical representations via real-world interactions aided by AR. Results indicate measurable improvement in both concept comprehension and learner engagement, highlighting the potential of AR to enhance mathematical education.

Due to the very limited scope of the PoC in question, which focused on a single very basic concept in the early math learning process, the whole range of applicability of AR technology is not explored. Despite that, this chapter also provides examples of how it could be further integrated into educational applications with a wider scope, both in math and in other areas of knowledge.

2. Background

The integration of technology into education has encountered numerous challenges, primarily due to an overemphasis on portability and accessibility via screen-based platforms rather than the pedagogical efficacy of these media. Current educational technology frequently neglects the fundamental conditions necessary for effective learning, prioritizing digital accessibility over cognitive engagement and comprehension.

This section examines empirical studies that have shown effective and ineffective learning methodologies with a specific focus on mathematics education. This discussion serves as a foundation for understanding the potential role of emerging technologies, such as AR, in addressing existing limitations.

2.1 Semiotic representations of Duval

The theory of semiotic representations in mathematics, developed by French researcher Raymond Duval, explores the diverse ways mathematical concepts are conveyed. These representations include symbolic notation, natural language, graphical elements, and diagrammatic tools, all of which contribute to meaning construction and conceptual understanding. Duval categorizes these semiotic systems into iconic, discursive, and symbolic representations [1].

According to Duval, mathematical comprehension is deepened by transitioning between multiple semiotic representations, as each provides unique cognitive affordances. The interplay among these representations facilitates flexible problem-solving and a more profound grasp of mathematical structures. In early mathematics education, Duval advocates for integrating concrete actions with visual representations and symbolic manipulations to effectively scaffold learning [1].

One of the major pedagogical challenges is guiding learners through the transition from visual to symbolic representation systems, a process in which oral language plays a pivotal intermediary role. Young learners often struggle to independently establish these interconnections, necessitating instructional strategies that present multiple representations simultaneously. Ensuring that these associations are effectively developed is crucial to foster a robust mathematical foundation.

2.2 Screen inferiority

Research has demonstrated that contemporary virtual education often suffers from "screen inferiority," a phenomenon wherein students exhibit lower retention and comprehension when engaging with digital texts as opposed to printed materials. Empirical studies indicate that learners tend to perform worse on assessments following screen-based reading, often displaying overconfidence in their perceived knowledge, which results in shorter study durations and diminished outcomes compared to those who engage with print media. Psychological research [2] suggests that cognitive and behavioral disparities arise depending on the medium through which information is conveyed. Specifically, screen-based content presentation typically encourages faster, more superficial reading strategies, leading to reduced comprehension.

Moreover, findings suggest that digital reading is more conducive to scanning and keyword-based searching rather than deep engagement with textual content. Studies further propose that the medium itself serves as a contextual cue in information retrieval, prompting individuals to allocate fewer cognitive resources toward comprehension and metacognitive processes [2].

Neuro-scientific research [2] has underscored the cognitive benefits of physical engagement in learning activities. Studies reveal that movement and interaction with tangible materials stimulate more extensive neural connectivity than passive screen interaction. These enriched connectivity patterns are crucial for memory formation and the encoding of new information, thereby enhancing learning efficacy [2].

Further evidence from research on neural plasticity suggests that proprioceptive and visual integration, facilitated by controlled hand movements, play a significant role in shaping brain connectivity patterns relevant to learning [2]. For instance, studies comparing handwriting to typing have demonstrated that the intricate motor movements associated with handwriting elicit more widespread theta/alpha connectivity coherence patterns between critical neural hubs, reinforcing the cognitive benefits of multi-sensory engagement in learning [2].

While early research on screen inferiority predominantly focused on extended reading tasks, recent studies [3] have confirmed similar deficiencies in comprehension even for brief digital reading exercises. Evidence suggests that the contextual characteristics of electronic devices trigger cognitive patterns associated with shallow processing, ultimately impairing reasoning and problem-solving abilities [4]. Furthermore, these deficits appear to be modality-independent, affecting both multiple-choice and open-ended assessments alike. Interestingly, even individuals who express a preference for digital media tend to revert to paper when faced with complex mathematical problem-solving tasks. Research indicates that "while in-depth text processing is the default in print media, an external trigger is required to activate such engagement in digital formats" [3].

2.3 Multi-sensory approaches in mathematics education

Mathematics education presents unique cognitive challenges, requiring abstract reasoning and problem-solving skills that can induce anxiety and disengagement in young learners. Multi-sensory instructional approaches have been identified as effective in mitigating these challenges by engaging multiple sensory modalities—visual, auditory, kinesthetic, and tactile—to enhance comprehension and cognitive retention [5]. Empirical evidence supports the premise that integrating multi-sensory experiences fosters deeper neural connectivity, enabling students to approach mathematical concepts from multiple perspectives and solidify their understanding.

Pedagogically sound mathematics instruction incorporates physical manipulatives, interactive games, counters, and spatial models to facilitate the representation of abstract mathematical concepts. Such tools help construct mental frameworks that support various types of mathematical reasoning, including numerical systems, geometric structures, probabilistic analysis, and algebraic relationships [5]. A foundational aspect of early mathematics education involves fostering understanding of mathematical relationships and operations within meaningful problem-solving contexts.

Still, prevailing digital educational tools frequently fail to align with these pedagogical principles. According to Rojas [6], many mathematics software programs emphasize repetitive drilling over conceptual understanding, provide inadequate scaffolding, and restrict learner autonomy by relying predominantly on keyboard-based input. This unisensory approach undermines cognitive engagement and neglects the benefits of sensory integration.

To address these limitations, educational technology must evolve toward a paradigm that emphasizes embodied cognition and multi-sensory engagement. Mishra, Henriksen, and the Deep-Play Research Group [7] advocate for the development of digital learning environments that support transdisciplinary, interactive, and project-based learning experience. Such innovations should prioritize cross-modal sensory involvement to enhance cognitive processing and conceptual retention.

Traditional mathematics instruction has historically been unisensory, predominantly relying on visual inputs through textbooks and whiteboards. However, given that human cognition naturally integrates information from multiple sensory channels, incorporating multi-sensory learning strategies significantly enhances conceptual understanding [5]. Research has demonstrated that integration of all senses, though developing relatively late in early childhood, can be accelerated through deliberate educational interventions. There are also indications that early exposure to multimodal learning environments strengthens neural connectivity and facilitates acquisition of foundational mathematical competencies [5].

2.4 The role of manipulatives in mathematics education

The integration of manipulatives, physical objects used to explore mathematical concepts, has a long-standing tradition in mathematics education. Nemirovsky et al. suggest that engagement with manipulatives fosters deeper cognitive insights and more intense mathematical interactions compared to visual representations alone [8]. While the mere presence of manipulatives does not guarantee automatic learning, they provide a learning experience that is difficult to replicate through digital screens. A key distinction lies in their ability to incorporate tactile and proprioceptive (kinesthetic) feedback into mathematical problem-solving, enhancing depth of conceptual understanding.

A contemporary perspective, known as exploratory vision, posits that vision is inherently integrated with other sensory modalities and motor actions. According to this model, static visual representations alone fail to fully engage the perceptual system, whereas complementary sensory inputs enhance completeness of the information processed [8]. This perspective aligns with earlier work by Poincaré, who emphasized the critical role of bodily movement in spatial cognition, arguing that "the localization of objects in space is conceived through muscular sensations that accompany real or imaginary movements within that space" [9].

Empirical studies have demonstrated that children using manipulatives in mathematical problem-solving not only generate a greater number of solutions but also adopt more conceptually developed strategies. Their approaches exhibit systematic relational reasoning, whereby consecutive solutions are linked coherently within the problem space, fostering deeper exploration of permutations and variations [10]. These findings highlight the pedagogical value of manipulatives in cultivating abstract mathematical reasoning through embodied interaction.

2.5 Proprioception in learning

Proprioception, commonly referred to as kinesthesia, is the body's intrinsic ability to sense movement, position, and spatial orientation. Although it is often considered a distinct sensory modality, proprioception arises from the integration of kinesthetic, auditory, and visual inputs [11]. The brain continuously processes muscle contractions, spatial positioning, and environmental cues to construct an internal representation of body dynamics and spatial relationships.

Several studies suggest that proprioceptive development is fundamental to cognitive and academic success. Insufficient proprioceptive integration has been linked to attentional difficulties, as the brain prioritizes postural control and spatial awareness over higher-order cognitive tasks [11]. When proprioception remains underdeveloped, even minor balance instabilities can result in substantial cognitive resource allocation toward bodily coordination, thereby limiting focus and academic engagement.

Given its multi-sensory nature, proprioception is particularly relevant in early childhood education, where foundational learning experiences are shaped by bodily interaction with the environment. Educational activities that integrate movement and sensory engagement can, therefore, play a critical role in supporting both cognitive development and mathematical understanding. By leveraging proprioceptive feedback in learning environments, instructional strategies can foster more profound conceptual comprehension and improve students' capacity to engage with complex mathematical constructs.

3. AR in education

Augmented reality (AR) can be defined as "a technology that allows computer-generated virtual imagery information to be overlaid onto a live, direct, or indirect real-world environment in real time" [12]. It is recognized as a form of interaction that replaces screens of devices such as laptops with a more natural interface that enables a more natural interaction with virtuality [12]. It could be said that AR's objective is fundamentally different from Virtual Reality (VR) in that AR brings virtual information to a real environment, while VR transports the users' senses to another environment. Due to this, it has been said that "AR bridges the gap between the real and the virtual in a seamless way" [13].

According to Koumpouros [14], AR can be classified into different categories based on how they work, although many result in a combination of them. They can be categorized by tracking:

Marker-based AR: This type of AR uses optical markers captured by a video camera to add 3D effects to the scene; it is usually used to add information to a scene. ArUco library for Python uses marker-based AR.

Position-based AR: The device camera and sensors use GPS, accelerometer, magnetometer, and/or gyroscope to provide position, speed, acceleration, and orientation to the application. An example of this would be Pokémon Go,[1] which uses geo-location to place virtual images in the real world.

Or categorized by medium:

Projection-based AR: Through the use of projectors or smart glasses, digital images are projected onto real-world surfaces. Projections on buildings or on walls for art exhibits count as projection-based AR.

Superimposition-based AR: Applications of this type use overlay technology to replace an object with a virtual one using object recognition, usually by partially or completely replacing the view of an object with an augmented view. A common example of this is Social Media filters that superimpose images on a person's face using object recognition.

Mobile AR, which refers to AR that works through portable devices such as smartphones and tablets, has started to become more common and can range from simple experiences like camera filters to interactive games [14]. Due to not requiring expensive hardware, AR has started to be introduced as a practical technology in many industries. Its ability to provide more interactivity than a conventional screen while packing a lot of information in a small space has made it a point of interest in education, as a way to provide an exploratory experience for learning.

AR in education allows users to interact with virtual applications that use multimedia, simulations, and animations to explain and demonstrate concepts. It is usually used in conjunction with gamification, which creates highly rewarding and motivating lessons that can make learning less like a chore and more like a fun endeavor. Even repetitive tasks can become more engaging when treated as a form of progressive refinement through continued practice and when there is an immediate reward for getting an answer right. This technology "effectively complements the traditional forms of teaching and learning by promoting critical thinking and improving student engagement and perception" [15].

According to Fingent [15], teaching courses at primary and secondary levels through AR has been shown to increase motivation, improve learning performance,

---

[1] https://pokemongolive.com

and enable students to exert minimal effort to acquire the knowledge. Well-designed environments that use AR can decrease the cognitive load of students, ensuring effective learning, cultivate problem-solving skills, improve learning outcomes, and develop a positive attitude toward comprehending complex concepts [15]. AR also improves remote learning by allowing interactions in the classroom that provide an engaging experience regardless of the location of the students, making it an invaluable resource for remote learning.

There have been numerous documented uses of AR that have been designed and implemented for the purpose of teaching subjects such as Mathematics, Natural Sciences, Astronomy, Environmental Education, Language Skills, and more. The pedagogical approaches recorded include gamified learning, situated learning, constructivism (defined by Piaget as learners constructing understanding through experience), and investigative learning [14].

Some of the common applications of AR for education are:

Concept visualization: 3D models can be overlaid into the real world to help students see a concrete picture at a small scale. This could be used for anything from the Solar System to the human body. Allowing the manipulation of this 3D model through rotation or scaling can also help users create a more intricate mental representation. Examples of this are Human Anatomy Atlas 2025,[2] an application that uses AR to visualize the human body in 3D, allowing students to explore organs, systems, and structures in detail. Dinosaur 4D+[3] is another example that uses interactive AR flashcards to show dinosaurs and their features.

Virtual field trips: 3D visualization can help students learn about different environments from the comfort of their classrooms or homes by importing information from other places into close spaces. This approach was used in the now-discontinued Google Expeditions,[4] where users could “take virtual field trips” about many different topics guided by their teachers. ARZoo[5] is another application that focuses on bringing images of animals and their biomes to the student’s desk.

Gamification: AR can be used to create interactive games that promote problem-solving and collaboration while making the tasks more fun. Applications like Catchy Words AR[6] gamify the skill of spelling by having kids “catch” the letter blocks in the air to correctly build the words. QuiverVision[7] combines coloring pages with AR to bring student drawings to life in interactive, gamified ways, teaching concepts like geometry and biology.

Simulations: 3D visualization can be used to practice real-world scenarios to develop skills like decision-making. These simulations can even be used in real training. Microsoft HoloLens[8] is one of the greatest examples, being used in medical training to simulate surgeries or in engineering to visualize and interact with 3D models of machinery. Timelooper[9] is another app that lets users experience historical events in the locations where they occurred, such as walking through a medieval market or witnessing a famous speech.

---

[2] https://support.visiblebody.com/hc/en-us/categories/202598228-Human-Anatomy-Atlas

[3] https://play.google.com/store/apps/details?id=com.OctagonStudio.ARDinoVR

[4] https://artsandculture.google.com/project/expeditions

[5] https://www.monash.edu/mada/student-work/ar-zoo

[6] https://twiceapps.com/catchy/catchy.html

[7] https://quivervision.com

[8] https://learn.microsoft.com/en-us/hololens

[9] https://www.timelooper.com/

As the cost of AR hardware continues to decline, widespread adoption of this technology in educational settings is expected to increase. Advancements in AR, particularly through the integration of Artificial Intelligence (AI), have the potential to enhance adaptive learning by tailoring instructional content to individual students' progress and cognitive profiles. Additionally, incorporation of haptic feedback and multi-sensory interactions may further bridge the divide between digital and physical learning, fostering more immersive and effective educational experiences.

4. Exploration

A small-scale implementation was created to introduce an innovative educational approach, a mixed-media environment that integrates physical media with digital systems to teach foundational numerical concepts. By leveraging tangible elements, the system bridges the gap between abstract mathematical ideas and concrete experiences by focusing on the way humans have evolved to learn: through all senses at once. This approach aligns with pedagogical research emphasizing the importance of multi-sensory learning, which not only enhances engagement but also fosters a more profound understanding of numerical relationships and operations.

The topic chosen for the activities in this implementation was the concept of number, which is the basis of mathematical theory. Other math topics could have been considered for this demonstration, but the project intended to show how this technology can be applied even to fundamental concepts at the earliest ages, where abstract thinking represents a greater challenge for children.

This PoC identified essential achievement markers that guided the design of pedagogical activities for teaching the concept of number. These include recognizing different representations of numbers—such as numerals, words, and magnitudes—and the ability to switch between them. Additionally, learners must develop skills in representing quantities, understanding numerical order (cardinality), and counting. It also emphasized the importance of reading and writing numbers, as well as comparing numerical magnitudes to determine relations such as greater than, less than, or equal to. Finally, foundational arithmetic operations, including addition and division, were introduced, highlighting their real-world applications. While subtraction and multiplication were not explicitly implemented, their inclusion as inverse operations demonstrates their potential for seamless integration into the learning framework.

To keep the scope small but significant enough for the activities, the numbers from 0 to 10 were considered, including sums up to 10 and divisions of numbers 10 and below. The target audience for this evaluation consisted of bilingual children aged 6–10 who were in early stages of their mathematical education in English. These children had previously participated in a four-week intensive mathematics program due to persistent difficulties in foundational numerical concepts. Through sustained interaction and observation, it became evident that their struggles were rooted in deficits in their understanding of the concept of number. To assess their baseline proficiency, students completed fundamental numerical exercises using the digital platform provided by their school. The results indicated significant challenges, with some students requiring up to 2 hours to complete basic tasks. This preliminary assessment became the inspiration and base comparison for this exploratory study.

The decision to use English as the primary language of instruction was driven by several factors. First, it aligns with the language in which these students are learning mathematical concepts, ensuring consistency in their education. Additionally, presenting the study in English broadens its accessibility to a wider audience, facilitating the dissemination of findings. Furthermore, English was chosen due to the advanced capabilities of voice recognition and synthesis technologies in the language, enhancing interactive aspects of the application.

Physical media were prioritized over a screen-only approach due to their proven ability to stimulate multiple sensory pathways, facilitating deeper comprehension and more meaningful learning experiences. AR, in particular, plays a crucial role in making mathematics tangible by overlaying digital content onto physical objects, enabling learners to interact with numbers and operations in a hands-on manner. While this exploratory study does not constitute a rigorous controlled experiment with randomized trials or statistical modeling, it provides an initial appraisal of the potential benefits of an interactive, multimodal learning environment for early mathematical education.

4.1 Design

The design phase of this project consisted of gathering data from both students and teachers from first-hand and second-hand experience to understand the needs of the affected parties. This project follows human-centered design principles, prioritizing innovation and technology while ensuring a user-focused solution that enhances learning experiences in meaningful ways.

The Discover phase of the project commenced with the identification of key challenges in teaching numerical concepts, particularly the limitations of traditional educational tools. Existing screen-only applications were found to lack the engagement and cognitive depth required to effectively teach abstract concepts, especially to young learners. Research indicated that students frequently struggled to comprehend mathematical relationships when lessons relied exclusively on digital methods, as these tools failed to engage multiple senses or provide hands-on experiences. Additionally, screen devices introduced the challenge of retaining the student's attention against the accessibility of other unrestricted applications installed on it.

To address these challenges, interviews and surveys were conducted with educators, parents, and students to gain insights into the difficulties of integrating technology into classrooms. Observations of current teaching practices revealed an over-reliance on repetitive and passive learning techniques, such as mechanical drilling, which limited opportunities for active participation and reflective learning.

User insights emphasized the need to evaluate the types of interactivity that current hardware and software either foster or fail to foster in digitally mediated learning experiences. Challenges related to interfaces, data processing issues, and difficulties with attention and memory when working on screens, alongside the passive roles often assumed by students, influenced the development of initial ideas for potential solutions.

The Define phase consisted of establishing clear objectives and solution requirements based on insights from the Discover phase. Research highlighted the importance of multi-sensory interactions for children, as these stimulate neural pathways and improve memory retention. This insight shaped the project's focus on blending physical and digital media to create an immersive learning experience.

The goal was to design an educational tool that eliminated screen limitations by shifting the focus from screens to an interactive environment with physical objects. The design emphasized engaging multiple senses, including touch and proprioception, alongside traditional audiovisual stimuli, to enhance comprehension through varied neurological associations. Another focus was removing the distractions from devices such as tablets and laptops by creating an isolated screen in a space where all elements refocused students' attention on the activities.

The project also prioritized accessibility, affordability, and ease of use, ensuring compatibility with common hardware such as projectors and cameras. The interface was tailored for young learners with vibrant visuals, simple instructions, and child-friendly interactions to maintain engagement and foster independent exploration. The different types of interactions considered for this project, along with the technologies taken into account for each type, were as follows:

1. Visual interactions are those that rely on visual perception, such as seeing images, colors, shapes, and text on a screen or through other visual media. This includes Graphical User Interfaces (GUI) and technologies such as AR that overlay digital images onto the physical world.

2. Auditory interactions engage hearing and involve the perception of sound, including spoken language, music, tones, and other auditory cues. Using spoken command, receiving auditory feedback, whether in words or sound effects, and sonification, representing data through sound, all represent auditory interactions.

3. Kinesthetic interaction involves physical movement or manipulation of objects to interact with technology. It encompasses gestures, motion, and other physical actions. Kinesthetic interactions involve the sense of proprioception, or the awareness of one's own body parts in relation to other elements and the world. Using physical elements, such as controllers or objects to navigate through the digital interfaces by moving or manipulating said elements, and using AR to move digital images through physical media are all examples of kinesthetic interactions.

4. Tactile interaction involves physical contact with objects or surfaces, providing sensory feedback through the sense of touch. It encompasses the feel of different textures, pressures, and temperatures. The tactile experience in writing by hand includes feeling the texture of the writing surface, the pressure exerted by the writing instrument, and the movement of the hand when forming letters and shapes.

In the process of mapping out how existing technologies could be integrated into the system, AR emerged as one of the most versatile options due to its ability to enable complex interactions using simple tools, such as a printed marker. AR was chosen not only for its accessibility and the maturity of its implementations but also for its capacity to provide extensive data about the spatial position of objects, their distance from the user, and their orientation, including movement, inclination, and rotation.

The choice of AR was also influenced by its ability to seamlessly integrate physical and digital interactions without requiring expensive or complex hardware. While AR systems often leverage screen-based features, such as projecting objects or animations on top of markers, these functionalities were deliberately excluded from this project to align with its "screen-less" philosophy. The aim was to emphasize tactile and physical engagement, minimizing distractions that screens might introduce. Nevertheless, it is worth noting that these screen-based features hold significant potential for future educational applications, particularly in scenarios where visualizing three-dimensional objects or dynamic simulations could enhance learning.

The Develop phase focused on building and refining the application through iterative prototyping. Python was chosen as the core development language for its impressive array of libraries that could cover all technological needs of the project. Pygame[10] was used as the base engine to manage audio and visual aspects of the application, while OpenCV[11] was in charge of handling video capture and processing, and gTTS[12] was used as a speech synthesizer to create the spoken commands that guide the user. Specific libraries like speechrecognition[13] and the ArUco[14] library were used to provide complete features to the application. Even more complex technologies, such as Tensorflow,[15] were used to create a model trained with data from MNIST (Modified National Institute of Standards and Technology),[16] a publicly available source of handwritten characters, to recognize handwritten digits captured by the camera.

The hardware setup was designed to accommodate the various inputs required for the system to function effectively. It consisted of a web camera, a projector, a microphone, and speakers, all arranged to facilitate seamless interaction between the user and the application. A custom-designed button with an enlarged contact area, doubling as a left mouse button, replaced traditional input devices to better suit young learners; this button is examined in the next subsection. The devices were strategically positioned to allow the application to be projected onto a defined surface that simultaneously served as the camera's capture area. This designated surface became the primary workspace for users, enabling them to interact with the system.

4.2 Delivery

The Delivery phase focused on transforming the system's design into a functional and user-friendly educational tool. Taking into account the research and the key points designated in the design phase, the following digital interactions were implemented to provide a suitable dynamics for teaching math through physical objects. The result was a design, shown in **Figure 1**, that integrated both hardware and software and which allows inclusion of the designated manipulatives. The implementation of the screen being projected onto a surface (be it a table or the floor, or even a board on which to write) instead of a digital screen can be categorized as Projection-based AR. The basic interface turns real-life elements into part of the application.

4.2.1 ArUco markers as a quantity

ArUco markers are a type of fiducial marker system used in computer vision, consisting of square black-and-white patterns that cameras can detect and identify. Each marker has a unique ID, but in this interaction, the focus is on counting how many markers are fully within a designated rectangle, rather than identifying individual markers. This method assigns a numerical value based on the number of detected markers, ignoring those that are only partially inside the area, as can be seen in **Figure 2**.

---

10 https://www.pygame.org

11 https://opencv.org

12 https://pypi.org/project/gTTS

13 https://pypi.org/project/SpeechRecognition

14 https://github.com/cmower/aruco_markers

15 https://www.tensorflow.org

16 https://www.kaggle.com/datasets/avnishnish/mnist-original

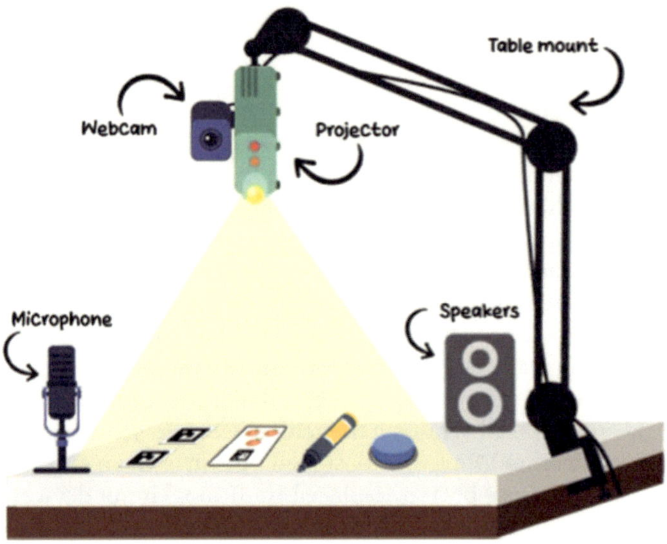

Figure 1.
Image of the hardware setup.

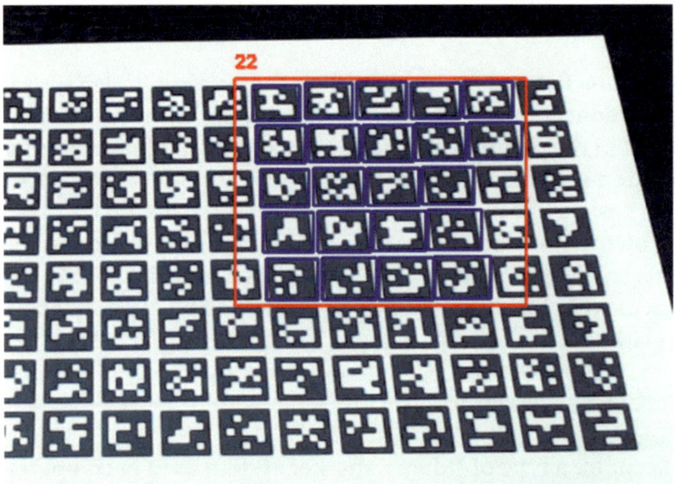

Figure 2.
The camera recognizes the markers inside the specified rectangle. The number of items is shown on the top left.

This approach helps children understand numbers as representations of real-world objects, making abstract mathematical concepts more tangible. By physically moving the markers, children can perform basic arithmetic operations such as addition, subtraction, and grouping, reinforcing the connection between numbers and everyday actions.

This marker-based AR interaction was implemented in educational activities, shown in **Figure 3**, where users determined the number of items needed to answer a question. The representation is very straightforward, with each printed marker representing one item. Putting markers in a single group represents a quantity, and this quantity is then associated with the numeral on the screen. This works for any

Figure 3.
Activities that use markers as interactive items that users must place inside rectangles.

quantity, including zero (0), where the representation is an empty group. In the Feeding Animals activity, users matched the number on the screen by placing the correct number of markers in a designated area, linking symbolic numerical representation to real-world quantities. A more advanced version introduced division by having users not only count the correct amount but also group items into equal sets, helping them grasp the concept of division as distributing elements into groups.

4.2.2 ArUco markers as cards

Another application of the ArUco library involves using the unique IDs of markers to create special cards for mathematical learning. Instead of counting markers, this interaction recognizes individual marker IDs within a designated rectangle, allowing only one card to be detected at a time. Number cards (0–10) are identified as digits, while special cards represent comparison relations (less than, greater than, and equal to), helping children understand mathematical notation and relationships between quantities. **Figure 4** shows cards being recognized by the application.

These cards follow a well-documented educational approach, with one side displaying a numeral or symbol and the other showing its corresponding visual

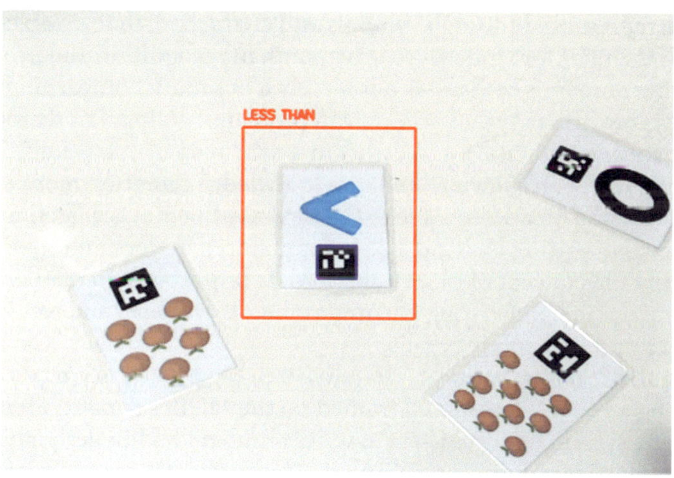

Figure 4.
The relation card is being recognized by the application.

Figure 5.
Activities that feature cards with printed markers as playing cards.

representation. Number cards feature a numeral on one side and a quantity image on the other, while operator cards pair mathematical symbols with their written names. This dual representation helps children grasp abstract concepts and allows for offline practice, extending their learning beyond the application's runtime.

The cards were used in the activities in **Figure 5** that required recognizing numbers and mathematical relations. In "Sequence Trucks," users identified missing numbers in a sequence, switching between numeral and visual representations. This activity helps kids understand cardinality by locating numbers in a sequence and by using the physical cards to go through the numbers while they search for the right card, sometimes turning the cards to the other side to check the number of items each numeral represents. In "Comparing Trees," children determined the relationship between two quantities and selected the correct relation card (less than, greater than, or equal to) to represent the comparison. This activity served the purpose of helping kids understand magnitudes from visual representations and, at the same time, understand the symbolic representation of the comparison relations.

4.2.3 Handwriting recognition

Mathematical notation is a crucial aspect of mathematics, allowing abstract concepts to be represented through symbols and characters. Indo-Arabic numerals, in particular, are essential for students to learn, both in recognition and proper handwriting. Writing numerals by hand is not merely a byproduct of learning to write, but also plays a key role in clarity and accuracy in problem-solving. Poorly formed numerals can lead to misinterpretation and errors in mathematical operations.

Handwriting has been shown to enhance knowledge retention more effectively than typing or tracing on a screen due to the increased neural connections formed during the process. Writing by hand also helps children understand spatial distribution, reinforcing the concept of place value and its importance in mathematical operations. Practicing handwriting ensures numerals are clean and well-formed, fostering better problem-solving skills.

To support this learning process, a handwritten digit recognition system was developed using a TensorFlow model trained on the MNIST dataset, focusing on digit recognition. The system requires users to write numbers within designated rectangles, with each rectangle identifying a single digit. This interaction is exhibited in **Figure 6**.

This interaction was used in educational activities (seen in **Figure 7**) where students manually wrote numerals in designated locations. In "Counting Animals,"

DOI: http://dx.doi.org/10.5772/intechopen.1011787

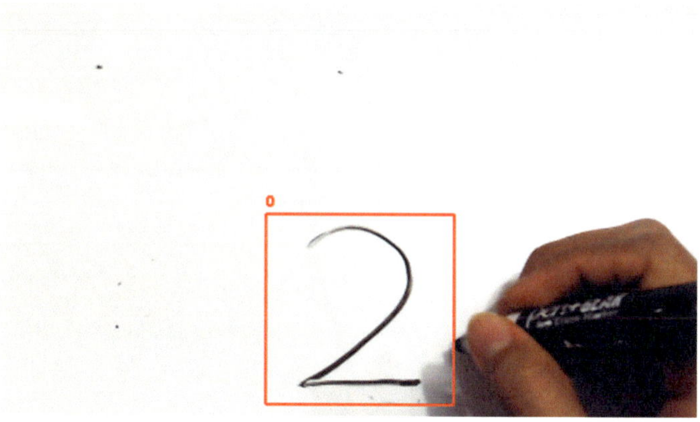

Figure 6.
The user writes a number on paper inside the bounds drawn by the application.

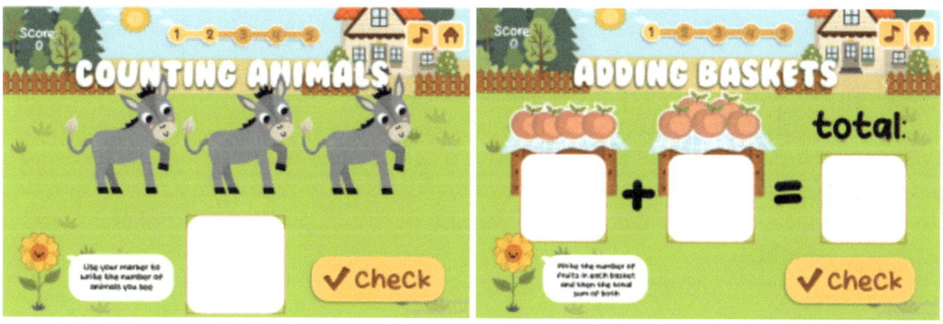

Figure 7.
Activities where the student had to manually write the numbers on paper.

users practiced writing clear and proportional numerals recognizable by the software, reinforcing spatial organization in mathematics. "Adding Baskets" expanded on this by having students place handwritten numerals correctly within an equation, helping them develop structured problem-solving skills.

4.2.4 Beat recognition

Sonification is the process of converting information into sound. In "Rhythm Cow," numbers are represented through beats, which users must count and interpret into movement or visual representations on screen. The beats are played in patterns, separated by short silences within groups and longer silences between groups. Users must listen carefully to identify group boundaries and count the beats, engaging multiple cognitive processes such as auditory-to-numerical conversion, time interval differentiation, and working memory retention.

To interact, users position their mouse over rectangles representing pattern groups, clicking to increase the stored count. A specially designed button, pictured in **Figure 8**, requires larger arm movements instead of simple clicks, engaging more muscles and enhancing proprioception. This increased physical effort activates additional neural pathways, reinforcing cognitive engagement with the activity.

Figure 8.
Left: Button used in this activity. Right: Interface of the activity.

4.2.5 Speech recognition

Speech recognition is commonly used in language learning applications to assess pronunciation, provide immediate feedback, and improve learning. In a math teaching application, it helps users learn the verbal representation of numbers, reinforcing their ability to switch between representations.

Modern speech recognition is highly accurate, even accommodating different accents, making it beneficial for both native English speakers and students learning math in English. While the "Reading Numbers" activity currently focuses on number pronunciation, it could be expanded to verbalizing math problems to enhance reasoning and comprehension.

The implementation activates the microphone on click, records the uttered speech, transcribes it into text, and compares it to the correct answer. If mispronounced, the system prompts the user to try again, reinforcing accurate pronunciation and understanding. The following **Figure 9** shows the interface of this activity in the application.

Figure 9.
The interface of the speech recognition activity.

4.3 Evaluation

The evaluation phase tested the system's impact on children, conducted in their homes to reflect real-world conditions. This approach provided insights into how the application performed in diverse environments, even if ideal conditions were not always met. The evaluations were done in two iterations, with children engaging in activities while their interactions were observed and recorded, as seen in **Figure 10**. After each session, the children provided feedback on the usability and comprehension of the app.

The testing revealed that the users enjoyed the variety of activities and actively engaged with them, eagerly awaiting results. They particularly enjoyed using the manipulatives to solve problems and even continued to engage with them during their free time, suggesting that physical elements helped students transfer knowledge beyond the lesson. The children, especially those who had previously struggled with traditional methods, showed significant improvements in confidence and problem-solving abilities. Progress was observed in counting, number recognition, and solving simple equations, with notable reductions in error rates and faster completion times. A comparison was made between the performance of the students based on 30 total exercises related to the concept of number resolved through both the digital platforms and the interactive environment to measure the improvement in time and accuracy of the children when confronted with similar types of exercises. This comparison is shown in **Table 1**.

The multi-sensory approach, combining visual, auditory, and tactile stimuli, proved to be highly effective in helping students grasp and retain abstract mathematical concepts. One of the factors most thought to have influenced these results is the level of engagement and interest the children showed when it came to solving the same exercises through objects. Kids who were usually disinterested and even frustrated by the math exercises showed evident motivation and initiative in using the system to do math.

Figure 10.
Users engaged in the activities during the evaluations.

Measurement	Digital platforms	Interactive system	Improvement
Time spent in the activities	68.1 min	23 min	66.2%
Number of correctly solved exercises	39%	77%	97.4%

Table 1.
Comparison between initial assessment and performance of the students with the interactive system.

The evaluation concluded that the system successfully created an interactive and tactile learning environment that fostered meaningful engagement and measurable learning outcomes. This demonstrated the system's potential for broader educational applications, providing a promising model for future learning tools.

5. Conclusions

This PoC implementation has demonstrated the potential of AR as a transformative tool in early mathematics education. By integrating AR into a mixed-media learning environment, we addressed key challenges associated with traditional digital and physical learning methods, such as a lack of engagement, limited sensory stimulation, and shallow cognitive processing. The results of our case study support that interactive, multi-sensory learning experiences improve mathematical comprehension, enhance retention, and increase motivation.

The evaluation reinforced the idea that learning mathematics is most effective when it engages multiple senses. Our findings align with existing research on multisensory education, indicating that combining visual, auditory, and kinesthetic interactions significantly enhances cognitive processing and conceptual understanding. The use of tangible objects, handwriting recognition, and interactive tasks facilitated deeper engagement and comprehension of numerical concepts among young learners.

Integration of augmented reality (AR) with traditional manipulatives marks a transformative shift in both teaching and learning paradigms. Technologically, AR extends the capabilities of physical materials by offering dynamic, immersive, and interactive learning experiences that enrich student understanding. Pedagogically, it fosters deeper engagement, comprehension, and retention through a multi-sensory, experiential approach, enhancing students' ability to connect with abstract concepts. The potential of AR in education, though still unfolding, is already reshaping how students engage with complex subjects, particularly those requiring visualization of abstract ideas. As AR, AI, and machine learning continue to advance, they are paving the way for a new horizon in human-machine collaboration. Ongoing evolution of these technologies promises to further elevate the effectiveness and depth of learning, creating richer, more individualized educational journeys in the future.

The results of the exploratory study indicate that the use of a mixed-device system significantly improved task completion time and accuracy compared to the existing digital platforms that use a screen-focused approach. These findings align with existing research [2, 5, 7] on the benefits of interactive and embodied learning in mathematics education. The observed improvements in this implementation suggest that integrating interactive systems into early mathematics education has the potential to enhance learning outcomes and task efficiency. Future research should further explore these findings through controlled studies with larger sample sizes to validate and expand upon these initial results.

Traditional teaching methods often struggle to capture students' attention, particularly when dealing with abstract or complex topics. AR introduces an interactive, hands-on component that encourages active participation rather than passive learning. By allowing students to manipulate objects, experiment with variables, and explore concepts in a hands-on manner, AR transforms learning into an immersive experience. This level of engagement can lead to increased retention rates, deeper understanding, and a more positive attitude toward learning.

By integrating AR into education, institutions can enhance learning experiences across multiple disciplines, making complex concepts more accessible and engaging. Its ability to merge visualization, interactivity, and real-world application underscores its transformative potential in reshaping how students learn and apply knowledge.

Abbreviations

AI	Artificial Intelligence
CV	computer vision
GPS	Global Positioning System
GUI	Graphical User Interface
ID	identification
MNIST	Modified National Institute of Standards and Technology
PoC	Proof-of-concept
TTS	Text-to-speech
VR	virtual reality

Author details

Ghina-Alexandra Garcés-Rojas*† and Gerardo-M. Sarria-M.†
Pontificia Universidad Javeriana Cali, Colombia

*Address all correspondence to: ghina.garces@gmail.com

† These authors contributed equally.

References

[1] Duval R. A cognitive analysis of problems of comprehension in a learning of mathematics. Educational Studies in Mathematics. 2006;**61**:103-131. DOI: 10.1007/s10649-006-0400-z

[2] Van der Weel FR (Ruud), Van der Meer ALH. Handwriting but not typewriting leads to widespread brain connectivity: A high-density EEG study with implications for the classroom. Frontiers in Psychology. 2024;**14**. DOI: 10.3389/fpsyg.2023.1219945

[3] Ackerman R, Sidi Y, Ophir Y. Generalizing screen inferiority - Does the medium, screen versus paper, affect performance even with brief tasks? Metacognition and Learning. 2016;**11**: 15-33. DOI: 10.1007/s11409-015-9150-6

[4] Wang X, Chen L, Liu X, Wang C, Zhang Z, Ye Q. The screen inferiority depends on test format in reasoning and meta-reasoning tasks. Frontiers in Psychology. 2023;**14**:067577. DOI: 10.3389/fpsyg.2023.1067577

[5] Cuturi LF, Cappagli G, Yiannoutsou N, Price S, Gori M. Informing the design of a multi-sensory learning environment for elementary mathematics learning. Springer Link. 2022;**16**:155-177. DOI: 10.1007/s12193-021-00382-y

[6] Rojas D. The Evolution of Hardware and Software in Education: What Is the Next Step? Nice, France: MSc SmartEd Tech, Co-Creativity and Digital Tools for Educational Innovation, Université Côte-D'Azur; 2024

[7] Henriksen D, Creely E, Henderson M, Mishra P. Creativity and technology in teaching and learning: A literature review of the uneasy space of implementation. Educational Technology Research and Development. 2021;**69**(4):2091-2108. DOI: 10.1007/s11423-020-09912-z

[8] Nemirovsky R, Borba M, DiMattia C, Arzarello F, Robutti O, Schnepp M, et al. Introduction: PME special issue: Bodily activity and imagination in mathematics learning. Educational Studies in Mathematics. 2004;**57**(3):303-321

[9] Poincaré H. Mathematics and Science: Last Essays (Dernieres Pensees). (J. W. Bolduc, Trans.). New York: Dover Publications, Inc; 1963

[10] Manches A, O'Malley C. The effects of physical manipulatives on children's numerical strategies. Cognition and Instruction. 2016;**34**(1):27-50. DOI: 10.1080/07370008.2015.1124882

[11] Kasterko D. Why Developing Proprioception Might Be the Most Important Step to Overcoming Specific Learning Disabilities. Learning Success; n.d. Available from: https://www.learningsuccesssystem.com/system/proprioception [Accessed: February 26, 2024]

[12] Azuma RT. A survey of augmented reality. Presence: Teleoperators and Virtual Environments. 1997;**6**(4):355-385. DOI: 10.1162/pres.1997.6.4.355

[13] Chang G, Morreale P, Medicherla P. Applications of augmented reality systems in education. In: Proceedings of the Society for Information Technology & Teacher Education Int. Conf. San Diego, CA, USA; 2010. ISBN: 978-1-880094-78-5

[14] Koumpouros Y. Revealing the true potential and prospects of

augmented reality in education. Smart Learning Environments. 2024;**11**(1):2. DOI: 10.1186/s40561-023-00288-0

[15] Fingent. What Is Augmented Reality in Education? 2023. Available from: https://www.fingent.com/blog/augmented-reality-in-education-training-use-cases-and-business-benefits/ [Accessed: January 15, 2025]

Chapter 3

Learning in Informal Educational Spaces: Augmented Reality and Merge Edu in Natural Science Museums

Delsa Silva Amino Cufuna, Gizeh Rangel-de Lazaro and Josep M. Duart

Abstract

The integration of augmented reality (AR) into science museums has emerged as a novel approach to enhancing visitor experiences. This chapter presents a framework to use the AR user-friendly Merge Edu application to facilitate interactive, inquiry-based learning in museums as spaces for informal education. For this pilot analysis, CosmoCaixa in Barcelona is proposed as a case study. In this chapter, we discuss the potential of AR to visualise natural science museum artefacts in 3D, highlighting how the merging of digital content and physical exhibits sparks curiosity and inquiry. We propose that AR-powered interactions, such as those enabled by Merge Edu, offer immersive possibilities for small-group experiences, making complex scientific concepts more accessible. Challenges include developing digital infrastructure, training staff, and striking a balance between technology and the museum's cultural mission. Ultimately, this chapter argues that adopting AR in museums can enhance visitor engagement and democratise the learning of natural science concepts in a tangible, inclusive manner.

Keywords: augmented reality (AR), pedagogy, museology, Merge Edu, interactive learning

1. Introduction

Museums play a fundamental role in the conservation and dissemination of knowledge, serving as spaces where communities can explore cultural and scientific heritage. With time, their educational models have evolved to actively engage visitors in meaningful learning processes [1]. This shift has led to the adoption of practical and immersive activities [2]. Functioning as dynamic centres of culture and informal education, museums encourage visitors to construct knowledge actively [2–4]. Museums have incorporated contemporary pedagogical dynamics to provide alternative learning experiences that stimulate inquiry, encourage manipulation of real objects, and integrate digital tools to explain complex scientific and cultural concepts [3]. This evolution toward more participatory approaches reflects the growing demand for inclusive, accessible, and engaging educational spaces [5].

As part of this trend, augmented reality (AR) has gained followers by overlaying immersive digital content onto physical objects or exhibits [6, 7]. The introduction of AR has revolutionised the visitor experience by facilitating interaction with digital reconstructions and simulated real environments [8]. This digital overlay enriches knowledge by transforming static exhibits into dynamic learning initiatives. For example, AR can incorporate animations to demonstrate how an extinct creature moved or how an artefact was used in its original context. This approach enriches the scene with temporal and interactive content that a static display cannot provide.

Museums in the United States, such as the Smithsonian National Museum of Natural History, have incorporated AR technologies into their exhibits, allowing visitors to interact with digital reconstructions of fossils and historical artefacts, which enriches the understanding of natural history [4, 9]. Similarly, the British Museum in London has experimented with digital layers overlaid on historical objects, enabling dynamic and contextualised interaction with cultural heritage, which has contributed to renewing the museum experience for diverse audiences.

Likewise, institutions such as the Louvre in Paris and the Museum of Modern Art (MoMA) in New York have integrated immersive experiences that combine AR and other digital technologies. For example, the Louvre has utilised AR to reimagine its collections, enabling visitors to access interactive and personalised narratives that add an extra dimension to their encounter with the artworks [10]. At MoMA, digital interfaces have been developed to encourage active participation, sparking exploration and dialogue around contemporary art [11]. These initiatives reflect a trend toward reinventing museums as spaces for interactive and multisensory learning, expanding their educational reach.

In Spain, museums are progressively transforming traditional exhibition spaces to introduce dynamic environments that foster active learning, playing a key role in the informal education of visitors [2, 12]. The CosmoCaixa Science Museum in Barcelona is an example of this transformation. Created in 2004 by the 'la Caixa' Foundation, its exhibits feature interactive displays showcasing palaeontological remains and fossils from the plant and animal worlds, including the *Protoceratops*, *Chilotherium* (fossil rhinoceros), and *Triceratops horridus* (**Figures 1** and **2**).

Visitors can observe palaeontological skeletal remains and learn about palaeoecology and the changes the Earth has undergone throughout its history, fostering curiosity and interest in natural sciences. The educational philosophy of CosmoCaixa emphasises active learning, where visitors physically interact with the displayed objects and directly experience scientific principles. This reflects the strategies currently observed in many Spanish museums, where tangible interactions and immersive technologies create memorable learning environments [2, 6]. The institution collaborates with schools to reinforce formal curricula, providing educational materials and organising field trips that serve as a bridge between classroom theory and museum practice [3, 4, 6].

Using CosmoCaixa as a case study, this chapter presents a framework for integrating AR into the dynamics of informal education in museums, facilitating interactive, object-based learning.

The methodology presented here can be applied to other institutions seeking to integrate inquiry-based and constructivist learning into their visitor experiences (**Figure 2**). Particularly in science museums, where AR can be integrated into

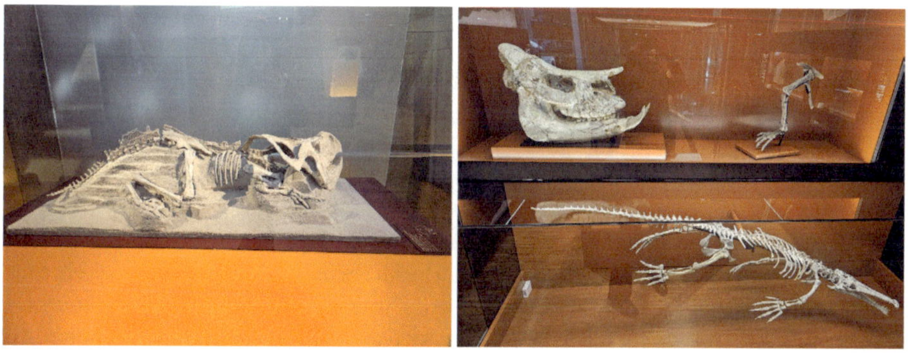

(A) (B)

Figure 1.
Visitor interaction with fossils and extinct species remains at CosmoCaixa. Note. On the left (A), a Protoceratops skeleton; on the right (B), a Chilotherium (fossil rhinoceros) skull, limb bones, and a partial skeleton. Also, on the lower right, there is a complete crocodile skeleton. Source: Photograph taken by the authors at the CosmoCaixa Museum, Barcelona.

(A) (B)

Figure 2.
Visitor interaction with a digital reconstruction in Merge Edu, featuring a Triceratops at the CosmoCaixa Museum in Barcelona. Note. The AR experience overlays the model into the exhibition space (A), allowing realistic exploration (B). Source. Photograph taken by the authors at the CosmoCaixa Museum, Barcelona.

exhibitions and educational activities to enhance hands-on, interactive experiences and encourage visitors to explore and familiarise themselves with scientific concepts.

2. Object-based learning activity proposal

In designing this framework, we utilised the Merge Edu app, along with the integrated applications 'Merge Explorer' and 'Object Viewer' [13]. Using the 'World' feature, this is low-cost and compatible with numerous device applications, enabling users to manipulate and view three-dimensional objects through the camera of a mobile device.

In this way, the user can observe and explore these AR models in their own space, interacting with them from different perspectives (**Figure 3**) [13]. Our proposed activity aims to foster object-based scientific learning using artefacts from the CosmoCaixa Museum of Science. This is achieved through the sensory and visual exploration of fossils, complemented by AR visualisation using the Merge Explorer and Object Viewer. **Table 1** defines, and **Figure 1** exhibits, the objective of the activity, focusing on interaction with authentic fossils and integrating technology. This proposal is framed within active learning methodologies that promote student participation through exploration and hypothesis formulation [4].

The activity structure is based on the 'See, Think, Wonder' approach, a method used in education to stimulate observation, critical thinking, and questioning [14]. In the 'See' phase, participants will explore the fossils without prior knowledge of their identity, using touch and observation as a first encounter. In the 'Think' phase, they will be provided with contextual information and encouraged to reflect on the objects, their origin, and their evolutionary background. Finally, in the 'Wonder' phase, the use of AR resources will allow them to visualise the reconstruction of the fossils in their original state, raising new questions about their life, appearance, evolutionary adaptations, and preservation [12, 15, 16].

This approach enables participants to connect the past to the present through technology, thereby strengthening understanding of scientific concepts and fostering a deeper curiosity about history. The combination of sensory exploration and digital tools makes the activity an immersive experience that drives scientific inquiry [17]. Thus, a balance is achieved between interaction with physical elements and digital visualisation, allowing for a more comprehensive educational experience.

To engage with fossils and the Merge Edu 'World' feature in a hands-on storytelling scenario, participants will work in small groups to create a personalised, immersive learning environment where each one can directly interact with both the physical fossils and the AR application (**Figure 4**).

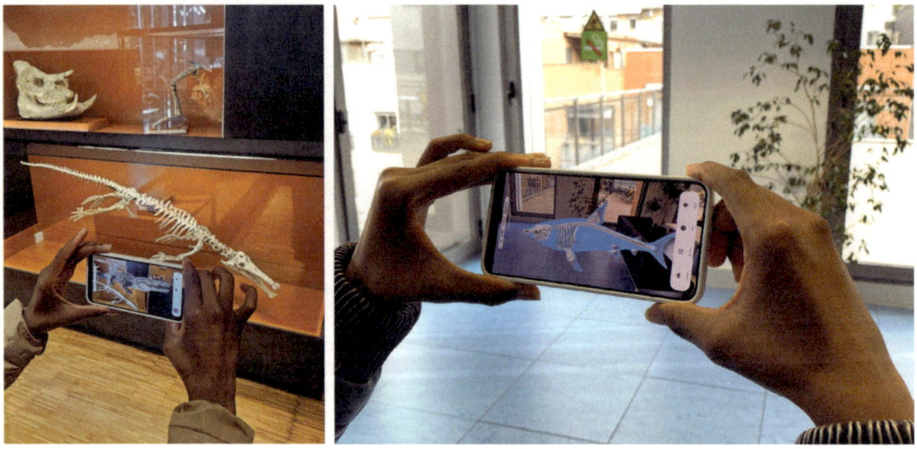

(A) (B)

Figure 3.
Visitor interaction with 3D models in the physical environment using the Merge Edu 'World' function. Note. The participant has placed a virtual 3D model of a fossil in real space via the mobile device. AR view and is moving around it to observe the object from various angles (A and B). Source. Photograph taken by the authors at the CosmoCaixa Museum, Barcelona.

See (discovering and touching the past)	**Think (about the objects)**	**Wonder (about the past, present, and future)**
The participants find themselves facing a mysterious box. They know that inside are ancient fossils, fragments of the past that tell stories of a world that existed millions of years ago. But, • What will it be? • What will it look like? • What creature does it come from? With one hand, without looking, they explore the texture, the shape, and the weight. They perceive the roughness of a sharp tooth, the hardness of a fossilised piece, and the spiral shape of an ammonite. The first contact is sensorial, awakening imagination and expectation. Each participant takes out a fossil without yet knowing what it is.	Now, a brief history is presented: 'Millions of years ago, a predator ruled the seas. Its teeth were as big as a human hand and could crush bones with ease...' Questions are asked to guide them: • What do you think you are holding in your hands? • What do you think it looked like in its natural environment? • What do you think this creature ate or lived like? • How do you think this fossil was acquired? The answers are varied, ideas are exchanged, and hypotheses emerge from the participants. These are discussed as a group and compared with what others have perceived.	Finally, the fossil box is transformed into a window into the past. Using AR, participants see in actual size what once was that tooth, that ammonite, that coprolite. The tiny fragment in their hands now comes to life on the screen, visually revealing its actual size, and they can see representations of such fossils as they would have been in life. They can generate a 3D model in their environment using the AR application and the Merge Edu tool, rotate the 3D image, zoom in, and view the megalodon or sea urchin as a real urchin, rather than a fossil. His initial questions find answers, but new ones also emerge: • How can we protect these vestiges of the past? • What other amazing creatures existed that we have not yet found? Thus, the activity concludes with a bridge between the past and the present, where science and technology combine to awaken curiosity and the desire to explore further.
Summary of activity phases		
In this phase, participants will have the opportunity to formulate initial hypotheses, encouraging them to interact with the fossils and reflect on their physical characteristics.	Here, participants will reflect on the evolutionary history of the fossils and provide additional context that helps participants connect their observations with scientific theory.	In this phase, they will actively explore by manipulating 3D models, which will increase their understanding and interest in the fossils, transforming them into a complete representation when viewed in an interactive format.
Finally, after implementing the three (3) phases, students will reflect on what they have learned and discuss new questions that have arisen from the experience. Open-ended questions that stimulate critical thinking will be encouraged. The discussion will focus on evolutionary adaptations and ecological changes that led to the extinction of species like the ammonite.		

Table 1.
See, think, wonder: A multisensory journey into fossil exploration with AR.

By reducing group size, sensory exploration and hypothesis formulation could occur in a more structured manner, encouraging participants to share observations and ask probing questions without feeling rushed. Moreover, such a facilitator can provide targeted guidance, ensuring everyone masters the 'World' feature's interactive capabilities and fully experiences the 'See, Think, Wonder' methodology.

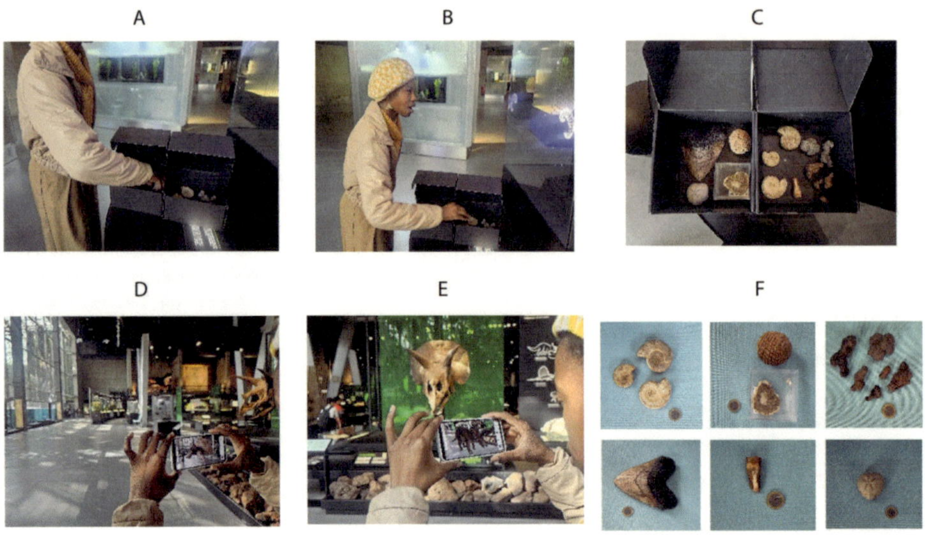

Figure 4.
Storytelling with Fossils and AR at CosmoCaixa Museum of Science. Note. A composite of six moments from the activity: exploring fossils blindly, forming hypotheses, and visualising 3D reconstructions with Merge Edu. Source. Photograph taken by the authors at the CosmoCaixa Museum, Barcelona.

Furthermore, a small number of participants allows the facilitator to provide more effective pedagogical support, ensuring that each student receives the guidance necessary to maximise their experience in the activity. This method will allow for more meaningful interaction with the learning objects, promoting a deeper understanding and a clearer connection between initial observation, critical reflection, and digital visualisation. In this way, the educational approach based on the 'See, Think, Wonder' model is reinforced, enabling students to engage in an active learning process.

2.1 Proposed evaluation methods

Here, we outline the potential evaluation methods that can be used to assess the impact of the proposed framework, utilising the AR Merge Edu app, on the learning experience in science museums.

Quantitative Analysis:

Pre- and post-activity surveys will be used to measure the impact of the educational experience on the visitors' understanding.

- Pre-activity survey: Before the activity, participants will complete a diagnostic survey that assesses their prior knowledge of fossils and evolution. This survey will serve as a baseline to compare knowledge before the educational intervention [18].

- Post-activity survey: After the AR activity, participants will complete a similar survey to measure the change in their understanding of fossils and evolution [18]. The survey will include closed-ended questions using a Likert scale (from 1 to 5), which will assess aspects such as:

- o The degree of understanding of concepts related to fossils and evolution.
- o The level of enjoyment of the activity.
- o The perception of the effectiveness of AR in enhancing understanding.

The pre- and post-activity surveys will enable the analysis of changes in participants' knowledge and understanding. Additionally, the responses will be compared to assess the impact of interacting with AR on their knowledge of scientific concepts.

Qualitative analysis:

For the qualitative analysis, this study will employ data collection techniques recommended by [18, 19].

- Interviews: Semi-structured interviews will be conducted with participants to capture their subjective experiences, opinions, and insights regarding the use of AR and Merge Edu tools in informal learning environments, such as museums.
- Focus groups/workshops: Will be utilised to facilitate collective discussions and interactions, allowing a deeper exploration of participants' perceptions and collaborative reflection on their learning process.
- Observation: Observation will also be carried out during the AR activity to record group interactions and participants' interactions with both physical museum artefacts.

The data obtained from these qualitative methods will be thematically analysed to identify recurring patterns, key insights, and emerging themes. This will help to gain a deeper understanding of participants' learning experiences and perceptions regarding the integration of AR in informal educational settings.

3. Discussion

As museums evolve into dynamic and participatory learning environments, the integration of AR has emerged as a powerful tool for enhancing educational engagement [20]. AR facilitates interactive and multisensory exploration of complex scientific and historical content, encouraging inquiry-based learning and promoting deeper engagement among visitors [21, 22]. Unlike traditional exhibits, which are characterised by passive observation, AR enables active participation, fostering curiosity and reflection.

Platforms such as Merge Edu exemplify this pedagogical shift by allowing visitors to engage directly with 3D models of artefacts. These experiences align with frameworks like 'See, Think, Wonder', guiding users from initial observation through reflective analysis to question generation. Such methods not only support knowledge retention but also foster meaningful connections with the material. AR's capacity to democratise learning is particularly significant. By making content accessible to diverse audiences—including young learners, individuals with disabilities, and those with limited access to formal education—AR supports inclusivity and differentiated learning. Its compatibility with standard mobile devices, such as in the case of Merge

Edu's 'World' feature, minimises financial and logistical barriers while maximising accessibility [7, 23, 24].

In natural science museums, AR enhances experiential learning by integrating digital content with physical exhibits, allowing for the visualisation of complex phenomena without compromising the integrity of original specimens [25, 26]. Research has shown that such interactive exhibits significantly improve knowledge retention and visitor engagement [27], aligning with contemporary pedagogical approaches that emphasise hands-on learning, curiosity, and scientific literacy [10]. Institutions like CaixaForum are leading this transformation, redefining museums as active facilitators of informal education. Merge Edu's 'World' feature, for instance, enables visitors to scan their surroundings and visualise 3D objects in situ, enhancing spatial understanding and immersion. While the use of AR glasses could offer a more seamless experience, the tool remains highly effective with basic technology.

Object-based learning through AR further deepens understanding of scientific principles. For example, enabling users to compare the skeletal structures of prehistoric and modern species supports the study of evolution and adaptation mechanisms [28]. This aligns with what [29] points out, highlighting that AR can also strengthen visitor social interaction and enhance the collective experience within exhibitions. Additionally, collaborative features—such as AR-guided tours and gamified experiences like scavenger hunts—promote group learning and dialogue, making AR especially beneficial for school groups and family visits [7, 25, 26, 30].

AR also significantly improves accessibility. Many applications offer features such as multilingual support, sign language narration, and audio descriptions for visually impaired users [13]. Providing sign language narration can be preferable to text descriptions for Deaf visitors, as it delivers information in their primary language and more directly conveys the content than written text. The integration of QR codes within exhibitions provides supplementary information, enriching visitors' understanding and engagement with the material.

Despite its clear benefits, implementing AR in museums poses challenges. High development costs, the need for staff training, and technical limitations such as internet dependency and device compatibility may hinder widespread adoption [7]. To ensure successful and sustainable integration, museums must adopt a strategic approach that includes:

- Budget planning for infrastructure and long-term content updates [7].
- Inclusive design, incorporating accessibility features such as audio narration and sign language [13].
- Pedagogical alignment, ensuring AR supports and enhances institutional educational goals [13].

The sustainability of AR applications also depends on the continual updating of 3D models and digital content. Emerging technologies, such as artificial intelligence and machine learning, present promising opportunities for personalising AR experiences based on user profiles, including age, interests, and prior knowledge [31]. Studies show that AR increases visitor engagement and time spent in exhibitions, indicating a stronger educational impact [26].

In natural history museums, augmented reality (AR) transforms exhibitions into immersive environments that enhance visitor collaboration and foster a deeper appreciation for science and conservation. To ensure long-term success, institutions must adopt adaptive and inclusive strategies that align with their missions. Overcoming technical barriers, such as software calibration and infrastructure optimisation, is crucial for fully democratising these experiences. Future research should evaluate the long-term educational impact of AR, compare the 'World' feature of Merge Edu with similar tools, and explore its integration with other immersive technologies, such as virtual reality.

However, AR has limitations in certain exhibits. Large-scale architectural works or aesthetic pieces like expansive paintings and sculptures may not benefit much from digital augmentation. Overlaying AR content on these objects can sometimes distract from the original artwork. In contrast, small and midsized objects like fossils or anatomical models are well-suited for augmented reality (AR), providing detailed and dynamic experiences. However, scaling 3D models in AR presents challenges. Incorrect scaling can reduce visual quality and realism, particularly with larger objects. For example, when representing a life-sized dinosaur on a handheld device, its scale must be reduced, which may lessen the viewer's perception of its actual size. Conversely, if the object is not scaled down at all, only a portion of the dinosaur would be visible on the screen. Therefore, achieving the appropriate scale requires balancing practical limitations to accurately convey size and proportions.

Despite the availability of AR content for personal devices at home, in-person museum visits remain essential. Museums provide sensory engagement with authentic artefacts and social interaction that virtual experiences cannot fully replicate. AR can enhance these aspects but cannot replace them. Lastly, AR fosters collaborative learning in museum spaces. With tools like the Merge Edu 'World' feature, multiple visitors can engage with the same AR objects simultaneously, promoting shared exploration, discussion, and collaborative meaning-making. For example, a single Merge Edu 'World' can be utilised by a small group. Each member can use their own device to view the augmented reality content from various angles. Alternatively, they can take turns using one device, allowing the entire group to experience the same digital model together. This shared AR interaction enriches both the learning and social experiences of museum visits.

4. Conclusions

This chapter argues that AR, through the 'World' function of Merge Edu, can transform visitor experiences in science museums by fostering inquiry-based learning. AR allows visitors to interact with digital models of fossils in real time, bridging tangible artefacts with intangible concepts. It is especially effective in small group activities, promoting discussion and meaning-making.

While challenges such as staff training and hardware maintenance remain, AR stands out as a democratising technology that expands access to diverse audiences. By reducing conceptual distance, such as showing how a fossil fragment belonged to a large extinct creature, AR creates an immersive sense of wonder. When integrated into a museum's pedagogical strategy, AR enhances both knowledge retention and emotional engagement.

The value of AR goes beyond novelty, aligning with the evolving role of museums as active facilitators of knowledge. Future research should focus on long-term knowledge retention, inter-institutional collaborations, and improving group experiences to help visitors establish lasting connections with science and heritage.

However, AR has limitations in certain exhibits. Large-scale architectural works or aesthetic pieces, such as paintings and sculptures, may not benefit from digital manipulation. In contrast, small objects such as fossils or anatomical models are ideal for AR, offering detailed and dynamic experiences. Scaling 3D models in AR is also challenging—incorrect scaling can compromise visual quality, especially for large objects; however, scaling enables a better understanding of size and proportions.

Despite the availability of AR at home, in-person museum visits remain essential. They provide sensory engagement, authentic artefacts, and social interaction that virtual experiences cannot replicate. AR enhances these aspects but cannot replace them. Lastly, AR fosters collaborative learning in museum spaces. With tools like the Merge Edu 'World' feature, multiple visitors can engage with the same AR objects, promoting shared exploration and discussion and enriching both the learning and social experiences of museum visits.

Acknowledgements

We sincerely thank María Luisa Gómez Martínez, Eduard Novell, and Roger Taixes from the CosmoCaixa Science Museum in Barcelona for their invaluable support and contributions.

Funding

This research was supported by AGAUR-FI ajuts (2025 FI-2 00899) Joan Oró of the Secretaria d'Universitats i Recerca del Departament de Recerca i Universitats de la Generalitat de Catalunya, i del Fons Europeu Social Plus.

Author contributions

Delsa Silva Amino Cufuna: conceptualization, data curation, formal analysis, funding acquisition, investigation, methodology, project administration, software, resources, supervision, validation, visualisation, writing – original draft, writing – review and editing. Gizeh Rangel-de Lazaro: conceptualization, writing – review and editing, supervision, validation. Josep M. Duart: supervision, validation.

Competing interests

We declare no conflicts of interest.

Author details

Delsa Silva Amino Cufuna[1*], Gizeh Rangel-de Lazaro[2] and Josep M. Duart[3]

1 Doctoral School, Universitat Oberta de Catalunya, Barcelona, Spain

2 School of Arts, College of Humanities, SOAS, University of London, London, UK

3 Faculty of Psychology and Educational Sciences, Universitat Oberta de Catalunya, Barcelona, Spain

*Address all correspondence to: scufuna@uoc.edu

References

[1] Freire P. Pedagogy of the Oppressed. New York: Continuum; 1970. ISBN: 9780826400475

[2] Luna U, Ibáñez-Etxeberria A. Cuando el museo se convirtió en espacio de aprendizaje. Educación y museos en Guipúzcoa en los años 80 [When the museum became a learning space. Education and museums in Guipúzcoa in the 1980s]. Arte, Individuo Y Sociedad. 2020;**32**(3):641-659. Available from: https://revistas.ucm.es/index.php/ARIS/article/download/64869/4564456553619

[3] Trujillo MAM. El Museo, Un Espacio De Educación No Formal [The Museum, a Space for Nonformal Education]. Bogotá, Colombia: Corporación Ima; 2017. Available from: https://www.corporacionima.com/wp-content/uploads/2017/05/El-museo-un-espacio-de-educaci%C3%B3n-no-formal.pdf

[4] Falk JH, Dierking LD. The Museum Experience Revisited. New York: Routledge; 2018. ISBN: 9781611320459

[5] Roitman D. El museo Como instrumento educativo hacia la diversidad: la experiencia del Museo Judío de Chile [The museum as an educational tool towards diversity: The experience of the Jewish Museum of Chile]. Cuadernos Judaicos. 2019;**36**:135-149

[6] Hernández Á. La educación museal para enriquecer la enseñanza y el aprendizaje [Museum education to enrich teaching and learning]. Bogotá, Colombia: Pontificia Universidad Javeriana; 2023

[7] Billinghurst M, Clark A, Lee G. A survey of augmented reality. Foundations and Trends® in Human–Computer Interaction. 2015;**8**(2-3):73-272. DOI: 10.1561/1100000049

[8] Chiappini L, Boccardi G, Wagensberg J. Museums as Educational Environments: The Role of Interactive Displays in Science Learning. New York: Springer; 2020

[9] Azuma RT. A survey of augmented reality. Presence: Teleoperators and Virtual Environments. 1997;**6**(4):355-385. DOI: 10.1162/pres.1997.6.4.355

[10] Hein GE. Learning in the Museum. New York: Routledge; 1998. ISBN: 9780415097765

[11] Billinghurst M, Dünser A. Augmented reality in the classroom. Computer. 2012;**45**(7):56-63. DOI: 10.1109/MC.2012.111

[12] Janis CM, Theodor JM, Boisvert B. Evolution of the grazing niche in Pleistocene mammals. Journal of Vertebrate Paleontology. 2012;**32**(5):1154-1166

[13] Voštinár P, Ferianc P. Merge cube is a new teaching tool for augmented reality. IEEE Access. 2023;**11**:81092-81100. DOI: 10.1109/ACCESS.2023.3301399

[14] Ritchhart R, Church M, Morrison K. Making Thinking Visible: How to Promote Engagement, Understanding, and Independence for all Learners. New York: Wiley; 2011. ISBN: 9780470915516

[15] Taylor EL, Taylor TN, Krings M. Paleobotany: The Study of the Biology and Evolution of Fossil Plants. New York: Academic Press; 2009. ISBN: 9780123739728

[16] Dunleavy M, Dede C. Augmented reality teaching and learning. In: Handbook of Research on Educational Communications and Technology. New York: Springer; 2014. pp. 735-745. ISBN: 9781461431848

[17] Gee JP. The Anti-Education Era: Creating more Innovative Students through Digital Learning. New York: Palgrave Macmillan; 2013. ISBN: 9780230342095

[18] Creswell JW. Research Design: Qualitative, Quantitative, and Mixed Methods Approaches. 4th ed. Thousand Oaks: SAGE Publications; 2014. ISBN: 9781452226101

[19] Hernández Sampieri R, Fernández Collado C, Baptista LP. Research Methodology. 6th ed. New York: McGraw-Hill Education; 2014. ISBN: 9781456223960

[20] Craig AB. Understanding Augmented Reality: Concepts and Applications. 2nd ed. New York: Morgan Kaufmann; 2021

[21] Magrinyà i Clos E. La Realidad Virtual y Aumentada en la jornada de puertas abiertas del instituto mostrando el proyecto de “Cultural Merge Cubes” [Virtual and augmented reality on the open day at the institute showcasing the “Cultural Merge Cubes” project]. Ciberespiral; 2024. Available from: https://ciberespiral.org/es/__trashed/

[22] Ruiz TD. Realidad Aumentada, educación y museos. Revista ICONO 14. 2011;**9**(2):212-226. Available from: http://www.icono14.net

[23] Ferrer-Torregrosa J, Torralba J, Jiménez M, García S. ARBOOK: Development and assessment of a tool based on augmented reality for anatomy. Educational Technology & Society. 2015;**18**(2):19-28

[24] Rodríguez F. AR 101– Augmented reality. AR/VR Journey. 2020. Available from: https://arvrjourney.com/ar-101-augmented-reality-6bc92a863b2e

[25] Herrera D. Metaverse in a virtual education context. Metaverse. 2022;**3**(1):1-7. DOI: 10.54517/met.v3i1.1807

[26] Jung T, tom Dieck MC, Lee H, Chung N. Augmented reality and the museum visitor experience. Journal of Heritage Tourism. 2020;**15**(1):1-15

[27] Eberbach C, Crowley K. From everyday to scientific observation: How children learn to observe the biological world. Review of Educational Research. 2009;**79**(1):39-68. DOI: 10.3102/0034654308325899

[28] Dodson P. The Horned Dinosaurs: A Natural History. Princeton: Princeton University Press; 2018. ISBN: 9781400887446

[29] Asogwa JI. The role of augmented reality in museum exhibitions: Enhancing visitor engagement and learning. Research Output Journal of Arts and Management. 2024;**3**(2):46-49. Available from: https://www.researchgate.net/publication/383084216

[30] Dünser A, Walker L, Horner H, Bentall D. Creating interactive physics education books with augmented reality. In: Proceedings of the 24th Australian Computer-Human Interaction Conference (OzCHI 2012); 2012; Melbourne, Australia. New York: ACM (Association for Computing Machinery); 2012. pp. 26-30

[31] Ibáñez MB, Delgado-Kloos C. Augmented reality for STEM learning: A systematic review. Computers & Education. 2018;**123**:109-123. DOI: 10.1016/j.compedu.2018.05.002

Section 2

Technical Approaches: Sensory Modalities, Perception, and Interaction

Chapter 4

Auditory Augmented Reality for Well-Being

Michael Frishkopf and Scott Smallwood

Abstract

Augmented reality (AR) harbors an ocularcentric bias toward visual augmented reality (VAR), at the expense of auditory augmented reality (AAR). The latter is more readily available, technologically simpler and lower cost, with great potential for improving human well-being, what we call AAR for Well-being (AAR4W). In our chapter, we discuss the history of AR from this perspective, then present several AAR4W projects, each extending reality with acousmatic sound, as informed, in varying proportions, by disciplines of sound art, electroacoustic composition, ethnomusicology, and health sciences, including context, technical descriptions, experience, and future implications. Each is designed to enhance well-being using soundscapes, which we define as steady-state, nonperiodic sound, primarily admixtures of natural, musical, and synthetic sounds. Soundscapes offer enormous potential to alter mood and promote mental health, while remaining subliminal. Our projects are designed to support reflection, meditation, relaxation, and focus, with explicit intentions ranging among aesthetic priorities of sound artists, multicultural educational priorities of ethnomusicologists, and therapeutic priorities of health care providers. We consider soundscapes an ideal AR vehicle for well-being, as they naturally blend seamlessly with the real world, mixing harmoniously with each other, requiring minimal technological intervention or cost, and fading non-distractively into the perceptual background, unlike VAR presentation of visual information, which tends to be perceptually and cognitively disruptive.

Keywords: augmented reality, sound, soundscapes, sound art, mental health, well-being, machine learning, soundwalking

1. Introduction: The varieties of AR experience

1.1 Definitions: AR, VAR, AAR

In a broad sense, augmented reality (AR) can be defined as a simulated sensory environment seamlessly superposed upon ordinary reality, rather than replacing it entirely, as in virtual reality (VR), such that the user perceives this environmental fusion through sensory channels. While the human senses are more numerous than the Aristotelian five,[1] AR encompasses primarily visual and auditory channels; olfactory, haptic, and gustatory channels are rarely addressed due to technological obstacles. But for the most part, AR combines possibilities offered by visual augmented reality (VAR) and auditory augmented reality (AAR).[2] AAR and VAR may aim for coordinated, congruent sensory fusion, providing auditory and visual perspectives on a common multisensory simulated environment (e.g., matching sights and sounds of wild animals, a moving vehicle, or a trumpet player), or they may generate independent auditory and visual environments.

Frequently, AR is narrowly equated (sometimes tacitly) with VAR. As Yang, Barde, and Billinghurst state in their review, referencing earlier authors: "...the overwhelming majority of AR research has been focusing on visual augmentation" [6, 9–11]. Prevailing definitions center on computer technology generating graphical images augmenting natural vision, using optical see-through displays to superimpose virtual visual objects over reality [12]. The following entry in a technical dictionary is typical of the ocularcentric bias:

> **augmented reality** *the idea that an observer's experience of an environment can be augmented with computer generated information. Usually this refers to a system in which computer graphics are overlaid onto a live video picture or projected onto a transparent screen as in a head-up display [13].*

Modern VAR is predicated upon high-tech devices developed only in recent decades—such as stereographic (binocular) head-mounted or head-up displays (HMDs, HUDs), AR eyeglasses and contact lenses, and virtual retinal displays (VRDs)—to present virtual images to the user [14, 15]. Indeed, though AR dates to Morton Heilig's 1962 Sensorama, which combined visual, acoustic, and olfactory stimulation [16, 17], and Sutherland's early HMD [18], the term "augmented reality" was not coined until 1992, with the development of digital HMD technologies [19], which came to be intimately associated with the concept [20]. Textbook treatments of AR generally pay short shrift to sound, limiting it to a support role in the service of virtual images [15] (for instance, both virtual avatars and NPCs may need to speak) despite the fact that AAR is, in many respects, simpler, less expensive, and more emotionally powerful.

Actually, Mavor and Durlach's foundational 1995 edited volume on virtual environments devotes its entire third chapter to the auditory channel, following prefatory remarks, presciently echoing our own observations on low-tech AAR:

> *As indicated previously, the accomplishments and needs associated with the auditory channel differ radically from those associated with the visual channel. Specifically, in the auditory channel, the interface devices (earphones and loudspeakers) are essentially adequate right now. In other words, from the viewpoint of synthetic environment (SE) systems, there is no need for research and development on these devices and no need to consider the characteristics of the peripheral auditory system to which such devices must be matched. What is needed, however, is better understanding of*

[1] As Aristotle enumerated and affirmed in his *De Anima*, Book 3, Part 1, "one may be satisfied that there are no senses apart from the five (I mean vision, hearing, smell, taste, and touch)..." [1, 2]. Modern perceptual science recognizes at least seven senses, including proprioception and the vestibular sense [3, 4].

[2] Others have used the same initialism for the roughly synonymous terms audio augmented reality [5–7] or augmented aural reality [8].

> *what sounds should be presented using these devices and how these sounds should be generated. Accordingly, most of the material presented in this section is concerned not so much with auditory interfaces as with other aspects of signal presentation in the auditory channel [21].*

There follows a discussion of how to communicate information to the user through the auditory channel, including (on p. 136) the related but distinct techniques of data audification and sonification (these terms are elaborated below), as well as spatial sound, all within the broader field of auditory display technology [22], while noting that "...relatively little attention has been given to augmented reality in the auditory channel" [21].

However, despite this broad "vision" for AAR early in AR's history, in practice most subsequent AR research has focused on the visual field, as well as practical informational applications (medical, robotic, etc.), rather than creative or therapeutic ones, at least until the more recent era of AR gaming. Several widely cited overviews of AR exclude the auditory field entirely. Thus, Dey et al., citing Azuma: "Augmented Reality (AR) is a technology field that involves the seamless overlay of computer generated virtual images on the real world, in such a way that the virtual content is aligned with real world objects, and can be viewed and interacted with in real time (Azuma, 1997)" [9], or Zhou et al.: "Augmented Reality (AR) is a technology which allows computer generated virtual imagery to exactly overlay physical objects in real time" [10].

Yet, in his pioneering article, Ronald Azuma himself defined AR broadly as a system with three characteristics: "1) Combines real and virtual; 2) Interactive in real time; 3) Registered in 3-D" ([23], section 1.2). And while nearly all his examples are visual, he also emphasizes AR's multisensory nature, specifically mentioning the possibility of AAR:

> *Augmented Reality might apply to all senses, not just sight. So far, researchers have focused on blending real and virtual images and graphics. However, AR could be extended to include sound. The user would wear headphones equipped with microphones on the outside. The headphones would add synthetic, directional 3–D sound, while the external microphones would detect incoming sounds from the environment. This would give the system a chance to mask or cover up selected real sounds from the environment by generating a masking signal that exactly canceled the incoming real sound (Durlach and Mavor 1995). While this would not be easy to do, it might be possible [23].*

Azuma's definition of AR emphasizes an important ingredient noted by many other authors (e.g., [20]), namely interactivity: the simulated sensory environment (whatever its modalities) is required to respond to the subject's spatio-temporal environment: location, orientation, movement, time, and potentially internal physiological variables (e.g., heart rate) as well. While perhaps "not easy to do" at the time of his writing (1997), interactive augmentation in the auditory field is readily available today. For instance, earbuds can directionalize sound depending on head orientation or cancel unwanted noises, enabling greater focus on desired sounds. Hearing aids are a case in point. AAR may also interact with the visual field, for instance, reading visible texts aloud [8] or providing an audible dimension to virtual images. Several projects have developed sophisticated AAR for the blind and visually impaired, rendering the world as sound [24–29]. But AAR need not be technologically complex to be effective. Unfortunately, nearly 30 years after Azuma's speculations, comprehensive explorations of AAR concepts, technologies, applications, taxonomies, and potentials remain scarce, though several recent articles and one book (by a sound designer) herald an emerging disciplinary maturity (see [5–7, 30]).

1.2 AAR and VAR compared

VAR generally entails the technological complexity and cost of a mobile, head-mounted visual display in order to effectively fuse the simulated visual field with the real one. But when AR is defined as a computer-generated overlay occupying any sensory modality [31], a far lower-tech version is possible in the acoustic domain, where "...virtual auditory content is blended into the physical world to augment the user's real acoustic environment." Yet, "audio augmented reality (AAR) remains relatively under-explored" [6] as well as under-theorized, though the recent grounded theory taxonomy by Dam et al. [5, 30] represents a salutary step toward establishing AAR on a more solid foundation. As in feature film or video game soundtracks, auditory channels, though universally acknowledged as critical, tend to be subordinate to the visual ones. But, like VAR, AAR is powerful, though in a different way, and presents a much lower technological bar.

In its broadest form, AAR is familiar as recorded audio content played over a loudspeaker. Such AR offers a potentially enormous range of content without the need for more advanced technology, and thus at a much lower cost, with fewer barriers to entry. No digital technology is required for AAR; open-backed or bone-conduction headphones suffice, allowing the audio stream to blend seamlessly with the real environment. Indeed, any acousmatic[3] sound fulfills AR's broad sense definition. With the advent of portable, personal listening devices starting with the cassette-based Walkman (1979), through the portable CD and MP3 players, to the contemporary smartphone and the latest crop of smart glasses and lightweight speakers (headphones or earbuds), the radical impact of acousmatic environmental augmentation became portable too [33–36].

Played through loudspeakers, sound is broadcast relatively omnidirectionally, providing a collective augmented reality by diffusing, reflecting, and diffracting throughout a space, circumnavigating solid objects that would block light, and thereby affecting all who inhabit it, as well as drawing them together through shared auditory experience. Played through personal listening devices, sound becomes mobile and can be personalized. Either way, acousmatic sound can transform mood and color other perceptual modalities far more readily than in the visual domain. The low-tech VAR equivalent to the loudspeaker, for instance, projecting images on one wall of a room,[4] is far less immersive. Even when the projected image is large enough to encompass peripheral vision, the user is required to look in a particular direction. But augmentation of visual reality *via* smart eyewear, the equivalent of a personal listening device, requires the complexity and expense of an HMD in order to blend

[3] The acousmatic, a concept developed by Pierre Schaeffer, founder of *musique concrète*, is that which is heard without the cause being seen [32].

[4] It is possible, if expensive and usually impractical, to project omnidirectionally across walls and ceilings of special-purpose spaces, such as a planetarium, or the projective VAR popular at location-based entertainment (LBE) venues such as Meow Wolf (USA) and TeamLab (Japan), thereby obviating special eyewear.

seamlessly with visual reality.[5] Furthermore, at its simplest, the auditory modality is emotionally powerful, widely viewed as more affective, unmediated, soulful, or embodied than the visual, as numerous philosophers and neuroscientists have variously discussed across the ages ([40–43]; [44] book 3, section 402). Even newer AR technologies have begun to recognize the advantages of AAR. Indeed, Meta's first foray into the world of AR glasses, the Ray-Ban Meta smart glasses, has resulted in a system that is mostly geared toward sound and lacks an HMD due to current constraints of technology and cost.[6]

One technology critic has noted that music is the simpler, original AR: "Augmenting our visual field is a new feat, but augmenting our sense of sound is one of the oldest human tricks... When music plays in the background, it provides an emotional undertone for everyone in its presence." And it does so without the need for intrusive, distracting devices strapped to one's body. "Having music at our fingertips gives us something many of us lack but crave–control over our environment as well as control of our emotions... Even Google may have realized that augmented reality solutions don't need a screen. They just need sound" [46].

AAR's relative simplicity and lower cost depend in part on the fact that providing an immersive auditory field does not require bringing auditory objects into spatial focus, unlike the visual field, where reality augmentation requires spatial focusing on the retina. Indeed, the power of acoustic AR lies partly in the unfocused nature of sound, which tends to permeate enclosed spaces without casting sharp shadows. The tonotopic cochlea performs frequency analysis, and while auditory spatialization follows in the auditory cortex, sonic spatialization is relatively crude compared to spatialization of the visual field. Acousmatic sound takes advantage of these facts while radically widening the range of sonic possibility to anything that has been recorded. Acoustically transparent headphones are thus a simple, relatively low-tech way to augment acoustic reality without blocking it.

However, simply playing music or other sounds in the background does not satisfy everyone's definition of AR. As stated earlier, in a narrower sense, AR (and VR) require a simulated *interactive* sensory environment responsive to, as well as superposed upon, the real one. To meet this definition, both AR and VR must respond to the user's *spatial* attributes, location, and orientation, using sensors and processors to track GPS position, as well as head, hand, eye, or body movements. Interactivity makes both VAR and AAR more difficult and costly: simulated visual and acoustic fields must be continuously recomputed with corresponding changes in the user position. Such requirements entail additional input and output technology: cameras, accelerometers, magnetometers, gyroscopes, microphones, and GPS to map the environment and detect body and eye location, orientation, and movement; binocular displays and binaural speakers to render the virtual sensible. AR can thereby adjust the projected scene according to the real scene, combined with subject movement.

But even subject to this narrower definition, AAR is simpler than VAR. Given a user trajectory within an AV environment, each AR audio channel is a map from time to amplitude, while each video channel is a map from time and 2D raster pixel space

[5] Excellent earbuds are available for around $100 USD, headphones for around $300, while a good HMD costs over $1000. Within Apple's pricier product line, the AirPods 4 earbuds retail for $129, AirPods Max headphones for $549, and Apple Vision Pro HMD for $3499 [37–39].

[6] Meta's new augmented reality system, Orion, is deemed "too complicated and expensive to manufacture right now" [45].

to the four channels defining each pixel (e.g., R, G, B, alpha). And displaying visual information is far more complex than displaying acoustical information, as has been noted. Furthermore, when performing realistic AR modeling through binaural and binocular representations, auditory channels are less variable than the visual due to the more omnidirectional propagation of sound compared to light in the real domain and therefore also in the virtual one. Vision is highly directional, while audition is more omnidirectional and diffused, even when fully modeling binaural hearing by computing a head-related transfer function (HRTF). When the subject moves or turns, VAR necessitates rapid computations corresponding to the quickly changing spatial visual field; in contrast, the spatial auditory field remains more constant, even when computing binaural sound as a function of position, at least when simulating realistic sensory environments.

Interactive sonic technologies have been developed with far fewer technological machinations than required for their visual counterparts. To quote the same technological critic: "Further augmenting its effect, the music we hear can now be responsive to our environments. Spotify allows users to discover popular tracks in their cities or even sync their music to their run. Technology also exists to sync music with gaming experiences or to soundtrack your surroundings" [46–50].

But interactivity may also entail responsiveness to a user's physiological attributes by means of biometric data, including heart rate (HR, indicating physiological arousal), heart rate variability (HRV, reflecting stress and autonomic nervous system activity), galvanic skin response (GSR, measuring emotional arousal), respiration rate (RR, related to stress and relaxation), and skin temperature, as well as data from electroencephalography (EEG, indicating brain activity) and electromyography (EMG, indicating muscle activation). This sort of interactivity is crucial in several AAR applications we discuss in this chapter.

VAR and AAR also differ in relation to cognitive (informational) communication versus emotional (affective) evocation: mentation vs. mood. The visual field superimposed in VAR is highly effective for the former, for instance, conveying airspeed to a pilot *via* a HUD, rendering critical data as a colored plot, or indicating positions of monsters in Pokémon Go [51]. AAR may function in the same way, carrying cognitive content *via* language (for instance, a synthesized voiceover describing a scene, virtual or real), as well as nonverbal auditory displays, including sonification (data-controlled sound) and audification (data rendered as sound) [22]. Using sonification, one might detect patterns in a dataset (perhaps a lengthy DNA sequence) by hearing it, while audification can render bounded oscillations (seismological data, say) audible. Whole research labs are dedicated to such topics [52]. Likewise, both VAR and AAR evoke mood and arouse emotion. But here the latter is more effective. Perhaps the affective power of sound is most widely recognized in the form of music. However, in our projects, we focus not on music as usually understood, but rather on "soundscapes."

The soundscape concept first came to prominence through the work of Canadian composer and environmentalist R. Murray Schafer, who in the early 1970s wrote an influential text, *The Tuning of the World*, in which he introduced the term, encouraging the reader to consider the world soundscape as "a macrocosmic musical composition" [53]. With this text, along with a series of research projects out of Simon Fraser University, Schafer and his colleagues founded the field of acoustic ecology, along with the World Forum for Acoustic Ecology, an organization that still exists today, with its own journal, entitled *The Soundscape*. Schafer's project, part activism and part artistic inquiry, inspired a new generation of listeners who combined this "world soundscape" sensibility with *Deep Listening* methodologies of Pauline Oliveros, an

American composer and improviser who cultivated an immersive life practice of listening that complemented many of Schafer's ideas [54].

Our projects center on soundscapes not as occurring naturally in the world, but rather soundscapes that are deliberately fashioned for aesthetic-educational-therapeutic purposes and generated acoustically. Therefore, our definition is much narrower. For our purposes, we succinctly define a soundscape as a stochastically steady-state, non-periodic (and hence extensible), non-distractive (hence non-denotative[7]) acousmatic sound. Such sounds include collages of static natural sounds, such as rain, wind, surf, insects, or dawn choruses; sounds of human activity (e.g., highway traffic, cafe babble); synthetic "colored" noise (white, brown, pink, etc.; see [55]); as well as ambient and minimalist music, especially drones, and so-called sonic or acoustic "wallpaper" [56, 57]. Brian Eno, for example, who coined the term *ambient music* in the 1970s, conceived of room ambiences enhanced through musical processes, by which spaces could be suffused with "an atmosphere, or a surrounding influence: a tint" [58]. A great variety of sounds fit, or can be made (through judicious editing) to fit, our definition of soundscape, including various combinations of natural sounds, synthetic sounds, and musical sounds in genres such as ambient, drone, or minimalism, though not the broader category of music as usually conceived (and especially not song!). Following from their definition, it is easy to see that the set of all soundscapes (quite unlike music) is additively closed: mixing two soundscapes produces a third. This closure property—not shared with music—is quite useful, as we will observe. Furthermore, again, unlike most music, soundscapes tend to be non-distractive, fading into the perceptual background, rendering them more suitable for inducing mental calm and focus.

While visual content may trigger emotional responses, as in the visual arts, and especially *via* emotionally disturbing imagery, the auditory channel is widely regarded as far more potent in this regard [59, 60], generating an affective response by indexing environment features, carrying paralinguistic emotion, evoking affective memory, or setting a mood *via* musical properties like timbre, melody, and harmony. Our response to natural soundscapes is probably shaped by evolution, stimulating the autonomic nervous system directly, triggering a stress response (sympathetic nervous system) for some sounds (e.g., roaring lion) and a relaxation response (parasympathetic nervous system) for others (e.g., chirping crickets) [61–67]. Further, audition is naturally immersive; unlike light, sound waves suffuse an enclosed space, and our auditory system is, correspondingly, always "open." There is no auditory counterpart to "looking away" ("hearing away"?); as Schafer famously remarked, "there are no earlids" [68].

Yet another contrast between VAR and AAR lies in the possibilities for a collective social media experience. VAR can, of course, be synchronized across users, but for the purposes of realism, the technology must uniquely tailor visual imagery to each user in order to achieve perspectival interactivity; unless similarly positioned, no two people will receive the same signal (though they may access different perspectives on the same virtual space, by which the technology can nevertheless induce mediated socialization). However, AAR opens the possibility of a realistic collective social experience

[7] This attribute—required because all denotative reference tautologically entails distraction, through the cognitive shift from sonic signifier to signified—is relative to the listener. In particular, any verbal content must be incomprehensible, either due to dense polyphony (the buzz of a crowded cafe) or linguistic unfamiliarity (a monolingual English speaker hearing Mandarin, though even the uncomprehending perception of *meaningfulness* may be distracting).

in which a group of people simultaneously hears the same sounds. This collective experience enables AAR to generate broad social connections in a way that VAR does not, just as a concert, which may gather thousands to participate in a synchronous communal aural event, is a more effective generator of collective experience than a museum exhibit, in which shared experiences are scarce and largely unsynchronized.

1.3 Auditory augmented reality for well-being (AAR4W)

In this chapter, we are primarily interested in the use of AAR to generate an independent simulated auditory environment, without any coordinated VAR analog, to enhance well-being. Compared to VAR, the relative technical simplicity, immersiveness, emotional power, and collective experience of AAR render it more effective, as well as more practical and economical, toward the promotion of well-being.

Well-being admits a wide array of definitions; here we focus on its broadest psychological and sociological dimensions: human health in a general sense—physical, mental, and social—particularly stress reduction, serenity, focus, insight, and interpersonal connection. Soundscapes appear to be ideal for well-being in this general sense. In our work, we therefore focus upon soundscapes, either as intentionally therapeutic tools or as sound art compositions inducing well-being as a side effect of an intended aesthetic experience. Being steady-state and non-distractive, soundscapes are extensible to arbitrary length, fading into the sensory background while strongly, if subliminally, shaping mood. The closure property mentioned earlier enables sonic mixing and collaging, opening new possibilities for their creation, deployment, and optimization: effective soundscapes can be combined and composited.

Such soundscapes serve to alter the intersensory perception of one's environment, powerfully and unobtrusively shaping consciousness as surely as other environmental factors, such as lighting, temperature, and wall color. While both sounds and the AR devices that produce them may become objects of perceptual focus, they can also recede into the background realm of utility as naturalized practical instruments for interacting with the world, what Heidegger called "ready-to-hand" [69]. Just as a seasoned pianist, for whom the piano is a virtual bodily extension, needn't think about her musical tool, neither must the wearer of a portable acousmatic playback device, which likewise becomes a bodily extension.

There is a large literature on the value of music and sound for well-being [63, 70–74], including among students [75–80]. Many of these studies focus on soundscapes using a definition comparable to ours (steady-state aperiodic), though typically they do not describe these possibilities as AR. Sounds that activate the parasympathetic autonomic nervous system and thus elicit a relaxation response are widely regarded as therapeutic in a broad as well as specific sense, from accelerating convalescence in the hospital to enhancing focus in the classroom and generally improving mood [81–83]. Soundscapes (by our definition) tend to have this effect. The literature suggests that colored noise [84, 85] and predictable natural soundscapes are particularly effective [86–92]. No doubt human beings have evolved over millennia to interpret predictable (hence low-information) nature soundscapes featuring stochastically steady-state sounds resulting from the sonic summation of myriad unthreatening agents (such as chirping crickets, croaking frogs, rustling leaves, light rain, and gentle surf) as auditory streams requiring minimal perceptual attention, to which we therefore respond with decreased stress, increased relaxation, and improved mood. Such sounds contrast with unpredictable high-information impulse sounds emitted by potentially dangerous agents, like the roar of a wild animal or unexpected footsteps in one's home, which trigger a high perceptual alert, requiring rapid processing and stimulating a stressful fight-flight response[8] [86, 94–96].

Another immersive practice, *soundwalking*, adds to the already recognized practice of walking (for physical and mental health): a method of listening and attunement to the sense of place through a specific, often artistically curated pathway. Soundwalks can be self-directed or curated and guided, and at a basic level involve moving attentively through an environment and practicing what Pauline Oliveros called *Deep Listening*, or listening with attention to analytical detail, intentionally [54]. Hildegard Westerkamp—an original member of the aforementioned acoustic ecology movement of R. Murray Schafer, Barry Truax, and others—has written extensively on soundwalking as a practice, describing it as an "intense introduction to the experience of uncompromised listening" [97].

Soundwalking can also be mediated through technology, and this is where it leans into an AR practice. For example, Janet Cardiff's audio walks, a huge part of her oeuvre since the 1990s, require the listener to wear open-backed headphones, which allow the local soundscape to leak through a mediated version of that same soundscape Cardiff recorded earlier, alongside her reflections, instructions, musings, and storytelling [98]. In another example, Christina Kubisch's *Electrical Walks* uses special headphones and instructions for listening to sounds that are created through magnetic induction noises in modern electronics spread throughout cities, including ATMs, security electronics, and other electronic equipment found in everyday urban environments. For this work, the listener is hearing sounds that normally would not be possible to hear, bringing into sonic awareness a whole layer of existence that we normally would not notice [99]. These two examples differ in their approaches to the normative soundscape of the environments in which they happen, Cardiff's being more attuned to the sense of place and its potential for narrative and historical reflection, whereas Kubisch's work brings us into a hidden layer where our imaginations can interpret the experience in personal ways. Additionally, both of these examples involve solo reflections, although often they are presented in groups of individual listeners who walk together.

Soundwalks can be mediated by older technologies as well, such as musical instruments or other sounds. One of the current authors experienced such a soundwalk in Koli National Forest in Finland, led by Pessi Parvianinen in 2010. In this walk through the forest, Parvianinen secretly populated the trail with musicians, each in a solo environment playing excerpts of music by Finnish composers or improvising with birds. It was a lovely way to bring an additional sonic layer into the natural sounds of the environment, inviting the participants to consider generations of musicians whose music was influenced by this environment.

Whether intended as aesthetic, therapeutic, or wellness interventions, and whether deliberately combined with real sounds (as in soundwalks) or not, AR soundscapes can contribute to well-being.

2. AAR4W: Past and present

Soundscape-based AR for well-being lies on a continuum between art and utility. At the former pole, projects seek to extend the scope of music composition by integrating

---

[8] Or perhaps also the unpredictability of most music, requiring intensive perceptual processing, triggering an affective response by undercutting expectations, as hypothesized by Leonard Meyer [93].

sound with the lived environment, beyond the concert hall, embedding sound through installations. At the latter, projects explicitly seek to enhance well-being, using AR soundscapes to support mental health, especially mitigating stress and promoting calm focus. What follows is a review of some representative case studies.[9]

2.1 *Coronium 3500 (Lucie's Halo)*

In 2014, the second author (Smallwood) created an environmental, site-specific sound installation called *Coronium 3500 (Lucie's Halo)* on the site of Caramoor Center for Music and the Arts in Katonah, New York [101–103]. Part of a larger group of sound installations by various artists, this piece sought to tie the soundscape directly to the environment by (a) creating sounds inspired by the natural sounds of the site's birds and insects and (b) creating sounds that were entirely dependent on available sunlight (see **Figure 1**). The resulting "solarsonic" voices, which used custom electronics, played through several small speakers distributed around a grassy area. These speakers were powered by solar panels without batteries, which thus produced a variable level of real-time energy, affecting both the intensity and tempo of musical phrases (see [101] for technical details).

Although it has since been exhibited elsewhere, the original intention was to create a piece tied directly to Caramoor, incorporating its sounds into a mix of other sounds. Field recordings of the installation site were used to create the sound-making circuitry in order to engineer a soundscape inclusive of the local one. Then, when the piece was installed, the environment itself "played" the piece through a combination of sunlight and shadows created by large deciduous trees surrounding the site. Indeed, even the changing seasons played a role in the resulting soundscape, since the sun's angle, the presence or lack of leaves on the trees, and other environmental factors had a direct bearing on the sounds of the electronic "critters." This was a risky proposition, since the piece was exhibited on-site for 2 years, and the visitor's aural experience of the piece could not be controlled or determined. On a cloudy day, for example, the piece would be very quiet, with some voices never sounding at all. It was

Figure 1.
Coronium 3500 (Lucie's Halo)*, installed at the Caramoor Center for the Arts in Katonah, NY, in 2014 and 2015. Photograph by Scott Smallwood.*

[9] Descriptions of Scott Smallwood's projects are available in greater detail online [100].

fun to watch people experiencing the piece, especially when the sun would suddenly come out from behind clouds to awaken previously silent voices, to the surprise and delight of the visitors.

2.2 *Emergences/Expanded Anatomies*

In another work from 2024, entitled *Emergences/Expanded Anatomies*, Smallwood collaborated with visual artist Sean Caulfield on a site-specific installation on the historic townsite of Malvina, Quebec, a colonial-era village near the New Hampshire border [104]. In this work, combining multichannel audio with Caulfield's prints and drawings, many of which were made on-site, the piece captured the historic and current reality of Malvina, inclusive of a garden with its wooden fence and small garden cottage (see **Figure 2**). The sound piece included sounds of found objects, including many historical objects from the original town, loaned by local residents, and worked into drones and textures created on-site by the artist. In addition to these sounds, the idea was to also include the remarkable sounds of Malvina's birds, the wind and rain, the creek running by, and occasional tractors driving down the gravel road. Due to the lack of highway noise, these sounds were ever present in this "high fidelity" environment, and so rather than attempting to record them, the piece simply left room for them by including sparse spaces and silences through which they could be heard.

In both of these examples, the "AR" is clear: the pieces incorporate the sounds of the place where the piece happens, making the *place* itself integral to the work. This work owes some inspiration to many of Schafer's concert works, in which he eschewed the "temples of silence" that are concert halls in favor of natural environments that become part of the music and stories told in the work, often requiring the audience to travel to remote locations in northern Ontario and elsewhere [105]. Schafer's work reflects a more general shift towards inclusion of space and place as active parameters, due, in part, to the rise of multichannel sound, but also to the opening up of sonic materials to include our human soundscape. In fact, the rise of sound art in the 1980s, a genre of art born in visual art culture in which sound is an artistic medium, introduced ways of thinking about the artistic uses of sound beyond music, and this includes sound in the context of site-specificity.

2.3 Sounding the Garden

Sounding the Garden [106] is an interdisciplinary, educational AR sound art project situated at the intersection of fine arts, humanities, social sciences, artificial

Figure 2.
Emergences, *a 4-channel audio piece, with Sean Caulfield's* Expanded Anatomies, *in Malvina, Quebec, August and September 2024. Photographs by Scott Smallwood.*

intelligence, and engineering. It draws on student contributors, including electroacoustic music composers, world music performers, designers, and ethnomusicologists, aiming to support their development as artists and scholars.

In 2013, the Canadian Centre for Ethnomusicology (CCE) [107] and the Aga Khan Trust for Culture [108] collaborated on an international event entitled "I am a bird from Heaven's Garden: Music, Sound, and Architecture in the Muslim World," heralding the creation of a new Islamic garden (later named the "Aga Khan Garden") to be funded by the Aga Khan and located on the site of the University of Alberta's Botanic Garden [109, 110]. Out of this initiative emerged an AR project funded by the Canadian government's Social Science and Humanities Research Council (SSHRC) entitled "Evolving the Botanic Garden," which provided AR overlays as educational and aesthetic enhancements of the garden experience *via* visitors' mobile devices [111].

As CCE director, the first author (Frishkopf) led construction of an AAR layer, *Sounding the Garden* [106], aiming to enhance the garden experience with poetry, music, and other sound, with a Sufi interpretation: the garden stroll becoming a mystical-aesthetic path. A team was recruited, including both authors along with graduate students in composition, ethnomusicology, computer science, design, and drama.

Sounding the Garden is a spatial mapping of mystical language, projecting a famous poem by the Persian Sufi poet Farid al-Din Attar (c. 1145–c. 1221) entitled "Language of the Birds" (*Mantiq al-Tayr*), with its seven-stage spiritual journey toward enlightenment, onto the physical garden. We associated each stage—or "valley" (*wādi*), to adopt Attar's metaphor—with a section of the garden. An ensemble comprising students, alumni, and faculty of our music program then collectively created and recorded ambient improvisatory music in a Persian *dastgah* (melodic mode) corresponding (according to prominent Iranian music scholar, performer, and composer Majid Kiani) to each such "valley." We also embedded relevant tracks from a CD series, "Music of Central Asia" [112], at specific locations in the garden's augmented reality space, along with bird calls and poetic recitations of Attar's masterpiece in Persian, with English translations and interpretations.

Traversing the garden counterclockwise (aligning with Islam's spiritual direction), one progresses through the seven valleys in order while experiencing associated poetry, sounds, and music (see **Figure 3**). User position is tracked *via* GPS (or signaled by tapping on-screen icons), triggering the soundscape. In this way, the piece provides visitors a new sonic layer overlaid upon the remarkable soundscape of the garden itself, deepening affective understanding and enhancing well-being through sound.

2.4 Autonomous adaptive soundscapes

In 2012, sound artist and composer Yoko Senn found herself in the emergency room of a hospital in New York, and the sonic hellscape she described and sought to escape was almost more traumatic than her medical reason for being there. As an electronic musician and composer, Sen started to imagine ways that such a hospital soundscape could be "composed" by sound artists to create a calming space, rather than one of chaos. Her project to redesign hospital alarm sounds and noises has caught the attention of hospital administrators and researchers, and experiments are now underway to collaborate with equipment manufacturers to create a more supportive sonic environment [113].

Hospital environments are excellent candidates for augmenting a stressful reality with soothing sounds. High stress levels and anxiety, associated with

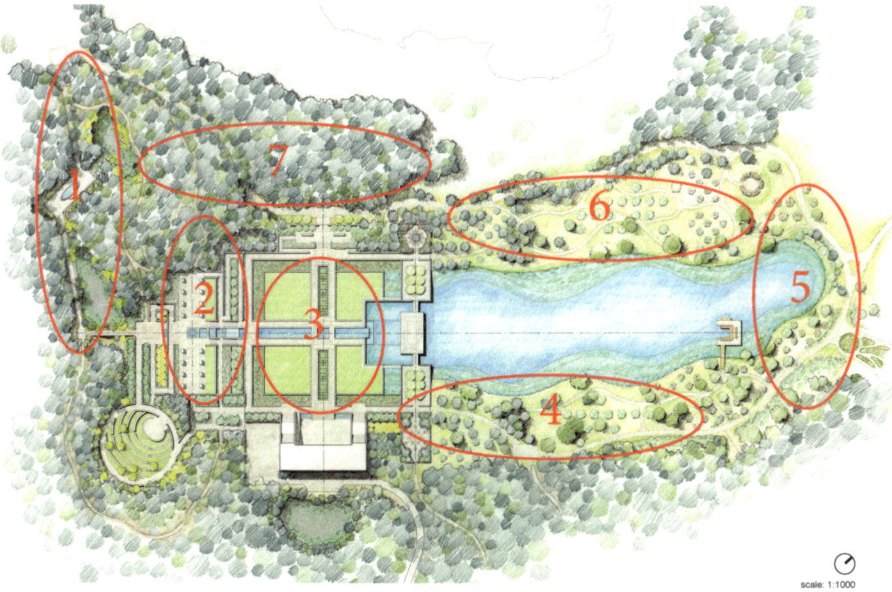

Figure 3.
Sounding the Garden entails mapping the seven mystical valleys of Attar's "Language of the Birds" onto the Aga Khan Garden in a counterclockwise circuit (starting from the Garden entrance, upper left): 1. The valley of the quest, 2. The valley of love, 3. The valley of insight into mystery, 4. The valley of detachment, 5. The valley of unity, 6. The value of bewilderment, 7. The value of poverty and nothingness.

delirium and sleep deprivation, are very common in critically ill patients and may compromise recovery and survival, as well as increase the length and costs of hospital stays [114–116]. Pharmacological approaches typically used to treat these conditions have non-negligible expense, limited effectiveness, and serious side effects. As a means to counter high stress levels and related effects, music and sound therapies are low-cost and noninvasive, with far more limited side effects than medication. Research (including our own systematic review) has shown them to be highly effective if customized to the patient [117, 118]. However, critically ill patients cannot be expected to communicate effectively with music therapists, who are scarce, frequently unavailable, and costly. Linguistic or cultural differences between the patient and therapist may also limit their effectiveness. Furthermore, as discussed above, soundscapes (as we define them) present many advantages over music.

Building on and integrating knowledge from multiple disciplines (music, music therapy, computer science, nursing, and critical care medicine), we developed *autonomous adaptive soundscapes* (AAS), an intelligent bio-algorithmic system generating therapeutic soundscapes for critically ill patients, using machine learning and biofeedback to induce relaxation, improve sleep, and reduce agitation, anxiety, and delirium [81]. AAS seeks to optimize a patient's sonic environment by dynamically selecting, tuning, and mixing soundscape files (currently around 10) drawn from an audio library spanning a wide range of recordings (natural, musical, and synthetic). A reinforcement learning approach [119] developed by computer scientist Martha Steenstrup guides the search of the soundscape space based on autonomic biosignals indicating the patient's current state, thereby delivering a customized soundscape to the patient (see **Figure 4**). No conscious, active engagement with the system is required from the patient. Our objective is a system suitable for the intensive care unit (ICU), one that is highly effective, always available, simple to operate, minimally intrusive, and low risk.

AAS also promises enormous potential beyond the ICU, as stress, anxiety, and insomnia are pervasive social problems. Recent evidence-based research supports the use of music and sound for sleep [121] and has led to the specification of sonic criteria (rhythm, pitch, frequency, volume, genre, and duration) suitable for relaxation [122]. However, this research has not yet been operationalized in autonomous adaptive soundscapes. Experimentation with AAS was difficult to conduct in practice due to restrictions surrounding ICU access, particularly during the pandemic, but we ran experiments using a medical simulation laboratory [123]; results are pending.

2.5 Mindful Social Listening (MSL)

We decided to modify AAS to provide adaptive soundscapes for relatively healthy subjects outside medical facilities but nevertheless in need of support, starting with those closest to us: our students. For *Mindful Social Listening* (MSL), we removed the constraint that no conscious, active engagement with the system is required. However, we also imposed a new one: the MSL system should select soundscapes suitable for group rather than individual listening in order to catalyze student socialization and reduce isolation, exacerbated by the use of headphones and earbuds while studying in the library.

The motivation for such a system stemmed from a simple observation: Academic life is replete with exploration, discovery, learning, creativity...and stress. How can soundscapes enhance student well-being and academic success? Across all disciplines, postsecondary students suffer from the stress that inevitably accompanies the harried occupation of university life, impeding learning and jeopardizing well-being. This dire situation has become a veritable mental health crisis. As university mental health programs are woefully under-resourced, students rely on various forms of self-care. Our pilot study revealed that over 75% of students experience high levels of stress, 94% use music and sound to cope, and about 80% find this use highly effective, wearing personal listening devices (headphones, earbuds) to enhance concentration, mask distractions, and reduce stress. However, students may not be optimizing their sonic environments for stress reduction and focus; often, their selected soundscapes, or

Figure 4.
The autonomous adaptive soundscape system (from poster session; see [120]).

preferred genres of music, are actually distracting them from work by demanding attention. Furthermore, personal listening devices can not only be deleterious to hearing but also contribute to social isolation. We sought instead to develop an autonomously evolving, shared, non-distracting augmented sonic reality: a soothing sonic factor analogous to such common (but nonadaptive) ergonomic factors as room temperature, lighting, seating, and interior design.

We address these limitations by developing an autonomous system that generates a responsive soundscape environment in a social listening space. Building on AAS, combining data mining, machine learning, and algorithmic composition, and drawing on field recordings, applied ethnomusicology, health science research, and creative sound art, we have designed a responsive soundscape environment that can autonomously adapt to feedback from socially interacting users, enhancing mindful calm and supporting academic well-being. Installed in a library study room on the University of Alberta campus, this octophonic system[10] operates by gathering conscious feedback from students, then compiling this information to update a "value" for each soundscape, as shown in **Figure 5**.

MSL deploys a "multi-armed bandit" reinforcement learning algorithm, balanced between exploration (seeking the optimal soundscape) and exploitation (making use of current knowledge), quite similar to that of AAS, and requiring calibration of three critical parameters:α, ε, and T. Each soundscape has a value $\in [-1,1]$, adjusted over time according to user feedback, comprising a vector. Initially, all values are set = 1. After playing a soundscape for T minutes, we compute its reward as the average user response: reward $\in [-1,1]$. Next, we recompute its value as a weighted average between the new reward (weight = α) and the old value (weight = $1-\alpha$). Finally, we select the next soundscape: with probability ε, select at random (exploration); with probability $1-\varepsilon$ select the highest-valued soundscape ("greedy" exploitation). Currently, we explore a small set of 10 (like AAS) but plan to develop the algorithm

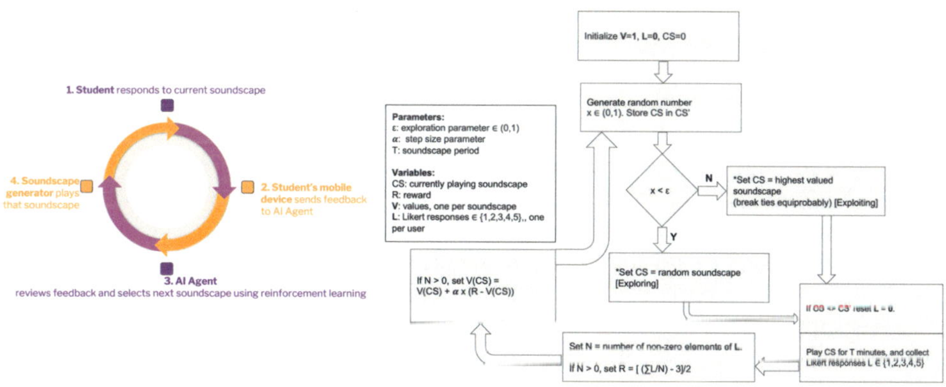

Figure 5.
Left: Autonomous adaptive feedback cycle to optimize soundscape selection. Right: Flowchart representation of the MSL algorithm [124].

[10] Actually 8.2, with all speakers securely mounted on walls and floor. Soundscapes are octophonic; subwoofer LFE channels are derived automatically *via* low-pass filtering. We have also developed a simpler, more portable stereo version that can be set up anywhere, in use for experimentation at the University of Calgary.

to enable exploration of larger sets (see below). Adaptation is difficult due to change: users may enter or exit, and their preferences may shift. Simulations show that with proper parameter settings, such a system can effectively adapt to play effective sounds addressing user preferences, provided the change is not too rapid.

3. Conclusion: Possible AAR4W futures

As Yogi Berra (or perhaps Niels Bohr) famously quipped, it is always difficult to make predictions, especially about the future. Yet, in our exploration of auditory augmented reality for well-being, many future avenues have suggested themselves, and we are currently exploring several.

AAS currently depends on heart rate alone, a biosignal that is easy to measure but does not fully capture stress. We are considering other noninvasive real-time metrics, including HRV, GSR, RR, EMG, and EEG, and currently experimenting with the latter outside the ICU. We are intending to extend MSL by incorporating a portal system, allowing users to log in so that individual value vectors can be computed and persistently retained from one session to another. Combining this concept with the idea of a single-user system would allow users to establish a value vector representing their own preferences prior to entry into a common listening environment. Then the social listening system would adjudicate among known preferences for the group of users presently inhabiting the space, rather than having to relearn for every group of users, as is now the case. Using collective or individual value vectors to identify the most popular soundscapes and then mixing them together (relying upon the additive closure property) is a possible strategy toward maximizing MSL's effectiveness, highlighting a distinct advantage of soundscapes over music.

For both AAS and MSL, it may be possible to estimate the value vector rather than learning it from scratch, given each user's demographic profile and sufficient data linking such profiles to sonic preferences. We have already conducted experiments along these lines, correlating various demographic parameters (including gender, age, place of birth, personality traits, education, musical preferences, and medical history) with sonic preferences, and all that is required is to gather more data.

It may also be possible to explore far larger collections of soundscapes if they can be arranged in a hierarchical or structured way, rather than as a flat data set, so as to facilitate heuristic search. For instance, if an algorithm can determine that users wish to hear sounds of water flowing rather than bird sounds, then the category of water flowing sounds can be explored through structured browsing, analogous to "drill-down" menus, or a progressive gallery exposure.

In any sort of social listening space, it may also be possible to localize soundscapes by spatially tracking users, delivering relevant sound to the subjects who prefer them (while avoiding others who do not). This sort of tracking is increasingly possible with advances in geolocation technologies together with the availability of directional loudspeakers, as well as recently emerging technologies for constructing audible enclaves that can be transmitted through curved paths in space [125], though taken to an extreme, personalized sound undermines the principle of social listening (and could be implemented more simply and effectively through headphones). MSL could also incorporate autonomic biosignal data, similar to AAS.

Moving beyond biosignals, nonhuman environmental signals in the listening space could also be included in an MSL-type system, including acoustic, optical, thermal, temporal, and geospatial sensors (e.g., adapting sound to the user's perceptual field, using cameras and AI to link to physical landmarks or lighting, as well as temperature, season, time of day, or place). Imagine a computer equipped with sensors for sound (microphones), lighting, temperature, humidity, GPS, and a clock, and a sensor to estimate how many people are in the room. All such data could be combined with biosignals and conscious responses as a means of determining, for example, that people prefer a certain kind of soundscape at dusk versus dawn.

MSL team member Khurram Javed has developed a prototype spatial sound single-user system, allowing the subject to position sounds relative to an on-screen avatar, then indicate the degree of satisfaction for each configuration [126]. The idea is that the system will explore the possibilities while bearing in mind configurations that have already been evaluated in this way. The same system can be used for social listening situations with public speakers, combining the spatial sound preferences of everybody in the room. Experimentation with this system, in collaboration with students at NYU's MARL [127], to address the needs of attention deficit hyperactivity disorder (ADHD) students is in its initial phases.

New soundscapes for these and other projects can be developed using audio resources gleaned by combing through archives, online and off, as well as new recordings made both in the studio and in the field, and new compositions in the emerging domain of sound art. Indeed, we have already curated over 700 soundscapes using online sources alone. Stacy Bliss [128]—educator, musician-improviser, and sound artist/therapist—specializes in the sonorities of gongs and bowls for sound baths of meditative healing. In 2023, we invited her to the University of Alberta to record improvised gong performances in our Sound3Lab recording studio. With these recordings, we generated a library of gorgeous textures, which we hope to use in future systems as layers for soundscape generation, potentially linked to user profiles and preferences. Two graduate students are currently working on 8-channel pieces utilizing these recordings. Similarly, composer and sound designer Greg Mulyk contributed field recordings, and he and composer Nicolás Arnáez composed soundscapes for MSL.

It is also possible to conceptualize generalizations of soundscapes that operate beyond the range of hearing, exploring low and infrasonic frequencies that are sensed haptically more than auditorily, or tapping into the auditory system directly in a manner analogous to retinal displays. Not only are low frequencies known to be therapeutic, but also such a system would be advantageous for the hard-of-hearing or deaf community.

However, soundscapes extend beyond data in the form of sound files and could include procedural algorithms, including stochastic processes and generative AI. One of our graduate students, Deepak Paramashivan, is developing promising generative AI techniques to produce therapeutic soundscapes from smaller bits of sound, granular synthesis, potentially down to the level of an individual sample. Such a system might also be able to generate a soundscape given a user's stated musical preferences. Although music and soundscapes are different according to our definitions, it may be possible to transform music into a soundscape using AI or other techniques, focusing on static aspects, such as timbre, sonority, harmony, and texture, rather than melody, rhythm, or developmental form.

Extending to other sensory systems, such soundscapes as have been described could be combined with visual displays. Projecting a soundscape into the visual field can be affected in a variety of ways, from the low-tech (e.g., variable lighting in the room, including color, or corresponding images on a display screen) to the high-tech (all the apparatus of AR, from glasses to retinal projection).

As we enter an age of increasing use of wearable technology with lower costs, lighter weight, and better quality, sounds tied to bodily states and daily function are increasingly likely use cases. Already, one can walk to the gym, swim laps, and walk from there to work, while one's smartwatch tracks every step and stair climb and knows how many strokes one swam and how many calories one burned, all with very little prompting. And already, one's wireless earbuds serve endless musical and podcast content, often controlled through voice commands and no physical interfacing. Features such as noise cancelation can shut out much of the world, while bone-conductive technologies can provide good-quality sound without blocking the ears' listening mechanisms.

The technologies of sound production are also now linked to technological forms of personalization, including physiological responses through sensors, but also to our social media data; yet, the linking of these things has only just begun to come into focus.[11] One aspect of this is the personal space of the phone/earphone-scape, but what is really exciting to us is the possibility of group soundscape generation, where the soundscape is linked to a group of individuals in real time, reflecting a kind of "public hum," inside of which would be places for individual escape or contemplation.

In addition to technological affordances, cultural use of sound has expanded beyond music produced in "temples of silence" [105] and includes a whole panoply of soundscape and nature recordings, ambient music, site-specific sound art, and other sound designs meant to enhance one's mood within their current environment. We have surveyed some artists who work in these realms, but it is also worth noting the various genres of meditative practices that commonly use music designed specifically for mindfulness and healing. Many artists have found places for themselves within the larger ecosystems of mindfulness practices. For example, Kaitlyn Aurelia Smith's 2013 album *Tides: Music for Meditation and Yoga* was commissioned by her mother for use in her meditation practice and became a sensation in the electronic music community, being rereleased with special vinyl editions in 2019. Much of this music is created with analog synthesizers and harmonized vocals, which create uniquely rich forms of droning textures.

In summary, whether explicitly geared toward meditation, mental health, or aesthetic experience, or whether conceived as sound art, music, education, or therapy, the affective power of acousmatic auditory augmented reality presents innumerable possibilities for creative innovation, experimentation, and deployment, ranging far beyond AR's usual ocularcentric limitations, to support human well-being in the widest possible sense.

Acknowledgements

Martha Steenstrup developed the ML algorithms for AAS, with system programming from Yourui Guo and Marc-André Haley, using Health Gauge watches for heart rate measurement; Martha led AAS experimentation at the NAIT medical simulation unit with support from Mariia Ostroha, Marc-André, Shaista Meghani, and Usha Pant. Greg Mulyk and Corona Wang gathered online soundscape recordings; Greg also recorded new ones *in situ*. Octophonic soundscapes were edited and composed

[11] *Ed. note: Sony has a demo in their Sony Park showroom in the Ginza that samples the heartbeats of about a dozen listeners, then composes music and icons that express that pulse, displayed in a shared space: https://www.sonypark.com/e/activity/003/*

by Greg and Nicolás Arnáez. Greg programmed MSL, and Khurram Javed developed the spatial sound version. MSL experimentation at the University of Alberta could not have proceeded without support from the library, which authorized speaker installation in a study room funded by a grant from United Way. MSL research at the University of Calgary was led by Chelsea Taylor, supervised by Stephanie Plamondon. Sounding the Garden ambient music recordings were organized by Hossein Hosseiniparvar, with sound design by Greg Mulyk and GPS programming by Yourui Guo. Central Asian tracks are courtesy of Fairouz Nishanova, Director of the Aga Khan Music Programme, and Smithsonian Folkways Recordings. The larger Aga Khan Garden web app project was led by Hussein Keshani. Tom Merklinger's tireless work keeps the Sound Studies Institute running. We also wish to acknowledge and deeply thank our funders: the University of Alberta's Killam Foundation (MSL) and Vice President Research and Innovation Pilot Seed Grant (AAS), as well as two of Canada's federal research programs, the New Frontiers in Research Fund (AAS) and the Social Sciences and Humanities Research Council (Sounding the Garden).

Thanks

The authors would like to express their sincere gratitude to the editor of this volume, Michael Cohen, for his incisive critiques, valuable recommendations, and exemplary editorial precision.

Abbreviations

AAR	auditory augmented reality, audio augmented reality, or augmented aural reality
AAR4W	auditory augmented reality for well-being
AAS	autonomous adaptive soundscapes
AR	augmented reality
CCE	Canadian Centre for Ethnomusicology
EEG	electroencephalography
EMG	electromyography
GPS	global positioning system
GSR	galvanic skin response
HR	heart rate
HRTF	head-related transfer function
HRV	heart rate variability
HUD	head-up display
ICU	intensive care unit
LBE	location-based entertainment
LFE	low-frequency effects
MSL	Mindful Social Listening
RR	respiration rate
VAR	visual augmented reality

Author details

Michael Frishkopf* and Scott Smallwood
University of Alberta, Edmonton, Canada

*Address all correspondence to: michaelf@ualberta.ca

References

[1] Polansky RM. Aristotle's De Anima. New York: Cambridge University Press; 2007

[2] Aristotle. On the Soul: On Breath; Parva Naturalia. Cambridge, Mass./ London: Harvard University Press/W. Heinemann Ltd.; 1935. (Loeb Classical Library)

[3] Brandt T, Dieterich M, Huppert D. Human senses and sensors from Aristotle to the present. Frontiers in Neurology. 2024;**15**:1404720

[4] Fritzsch B, editor. The Senses: A Comprehensive Reference. 2nd ed. Cambridge, MA: Academic Press; 2021. Available from: https://www.sciencedirect.com/science/referenceworks/9780128054093

[5] Dam A, Siddiqui A, Leclercq C, Jeon M. Taxonomy and definition of audio augmented reality (AAR): A grounded theory study. International Journal of Human-Computer Studies. 2024;**182**:103179

[6] Yang J, Barde A, Billinghurst M. Audio augmented reality: A systematic review of technologies, applications, and future research directions. Journal of the Audio Engineering Society. 2022;**70**(10):788-809

[7] Harju M. Audio Augmented Reality: Concepts, Technologies and Narratives, Technologies and Narratives. London: CRC Press; 2025

[8] Manthorpe R. Listen Up: Augmented Reality is Coming to Your Ears. Wired; 2016. Available from: https://www.wired.com/story/aural-augmented-reality/

[9] Dey A, Billinghurst M, Lindeman RW, Swan JE. A systematic review of 10 years of augmented reality usability studies: 2005 to 2014. Frontiers in Robotics and Artificial Intelligence. 2018;**5**:1-28. Available from: https://www.frontiersin.org/journals/robotics-and-ai/articles/10.3389/frobt.2018.00037/full

[10] Zhou F, Duh HBL, Billinghurst M. Trends in augmented reality tracking, interaction and display: A review of ten years of ISMAR. In: 2008 7th IEEE/ACM International Symposium on Mixed and Augmented Reality. New York City: ACM; 2008. pp. 193-202. Available from: https://ieeexplore.ieee.org/document/4637362

[11] Kim K, Billinghurst M, Bruder G, Duh HBL, Welch GF. Revisiting trends in augmented reality research: A review of the 2nd decade of ISMAR (2008-2017). IEEE Transactions on Visualization and Computer Graphics. 2018;**24**(11):2947-2962

[12] Butterfield A, Ngondi GE, Kerr A, editors. Virtual reality. In: A Dictionary of Computer Science. Oxford, UK: Oxford University Press; 2016. Available from: https://www.oxfordreference.com/display/10.1093/acref/9780199688975.001.0001/acref-9780199688975-e-5714

[13] Laplante PA, editor. Dictionary of Computer Science, Engineering and Technology. Boca Raton: CRC Press; 2017

[14] Mohn E. Augmented reality. In: Salem Press Encyclopedia of Science. Amenia, NY: Salem Press; 2024

[15] Peddie J. Augmented Reality. Cham: Springer International Publishing; 2017. Available from: http://link.springer.com/10.1007/978-3-319-54502-8

[16] Rheingold H. Virtual Reality. Ann Arbor: Summit Books; 1991. Available from: http://archive.org/details/virtualreality00rhei_0

[17] Heilig M. Sensorama stimulator. Patent #3,050,870. 1962.

[18] Sutherland IE. A head-mounted three dimensional display. In: Proceedings of the December 9-11, 1968, Fall Joint Computer Conference, Part I. New York, NY, USA: Association for Computing Machinery; 1968. pp. 757-764. (AFIPS '68 (Fall, part I))

[19] Caudell TP, Mizell DW. Augmented reality: An application of heads-up display technology to manual manufacturing processes. In: Hawaii International Conference on System Sciences. New York City: ACM; 1992. pp. 659-669. Available from: https://tweakers.net/files/upload/329676148-Augmented-Reality-An-Application-of-Heads-Up-Display-Technology-to-Manual-Manufacturing-Processes.pdf

[20] Rampolla J, Kipper G. Augmented Reality: An Emerging Technologies Guide to AR. Waltham, MA: Syngress; 2013

[21] Mavor AS, Durlach NI. Virtual Reality: Scientific and Technological Challenges. Washington, D.C.: National Academies Press; 1995. (Committee on Virtual Reality Research and Development, Computer Science and Telecommunications Board, National Research Council)

[22] Kramer G. Auditory Display: Sonification, Audification, and Auditory Interfaces. Reading, Mass: CRC Press; 1994

[23] Azuma RT. A survey of augmented reality. Presence: Teleoperators & Virtual Environments. 1997;**6**(4):355

[24] Loomis JM, Golledge RG, Klatzky RL. Navigation system for the blind: Auditory display modes and guidance. Presence: Teleoperators and Virtual Environments. 1998;**7**(2):193-203

[25] Meijer PBL. An experimental system for auditory image representations. IEEE Transactions on Biomedical Engineering. 1992;**39**(2):112-121

[26] Capelle C, Trullemans C, Arno P, Veraart C. A real-time experimental prototype for enhancement of vision rehabilitation using auditory substitution. IEEE Transactions on Biomedical Engineering. 1998;**45**(10):1279-1293

[27] Auvray M, Hanneton S, O'Regan JK. Learning to perceive with a visuo — Auditory substitution system: Localisation and object recognition with 'the voice'. Perception. 2007;**36**(3):416-430

[28] Liu Y, Stiles NR, Meister M. Augmented reality powers a cognitive assistant for the blind. Rieke F, Marder E, editors. eLife. 2018;**7**:e37841

[29] Albouys-Perrois J, Laviole J, Briant C, Brock AM. Towards a multisensory augmented reality map for blind and low vision people: A participatory design approach. In: Proceedings of the 2018 CHI Conference on Human Factors in Computing Systems. New York, NY, USA: Association for Computing Machinery; 2018. pp. 1-14. (CHI '18)

[30] Dam A, Siddiqui A, Leclerq C, Jeon M. Extracting a definition and taxonomy for audio augmented reality (AAR) using grounded theory. Proceedings of the Human Factors and Ergonomics Society Annual Meeting. 2022;**66**(1):1220-1224

[31] Cipresso P, Giglioli IAC, Raya MA, Riva G. The past, present, and future of virtual and augmented reality research: A network and cluster analysis of the literature. Frontiers in Psychology. 2018;**9**:2086

[32] Schaeffer P. Treatise on Musical Objects: An Essay across Disciplines. Berkeley, California: University of California Press; 2019. Available from: https://www.degruyter.com/document/doi/10.1525/9780520967465/html

[33] Hosokawa S. The Walkman effect. Popular Music. 1984;**4**:165-180

[34] Bull M. Sound Moves: iPod Culture and Urban Experience. New York: Routledge; 2008. (International Library of Sociology)

[35] Sterne J. MP3: The Meaning of a Format. Durham: Duke University Press; 2012. (Sign, storage, transmission)

[36] Sterne J. The Audible Past: Cultural Origins of Sound Reproduction. Durham: Duke University Press; 2003

[37] AirPods 4. Apple. 2025. Available from: https://www.apple.com/airpods-4/

[38] AirPods Max. Apple. 2025. Available from: https://www.apple.com/airpods-max/

[39] Apple Vision Pro. Apple. 2025. Available from: https://www.apple.com/apple-vision-pro/

[40] Langer SK. Feeling and Form; A Theory of Art. 1st ed. First printing ed. New York: Scribner; 1953. Available from: https://bac-lac.on.worldcat.org/oclc/301358920

[41] Schopenhauer A. The World as Will and Representation. New York: Dover Publications; 1966. (Dover books of general interest)

[42] Tsushima Y, Nakayama K, Okuya T, Koiwa H, Ando H, Watanabe Y. Brain activities in the auditory area and insula represent stimuli evoking emotional response. Scientific Reports. 2024;**14**(1):21335

[43] Barthes R. Image, Music, Text. London: Fontana; 1977

[44] Plato JB. The Republic: The Complete and Unabridged Jowett Translation. Vintage classics ed. New York: Vintage Books; 1991. (Vintage classics). Available from: http://catdir.loc.gov/catdir/enhancements/fy0703/90055688-d.html

[45] Heath A. Meta's Big Tease. The Verge; 2024. Available from: https://www.theverge.com/24253908/meta-orion-ar-glasses-demo-mark-zuckerberg-interview

[46] Bair T. Augmented Reality is Already Here. It's Called Music. Medium; 2015. Available from: https://medium.com/@TorBair/augmented-reality-is-already-here-it-s-called-music-fe60113bcdfc

[47] Meilus L. Spotify's Musical Map - The Most Popular Songs in 1,000 Cities - Thrillist. 2015. Available from: https://www.thrillist.com/travel/nation/spotify-s-musical-map-the-most-popular-songs-in-1-000-cities

[48] Spotify Running. Available from: https://www.spotify.com/us/running/

[49] Aurora. 2016. Available from: https://www.auroraapp.com/

[50] Sonic Bloom. Sonic Bloom. 2023. Available from: https://www.koreographer.com

[51] Pokémon GO. Available from: https://pokemongo.com/en

[52] Georgia Tech Sonification Lab -- home. Available from: http://sonify.psych.gatech.edu/

[53] Schafer RM. The Tuning of the World. New York City: Knopf; 1977

[54] Oliveros P. Deep Listening: A Composer's Sound Practice. New York, NY: iUniverse; 2005

[55] Zhivomirov H. A method for colored noise generation. Romanian Journal of Acoustics and Vibration. 2018;**15**(1):14-19

[56] Kivy P. The fine art of repetition. In: The Fine Art of Repetition: Essays in the Philosophy of Music. Cambridge [England]: Cambridge University Press; 1993. pp. 327-359

[57] Makomaska S. "Acoustic wallpaper" under control – The case of musique d'ameublement and Muzak. Interdisciplinary Studies in Musicology. 2021;**21**:39-55

[58] Eno B. Ambient: Music for Airports. New York: Polydor EG Records; 1978

[59] Chua P, Makris D, Herremans D, Roig G, Agres K. Predicting emotion from music videos: Exploring the relative contribution of visual and auditory information to affective responses. arXiv. 2022. Available from: http://arxiv.org/abs/2202.10453

[60] Bradley M, Lang P. Affective reactions to acoustic stimuli. Psychophysiology. 2000;**37**:204-215

[61] Valenti VE, Guida HL, Frizzo ACF, Cardoso ACV, Vanderlei LCM, de Abreu LC. Auditory stimulation and cardiac autonomic regulation. Clinics (São Paulo, Brazil). 2012;**67**(8):955-958

[62] Joyner MJ, Charkoudian N, Wallin BG. The sympathetic nervous system and blood pressure in humans: Individualized patterns of regulation and their implications. Hypertension. 2010;**56**(1):10-16

[63] Erfanian M, Mitchell AJ, Kang J, Aletta F. The psychophysiological implications of soundscape: A systematic review of empirical literature and a research agenda. International Journal of Environmental Research and Public Health. 2019;**16**(19):3533

[64] Michels N, Hamers P. Nature sounds for stress recovery and healthy eating: A lab experiment differentiating water and bird sound. Environment and Behavior. 2023;**55**(3):175-205

[65] Jo H, Song C, Ikei H, Enomoto S, Kobayashi H, Miyazaki Y. Physiological and psychological effects of forest and urban sounds using high-resolution sound sources. International Journal of Environmental Research and Public Health. 2019;**16**(15):2649

[66] Patel AD. Music, Language, and the Brain. Oxford: Oxford University Press; 2008

[67] Horowitz SS. Universal Sense: How Hearing Shapes the Mind. Paperback ed. New York: Bloomsbury; 2013

[68] Schafer RM. The Soundscape: Our Sonic Environment and the Tuning of the World. Rochester, VT: Destiny Books; 1994

[69] Heidegger M. Being and Time. Oxford: Blackwell; 2006

[70] Ahonen H, Deek P, Kroeker J. Low frequency sound treatment promoting

physical and emotional relaxation qualitative study. International Journal of Psychosocial Rehabilitation. 2012;**17**(1):45-58

[71] Cockerham D, Lin L, Chang Z, Schellen M. Cross-sectional studies investigating the impacts of background sounds on cognitive task performance. In: Parsons TD, Lin L, Cockerham D, editors. Mind, Brain and Technology: Learning in the Age of Emerging Technologies. Cham: Springer International Publishing; 2019. pp. 177-194. (Educational Communications and Technology: Issues and Innovations). DOI: 10.1007/978-3-030-02631-8_10

[72] Lesiuk T. The effect of music listening on work performance. Psychology of Music. 2005;**33**(2):173-191

[73] Shih YN, Huang RH, Chiang HY. Background music: Effects on attention performance. Work. 2012;**42**(4):573-578

[74] Zhu Y, Huang N, Weng Y, Tong H, Wang X, Chen J, et al. Does soundscape perception affect health benefits, as mediated by restorative perception? Forests. 2023;**14**(9):1798

[75] Dolegui AS. The impact of listening to music on cognitive performance. Inquiries Journal. 2013;**5**(09). Available from: http://www.inquiriesjournal.com/articles/1657/the-impact-of-listening-to-music-on-cognitive-performance

[76] Kiss L, Linnell KJ. The effect of preferred background music on task-focus in sustained attention. Psychological Research: An International Journal of Perception, Attention, Memory, and Action. 2021;**85**(6):2313-2325

[77] Kumar N, Wajidi MA, Chian YT, Vishroothi S, Ravindra S, Aithal A. The effect of listening to music on concentration and academic performance of the student: Cross-sectional study on medical undergraduate students. Research Journal of Pharmaceutical, Biological and Chemical Sciences. 2016;**7**:1190-1195

[78] Morgan E. Music: A weapon against anxiety. Music Educators Journal. 1975;**61**(5):38-91

[79] Muslimah M, Apriani W. The effect of listening to music on concentration and academic performance of the students: Cross-Selectional on English education college students. Journal of English Teaching, Applied Linguistics and Literatures (JETALL). 2020;**3**(1):27-32. Available from: https://ppjp.ulm.ac.id/journal/index.php/jetall/article/view/7779

[80] Peretti PO, Swenson K. Effects of music on anxiety as determined by physiological skin responses. Journal of Research in Music Education. 1974;**22**(4):278-283

[81] Frishkopf M. Autonomously adaptive soundscapes for stress reduction in the intensive care unit and beyond. AIP Conference Proceedings. 2023;**2909**(1):110001

[82] Shu S, Ma H. Restorative effects of classroom soundscapes on children's cognitive performance. International Journal of Environmental Research and Public Health. 2019;**16**(2):293

[83] Iyendo TO. Exploring the effect of sound and music on health in hospital settings: A narrative review. International Journal of Nursing Studies. 2016;**63**:82-100

[84] Boggs LJ, Fisher D, Flint GA. Technical note: The "pink" noise generator— An apparatus for inducing

relaxation. Behavior Therapy. 1973;**4**(2):267-269

[85] Singh D, Jain A, Jain D, Goyel V. Effect of white, brown and pink noises on anxious pediatric dental patients. Cardiometry. 2022;**25**:1252-1258

[86] Buxton RT, Pearson AL, Allou C, Fristrup K, Wittemyer G. A synthesis of health benefits of natural sounds and their distribution in national parks. PNAS. 2021;**118**(14):1-6. Available from: https://www.pnas.org/content/118/14/e2013097118

[87] Cutshall SM, Anderson PG, Prinsen SK, Wentworth LJ, Olney TL, Messner PK, et al. Effect of the combination of music and nature sounds on pain and anxiety in cardiac surgical patients: A randomized study. Alternative Therapies in Health & Medicine. 2011;**17**(4):16-23

[88] Davis C, Nussbaum GF. Ambient nature sounds in health care. Perioperative Nursing Clinics. 2008;**3**(1):91-94

[89] Febriandirza A. The effect of natural sounds and music on driving performance and physiological. Engineering Letters. 2017;**25**:455-463

[90] Gatti MFZ, da Silva MJP. Ambient music in the emergency services: The professionals' perception. Rev Latino-Am Enfermagem. 2007;**15**:377-383

[91] Medvedev O, Shepherd D, Hautus MJ. The restorative potential of soundscapes: A physiological investigation. Applied Acoustics. 2015;**96**:20-26

[92] Nishida K, Oyama-Higa M. The influence of listening to nature sounds on mental health. In: Pham TD, Ichikawa K, Oyama-Higa M, Coomans D, Jiang X, editors. Biomedical Informatics and Technology. Berlin, Heidelberg: Springer; 2014. pp. 319-323. (Communications in Computer and Information Science)

[93] Meyer LB. Emotion and Meaning in Music. Chicago: University of Chicago Press; 1956

[94] Gould van Praag CD, Garfinkel SN, Sparasci O, Mees A, Philippides AO, Ware M, et al. Mind-wandering and alterations to default mode network connectivity when listening to naturalistic versus artificial sounds. Scientific Reports. 2017;**7**(1):45273

[95] Ulrich RS, Simons RF, Losito BD, Fiorito E, Miles MA, Zelson M. Stress recovery during exposure to natural and urban environments. Journal of Environmental Psychology. 1991;**11**(3):201-230

[96] Kaplan R, Kaplan S. The Experience of Nature: A Psychological Perspective. Cambridge: Cambridge University Press; 1989

[97] Westerkamp H. Soundwalking. In: Carlyle A, editor. Autumn Leaves: Sound and the Environment in Artistic Practice. Paris, France: Association Double-Entendre in Association with CRISAP; 2007

[98] Cardiff J, Schaub M. Janet Cardiff: The Walk Book. 1. Aufl. Köln: König, Walther; 2005

[99] Kubisch C. Christina Kubisch: Inaudible, Invisible: 1974 ->2023. Bourogne: Espace Multimédia Gantner; 2023. Available from: http://catalogue.bnf.fr/ark:/12148/cb47341119q

[100] Smallwood S. Scott Smallwood Homepage. 2025. Available from: http://scott-smallwood.com/works.html

[101] Smallwood S. Coronium 3500: A solarsonic installation for Caramoor. In: NIME: Proceedings of the International Conference on New Interfaces for Musical Expression. 2016. Available from: https://zenodo.org/record/1176127

[102] Coronium 3500 (Lucie's Halo). 2016. Available from: https://vimeo.com/196516663

[103] Caramoor | Katonah, NY | In The Garden of Sonic Delights. Caramoor. 2014. Available from: https://caramoor.org/in-the-garden-of-sonic-delights/

[104] Emergences. Instagram. 2024. Available from: https://www.instagram.com/p/C_yCzLTJ0ku/

[105] Schafer RM. Voices of Tyranny: Temples of Silence. Ontario, Canada: Arcana Editions; 1993

[106] Frishkopf M. Sounding the Garden – Canadian Centre for Ethnomusicology. 2019. Available from: http://bit.ly/soundingthegarden

[107] The Canadian Centre for Ethnomusicology. Available from: https://www.artsrn.ualberta.ca/ccewiki/index.php/The_Canadian_Centre_for_Ethnomusicology_(CCE)

[108] Aga Khan Trust for Culture. Aga Khan Development Network. Available from: https://the.akdn/en/how-we-work/our-agencies/aga-khan-trust-culture

[109] Anonymous. New Sounds from the Arab Lands - I'm a Bird from Heaven's Garden, 7 Min. 2014. Available from: https://vimeopro.com/akmp/new-sounds-from-arab-lands/video/96997112

[110] Aga Khan Garden, Alberta | University of Alberta Botanic Garden. Available from: https://www.ualberta.ca/en/botanic-garden/whats-on/gardens/aga-khan-alberta.html

[111] Aga Khan Garden Web App. Available from: https://akg.ok.ubc.ca/

[112] Music of Central Asia Series (Co-produced by Smithsonian Folkways and Aga Khan Music Programme). Smithsonian Folkways Recordings. Available from: https://folkways.si.edu/music-of-central-asia-series

[113] Rueb E. To Reduce Hospital Noise, Researchers Create Alarms that Whistle and Sing. Vol. 3. New York Times; 2019. Available from: https://www.nytimes.com/2019/07/09/science/alarm-fatigue-hospitals.html

[114] Canadian Institute for Health Information. Care in Canadian ICUs. Ottawa, Ontario: Canadian Institute for Health Information; 2016

[115] Devlin JW, Skrobik Y, Gélinas C, Needham DM, Slooter AJC, Pandharipande PP, et al. Executive summary: Clinical practice guidelines for the prevention and management of pain, agitation/sedation, delirium, immobility, and sleep disruption in adult patients in the ICU. Critical Care Medicine. 2018;**46**(9):1532-1548

[116] Cuesta JM, Singer M. The stress response and critical illness: A review. Critical Care Medicine. 2012;**40**(12):3283-3289

[117] Chlan L, Tracy MF. Music therapy in critical care: Indications and guidelines for intervention. Critical Care Nurse. 1999;**19**(3):35-41

[118] Papathanassoglou E, Pant U, Meghani S, Saleem Punjani N, Wang Y, Brulotte T, et al. A systematic review of the comparative effects of sound and music interventions for intensive care

unit patients' outcomes. Australian Critical Care. 2025;**38**(3):101148

[119] Sutton RS, Barto AG. Reinforcement Learning: An Introduction. 2018. Available from: http://incompleteideas.net/book/the-book-2nd.html

[120] Frishkopf M, Papathanasoglou E, Steenstrup M. Autonomously Adaptive Soundscapes for Reducing Stress in Critically-Ill Patients. Toronto Metropolitan University; 2021. Available from: https://www.torontomu.ca/canadian-srs/program/

[121] Chang ET, Lai HL, Chen PW, Hsieh YM, Lee LH. The effects of music on the sleep quality of adults with chronic insomnia using evidence from polysomnographic and self-reported analysis: A randomized control trial. International Journal of Nursing Studies. 2012;**49**(8):921-930

[122] Chi GCHL, Young A. Selection of music for inducing relaxation and alleviating pain: Literature review. Holistic Nursing Practice. 2011;**25**(3):127-135

[123] Centre for Advanced Medical Simulation. NAIT.ca. Available from: https://www.nait.ca/centre-for-advanced-medical-simulation

[124] Frishkopf M. Mindful Social Listening: Intelligent Immersive Soundscape Environments for Student Wellbeing. Berlin: IAMM-ISfAM: The Future of Music and Arts in Medicine and Health; 2024. Available from: https://iammonline.com/berlin2024/program/

[125] Zhong J, Jing Y. Researchers created sound that can bend itself through space, reaching only your ear in a crowd. The Conversation. 2025. Available from: http://theconversation.com/researchers-created-sound-that-can-bend-itself-through-space-reaching-only-your-ear-in-a-crowd-252266

[126] Javed K. PersonalScapes. 2024. Available from: https://soundscape-4937f.web.app/index.html

[127] Music and Audio Research Laboratory | NYU Steinhardt. Available from: https://steinhardt.nyu.edu/marl

[128] Stacey Bliss, PhD. Stacey Bliss, PhD. Available from: https://blissresearch.org/

Chapter 5

Spatial Sound Rendering for Audio Augmented Reality

Jean-Marc Jot and Michael Cohen

Abstract

Interactive audio spatialization technology is an essential component of platforms supporting shared immersive virtual experiences, including co-presence, remote collaboration, and entertainment. Modern wearable virtual and augmented reality display devices integrate real-time binaural audio engines that dynamically render multiple sound objects and allow users and their avatars to navigate seamlessly across real and virtual acoustic environments. To support such experiences, a shared audio scene rendering interface facilitates the creation and exchange of immersive, interactive, and persistent 3D soundscapes across multiple independent applications. This chapter presents a practical approach for realizing parametric, six-degree-of-freedom (6-DoF) interactive audio rendering engines that deliver to a user the perceptual auditory cues ensuring audio–visual congruence and virtual-real coherence in extended reality experiences. The description model accounts for the effects of room acoustics, reflective surfaces, and obstacles in "acoustic digital twins" of real or virtual spaces. The rendering interface is interoperable across diverse applicative platforms and allows modeling each audio object as a natural sound source with controllable attributes such as distance, orientation, size, and acoustic radiation properties. By facilitating the interoperability of augmented audio reality applications with generic audio display devices, this solution enables seamless integration of immersive audio into the evolving XR ecosystem, enabling engagement, personalization and free-viewpoint navigation in both interactive experiences and recorded or broadcast media.

Keywords: spatial audio, augmented reality (AR), virtual reality (VR), extended reality (XR), room acoustics, reflections, reverberation, application programming interface (API), auditory rendering, Audio Metaverse

1. Introduction

We begin this chapter by considering the applicative context of augmented audio reality (AAR), and of 3-DoF or 6-DoF immersive audio content creation and distribution. Section 3 reviews the progression of interactive audio application programming interfaces (APIs) since their inception in the late 1990s, leading to a 6-DoF audio scene description interface suitable for representing sonic digital twins of virtual or physical environments in modern AAR applications.

 IntechOpen

Section 4 outlines the composition of a rendering engine compliant with this general audio scene description interface, suitable for implementation in wireless power-constrained devices such as head-worn AAR displays.

The immersive audio scene description and rendering model presented here was introduced in Ref. [1]. In a subsequent elaboration [2], its application to esthetics-driven music production was examined, showing that this model is compatible with the reproduction of immersive music or soundtracks created with IRCAM `Spat`—an audio spatialization tool for the creation and performance of immersive music and soundtracks in flexible audio formats [3–5]. In more recent publications complementing the present chapter [6, 7], the notion of an *Acoustic Object* is introduced, extending object-based immersive audio interchange and transmission file formats to support the distribution of linear content (such as recorded music or cinema soundtracks), as well as interactive AAR experiences, to generic consumer devices. Independent content generation applications can deliver sounds presented to end users employing compatible AAR or immersive audio playback appliances (such as automotive sound systems, for instance) and can enable user-end customization or interaction features such as remixing, karaoke, language dubbing, or virtual navigation within the immersive audio scene.

2. From 3- to 6-DoF object-based audio

In this section, based on Ref. [1], we review developments in immersive audio creation and distribution technology and its applications, including recorded music and cinema soundtracks, as well as AAR experiences in which the spectator is able to navigate and communicate within a digitally rendered virtual world.

2.1 Recent developments in 3-degree-of-freedom media

Spatial audio reproduction technology has evolved since the mid-twentieth century, progressing from mono through stereo and surround to immersive formats [8]. George Lucas famously observed that audio constitutes "half the experience" when integrated with visual display in cinema [9]. The adoption of new immersive multichannel audio formats in the cinema industry has enabled a greater degree of spatial alignment between on-screen visual cues and audio localization cues. These advancements, delivered *via* loudspeakers to fixed (seated) audience members in theaters or location-based entertainment (LBE) venues, enhance perceptual congruence and deepen the viewer's sense of immersion.

These emerging multichannel audio formats enable the distribution of immersive cinematic VR experiences, where content is experienced *via* head-mounted display (HMD) systems. Such systems incorporate head-tracking technology, enabling a three-degree-of-freedom (3-DoF) experience, in which changes in the user's head orientation are dynamically accommodated in both the visual and auditory domains. These formats have introduced immersive and positional audio features to mainstream consumers and to the entertainment industry [10–12], surpassing the limitations of traditional stereo or multi-channel audio:

- Enhanced spatial audio resolution and coverage, incorporating elevation ("height") cues and realistic rendering of spatially diffuse room reverberation.

- Flexible loudspeaker playback configurations, supporting encoding and reproduction of audio scenes using object-based or ambisonic techniques [13].
- The ability to substitute or modify selected elements of the audio mix, represented as discrete audio objects, enabling content customization for applications such as language localization and hearing enhancement [14].

Some limitations persist. For instance, in current 3-DoF immersive audio formats (such as Dolby Atmos and MPEG-H [10, 12]), it is not practical to allow the consumer to substitute audio objects that carry spatially diffuse reverberation, or to allow free listener navigation "inside the audio mix" at playback time. Essentially, a 3-DoF audio object mimics a virtual loudspeaker permanently oriented toward the listener and allowed variable position on a surrounding surface, as illustrated in **Figure 1** (see Refs. [6, 7] for an analysis of this limitation in modern immersive audio formats).

2.2 Toward the 6-degree-of-freedom audio Metaverse

In interactive AR experiences, audiovisual presentation must accommodate both rotational motion of the user about three axes (*yaw*, *pitch*, and *roll*) and translational movement along three directions (*x*, *y*, *z*). This enables simulated 6-Degree-of-Freedom (6-DoF) navigation within networked virtual environments, hereafter referred to collectively as the "Metaverse" [16, 17]. Similar to the physical world, the Metaverse can be modeled, from a human perception and cognition perspective, as a collection of audiovisual objects. Each of these objects may function as a sound source or reflector, or as a light emitter or reflector, coexisting within an environment that manifests itself to the observer through ambient lighting, acoustic reflections, and reverberation.

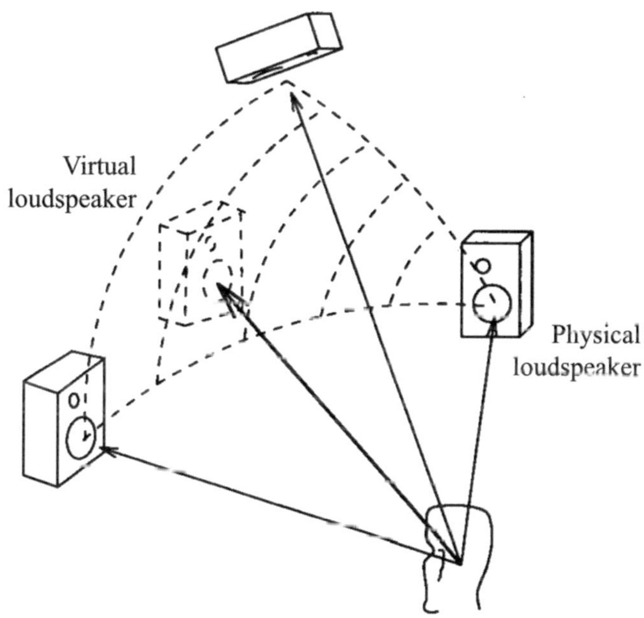

Figure 1.
In 3-DoF object-based immersive audio formats, each mono-waveform audio object represents a virtual loudspeaker with a dynamically adjustable angular position (drawing adapted from Ref. [15]).

Unlike 3-DoF experiences, 6-DoF scenarios allow a user to approach an object or move around it, and allow an object to be freely repositioned. Properties of an audio object should include its directivity pattern, so that acoustic intensity and spectral changes are modulated convincingly upon variation in its orientation relative to the position of the listener [18]. Existing 6-DoF scene representation formats and technologies for authoring and rendering navigable virtual worlds include VRML (for web applications) [19, 20], MPEG-4 (for synchronized multimedia delivery) [21], and game engines [22]. More recent standards—such as OpenXR [23], WebXR [24], and MPEG-I [25]—address AR content and devices (the latter including support for listener navigation across multiple ambisonic audio scene capture locations [26]).

2.3 The coming-of-age of wearable 3D audio appliances

On the device side, several technological advancements have accelerated the adoption of 6-DoF immersive audio technology [27]:

- 3-DoF spatial audio formats and devices have brought head-tracking technology into the mainstream, enriching traditional "head-locked" headphone listening with dynamic spatial audio, even in the absence of visual display. A prominent example is gyroscope-equipped earbuds. The emergence of low-latency wireless audio transmission technologies such as Bluetooth has enabled unleashed mobile listening, granting users increased freedom of movement without sacrificing audio synchronization.

- Acoustically transparent binaural playback devices now support AR audio reproduction [28]. These include hear-through earbuds, bone conduction headsets [29], AR eyewear, audiovisual HMDs, and hearables. Hearables are wearable devices worn on or near the ear that may integrate conventional transducers (e.g., loudspeakers and microphones) with computational capabilities, biometric sensors, and wireless communication features. Also associated with personal sound amplification products (PSAPs) or hearing-enhancement earbuds, such devices enhance auditory perception for both entertainment and accessibility purposes [30].

In traditional headphone audio reproduction, binaural processing has often been considered optional, intended to "help the listener forget that they are wearing headphones" by delivering natural, externalized listening experiences [31].

Breaking with this traditional assumption, the latest generation of non-intrusive wireless wearable playback devices *requires* binaural 3D audio processing, not as an enhancement but as a fundamental necessity, ensuring that the audio playback system remains unobtrusive and seamless [28, 32].

2.4 Shared immersive experiences in the Audio Metaverse

Categories of applications enabled by this technological evolution include:

- Social co-presence, encompassing virtual meetings, remote collaboration, and interaction with virtual assistants

- Assisted training and education, as well as applications in diagnosis, surgery, design, and architecture

- Virtual travel, including immersive navigation, tourism, and enhanced situational awareness

- Immersive entertainment, spanning movies, interactive games, music experiences, and virtual concerts.

In some of these use cases, as illustrated in **Figure 2**, a portion or layer of the Metaverse may be experienced simultaneously by multiple connected users, each navigating independently or actively engaging in communication or collaboration. Portions of the audio environment data may be served or updated at runtime by multiple independent applications, which employ a common syntax and protocol to transmit compatible partial scene descriptions. These descriptions must then be parsed, consolidated, and processed by each local rendering device.

A general, versatile audio technology solution supporting these applications should accommodate both *"you are there"* experiences (VR, teleportation to a virtual world) and *"they are here"* use cases (AR, digitally extending the user's physical world without obstructing their environment). From an ecological perspective, the goal of this technology is to *suspend disbelief*: reducing the user's cognitive effort by aligning with implicit expectations formed through prior natural experience.

2.5 Environmental 6-DoF audio for VR and AR

Regarding the modeling of acoustic reverberation and sound propagation, an application programming solution for the Audio Metaverse should meet the following criteria:

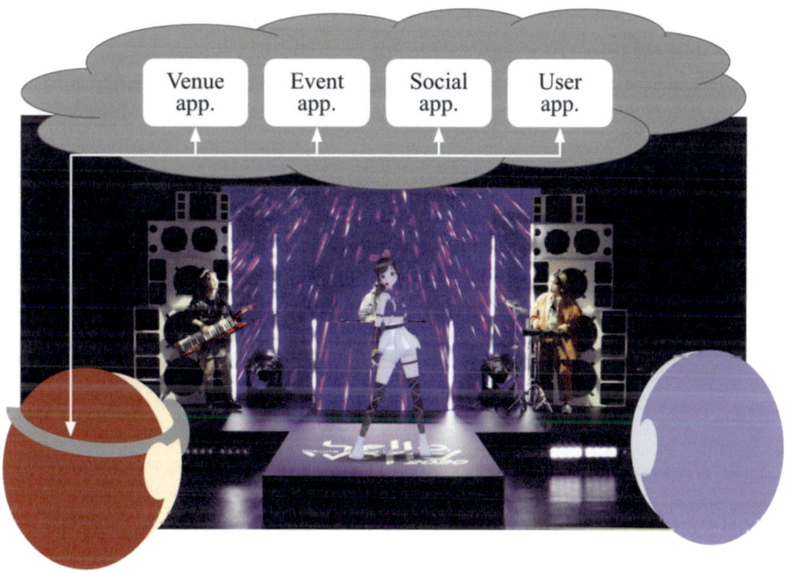

Figure 2.
Example of a 6-DoF Metaverse experience: attending a virtual live music event together with real and/or virtual audience members, performers, and environmental elements, using a wearable AAR display device connected to multiple cloud-hosted applications (background image credit: restofworld.org/2021/vtubers).

- In VR applications, reverberation characteristics should be adjustable by the sound designer *via* perceptually meaningful parameters—thereby expanding creative flexibility beyond the limitations of strictly physics-based environmental simulation [2, 6, 7].

- In AR applications, acoustic scene representations must dynamically adapt to real-time environmental data. This includes matching local reverberation profiles, and accounting for the spatial layout and material properties of both real and virtual acoustic elements such as reflectors and obstacles.

Accordingly, the following capabilities should be supported by a versatile programming and rendering solution:

At creation, defining a collection of virtual sound sources along with their intrinsic properties, including acoustic directivity and an audio generation method. Possible generation methods include prerecorded audio, real-time voice communication (such as VoIP), procedural audio synthesis, AI-generated sound, and deep learning-based audio [22].

At runtime, dynamically adjusting source and sink (virtual listener) positions, modifying reverberation properties, and tuning acoustic simulation parameters to align with conditions of the local or virtual environment, based on the application scenario and triggered events.

2.6 Spatial sound rendering technology for audio augmented reality

Binaural 3D audio rendering is essential for delivering realistic 6-DoF virtual experiences on wearable or head-mounted displays. Audio augmented reality (AAR) [33–36], also known as augmented audio reality, is an expression of AR that enhances the real world with auditory elements rather than (or in addition to) visual overlays. It features adaptively spatialized audio and real-time sound manipulation, rendered dynamically based on user or object movement to blend virtual sounds into one's environment for interactive experience, as in navigation assistance [37, 38], immersive storytelling, and museum guides. In this chapter, requirements for effective AAR are broken down as follows:

Binaural rendering: A perceptually grounded audio signal processing framework must efficiently allocate computational resources while requiring minimal processing footprint. To ensure compatibility with wearable and battery-powered devices, scalability is a key requirement (as in methods reviewed in Section 4 of this chapter). Predictability and consistency of audio fidelity across different platforms and operating conditions are essential design considerations. Additionally, rendering complexity should be prioritized based upon perceptual significance of audio features, optimizing the trade-off between computational efficiency and realism.

Application development can be advantageously structured around two distinct levels of application programming interface (API):

- *Low-level audio rendering* API providing fine-grained control over spatial audio rendering, adhering to psychoacoustically grounded principles. Section 3 outlines the iterative development of a practical and general interface, extending the established standards in PC and mobile game audio technology.

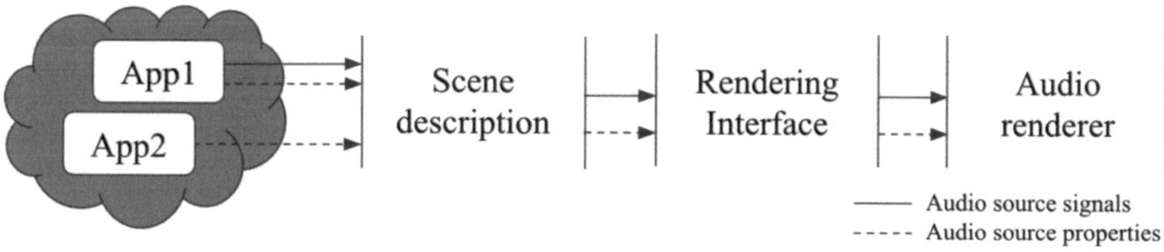

Figure 3.
Audio generation, transmission, and rendering for the Metaverse: high-level functional system synopsis.

- *High-level scene description* API designed to optimize development efficiency by exposing only critical functional elements required for spatial audio integration in application software.

Figure 3 illustrates the functional composition of the overall audio generation, transmission and rendering system considered in this chapter—proposing a practical, multi-application, multi-platform Audio Metaverse data model. This model includes a generic, object-based acoustic *rendering interface*, supported across interoperable AAR devices, and agnostic to the scene generation application. The high-level *scene description* interface, which derives per-object renderer property settings, performs a translation specific to each content generation application (labeled "App1" or "App2" in **Figure 3**)—which may be, for example, a VR game, teleconferencing platform, music streaming service, or live event broadcast.

By ensuring both flexibility in content generation paradigm and interoperability with any compliant consumer device, such a framework is instrumental to fully realize the promise of 6-DoF spatial audio technology innovation, outlined above in Section 2.4. The rendering model, described in the following sections of this chapter, is compatible with the encoding and transmission of recorded, broadcast, or linear immersive media exploiting the notion of *Acoustic Objects*—facilitating end-user interaction such as music remixing, language dubbing, or navigation in a free-viewpoint recorded immersive audio and video scene [6, 7].

3. Audio rendering interface for the Metaverse

Computer-generated audio display technology for VR and AR leverages several decades of signal processing advancements in interactive audio rendering systems and APIs, building upon prior developments in computer music and architectural acoustics. These include binaural sound reproduction techniques, artificial reverberation algorithms, physical room acoustics modeling, and auralization [5, 39–41].

We begin this section, largely based on Ref. [1], with an overview of early developments in interactive audio standards for PC, console, and mobile gaming, tracing their progression toward the OpenAL EFX API published in the mid 2000's [42]. In Section 3.2, we examine audio rendering model enhancements introduced more recently to support the development of modern AAR applications, illustrated by Magic Leap's Soundfield Audio API (MSA) [1, 43, 44]. In Section 3.3, we outline acoustic simulation principles that can be employed to govern the derivation of low-level generic renderer parameters from high-level physics-based Audio Metaverse scene descriptions.

Audio rendering API features	**(3-DoF)**	**I3DL1, DSound**	**I3DL2, EAX2**	**OpenAL EFX**	**AAR, MSA**
Direction of arrival *(per-object)*	✓	✓	✓	✓	✓
Distance or proximity *(per-object)*	o	✓	✓	✓	✓
Source orientation *(per-object)*	o	✓	✓	✓	✓
Source directivity *(per-object)*	o	✓	✓	✓	✓
Filtering effects *(per-object)*	o	o	✓	✓	✓
Listener's room *(global)*	o	o	✓	✓	✓
Multiple rooms *(global)*	o	o	o	✓	✓
Grouped reflections *(per-object)*	o	o	o	o	✓
Control frequencies *(global)*	o	o	`Fh`	`Fl, Fh`	`Fl, Fm, Fh`

Table 1.
Evolution of interactive object-based immersive audio rendering interface capabilities.

Table 1 summarizes the evolution of interactive audio rendering API standards, highlighting successive upgrades in object-based audio scene description capabilities. The final stage (labeled 'AAR' in **Table 1**) enables efficient per-source control of perceived source-to-sink distance, through the spatialization of "grouped" acoustic reflections (as described in Section 3.2.3). This improvement supports the creation of convincing 6-DoF interactive audio experiences, and unlocks sound design capabilities equivalent to those exposed in immersive audio creation tools such as IRCAM `Spat` [2–4, 7]. The functionality of the renderer technology described in this chapter is compatible with the creation and distribution of object-based immersive audio experiences whose narrative paradigm is nonlinear (as in VR or video games) or linear (as in TV or sport broadcast, recorded music, or cinema soundtracks) [6, 7].

3.1 Interactive audio standards for PC and mobile gaming

Technology standards for PC audio were established in the 1990s, followed later by mobile audio standards, to meet the demand for interoperable hardware platforms and 3D gaming software applications. This need parallels the motivation behind more recent XR industry initiatives, such as OpenXR [23] or file format X3D [45, 46]. Shared API conventions were developed for graphics rendering—most notably OpenGL—and analogously for audio rendering—including I3DL2 [47], EAX [48], and OpenAL [49].

3.1.1 Positional audio properties

In I3DL1/DirectSound3D [50], VRML97 [19, 20], OpenAL [49], and OpenSL ES [51], an acoustic scene is represented as a collection of sound sources and a single sink (listener), which are characterized by the following attributes:

- The *position* (including *location* and *orientation*) of the sink and each sound source, along with a per-source gain correction.

- *Velocity vectors* assigned to the listener and sound sources, with a `Doppler_factor` property that controls the strength of the pitch-shifting Doppler effect for moving objects (see, e.g., ([49], p. 28)).

- Automatic relative attenuation of acoustic intensity as a function of source-sink distance, beyond a `Reference_distance` (see **Figure 4**), configurable using a `Rolloff_factor` property.

- A simplified *source directivity* model (see **Figure 5**). Note that more general radiation models have also been proposed, such as those in Refs. [21, 52].

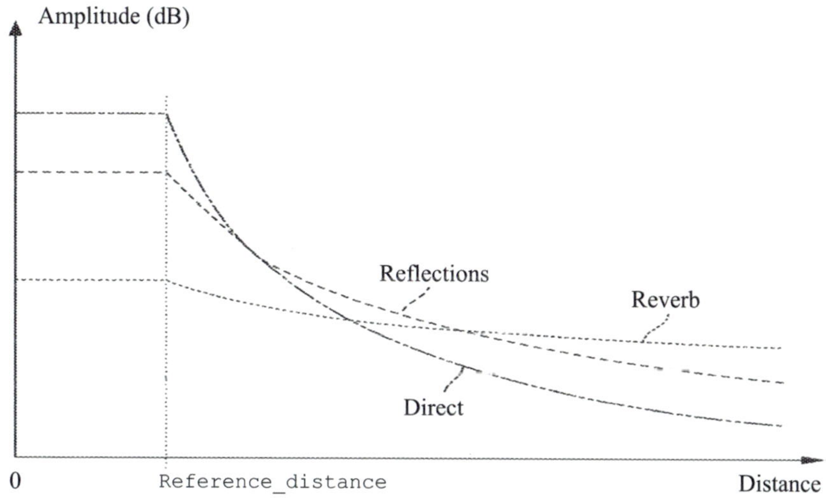

Figure 4.
Illustration of automatic range (distance) attenuation differentiated for direct sound, early reflections, and late reverberation.

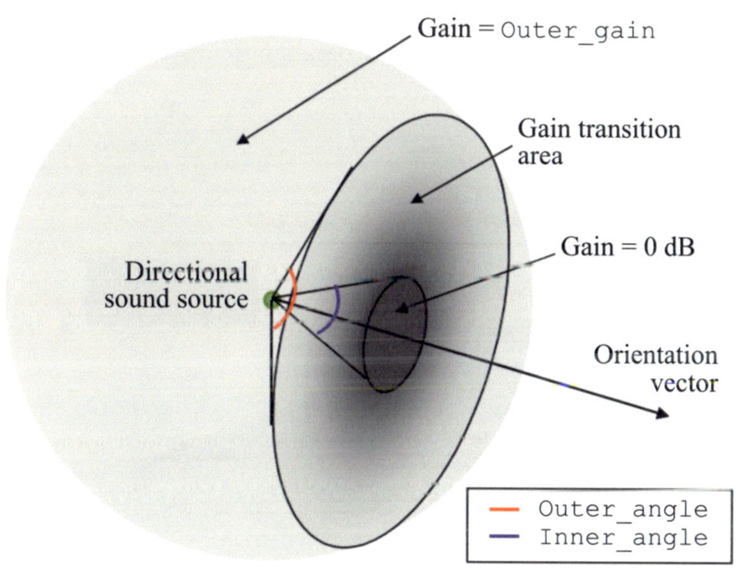

Figure 5.
Source directivity represented by axis-symmetric "radiation cone" model (adapted from Ref. [51]).

3.1.2 Environmental audio extensions (single room)

I3DL2 [47] and EAX 2.0 [48], followed by OpenAL EFX [42] and OpenSL ES [51], introduced properties to describe an "environment" (room) in which the virtual listener and virtual sound sources are situated. These frameworks decompose the rendered audio signal for each source into direct sound, early reflections, and late reverberation, while providing the following features:

- Room impulse response model (see **Figure 6**), parameterized by:
  - o A triplet of gain coefficients (`Direct`, `Reflections`, `Reverb`), specified at a `Reference_distance`.
  - o Onset times: `Reflections_delay` and `Reverb_delay`.
  - o Reverberation parameters: `Decay_time`, `Density`, and `Diffusion` (see Section 4.2).
- Reference frequency `Fh`, where high-frequency attenuations and the property `Decay_hf_ratio` are specified (the latter is defined as the high-frequency reverberation decay time divided by the mid-frequency reverberation decay time).
- Per-source control of gain and high-frequency attenuation for `Direct` and `Room` (the latter combining early `Reflections` and late `Reverb` decay tail).
- Spectral extension of the source radiation model: high-frequency attenuation `Outer_gain_hf`, which controls a low-pass filter (LPF) effect dependent on source orientation (detailed in Section 3.2.2).
- Globally defined air absorption model, controlling a distance-dependent low-pass filter effect.
- Extension of the distance-based model, automatically applying relative attenuation to reflections and reverberation for distances beyond the

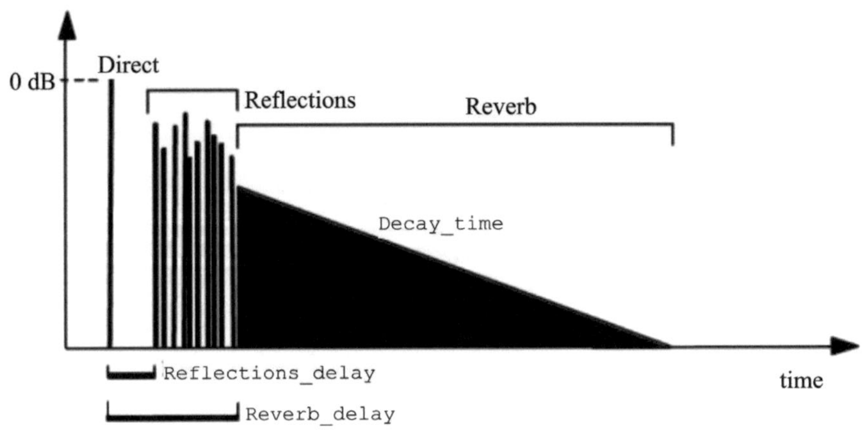

Figure 6.
The Reverberation response model in I3DL2, EAX, and OpenAL EFX, visualized here as an "echogram" articulating direct sound, early reflections, and late reverberation.

`Reference_distance`. This includes a per-source `Room_rolloff_factor` property and a physical simulation mode (reviewed in Section 3.2.4).

- Sound muffling effects for simulating sound transmission through a room partition (`Occlusion`) or through and around an obstacle inside the room (`Obstruction`).

3.1.3 Multi-room extensions

EAX 4.0 and OpenAL EFX enabled loading up to four concurrent I3DL2/EAX reverberator plugins into "auxiliary effect slots," while introducing the following capabilities [42, 53]:

- Indicating which of the four reverberators simulates the listener's environment at any given time.

- Independently controlled per-source contributions into multiple reverberators (see **Figure** 7).

- Reverberator output occlusion and diffuse panning model (see **Figure 8**).

- 3-band spectral effect control, using two reference frequencies, `Fl` and `Fh` (see Section 3.2.1).

3.2 From OpenAL to audio augmented reality

OpenAL and its EFX extension address a wide range of requirements for modern XR applications, supporting interactive reproduction of feature-rich audio scenes. In this section, we describe the details of EAX/OpenAL functions and examine their extension to provide a comprehensive yet efficient spatial rendering API for the Audio Metaverse:

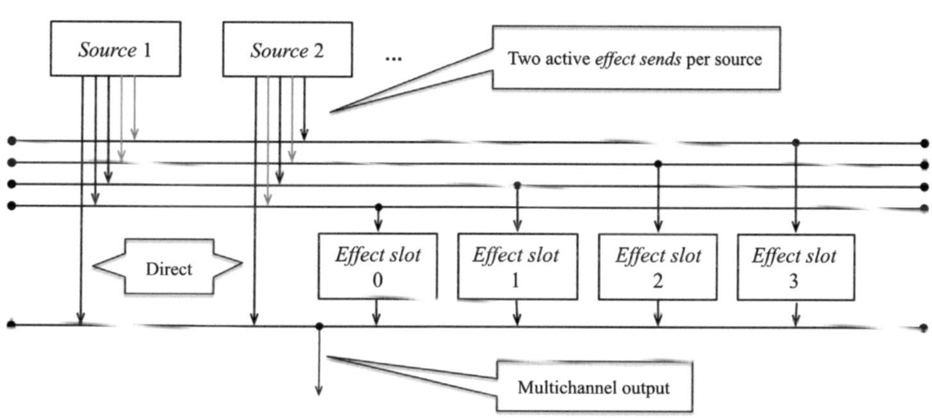

Figure 7.
In EAX 4.0 and OpenAL EFX, each source can contribute to multiple auxiliary effect slots, with each slot hosting a reverberator that simulates a room in the listener's surroundings. The reverberator generates a multi-channel output signal, which is then routed into the main output bus (adapted from Ref. [54]).

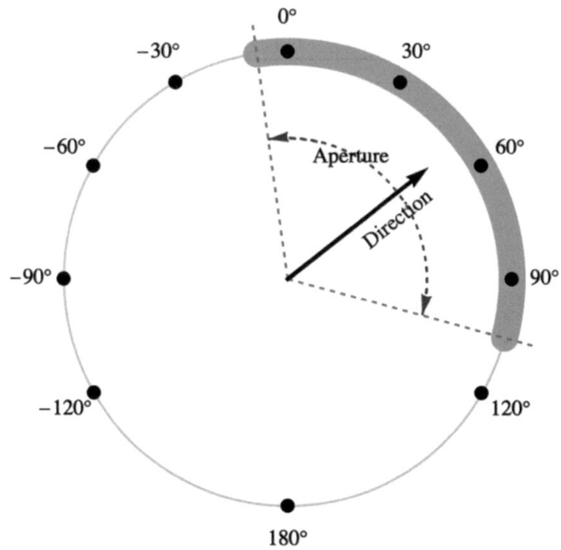

Figure 8.
Illustration of the "divergence panning" model for spatially extended sound source simulation and for optional reverberation output directional emphasis in EAX 4.0 and OpenAL EFX (adapted from Ref. [55]). Black circles represent head-locked equatorial-plane virtual loudspeakers.

- *Extended spectral control of source radiation patterns* allowing for more realistic modeling of 6-DoF objects.
- Per-source spatialization of *grouped reflections* for enhanced spatial rendering of distant audio objects and geometry-driven acoustic simulation.
- *Distance-dependent normalization and spectral attenuation* of reflections and reverberation, leveraging the acoustical characterization of rooms through their *reverberation fingerprint* [56, 57].

MSA differs from OpenAL EFX by more explicitly distinguishing between low-level API (audio object rendering) and high-level API (audio scene description)—a distinction introduced in Section 2.6. Scene geometry, including listener location and orientation tracking, is managed *allocentrically* (i.e., based on external references) within the high-level scene description API. In contrast, the low-level rendering API, described in this section, is *egocentric*, meaning that source location and orientation coordinates are defined as "head-relative."

3.2.1 3-band parametric spectral control

Three control frequencies (`Fl`, `Fm`, `Fh`) are specified globally and referenced throughout the audio rendering API to define or compute frequency-dependent properties and parameters. This approach—inherited from IRCAM `Spat`, I3DL2, and EAX—leverages the proportionality property of the shelving equalizer described in Ref. [58] and illustrated in **Figure 9**. This property enables the consolidation of multiple cascaded dual-shelving equalizer effects into a single second-order ("biquad") filter section, provided that they share a set of control frequencies [58, 59]. As a result, the rendering engine realizes computationally efficient implementation of global and per-source gain corrections across three frequency bands.

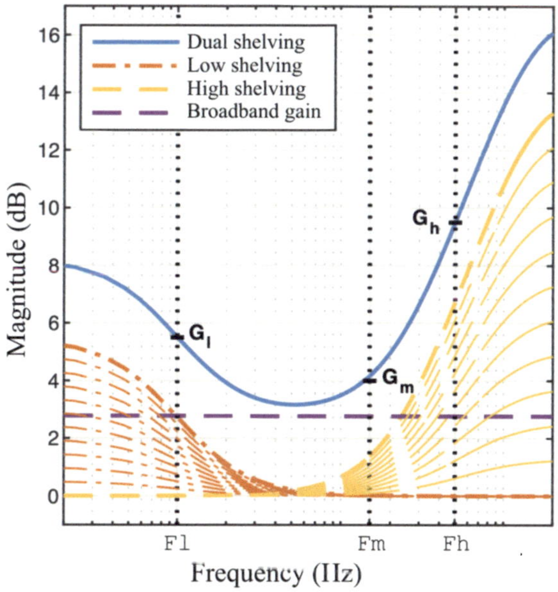

Figure 9.
Parametric frequency response equalization using a dual-shelving equalizer with three adjustable control frequencies (`Fl`, `Fm`, `Fh`). This filter is implemented by cascading two first-order proportional shelving equalizers into a second-order "biquad" IIR filter module [58, 59].

Acoustic obstruction and occlusion effects are modeled by the high-level API. The low-level API, in contrast, provides access to rendering filter gain offsets, which can also be utilized by the programmer for other purposes, including dynamic creative effects [43, 44].

3.2.2 Frequency-dependent source directivity

The `Outer_gain` property of a source is frequency dependent, allowing the direct sound component to be automatically filtered based on orientation of the source relative to the sink's location. This results in a dynamic spectral correction effect, which adapts to listener navigation or changes in source direction (increasingly muffled when the source points away from the listener).

Additionally, a dual-shelving filter approximating the *diffuse-field transfer function* of the sound source is derived and applied to its reflections and reverberation. As a result, simulating a source with greater directivity at higher frequencies, as is typical of natural sound sources, automatically introduces a LPF correction to its reverberation. This effect is a distinctive timbral characteristic of each sound source, determined by its frequency-dependent directivity and predicted by the statistical reverberation model developed in Ref. [60].

3.2.3 Grouped reflections spatialization

Plausible rendition of the effects of early reflections does not require exactly reproducing each one individually [61–63]. A computationally efficient method for grouped control and rendering of early reflections was proposed in

Ref. [55]. This approach utilizes a shared *grouped reflections* generator (see also Section 4.3), enabling independent control of the following properties for each sound source:

- `Reflections_delay`: Relative delay of the first reflection received by the listener for this sound source (expressed in ms).

- `Reflections_gain`: The gain of the early reflections group for each sound source is adjustable across three frequency bands, as described previously (array of three values expressed in dB).

- `Reflections_pan`: An azimuthal angle, measured in the head-related equatorial plane relative to the listener's gaze direction, reflecting the dominant direction of arrival of the early reflections group for this source.

- `Reflections_focus`: The magnitude of the Energy Vector [64] quantifies the directional concentration of grouped reflections relative to their average direction of arrival (illustrated in **Figure 8**). A value of 1.0 indicates maximum directional focus, with reflections arriving from a single direction, while a value of 0.0 signifies an isotropic distribution, with reflections arriving evenly from all directions around the listener.

By default, grouped early reflections are processed to emanate from a directional sector centered on the direct sound arrival for each source (see **Figure 8**). This behavior, inspired by the perceptual control model that underlies the design of IRCAM `Spat`, enhances the perception of source localization without relying on geometrical or acoustical environment data [2, 7]. In AAR applications where a physical environment description is provided, as discussed in Section 3.3, the properties of grouped reflections can be adjusted programmatically for each sound source.

3.2.4 Enhanced distance model

As shown earlier in **Figure 4**, automatic attenuation of sound components as a function of distance, if enabled by the developer, is extended to independently manage the differentiated intensities of direct sound, grouped reflections, and late reverberation for each sound source. For an unobstructed source positioned beyond the `Reference_distance` in the same room as the listener, the following default behavior applies:

- The direct sound component follows the conventional attenuation calculation model, referred to as the "inverse distance clamped" model in OpenAL [49, 50] (whose default effect is a 6-dB attenuation per doubling of metric distance).

- Early reflections undergo the same relative attenuation as the direct sound, emulating the perceptual model implemented in IRCAM `Spat` [2, 5, 7].

- Late reverberation is attenuated in a frequency-dependent manner, based on the reverberation decay time of the listener's room, as detailed below in Section 3.2.5.

3.2.5 Reverberation fingerprint of a room

Following an acoustic pulse excitation in a room containing both the sound source and the receiver (or listener), the reflected sound field builds up until it reaches a *mixing time*, after which the decaying residual acoustic reverberation energy is uniformly distributed throughout the enclosure [60, 65]. A numerical simulation example included in Ref. [1] (Appendix) illustrates this phenomenon, indicating that, in a typical mixing room, reverberation decay can be accurately simulated by considering the following properties, independent of source or sink position [57]:

- An intrinsic property of the room: its *reverberation fingerprint*, which encompasses the reverberation decay time as a function of frequency and the room's cubic volume, determining how the source's acoustic power is scattered across the room.

- An intrinsic property of the sound source: its *diffuse-field transfer function* (as described in Section 3.2.2), which describes the total acoustic power radiated by the source into the room, aggregated over all directions of emission.

The distance model described earlier (in Section 3.2.4) attenuates reverberation for each source using a frequency-dependent factor that decreases with source-sink distance and depends on the room's reverberation decay time, as illustrated in **Figure 10**. The `Reverb_gain` property can be interpreted as scaling the acoustic power of a sound generated by the user, such as their own voice or footsteps [56].

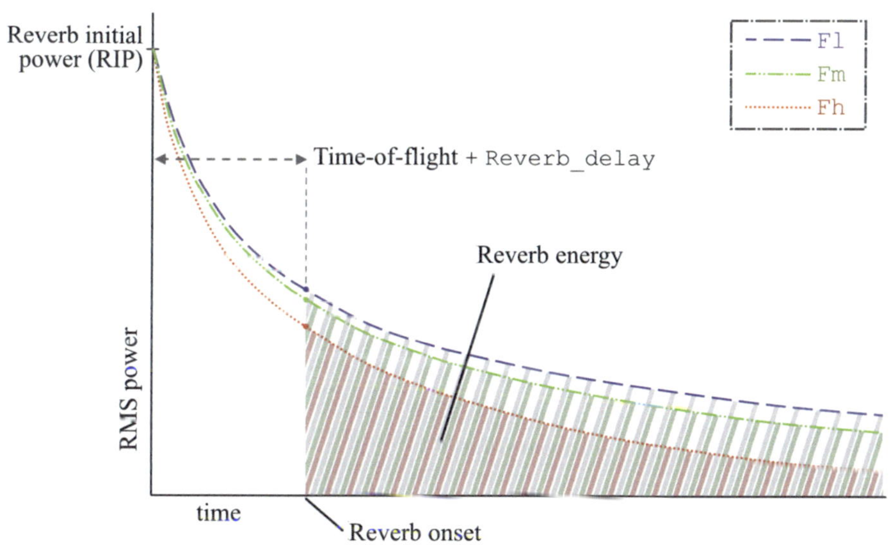

Figure 10.
Illustration of energy calculation yielding the relative Reverb attenuation vs. source-sink distance according to the reverberation decay time specified at three control frequencies (`Fl`, `Fm`, `Fh`), from Ref. [1].

3.3 From high-level physical scene description to low-level audio rendering parameters

In this section, we consider the automatic derivation of low-level audio rendering properties from high-level geometrical and physical environment descriptions, in accordance with the functional synopsis diagram shown in **Figure 3** and the distinction of API levels proposed in Section 2.6. As discussed in Refs. [6, 7], commercial dissemination of immersive audio content and experiences is facilitated by adopting a common low-level spatial audio rendering interface such as the one described in the present article, so that any compatible end user device can faithfully deliver the experience intended by a content creator or application developer—irrespective of narrative approach (linear or nonlinear) or sound design paradigm (e.g., an esthetics-driven musical production or a physics-driven XR experience).

In XR scenarios, congruence between the visual cues and the auditory cues delivered to the spectator can be maintained *via* physics-based simulation of acoustic propagation phenomena [1, 66–68]. Commercial solutions include Audiokinetic Wwise Reflect[1] and Apple PHASE[2]. To support realistic acoustic interactions, the simulation should account for the geometry of room boundaries and obstacles, and for properties of environment materials that determine their acoustic reflection, absorption, and transmission behaviors (see **Table 2**). For instance, transmissivity defines how much sound passes through an object, while reflectance governs the energy of reflected sound waves. Simplified spectral correction functions, such as described in Section 3.2.1, can approximate the resulting subjective effects, allowing for computationally efficient real-time rendering of acoustic obstruction, occlusion, or reflection phenomena. **Figure 11** shows an example of renderer architecture and illustrates mappings from some high-level physics-based audio scene parameters to low-level signal processing functions.

Real-time applications must balance computational load and perceptual accuracy to ensure seamless auditory realism without excessive processing overhead. Optimizing computational efficiency in acoustic propagation simulation remains a central challenge. One approach is to precompute certain properties, such as room impulse responses or diffraction coefficients, and store them as compact data representations for low-latency retrieval [69]. Hybrid models, which combine real-time physics-based simulation with precomputed perceptual parameters, have been explored in solutions such as Microsoft Project Acoustics [70]. Diffraction effects, which shape sound behavior when waves bend around edges or pass through narrow openings, can be simulated by a combination of precomputed lookup tables and runtime adjustments [71]. These approaches reduce the computational demands

Quality (property)	Physical process	Quantitative attribute
Reflectivity	Reflection	Reflectance
Absorptivity	Absorption	Absorbance
Transmissivity	Transmission	Transmittance

Table 2.
Acoustic material properties: The first column is the property or quality of conducting the physical process in the second column, which is quantitatively measured by the attribute in the third column.

1 https://www.audiokinetic.com/en/wwise/plugins/reflect

2 https://developer.apple.com/documentation/phase

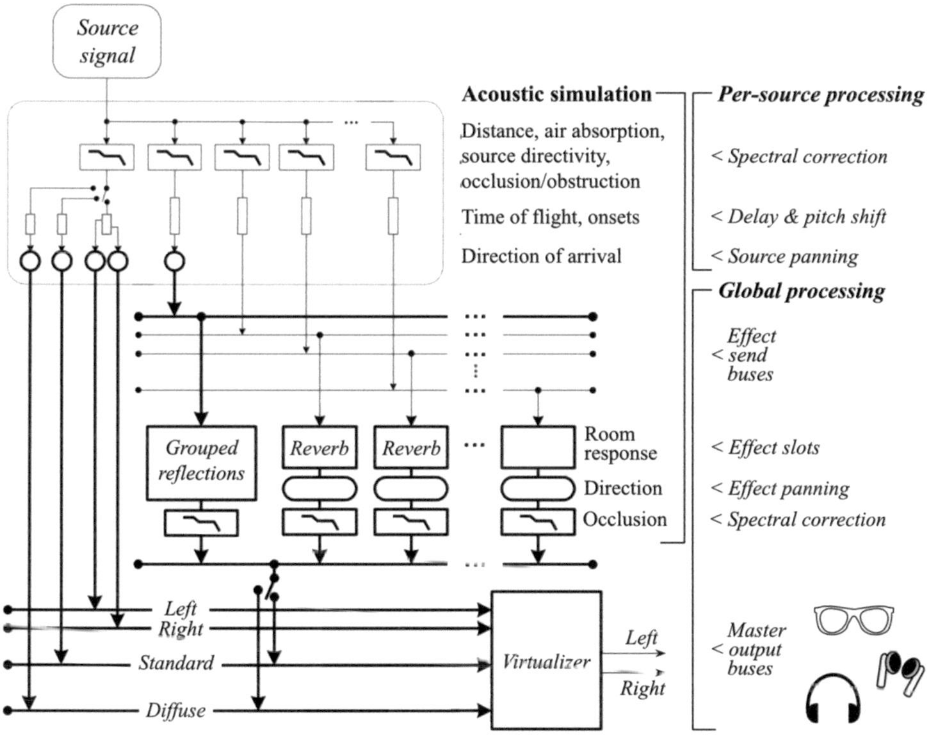

Figure 11.
Architecture of a generic 6-DoF binaural rendering engine including per-source and global processing, for computationally efficient multi-source/multi-room object-based spatial audio (adapted from Refs. [1, 55]). Thicker lines indicate multi-channel audio signal paths or processing functions. Acoustic simulation functionality is discussed in Section 3.3. Audio signal processing functionality is reviewed in Section 4.

to drive low-level rendering parameter settings from high-level scene description. Future developments in acoustic modeling solutions leveraging machine learning and edge computing may further optimize real-time spatial audio rendering for AAR applications [72].

3.4 Summary: Audio scene rendering for the Metaverse

We have presented a generic audio programming interface (API) for application-agnostic rendering of 6-DoF spatial audio and multi room reverberation, designed to balance auditory plausibility and computational efficiency. This rendering interface is compatible with flexible high-level scene description models, per the functional system synopsis diagram of **Figure 3**. For instance, as discussed in Refs. [2, 7], high-level control may be realized *via* perceptual or esthetics-driven paradigms. Alternatively or additionally, it may be accomplished *via* a physics-driven scene description interface, as outlined in Section 3.3. **Figure 11** shows an audio renderer architecture compatible with this rendering API and illustrates the derivation of audio signal processing parameters from acoustic phenomena such as occlusion and obstruction.

The Audio Metaverse can be modeled as a collection of rooms, each defined by a "reverberation preset" that characterizes its response to an omnidirectional sound source positioned near the receiver. This approach leverages the concept of *reverberation fingerprint*, which provides a data-efficient representation of perceptually relevant aspects of a room's reverberation that remain independent of source or receiver parameters [57]. Virtual sound sources, characterized by their position, orientation and directivity properties, can be seamlessly "dropped" into an environment at render time, functioning as audio objects with arbitrary dynamic positioning. The reverberation fingerprints of rooms within a given sector of the Audio Metaverse can be estimated through automated acoustic analysis [73, 74] or cataloged for future retrieval and rendering. The underlying multiple-reverberator topology is suitable for rendering anisotropic reverberation environments, such as open or semi-open spaces, coupled rooms, or corridors [75, 76]. Additionally, as described in Ref. [6], per-object parameters can be included in this rendering API to represent spatially extended sound sources by employing the divergence panning model illustrated in **Figure 8** [77, 78].

4. A binaural rendering engine for audio-augmented reality

Figure 11 displays the architecture of a computationally efficient binaural rendering engine, previously described in Refs. [1, 55], compatible with the API functionality reviewed in the previous section—including:

- *Per-source processing*: rendering of direct sound, acoustic reflections and reverberation sound field for arbitrarily complex audio scenes comprising multiple audio objects, including both point sources and spatially extended sound sources, with minimal incremental computation cost per audio object
- *Global effect processing*: a shared set of *effect slots* that can include several parallel reverberators to simulate complex acoustic environments, as well as one or more *grouped reflections* synthesis modules for computationally efficient rendering of per-source panned reflections
- *Anisotropic reverberation*: *effect panning* modules enable directionally weighted or spatially diffuse rendering of the acoustic reverberation emanating from the room in which the sink (virtual listener) is located, as well as adjacent virtual rooms simulated by additional reverberators.

In the following sections, we review known computationally efficient methods for binaural multi-source localization rendering and for synthetic reverberation. We then review the overall composition of a binaural rendering engine for AAR, which supports, for each sound source, spatial reflections rendering along with diffuse, anisotropic, or multi-room spatial reverberation.

4.1 Binaural 3D positional audio rendering for multiple sound sources

Many immersive audio application scenarios require binaural reproduction over wearable devices such as earphones or glasses. A per-object positional rendering function can be realized by implementing a pair of dynamic digital filters realizing head-related transfer functions (HRTFs) [62, 79, 80]. By delivering audio signals individually to the two ears of a listener, binaural rendering methods aim to produce an immersive sound impression comparable to real-world listening or to reproduction over a multichannel loudspeaker system. In headphone or wearable audio playback, factors that may impact the success of this illusion include HRTF personalization, head tracking, and listening room acoustic simulation [31, 79, 81]. An approach to enhancing externalization and front/back distinction in headphone immersive audio is introduced in Ref. [82].

In the following sections, we examine the binaural rendering of direct sound components for multiple audio objects, essential for accurately reproducing their individual position, loudness and timbre [83]. **Figure 12** illustrates the reference HRTF filter model for a source at a given location, consisting of frequency-independent bilateral delays cascaded with a minimum-phase filter pair [62, 84]. **Figures 13** and **14** present examples of HRTF filter specifications based on measurements conducted on artificial heads. We consider computationally efficient methods that support large object counts, minimizing per-object computation through a two stage process: (a) panning and mixing into an intermediate multichannel format, followed by (b) transcoding to binaural output (see, e.g., [55]).

Figure 11 illustrates per-source selection between three multichannel panning methods presenting different advantages and features, and supported by a shared global output *virtualizer* processing module (see Ref. [55] for more details):

4.1.1 Standard (channel-based or scene-based multichannel mixing)

The simplest and most common approach for computationally efficient binaural rendering employs a standard multichannel audio format for the intermediate mix,

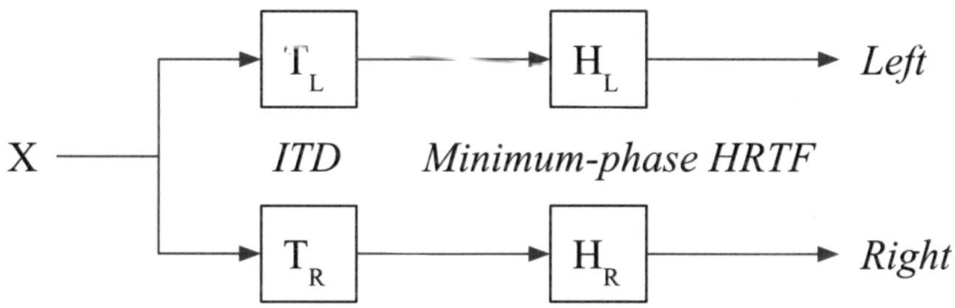

Figure 12.
Reference bilateral rendering model for single-point source, decomposing each HRTF filter as the cascade of a minimum-phase filter with a pure delay.

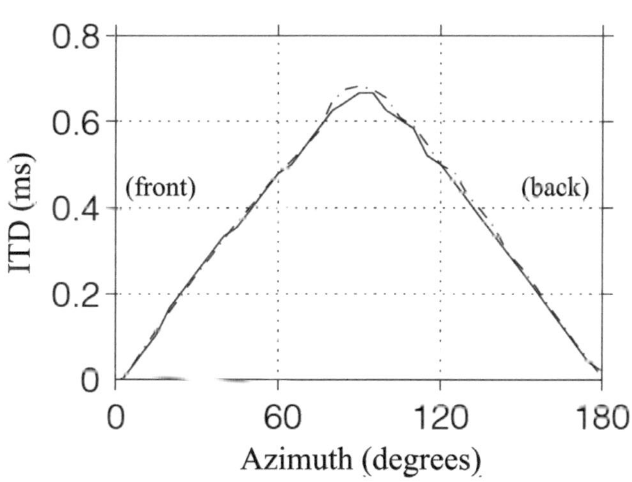

Figure 13.
Interaural Time Delay (ITD) derived from the interaural excess-phase difference in HRTF measurements collected on a Head Acoustics HMSII artificial head (after Ref. [84]).

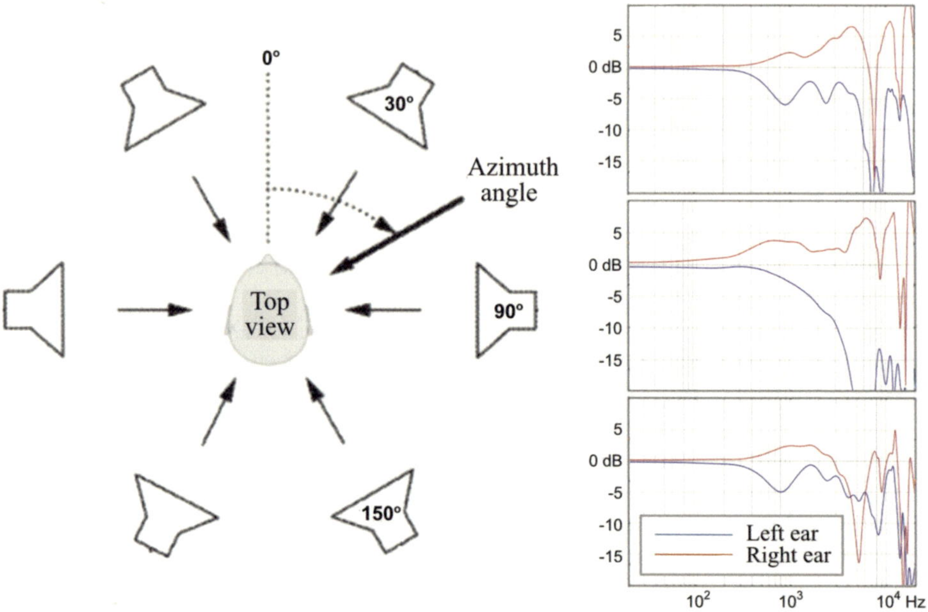

Figure 14.
Virtual loudspeakers rendering scheme using six equatorial directions, and corresponding diffuse-field equalized HRTF filter magnitude frequency responses for subject 55 in the HUTUBS database [85–87].

followed by transcoding *via* a virtual loudspeakers rendering scheme, as illustrated in **Figure 14**. Travis [88] proposed ambisonic-to-binaural transcoding for interactive audio, incorporating 3-DoF compensation of listener head orientation through rotation of an ambisonic-encoded global mix of all input sound sources. The *virtualizer* performs ambisonic decoding to a selected head-locked virtual loudspeaker layout, optionally preceded by automatic global sound field rotation responding to head-tracking coordinates (listener head orientation). This approach was later extended to high-order ambisonic (a.k.a. "scene-based") encoding in Ref. [89]. Alternatively, a "channel-based" amplitude panning technique such as VBAP [15] can be used, where listener head rotations are compensated globally or at the per-source panning stage.

For moderate channel counts (such as 10 to 20 channels), these standard binaural virtualization methods introduce inaccuracies in HRTF reconstruction, which can cause directional perception errors [90–92]. Frequency-domain parametric processing can mitigate this limitation, at the expense of increased *virtualizer* processing complexity [93–95].

4.1.2 Left, right (bilateral multichannel mixing)

A drawback of the standard approaches reviewed in Section 4.1.1 is that they rely on *virtualizer* processing to indirectly reconstruct per-source ITD cues in the output binaural signal. Alternatively, as illustrated in **Figure 15**, ITD synthesis is realized directly for each individual sound source, and a separate multichannel mix is computed for each ear. This approach is equivalent to linear decomposition of the minimum-phase HRTF filter using a basis of spatial panning functions [55, 84, 91]. Examples include first-order ambisonic panning (FOA) [91, 96], its extension to

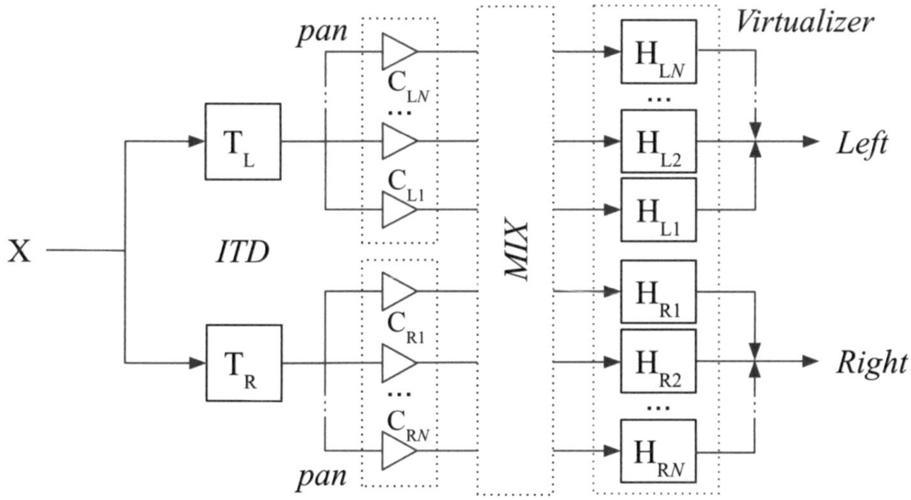

Figure 15.
Bilateral multichannel rendering signal flow for computationally efficient binaural rendering of multiple sound sources with per-source ITD preservation [55, 84, 91].

HOA (spherical harmonics of any order) [90], and bilateral pairwise amplitude panning [55]. These methods can be extended to incorporate per-source processing for near-field positional audio rendering [97], and to customize ITD, spatial, or spectral functions to match an individual listener's HRTF dataset [55, 84, 91]. However, compared to the standard approaches reviewed in Section 4.1.1, these more accurate binaural rendering methods incur additional per-object computation for ITD synthesis and do not readily support head-tracking by global sound field rotation. Computationally efficient realization of a *virtualizer* module is described in Ref. [55], wherein a shared set of static HRTF filters is employed for both the standard and bilateral multichannel methods.

4.1.3 Diffuse mixing

The third per-source multichannel panning method selectable in **Figure 11** enables the rendering of spatially extended sound sources (see [77]). As described in Ref. [55], the *virtualizer* applies an energy-preserving decorrelation filter bank to the set of audio signals that it receives *via* the *diffuse bus*, per the decorrelation filter bank design principle described, for example, in Refs. [98, 99]. The per-source *pan* function is designed according to the "divergence panning" method described in Ref. [55] and illustrated in **Figure 8**.

4.2 Simulating natural acoustic reverberation

Synthetic reverberation algorithms have been extensively studied, including techniques for analyzing, simulating, or "sculpting" recorded, simulated, or computed reverberation responses [100–108]. A computationally efficient parametrically controlled reverberator may be realized by a recirculating feedback delay network (FDN), mathematically equivalent to the canonical representation shown

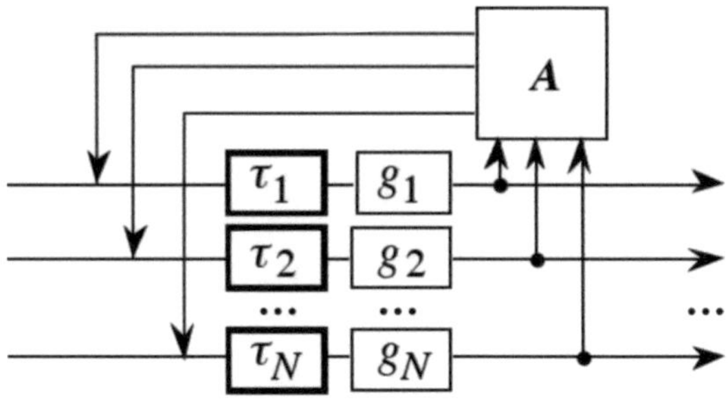

Figure 16.
Canonical Feedback Delay Network (FDN) representation: $\{(\tau i, gi)\} = \{(\tau_1, g_2), (\tau_2, g_2),\ldots,(\tau N, gN)\}$ *is a set of absorptive delay units with respective delay* τi *and frequency-dependent gain* gi*, coupled by matrix* **A** *(from Ref. [105]).*

in **Figure 16**—where, referring to the reverberation API properties introduced in Sections 3.1.2 and 3.1.3:

- $\{\tau_i\}$ represents a set of recirculating delay units, where the cumulative feedback delay length can be scaled *via* the modal `Density` property.

- A denotes a matrix of gain coefficients, whose sparsity can be controlled *via* the `Diffusion` property.

General principles for reverberation decay control are given, for example, in Refs. [104–106, 109]:

- Each g_i represents an absorptive filter that applies frequency-dependent attenuation, proportional to the ratio of the delay τ_i to the reverberation `Decay_time` specified at frequency `Fm`, and derived at `Fl` and `Fh` from the values of the properties `Decay_lf_ratio` and `Decay_hf_ratio`.

- Matrix A is such that, when all of the absorptive filters g_i are removed or neutralized (i.e., set to 1.0), the reverberation decay time is effectively infinite at all frequencies (i.e., the reverberator is a "lossless prototype" as defined in Refs. [105, 107]).

Each of the absorptive filters g_i may be realized as a proportional parametric equalizer, as described in Ref. [58] and Section 3.2.1. Additionally, cascaded *reverb* and *virtualizer* processing may be normalized to match the `Reverb_gain` [56] and to reproduce the low-frequency interaural coherence contour characteristic of natural diffuse fields [62, 108, 110], illustrated in **Figure 17** for a typical head size.

4.3 Multi-source, multi-room spatial reverberation rendering architecture

Spatial reverberation engine designs have been proposed in which a per-source early reflections processor feeds into a late reverberation processor shared among multiple sound sources positioned in the same room as the sink [101, 105]. In the architecture of **Figure 11**, the reflections processor is shared as well (*grouped reflections* module, described below), while the late reverberation is rendered separately by one or more *reverb* modules, each receiving a dedicated mix of

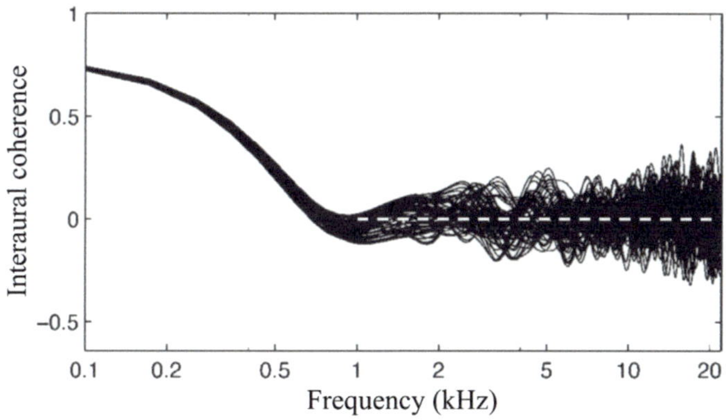

Figure 17.
Measured frequency-dependent interaural coherence (IC) in diffuse reverberation [110], and substitution above 1 kHz indicated by the dashed white line.

the source signals. As discussed in Section 3.1.3 and shown in **Figures** 7 and **11**, multiple reverberators can be dynamically instantiated in a set of *effect slots*, to simulate adjacent rooms and/or spatially anisotropic reverberation in the occupied room [75, 76]. The multichannel output signal of each reverberator is further processed by a directional emphasis module (*effect panning*), as mentioned in Section 3.1.3 and illustrated in **Figures 8** and **18**.

Figure 11 indicates the placement of dual-shelving equalizers, which apply per-source or global spectral corrections as specified in Section 3 and implemented in Section 3.2.1. The contribution of each sound source into a *reverb* module is automatically filtered according to this source's diffuse-field transfer function. As described in Section 3.2.2, this results in a natural-sounding LPF effect specific to each sound source, accounting for its frequency-dependent directivity index.

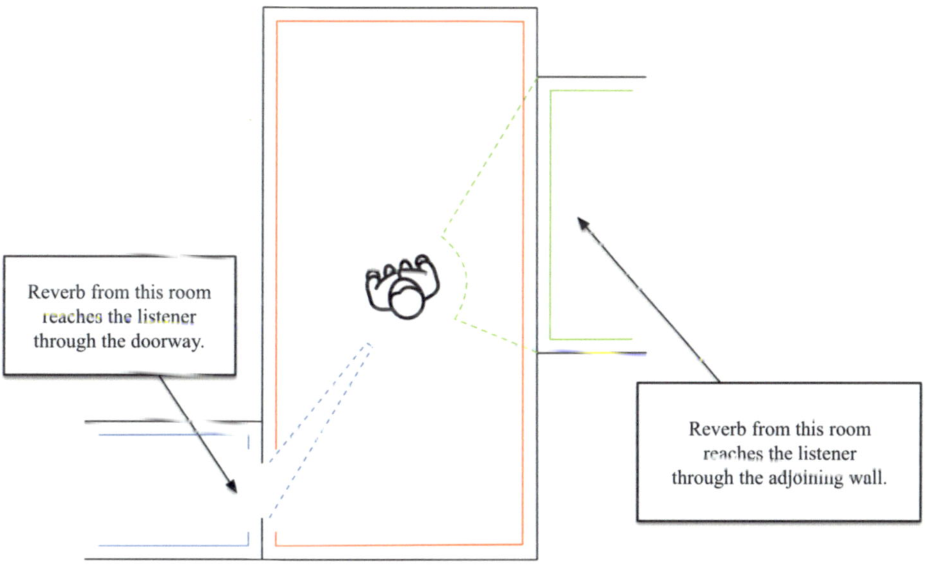

Figure 18.
Example illustrating reverb effect panning driven by high-level scene description (adapted from Ref. [54]).

To achieve differentiated control of early reflections for each sound source (see Section 3.2.3), a computationally efficient approach is enabled by the *grouped reflections* rendering method initially proposed in Ref. [55]. As illustrated in **Figure 11**, source signals are first scaled, panned and mixed into a multichannel reflections send bus, which sums the individually scaled and panned contributions of multiple sound sources to feed them to a shared *grouped reflections* processing module. An example implementation of this general scheme is detailed in Ref. [1], where the reflections send bus utilizes a 3-channel ambisonic format (*W, X, Y*) and per-source reflections panning is projected into the listener's head-relative equatorial plane.

In practical implementation (for instance embedded in a head-mounted AAR device system), the binaural renderer of **Figure 11** may be running continuously and can configure itself dynamically in response to system requests to start or stop rendering a given sound source for presentation to the listener. This involves incrementally instantiating or de-instantiating a *per-source processing module* and, if needed, one or more *effect slot* modules and associated *effect send bus* summation nodes.

5. Conclusion: Acoustic Object rendering interface

In combination with emerging wearable augmented audio reality (AAR) hardware, and with the expanding cloud-based ecosystem that supports the Metaverse, binaural immersive audio rendering technology serves as a fundamental enabler of co-presence, remote collaboration, and virtual entertainment experiences. In the present article, we have described an object-based spatial audio rendering interface that builds upon well-established interactive audio standards. It supports multi-source interactive 6-DoF spatial audio and multi-room reverberation, emphasizing auditory plausibility while minimizing computational footprint and application complexity. By favoring a perception-grounded construction of the rendered audio output, it achieves independence from application-level scene generation strategies, including both physics-driven environment models and esthetics-driven immersive music or soundtracks.

As discussed in Refs. [6, 7], the adoption of an application-agnostic *Acoustic Object* rendering interface enables compatibility between any end-user device and any immersive content source, including linear media broadcast or streaming services (e.g., live or recorded music, sports, or video), as well as interactive or navigable AAR experiences inhabiting digital twins of real or virtual worlds.

To support navigable Audio Metaverse experiences in which sound source positions and acoustic environment parameters may be dynamically modulated at runtime by multiple independent applications, this *Acoustic Object* rendering interface enables the decoupling of source vs. environment specifications, deferring their resolution until render time. This includes the positional coordinates of sound sources and sinks, the intrinsic radiation properties of sound sources, as well as the geometric and acoustic properties of rooms, obstacles, and reflectors, whether real or virtual. The acoustic environment may be managed dynamically as a navigable set of virtual rooms, each characterized by a "reverberation preset" that encodes its response to an omnidirectional sound source co-located with the sink (listener). This encoding is consistent with the notion of *reverberation fingerprint* of a room, affording a data-efficient characterization of acoustic reverberation, and thus facilitating the modeling of an "acoustic digital twin" of the Audio Metaverse.

Acknowlegments

This chapter is an abbreviated and updated version of a 2021 conference paper entitled "Rendering Spatial Sound for Interoperable Experiences in the Audio Metaverse" [1]. Jean-Marc is grateful to Rémi Audfray, Mark Hertensteiner, and Brian Schmidt for co-authoring this conference paper, and for their collaboration in the design of Magic Leap's Soundfield Audio technology (MSA) in 2017–2020.

Elements borrowed from the conference paper are reproduced here with the permissions of its authors and of its publisher. Jean-Marc also wishes to acknowledge the essential contribution of Sam Dicker to the development of the rendering engine presented here, as its principal software architect at Creative Labs and at Magic Leap. The research reported in the present article also benefits from collaborations with Jean-Michel Trivi, Daniel Peacock, Pete Harrison, and Garin Hiebert, for the development and deployment of the EAX and OpenAL APIs, and with Olivier Warusfel, Veronique Larcher, and Martin Walsh, for acoustic and rendering algorithm research.

Abbreviations

3-DoF	three degrees-of-freedom (orientation only)
6-DoF	six degrees-of-freedom (location and orientation)
AAR	audio augmented reality (or augmented audio reality)
API	application programming interface
AR	augmented reality
AV	audiovisual
EAX	Environmental audio extensions (creative technology)
FDN	feedback delay network
FIR	finite impulse response
FOA	first-order ambisonics
HMD	head-mounted display
HOA	higher-order ambisonics
HRTF	head-related transfer function
I3D (L1 & L2)	Interactive 3D Audio Rendering Guidelines (Levels 1.0 & 2.0)
IC	interaural coherence
IAC	interaural correlation
IACC	interaural cross-correlation coefficient
IIR	infinite impulse response
ITD	interaural time difference
LBE	location-based entertainment
LPF	low-pass filter
MSA	magic leap soundfield audio
MR	mixed reality
OS	operating system
PSAP	personal sound amplification product
RIP	reverb initial power
SDK	software development kit
VBAP	vector base amplitude panning
VR	virtual reality
X3D	extensible 3D
XR	extended reality

Author details

Jean-Marc Jot[1*] and Michael Cohen[2,3]

1 Virtuel Works LLC, Aptos, CA, USA

2 University of Aizu, Aizu-Wakamatsu, Fukushima, Japan

3 Highashi Nippon International University, Iwaki, Fukushima, Japan

*Address all correspondence to: jmmjot@gmail.com

References

[1] Jot J-M, Audfray R, Hertensteiner M, Schmidt B. Rendering spatial sound for interoperable experiences in the Audio Metaverse. In: I3DA: Proc. Immersive and 3D Audio: From Architecture to Automotive; Bologna, Italy. New York, NY, USA: Institute of Electrical and Electronics Engineers (IEEE); 2021. pp. 1-15. DOI: 10.1109/I3DA48870.2021.9610971

[2] Jot J-M, Carpentier T, Warusfel O. Perceptually motivated spatial audio scene description and rendering for 6-DoF immersive music experiences. In: I3DA: Proc. Immersive and 3D Audio: From Architecture to Automotive; Bologna, Italy. New York, NY, USA: Institute of Electrical and Electronics Engineers (IEEE); 2023. DOI: 10.1109/I3DA57090.2023.10289196

[3] Carpentier T. Orchestrating a software scosystem for the creation, manipulation, and distribution of spatial sudio [PhD thesis]. Paris, France: Sorbonne Université; 2024

[4] Carpentier T, Noisternig M, Warusfel O. Twenty years of IRCAM Spat: Looking back, looking forward. In: ICMC: 41st Int. Computer Music Conf. San Francisco, CA, USA: International Computer Music Association (ICMA); 2015

[5] Jot J-M. Real-time spatial processing of sounds for music, multimedia and interactive human-computer interfaces. ACM Multimedia Systems Journal. 1999;**7**(1):55-69. DOI: 10.1007/s005300050111

[6] Jot J-M, Carpentier T, Warusfel O. Acoustic objects: Bridging immersive audio creation and distribution systems. In: Audio Eng. Soc. 158th Conv. New York, NY, USA: Audio Engineering Society (AES); 2025

[7] Jot J-M, Carpentier T, Warusfel O. Creating and distributing immersive audio experiences. In: Roginska A, Geluso P, editors. Immersive Sound, Part 2. New York, NY, USA: Routledge; 2026

[8] Roginska A, Geluso P, editors. Immersive Sound: The Art and Science of Binaural and Multi-Channel Audio. New York, NY, USA: Routledge; 2017. DOI: 10.4324/9781315707525

[9] Blake L. George Lucas: Technology and the art of filmmaking. Mix Online. 2004:44-48

[10] Herre J, Hilpert J, Kuntz A, Plogsties J. MPEG-H 3D audio— The new standard for coding of immersive spatial audio. IEEE Journal of Selected Topics in Signal Processing. 2015;**9**(5):770-779. DOI: 10.1109/JSTSP.2015.2411578

[11] Recommendation ITU-R BS.2076-2. Audio Definition Model. Geneva, Switzerland: International Telecommunication Union (ITU); 2019. Available from: https://www.itu.int/rec/R-REC-BS.2076-2-201910-I/

[12] Robinson CQ, Mehta S, Tsingos N. Scalable format and tools to extend the possibilities of cinema audio. SMPTE Motion Imaging Journal. 2012;**121**(8):63-69. DOI: 10.5594/j18248XY

[13] Zotter F, Frank M. Ambisonics: A Practical 3D Audio Theory for Recording, Studio Production, Sound Reinforcement and Virtual Reality. Cham, Switzerland: Springer; 2019. DOI: 10.1007/978-3-030-17207-7

[14] Shirley B, Oldfield R. Clean audio for TV broadcast: An object-based approach for hearing-impaired viewers. Journal of the Audio Engineering Society. 2015;**63**(4):245-256. DOI: 10.17743/jaes.2015.00017

[15] Pulkki V. Virtual sound source positioning using vector base amplitude panning. Journal of the Audio Engineering Society. 1997;**45**(6): 456-466

[16] Ball M. The Metaverse: Building the Spatial Internet. New York, NY, USA: Liveright Publishing Corporation; 2024

[17] Stephenson N. Snow Crash. New York, NY, USA: Bantam Books; 1992

[18] Cohen M, Martens WL. Spatial soundscape superposition and multimodal interaction. In: Blauert J, Braasch J, editors. The Technology of Binaural Understanding, Modern Acoustics and Signal Processing, Chap. 13. Cham: Springer; 2020. pp. 351-390. DOI: 10.1007/978-3-030-00386-9 13

[19] Bell G, Parisi A, Pesce M, Mitra V, Hardenbergh YJC, Meyer T, et al. The Virtual Reality Modeling Language, Version 1.1 Specification Draft. New York, NY, USA: Institute of Electrical and Electronics Engineers (IEEE); 1995

[20] Pesce M. VRML: Browsing and Building Cyberspace. Indianapolis, IN, USA: New Riders Publishing; 1995

[21] Scheirer E, Väänänen R, Huopaniemi J. AudioBIFS: Describing audio scenes with the MPEG-4 multimedia standard. IEEE Transactions on Multimedia. 1999;**1**(3):237-250. DOI: 10.1109/6046.784463

[22] Somberg G, editor. Game Audio Programming 3: Principles and Practices. Boca Raton, FL, USA: CRC Press; 2021

[23] Khronos Group Inc. OpenXR Specification. Beaverton, OR, USA: Khronos Group; 2021. Available from: https://www.khronos.org/registry/OpenXR/specs/1.0/html/xrspec.html

[24] W3C. WebXR Device API. Wakefield, MA, USA: World Wide Web Consortium (W3C); 2024. Available from: https://w3.org/TR/webxr/

[25] Quackenbush S, Herre J. MPEG standards for compressed representation of immersive audio. Proceedings of the IEEE. 2021;**109**(9):1578-1589. DOI: 10.1109/JPROC.2021.3075390

[26] Patricio E, Ruminski A, Kuklasinski A, Januszkiewicz L, Zernicki T. Toward six degrees of freedom audio recording and playback using multiple ambisonic sound fields. In: Audio Eng. Soc. 146th Conv. 2019

[27] Rumsey F. Headphone technology: Hear-through, bone conduction, and noise canceling. Journal of the Audio Engineering Society. 2019;**67**(11):914-919

[28] Härmä A, Jakka J, Tikander M, Karjalainen M, Lokki T, Hiipakka J, et al. Augmented reality audio for mobile and wearable appliances. Journal of the Audio Engineering Society. 2004;**52**(6):618-639

[29] Lindeman RW, Noma H, de Barros PG. An empirical study of hear-through augmented reality: Using bone conduction to deliver spatialized audio. In: IEEE Virtual Reality. Reno, Nevada, USA: Institute of Electrical and Electronics Engineers (IEEE); 2008. pp. 35-42. DOI: 10.1109/VR.2008.4480747

[30] Gupta R, He J, Ranjan R, Gan W-S, Klein F, Schneiderwind C, et al. Augmented/mixed reality audio

for hearables: Sensing, control, and rendering. IEEE Signal Processing Magazine. 2022;**39**(3):63-89. DOI: 10.1109/MSP.2021.3110108

[31] Best V, Baumgartner R, Lavandier M, Majdak P, Kopco N. Sound externalization: A review of recent research. Trends in Hearing. 2020;**21**(1):2-10. DOI: 10.1177/23312165209483

[32] Roquet P. Acoustics of the one person space: Headphone listening, detachable ambience, and the binaural prehistory of VR. Sound Studies. 2021;**7**(1):42-63. DOI: 10.1080/20551940.2020.1750270

[33] Cohen M. Dimensions of spatial sound and interface styles of audio augmented reality: Whereware, wearware, and everyware. In: Barfield W, editor. Fundamentals of Wearable Computers and Augmented Reality, Chap. 12. 2nd ed. Boca Raton: CRC Press: Lawrence Erlbaum Associates; 2016. pp. 277-308. DOI: 10.1201/b18703

[34] Dam A, Siddiqui A, Leclercq C, Jeon M. Taxonomy and definition of audio augmented reality (AAR): A grounded theory study. International Journal of Human-Computer Studies. 2024;**182**:103179. DOI: 10.1016/j.ijhcs.2023.103179

[35] Cohen M, Aoki S, Koizumi N. Augmented audio reality: Telepresence/VR hybrid acoustic environments. In: Proc. Ro-Man: 2nd IEEE Int. Wkshp. on Robot and Human Communication; Tokyo. 1993. pp. 361-364. ISBN: 0-7803-1407-7. DOI: 10.1109/ROMAN.1993.367692

[36] Harju M. Audio Augmented Reality: Concepts, Technologies and Narratives. Waltham, MA, USA: Focal Press (Routledge, Taylor & Francis); 2025. ISBN 978-1040367971

[37] Cohen M, Villegas J. From Whereware to whence- and Whitherware: Augmented audio reality for position-aware services. In: ISVRI: Proc. Int. Symp. on Virtual Reality Innovations. Singapore: Institute of Electrical and Electronics Engineers (IEEE); 2011. pp. 273-280. DOI: 10.1109/ISVRI.2011.5759650

[38] Cohen M, Villegas J. Applications of audio augmented reality: Wearware, everyware, anyware, and awareware. In: Barfield W, editor. Fundamentals of Wearable Computers and Augmented Reality, Chap. 13. 2nd ed. Boca Raton: CRC Press: Lawrence Erlbaum Associates; 2016. pp. 309-330. DOI: 10.1201/b18703

[39] Chowning JM. The simulation of moving sound sources. Journal of the Audio Engineering Society. 1971;**49**(10):904-916. DOI: 10.2307/3679609

[40] Kleiner M, Dalenbäck B-I, Svensson P. Auralization – An overview. Journal of the Audio Engineering Society. 1993;**41**(11):861-875

[41] Puckette MS. The Theory and Technique of Electronic Music. Singapore: World Scientific Publishing; 2007. DOI: 10.1142/6277

[42] Peacock D, Harrison P, D'Orta A, Carpentier V, Cooper E. OpenAL Effects Extension Guide. Milpitas, CA, USA: Creative Labs, Inc.; 2006

[43] Audfray R, Jot J-M, Dicker S. Audio application programming Interface for mixed reality. In: Audio Eng. Soc. 145th Conv. New York, NY, USA: Audio Engineering Society (AES); 2018

[44] Magic Leap, Inc. Soundfield Components. Plantation, FL, USA: Magic Leap, Inc.; 2024. Available from:

https://developer-docs.magicleap.cloud/docs/guides/unity/soundfield-audio/soundfield-components/

[45] Brutzman D, Daly L. X3D: Extensible 3D Graphics for Web Authors. Burlington, MA, USA: Morgan Kaufmann Publishers; 2007. DOI: 10.5555/1214715

[46] Daly L, Brutzman D. X3D: Extensible 3D graphics standard. IEEE Signal Processing Magazine. 2007;**24**(6):130-135. DOI: 10.1109/MSP.2007.905887

[47] IA-SIG. Interactive 3D Audio Rendering Guidelines - Level 2.0. La Habra, CA, USA: MIDI Manufacturers Association; 1999. Available from: https://learn.microsoft.com/en-us/windows/win32/api/xaudio2fx/ns-xaudio2fx-xaudio2fx_reverb_i3dl2_parameters

[48] Jot J-M, Boom M. Environmental Audio Extensions: EAX 2.0. Singapore: Creative Technology Ltd.; 1999. Available from: http://en.wikipedia.org/wiki/Environmental_Audio_Extensions#References

[49] Hiebert G. OpenAL 1.1 Specification and Reference. Milpitas, CA, USA: Creative Labs, Inc.; 2005. Available from: https://openal.org/documentation/

[50] IA-SIG. 3D Audio Rendering and Evaluation Guidelines. La Habra, CA, USA: MIDI Manufacturers Association; 1998

[51] Khronos Group Inc. OpenSL ES Specification, Version 1.1. Beaverton, OR, USA: Khronos Group; 2017. Available from: http://khronos.org/registry/OpenSL-ES/specs/

[52] Savioja L, Huopaniemi J, Lokki T, Väänänen R. Creating interactive virtual acoustic environments. Journal of the Audio Engineering Society. 1999;**47**(9):675-705

[53] Peacock D, Harrison P. EAX 4.0 Programmer's Guide. Singapore: Creative Technology Ltd.; 2003. Available from: http://en.wikipedia.org/wiki/Environmental_Audio_Extensions#References

[54] Peacock D, Harrison P. EAX 4.0 Introduction. Singapore: Creative Technology Ltd.; 2003. Available from: http://en.wikipedia.org/wiki/Environmental_Audio_Extensions#References

[55] Jot J-M, Philp A, Walsh M. Binaural simulation of complex acoustic scenes for interactive audio. In: Audio Eng. Soc. 121st Conv. New York, NY, USA: Audio Engineering Society (AES); 2006

[56] Audfray R, Jot J-M. Reverberation loudness model for mixed-reality audio. In: Audio Eng. Soc. Conf. Headphone Technology. New York, NY, USA: Audio Engineering Society (AES); 2019

[57] Jot J-M, Lee KS. Augmented reality headphone environment rendering. In: Audio Eng. Soc. Conf. on Audio for Virtual and Augmented Reality. New York, NY, USA: Audio Engineering Society (AES); 2016

[58] Jot J-M. Proportional parametric equalizers — Application to digital reverberation and environmental audio processing. In: Audio Eng. Soc. 139th Conv. New York, NY, USA: Audio Engineering Society (AES); 2015

[59] Audfray R, Jot J-M, Dicker S. Practical realization of dual-shelving filter using proportional parametric equalizers. In: Audio Eng. Soc. 145th Conv. New York, NY, USA: Audio Engineering Society (AES); 2018

[60] Jot J-M, Cerveau L, Warusfel O. Analysis and synthesis of room reverberation based on a statistical time-frequency model. In: Audio Eng. Soc. 103rd Conv. New York, NY, USA: Audio Engineering Society (AES); 1997

[61] Gospodarek M, Warusfel O, Ripollés P, Roginska A. Methodology for perceptual evaluation of plausibility with self-translation of the listener. In: Proc. AES International Conference on Audio for Virtual and Augmented Reality. New York, NY, USA: Audio Engineering Society (AES); 2022

[62] Jot J-M, Larcher V, Warusfel O. Digital signal processing issues in the context of binaural and transaural stereophony. In: Audio Eng. Soc. 98th Conv. New York, NY, USA: Audio Engineering Society (AES); 1995

[63] Meyer-Kahlen N, Schlecht S, Amengual Garí S, Lokki T. Testing auditory illusions in augmented reality: Plausibility, transfer-plausibility, and authenticity. Journal of the Audio Engineering Society. 2024;**72**:11

[64] Gerzon MA. General metatheory of auditory localisation. In: Audio Eng. Soc. 92nd Conv. New York, NY, USA: Audio Engineering Society (AES); 1992

[65] Polack J. Playing billiards in the concert hall: The mathematical foundations of geometrical room acoustics. Applied Acoustics. 1993;**38**(2-4):235-244. DOI: 10.1016/0003-682x(93)90054-a

[66] Pind F, Einarsson J, Guojonsson S, Cosnefroy M, Pedersen J, Stefansson J, et al. A novel wave-based virtual acoustics and spatial audio framework. In: Proc. AES AVAR Conf. New York, NY, USA: Audio Engineering Society (AES); 2022

[67] Savioja L, Svensson UP. Overview of geometrical room acoustic modeling techniques. Journal of the Acoustical Society of America. 2015;**138**(2):503-516

[68] Vorländer M. Auralization: Fundamentals of Acoustics, Modelling, Simulation, Algorithms and Acoustic Virtual Reality. Berlin, Germany: Springer; 2008

[69] Liu S, Manocha D. Sound Synthesis, Propagation, and Rendering. Cham, Switzerland: Springer; 2022

[70] Raghuvanshi N, Snyder J. Parametric directional coding for precomputed sound propagation. ACM Transactions on Graphics. 2018;**37**(4):1-14. DOI: 10.1145/3197517.3201339

[71] Rungta A, Schissler C, Rewkowski N, Mehra R, Manocha D. Diffraction kernels for interactive sound propagation in dynamic environments. IEEE Transactions on Visualization and Computer Graphics. 2018;**24**:1613-1622. DOI: 10.1109/TVCG.2018.2794098

[72] Tang Z, Meng H-Y, Manocha D. Learning acoustic scattering fields for dynamic interactive sound propagation. In: IEEE Conf. on Virtual Reality and 3D User Interfaces. New York, NY, USA: Institute of Electrical and Electronics Engineers (IEEE); 2021. DOI: 10.1109/VR50410.2021.00111

[73] Gamper H, Tashev I. Blind reverberation time estimation using a convolutional neural network. In: IWAENC: Int. Workshop on Acoustic Signal Enhancement. New York, NY, USA: Institute of Electrical and Electronics Engineers (IEEE); 2018. DOI: 10.1109/IWAENC.2018.8521241

[74] Murgai P, Rau M, Jot J-M. Blind estimation of the reverberation fingerprint of unknown acoustic environments. In: Audio Eng. Soc.

143rd Conv. New York, NY, USA: Audio Engineering Society (AES); 2017

[75] Alary B. Analysis and synthesis of directional reverberation [PhD thesis]. Aalto, Finland: Aalto University; 2021

[76] Alary B, Massé P, Schlecht S, Noisternig M, Välimäki V. Perceptual analysis of directional late reverberation. The Journal of the Acoustical Society of America. 2021;**149**:3189-3199. DOI: 10.1121/10.0004770

[77] Potard G, Burnett I. Decorrelation techniques for the rendering of apparent sound source width in 3D audio displays. In: 7th Int. Conf. on Digital Audio Effects. Digital Audio Effects Conference (DAFx) Coordinated in Europe; Rotating Host Cities. DAFx Association; 2004

[78] Verron C, Aramaki M, Kronland-Martinet R, Pallone G. A 3-D immersive synthesizer for environmental sounds. IEEE Transactions on Audio, Speech, and Language Processing. 2010;**18**(6):1550-1561. DOI: 10.1109/TASL.2009.2037402

[79] Roginska A. Binaural audio through headphones. In: Roginska A, Geluso P, editors. Immersive Sound: The Art and Science of Binaural and Multi-Channel Audio, Chap. 4. New York, NY, USA: Routledge; 2017. pp. 88-123. DOI: 10.4324/9781315707525

[80] Zotkin D, Duraiswami R, Davis L. Rendering localized spatial audio in a virtual auditory space. IEEE Transactions on Multimedia. 2004;**6**(4):553-564

[81] Frankenbach C, Herzog C, Seitz J, Fels J. Evaluating localization accuracy of dynamic binaural synthesis: Differences between individual, estimated, and generic HRTFs. Journal of the Audio Engineering Society. 2025;**73**:219-223

[82] Jot J-M, Lukin A, Landschoot C. Binaural externalization processing – From stereo to object-based audio. In: Proc. 153rd AES Convention. 2022

[83] Blauert J. Spatial Hearing: The Psychophysics of Human Sound Localization. Revised ed. Cambridge, MA, USA: MIT Press; 1996. DOI: 10.7551/mitpress/6391.001.0001

[84] Larcher V. Techniques de spatialization des sons pour la réalité virtuelle [PhD thesis]. Paris: Université Pierre et Marie Curie; 2001

[85] Brinkmann F, Dinakaran M, Pelzer R, Grosche P, Voss D, Weinzierl S. A cross-evaluated database of measured and simulated HRTFs including 3D head meshes, anthropometric features, and headphone impulse responses. Journal of the Audio Engineering Society. 2019;**67**(9):705-718

[86] Larcher V, Jot J-M, Vandernoot G. Equalization methods in binaural technology. In: Audio Eng. Soc. 105th Conv. New York, NY, USA: Audio Engineering Society (AES); 1998

[87] Lladó P, Pollack K, Meyer-Kahlen N. Toward a standard listener-independent HRTF to facilitate long-term adaptation. Journal of the Audio Engineering Society. 2024;**72**(4):188-192

[88] Travis C. Virtual reality perspective on headphone audio. In: Audio Eng. Soc. 101st Conv. New York, NY, USA: Audio Engineering Society (AES); 1996

[89] Noisternig M, Sontacchi A, Musil T, Holdrich R. A 3D Ambisonic based binaural sound reproduction system. In: Audio Eng. Soc. 24th Conf.: Multichannel Audio, the New Reality. New York, NY, USA: Audio Engineering Society (AES); 2003

[90] Ben-Hur Z, Alon D, Mehra R, Rafaely B. Binaural reproduction based on bilateral ambisonics and ear-aligned HRTFs. IEEE/ACM Transactions on Audio, Speech, and Language Processing. 2021;**53**(7):620-631. DOI: 10.1109/taslp.2021.3055038

[91] Jot J-M, Larcher V, Pernaux J-M. A comparative study of 3-D audio encoding and rendering techniques. In: Audio Eng. Soc. 16th Int. Conf. New York, NY, USA: Audio Engineering Society (AES); 1999

[92] Wiggins B. Analysis of binaural Cue matching using Ambisonics to binaural decoding techniques. In: 4th Int. Conf. On Spatial Audio. Köln, Germany: Verband Deutscher Tonmeister (VDT); 2017

[93] Berge S, Barrett N. A new method for B-format to binaural transcoding. In: Audio Eng. Soc. 40th Int. Conf. New York, NY, USA: Audio Engineering Society (AES); 2010

[94] Breebaart J, Schuijers E. Phantom materialization: A novel method to enhance stereo audio reproduction on headphones. IEEE Transactions on Audio, Speech, and Language Processing. 2008;**16**(8):1503-1511. DOI: 10.1109/TASL.2008.2002983

[95] Goodwin MM, Jot J-M. Binaural 3-D audio rendering based on spatial audio scene coding. In: Audio Eng. Soc. 123rd Conv. New York, NY, USA: Audio Engineering Society (AES); 2007

[96] Jot J-M, Wardle S, Larcher V. Approaches to binaural synthesis. In: Audio Eng. Soc. 105th Conv. New York, NY, USA: Audio Engineering Society (AES). 1998

[97] Romblom D, Cook B. Near-field compensation for HRTF processing. In: Audio Eng. Soc. 125th Conv. New York, NY, USA: Audio Engineering Society (AES); 2008

[98] Bouéri M, Kyriakakis C. Audio signal decorrelation based on a critical band approach. In: Audio Eng. Soc. 117th Conv. New York, NY, USA: Audio Engineering Society (AES); 2004

[99] Kendall GS. The decorrelation of audio signals and its impact on spatial imagery. Computer Music Journal. 1995;**19**(4):71-87. DOI: 10.2307/3680992

[100] Carpentier T, Szpruch T, Noisternig M, Warusfel O. Parametric control of convolution based room simulators. In: ISRA: Int. Symp. on Room Acoustics. Berlin, Germany: International Symposium on Room Acoustics (ISRA) / EAA; 2013

[101] De Sena E, Hacıhabiboğlu H, Cvetković Z, Smith JO. Efficient synthesis of room acoustics via scattering delay networks. IEEE/ACM Transactions on Audio, Speech, and Language Processing. 2015;**23**(9):1478-1492. DOI: 10.1109/TASLP.2015.2438547

[102] Fagerström J, Alary B, Schlecht SJ, Välimäki V. Velvet-noise feedback delay network. In: DAFx: Proc. 23rd Int. Conf. on Digital Audio Effects. Digital Audio Effects Conference (DAFx) Coordinated in Europe; Rotating Host Cities. DAFx Association; 2020. pp. 219-226

[103] Fagerström J, Meyer-Kahlen N, Schlecht SJ, Välimäki V. Binaural dark-velvet-noise reverberator. In: DAFx: Proc. 27th Int. Conf. on Digital Audio Effects. Guildford, United Kingdom: Digital Audio Effects Conference Association (DAFx); 2024. pp. 219-226

[104] Gardner WG. Reverberation algorithms. In: Applications of Digital

Signal Processing to Audio and Acoustics. New York, NY, USA: Springer; 2002. DOI: 10.1007/0-306-47042-X 3

[105] Jot J-M. Efficient models for reverberation and distance rendering in computer music and virtual audio reality. In: ICMC: Proc. Int. Computer Music Conf. San Francisco, CA, USA: International Computer Music Association (ICMA); 1997

[106] Schlecht SJ. FDNTB: The feedback delay network toolbox. In: DAFx: Proc. 23rd Int. Conf. On Digital Audio Effects. Digital Audio Effects Conference (DAFx) Coordinated in Europe; Rotating Host Cities. DAFx Association; 2020. pp. 211-218

[107] Valimaki V, Parker JD, Savioja L, Smith JO, Abel JS. Fifty years of artificial reverberation. IEEE Transactions on Audio, Speech, and Language Processing. 2012;**20**(5):1421-1448. DOI: 10.1109/TASL.2012.2189567

[108] Xiang N, Trivedi U, Xie B. Artificial enveloping reverberation for binaural auralization using reciprocal maximum-length sequences. The Journal of the Acoustical Society of America. 2019;**145**:2691-2702. DOI: 10.1121/1.5095863

[109] Jot J-M, Chaigne A. Digital delay networks for designing artificial reverberators. In: Audio Eng. Soc. 90th Conv. New York, NY, USA: Audio Engineering Society (AES); 1991

[110] Menzer F, Faller C. Investigations on an early-reflection-free model for BRIRs. Journal of the Audio Engineering Society. 2010;**58**(9):709-723

Chapter 6

AR Applications That Fail to Support Proper Sensorimotor Coupling Can Result in User Disorientation and Disappointment

William L. Martens and Frederico Pereira

Abstract

Support for naturalistic sensorimotor contingencies is an essential component of successful augmented reality (AR) technology that superposes on a user's real world geometrically registered interactive media, such as 3D graphics and audio. For example, when AR system users move their heads while listening to spatially stabilized sounds that are superposed on the soundscape of the real world surrounding them, a highly realistic and immersive experience of displayed virtual sound sources can be enabled. In contrast, disorientation and disappointment result for a user when virtual sound sources are not properly modulated by the contingency of the dynamic causal coupling between user actions and auditory consequences of those actions. To examine the auditory contingency effect experimentally, an AR system's interactively displayed audio components were recorded for users engaged in typical head movements, and those same audio components were later replayed in a manner that was not properly coupled with head-tracking information for those users. In one test condition, the raw audio components were processed in a manner that depended upon angular head-tracking information with only two degrees of freedom, while a second test condition employed angular head-tracking information with three degrees of freedom. Both the resulting disorientation and disappointment of tested users were assessed after each user listened to the otherwise identical virtual sound sources under the two testing conditions.

Keywords: sensorimotor coupling, sensorimotor contingency, sounding objects, augmented reality audio, spatial hearing

1. Introduction

Users of an augmented reality (AR) system experience sensorimotor contingencies that confirm the permanent potential for natural auditory perception of the spatially stable virtual sounding objects that the AR system presents to them.

That is, the system must do more than simply reproduce a recording of the sound of an acoustical event for the user, even if what is heard sounds like a highly realistic event. The system must allow users to experience an expected change in auditory sensation that is contingent upon their actions (i.e., the user's sensations must change with the user's active head motion). Disappointment will typically result when a user hears static auditory display elements that do not change in response to that user's movement within the space containing the virtual sounding object. Now, it is manifestly obvious that change in the position of a stationary object relative to an observer's head will occur whenever an observer's head is moved past that stationary object; however, it is not a trivial decision whether an AR application should include all such obvious changes in the display of virtual sound sources that would occur when the observer's head is rotated in each of three planes, whether that rotation is in the midsagittal plane, the frontal (a.k.a. coronal) plane, or the horizontal plane. It should be noted at the outset of this discussion, that with the advent of head-tracking virtual auditory display (VAD) technology that was launched in the early 1980s, there was no consensus on the importance of including multiple degrees of freedom in the active coupling of spatial audio processing with head rotation (i.e., whether there should be one, two, or three degrees of freedom incorporated in angular head-tracking [1–3]). In fact, it was rare to find VAD systems with auditory processing that was coupled to head rotation that was tracked with a full three-degrees-of-freedom (3DoF).

A great deal of spatial hearing research has ignored the important contribution of head movements in supporting successful sound localization performance [4], despite the existence of strong evidence from early studies [5, 6] emphasizing the important role of head movements in sound direction of arrival discrimination. It cannot be overemphasized that Wallach's [5, 6] results, which were reported more than 80 years ago, have been repeatedly confirmed by modern studies using virtual auditory display technology.

This chapter explores the importance of head motion in resolving ambiguous directional hearing cues for AR system users facing challenging sound localization tasks, particularly those in which virtual sound sources arrive from angles of incidence that lie outside of the observer's visual field. Additionally, the relevance of sensorimotor coupling for natural interactions in AR environments is discussed.

1.1 The importance of tracking 3DoF angular variation in the orientation of the listener's head for successful AR system performance

A typical failure of AR auditory display concerns what happens during natural, unconstrained variation in the orientation of the listener's head. This failure stems from the mistaken assumption that AR systems can function adequately when using two-degree-of-freedom (2DoF) head-tracking technology that monitors head rotations of only two sorts (turning left to right, and tipping forward and backward), rather than the full complement of rotations about three spatial axes, described by Tait–Bryan angles (yaw, pitch, and also roll). These three types of angular variation have for many years been monitored using commercially available systems designed to track the orientation of a listener's head using 3DoF technology [1]. **Table 1** gives a more comprehensive account of how these orthogonal rotations of a listener's head relate to informal designations. The names typically given to representative head gestures are listed, along with the meanings typically associated with them when used in nonverbal communication.

The importance of head-movement-coupled variation in binaural head-related transfer function (HRTF)-based spatial audio processing for successful AR system performance must be carefully considered. It could be said that smooth and timely response to the AR system user's head movements play a pivotal role in creating satisfying illusions of spatially stable sounding objects in a displayed auditory scene. The most obvious support for this conclusion is found in examination of the resolution of front-back ambiguity enabled by proper coordination of interaural cues to source direction with monitored head turning. Whereas static HRTF-based processing is often plagued by front-back confusions, motion-coupled dynamic cues (contingent on head turning) eliminate such confusion, as is easily confirmed first hand by AR system users, and was clearly evidenced in the results of Wallach's experimental studies conducted over 80 years ago [5, 6].

Suffice it to say that there is incontrovertible evidence that human listeners can and do use the direction of the change in interaural cues that accompany head turning (change in yaw angle) as an unambiguous indicator of the proper hemifield of incident sound. Despite the incontrovertible evidence for this conclusion with regard to the resolution of front-back ambiguity [7], there are few reports of the importance of change in head roll angle as an unambiguous indicator of the above-versus-below hemifields of incident sound (although notable examples exist [8, 9]). A subsequent section of this chapter will present a more rigorous analysis of how human listeners can use these two types of head rotation to make these two hemifield distinctions. At this point, it should be emphasized that the third type of head rotation, identified in **Table 1** as angular variation in directional pitch, does not function in the same manner as head yaw and head roll, since changes in head pitch do not reorient the interaural axis of the listener's head. Before continuing with this exposition, systematic presentation of the relevant spatial geometry conventionally used in the sound localization literature will be reviewed here. This review includes the terminology used in describing the planes and angles of the two coordinate systems that have come to dominate the technical literature, the first of these two being the vertical-polar (VP) coordinate system.

According to the VP coordinate system, horizontal directions are specified by their azimuth angle: the angle subtended at the center of listener's head relative to the

Tait–Bryan angle	Plane of rotation	Informal designation	Head gesture	Nonverbal expression
Yaw	Horizontal Transverse (visuoaural) Plane (HTP)	turning to the left and right	shaking	denial, contradiction: "no"
Pitch	Median Sagittal (midsagittal) Plane (MSP)	tipping forward and backward	nodding	affirmation, concurrence: "yes"
Roll	Vertical Lateral (frontal, coronal) Plane (VLP)	pivoting leftward and rightward	wagging	uncertainty, questioning: "maybe"

Table 1.
Three types of angular variation in the listener's head orientation and the Tait–Bryan angles used to represent such rotations about three distinct axes and the orthogonal planes within which those rotations occur.

midsagittal plane. The vertical directions of stimuli are specified by the elevation: the angle subtended at the center of the head relative to the horizontal plane. Another head-related alternative to the VP coordinate system that was first introduced in 1979 [10] is the so-called spherical double polar (DP) coordinate system in which lateral and elevation angles are defined along independent axes. This double polar system was devised to align directly with the two main binaural cues for direction determination—interaural time differences (ITDs) and interaural level differences (ILDs). Surfaces of constant ITD/ILD form a listener's "cones of confusion" at each lateral angle. The lateral angle of a source is defined by its parasagittal plane, with the angular offset from the midsagittal plane measured on the visuoaural plane. The elevation angle of a source is defined by the transverse plane in which it is found, with the angular offset from the visuoaural plane measured in the parasagittal plane. For both systems, the radial distance complements directional information to fully describe source location. (In this text, the term *localization* is used to denote the complete determination of three-dimensional spatial coordinates, whereas the term *directionalization* may be used for sound direction-of-arrival determination, which can be reported via angular judgments that disregard the distance between source and receiver).

For moving listeners actively engaged in sound localization, satisfaction with an AR system will typically result when sensorimotor contingencies obey the tacitly understood rules that underly the head-movement-based dynamic interaural cues naturally used by those listeners in resolving ambiguities in source angular incidence (e.g., from which of a pair of opposing hemifields a source arrives). Note that head movements are not needed for left-right distinctions in source incidence, since sources incident from the left and right are virtually never confused with each other, as unambiguous lateralization cues ensue from a source's incidence from either side of the head. But for above-below and front-rear distinctions, there are two sets of analogous contingencies useful to binaural listeners who are actively engaged in determining source direction, and these constitute the governing laws that underlie the important role of head-movements in binaural spatial hearing. For a more complete treatment of these sensorimotor contingencies, the reader is referred to [11, 12]. The two types of these sensorimotor contingencies are those that disambiguate hemifield incidence by variation in yaw (A) and variation in roll (B):

(A) Variation in the yaw angle of the head (turning) produces variation in the lateral angle of incidence of a static sound source in a manner that depends on, and therefore can determine, whether the source originates in the frontward or rearward hemifield. A source is detected in the front hemifield when a leftward turn of the head is associated with a rightward shift in source lateral angle; conversely, a source in the rear hemifield is localized by a rightward shift in source lateral angle that is contingent on a rightward turn of the head.

(B) Variation in the roll angle of the head (rolling) produces variation in the lateral angle of incidence of a static sound source in a manner that depends on, and therefore can determine, whether a source originates in the upward or downward hemifield. A rightward shift in source lateral angle results when a head roll drops the right ear toward a source localized to the right in the downward hemifield; conversely, a leftward shift in source lateral angle results when a head roll drops the right ear downward, toward a source localized to the right in the upward hemifield, as illustrated in **Figure 1**.

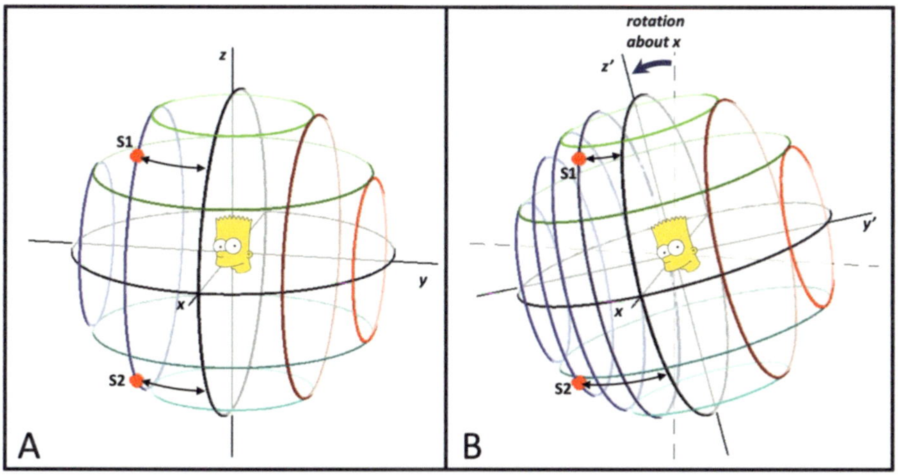

Figure 1.
In Panel A, two spatially stabilized sources (labeled 'S1' and, 'S2') are shown to be equidistant from the user's midsagittal plane, lying initially on the same parasagittal plane, but with elevation angles that are opposite in sign (above vs. below ear level). Panel B illustrates what happens when the user (a.k.a. Bart) rolls his head to the right while hearing these two stationary sources. With a rightward roll of the user's head source S1 shifts to a parasagittal plane toward the midsagittal plane, as it was well above the user's ear level. In contrast, for the same rightward headroll, at the same time, source S2 shifts to a parasagittal plane away from the midsagittal plane, as it was well below the user's ear level. Also apparent in this figure are the contrary shifts in elevation angle for the two sources, both of which were held stationary in world-centric coordinates: the head-centric elevation angle for S1 increases with the rightward headroll, as the head-centric elevation angle for S2 is shifted closer to the user's ear-level (i.e., the transverse plane containing the user's interaural axis y').

1.2 Assessment of wearable augmented reality audio systems performance

Listening tests have often been performed in order to assess the level of performance of deployed wearable augmented reality audio (WARA) systems, particularly in terms of their ability to support rendering of virtual sources that satisfy at least two *otorealistic* criteria. Of these two, the first is that the virtual sound sources should be accurately positioned in space; but, the second is that they should sound natural, so they will not be heard as glaringly different from actual sounds arriving from the physical space from within which they should seem to be arriving. One of the two most obvious ways in which virtual sources can sound very different from actual sources is in their tonal coloration (timbre). The other most glaring difference would be if virtual sources were to be heard as if located inside the user's head, unlike the externalization of actual sources that is typical in everyday listening. The reader is directed to a more comprehensive review of the methods used for perceptual evaluation of filters controlling source direction [13], which provides a context within which the assessments described herein can be understood.

An early example of such a WARA system assessment was reported in 2004 by developers at the Helsinki University of Technology [14]. For envisioned applications of a WARA system, they clearly identified failure of externalization as a most severe problem with binaural technology, as too often WARA systems exhibited the objectionable result described as the "perceived effect of having the virtual source localized inside the head." So, while also concerned with directional accuracy, their assessment included a direct comparison between actual sources and displayed virtual sources. In a series of experimental test trials, two identical test signals were presented for comparison, one of the two being reproduced by a loudspeaker, and the other filtered for display via the WARA system, processed using the appropriate HRTFs (HRTFs measured for angular incidence matching that of the reproducing loudspeaker). The test was a two-interval, two-alternative forced choice (2I2AFC) test, where the WARA system user was asked which of two temporal intervals contained the stimulus that was reproduced by the loudspeaker, rather than by the head-worn earspeaker. To avoid the influence of head movement on the results of their 2I2AFC tests, their experimental test setup included a head-supporting chair for the test subject wearing the WARA headset, and a loudspeaker that was not visible to the subject. With the user's head thus immobilized, they reported that it was nearly impossible for users to distinguish between loudspeaker and earspeaker stimuli when the presented sources were simple musical instrument sounds or speech. However, when broader-frequency-band sources were presented, better discrimination performance was observed, at significantly greater than chance levels (e.g., 68% correct rather than the 50% level expected by guessing alone).

Just as physical sound sources can be located anywhere in the 3D space surrounding a WARA system user, it should be possible to position virtual objects emitting sound in any location within that 3D space. To test the accuracy of virtual sound source positioning for WARA application, it would seem most straightforward to compare the apparent location of virtual sound sources to the visual location of potential sounding objects. Nonetheless, many WARA assessment studies, such as those in [14], ensured that no loudspeaker was visible to the user during assessment tests. Similar thought went into the selection of experimental conditions for the tests described in this chapter for the more recent studies conducted by the authors. The reasoning behind this experimental design choice is made clear in the following paragraph.

Were there an array of loudspeakers visible during localization testing, then potential operation of the "visual-capture effect" (a kind of "snap-to" adjustment) could strongly influence perceptual judgments of the location of virtual sound sources within the user's field of view. For this reason, and to avoid visual capture of sound by any visible object, all directionalization tests that were run in these experiments were executed for sound sources distributed throughout the space lying outside of the user's field of view (and never originated from within the frontal hemifield).

As users were instructed to attend during testing only to sources that arrived from the rear hemifield, the chance of observing front-rear confusion was also greatly reduced. Of course, other hemisphere confusions were possible, and could be observed primarily as confusion between sources arriving from above or below ear level. In practice, it is well established that it is extremely rare to observe confusion between sources arriving from the left versus the right hemifield. The only exception to this rule can be observed under the unusual circumstances of hearing simultaneously presented musical melodies with left-right interchanging of two musical instruments performing interleaved sequences of notes (a kind of gestalt streaming effect for auditory scene analysis in which a simplified mental model is not disturbed by occasional violation). In this case, even if a single note played on trumpet were interchanged in left-right position with a single note played on trombone, the sequence of notes played on trumpet might be heard as always arriving from the one side, as would all the notes played on trombone be heard always as arriving from the other side [15]. If perception of actual sound source were always veridical, then the "bundle of auditory attributes" associated with each sounding object would reflect both the character and location of each incident sound. However, as pointed out in [15], *"when multiple sequences of tones are presented simultaneously from different regions of space, these bundles of attribute values may fragment and recombine incorrectly, so that illusory conjunctions result."*

This concern with sound source fusion has plagued many studies of virtual sound source localization, even when it is not reported to have been an issue. The externalization of the auditory images displayed by an augmented reality audio (ARA) system is another concern that is not always adequately treated in studies designed to assess system performance. Therefore, in the authors' recent studies reported in this chapter, these issues were systematically evaluated in the preparation of stimuli for experimental investigation.

2. An experimental assessment of WARA system performance

To test the importance of 3DoF sensorimotor coupling to a WARA system, an experimental investigation of a particular system's performance was conducted in two stages. The first stage was executed to assess similarity of the earspeakers' delivered signals to the signals reproduced by loudspeakers that were positioned at the corresponding locations at which the HRTFs used for the spatialization process were measured. In the second stage, listeners completed two psychophysical tasks that required them to report both absolute and relative perceived directions of arrival for virtual sources delivered via calibrated earspeakers. Results of that psychophysical investigation are reported in a subsequent section of this chapter. What follows next is a discussion of the binaural synthesis methods that were employed for the investigation.

2.1 Binaural synthesis for WARA applications

Although measurement at the ear drum has long been regarded as the ideal procedure for capturing directional information contained within a set of HRTFs [16], it has been suggested in [15] that the ideal point for the measurement of HRTFs for WARA applications is that which offers a practical solution to the problem of obtaining confirmation of HRTF recreation when the WARA hardware is in place for typical use. The same reasoning applies in either case: All the transformations of an incident sound signal emitted from free field or reproduced source should be matched between the originally measured and then recreated HRTF, such that when two signals delivered to the ear drum are identical, there should be no perceptual differences between them. Of course, due to impracticalities of measuring at the ear drum, an alternative point at the entrance of the open-ear-canal may also be chosen, placing a probe that can be used either for free-field or reproduced sources. This option is based upon the assumption that the transformation due to the ear canal is independent of the sound emitter direction and distance [17].

The employed earspeaker [18] permitted HRTF measurement at an open-ear-canal entrance in the same configuration for which it would be used in a WARA application (a fitting design commonly termed *open-ear*, as seen in **Table 2**). Thus, for both measurement and usage, the same acoustic radiation impedance is seen from the ear canal and the same acoustic load will be presented to the earspeaker. In this particular case (more completely described in [25]), the same configuration was indeed used in the measurements for HRTFs and the equalization of an open-ear-canal earspeaker.

Such features are distinguished and regarded as an advantage of the more frequently investigated WARA systems that capture environmental sound by a pair

Product	AR supporting features	Form factor	Manufacturer description
OGS earspeaker, 2016 [18]	• Open-ear design	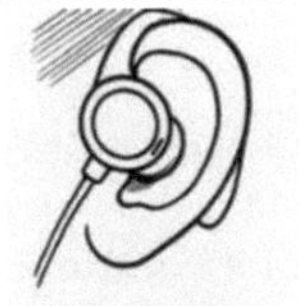	"Enjoy the audio you desire, while staying aware of the dangerous world around you."
JBL Soundgear Sense, 2023 [19]	• Open-ear design • Wireless	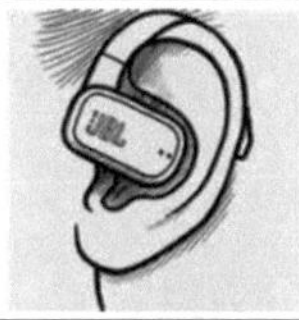	"...rest on the curve of your ears without obstructing your ear canal, so that you can hear both your sound and the world around in full comfort..."
Huawei FreeClip, 2024 [20]	• Open-ear design • Head tracking • Wireless	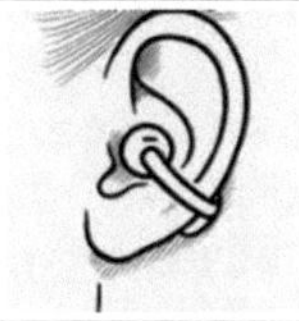	"Immerse yourself in music, while staying aware of changes in ambient sounds"
Apple AirPods 4, 2024 [21]	• Loose-fit design • Head tracking • Wireless	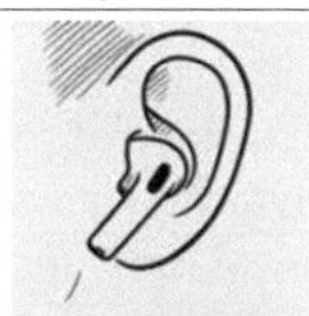	"Personalized Spatial Audio with dynamic head tracking ...open-ear design..."
Bose Ultra Open Earbuds, 2024 [22]	• Open-ear design • Head tracking • Wireless	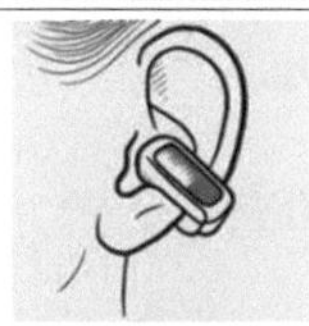	"...leave your ears open to hear the world around you while OpenAudio technology delivers rich, private sound..."
Oladance OWS Pro, 2024 [23]	• Open-ear design • Wireless	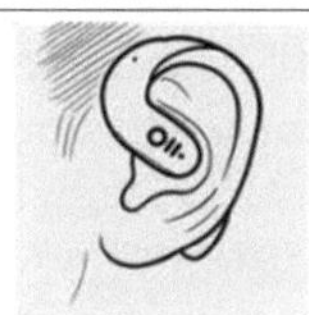	"With our patented open-ear design, the OWS Pro keeps you in sync with your surroundings, without sealing the ear canal"
Edifier LolliClip, 2025 [24]	• Open-ear design • Head tracking • Wireless	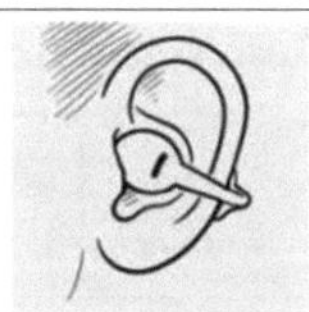	"The open-ear structure rests comfortably outside the ear canal, enabling fatigue-free listening while enhancing awareness of your surroundings..."

Each design is engineered to preserve natural hearing of environmental sounds by leaving the ear canal entrance unoccluded (at least partially) and exposing the pinna, while simultaneously enabling reception of the device-displayed sound. (Note that the Apple AirPods 4 do engage the ear canal entrance and so must be described as "loose-fit" rather than open-ear design).

Table 2.
Comparison of seven commercial products employing the open-ear design.

of miniature microphones, which sound is then digitally mixed with the binaurally processed virtual signal. In this case, the mix is presented via in-the-canal (ITC) transducers [26], resulting in successful matches of Anatomical Transfer Functions (ATF) and synthesized HRTF, although there are some disadvantages related to occlusion of the ear canal [27, 28].

The open-ear-canal measurement procedure is traditionally avoided due to high variability in responses resulting from the contribution of the ear canal via both intra-subject (left/right) and inter-subject variability. Due to difficulties in maintaining the point of measurement across different sessions (as in HRTFs and then Headphone Transfer Functions), it has been regarded as convenient to use generic "fits all" HRTF datasets most typically measured with blocked auditory meatus [17]. Many studies have been concerned mainly with verifying HRTF reconstruction for signals in the speech band (250–4000 Hz), where variations resulting from open-ear-canal measurements are small relative to blocked-meatus measurements [16]. The investigations reported herein were aimed at implementing a method for WARA applications using an unobstructive earspeaker that accommodates those who want to maintain their own natural spatial hearing abilities using their own ATFs.

Although the HRTF measurement, equalization, and synthesis methods employed in this study are commonplace (as they conform to conventional best practices [13, 29]), the application of these methods here is to the special case of observations made at the entrance to an unoccluded ear canal [30]. The advantage of reproducing binaural sound at the entrance to an unoccluded ear canal for WARA was already made clear above, but it could be asked whether this application really requires unoccluded ear canal HRTF measurements and equalization. Indeed, given the relative greater reliability with which blocked meatus measurements can be made, it should be made clear here why that approach was rejected. The key advantage of making observations at the entrance to the subject's unoccluded ear canal is the validity of its confirmation for binaural synthesis. Only when HRTFs are measured at the tip of the probe tube in free space can it be confirmed directly that the employed equalization method properly has reproduced that HRTF for the earspeaker application. Additionally, it is noted that open-ear-canal HRTF measurements have been shown to yield higher retained coherence with minimum phase HRTFs [31].

All measurements were done at the University of Sydney's Acoustics Research Laboratory 'Dome', an acoustically-treated room featuring a hemispherical array of 196 loudspeakers (Anthony Gallo Nucleus Micro), uniformly distributed at a distance of approximately 2 m from the center of the subject's head. The subject stood on a height-adjusted platform that positioned the head such that the lowest circle of loudspeakers was at an elevation of -11° below the visuoaural plane. The subject's head movement was restricted using molded dental impression material attached to a fixed angle-iron bracket (a "bite bar"). Although not strictly anechoic, the walls and speaker frame of the 'Dome' were covered with sound absorbing material, and the space exhibited an RT30 reverberation time at 1 kHz of only 0.18 s.

2.2 Perceived locations, precision and accuracy as measures of performance

It is important to emphasize here that the accuracy and precision of sound localization is expected to be greatly improved for envisioned WARA applications using the calibrated spatial auditory display system that was developed here, in that it uses both open-ear-canal HRTF measurements and correction for the earspeaker response that was based upon open-ear-canal earspeaker to ear-canal Transfer Functions (EETF) measurements (the same EETF-derived correction was applied for both channels). Of course, it has been well established in related fields that direction-identification performance should be better when the pinna is not occluded by an open-ear-canal transducer. An obvious field of research in which this has been established is that in which studies were done to evaluate the impact on direction-identification judgments due to the method of fitting hearing aids. In one such study [32] sound source direction judgments were tested in the vertical plane, using 10 loudspeakers arranged in a vertical arc directly to the side of the subjects, when listening unaided and when fitted bilaterally with Behind The Ear (BTE) hearing aids that were fitted with three earmold types: closed (occluded), open (partly occluded), and sleeve (non-occluded). The open and sleeve conditions supported better vertical judgments than did the closed condition, and, for the sleeve earmold, vertical judgments matched those observed when unaided. Readers interested in learning more about this related field of research are referred to the excellent review of the consequences of open versus closed hearing-aid fittings by Winkler, et al. [33], which emphasizes that open-fitting can yield improvements in perceived quality of one's own voice, as well as increased localization performance.

For the current study, the stimuli presented for the psychophysical tasks were a phonetically balanced speech samples, retrieved from the PN/NC corpus [34]. The binaurally processed signals were presented to listeners who perceived them to be positioned in well-defined locations. It has been deemed desirable to measure a listener's ability to report on the perceived location of the stimuli, in addition to their perceived angular incidence. Although the term has not always been used in this way, a consensus is growing to use the term location to indicate the making of both angular judgments and distance judgments. Furthermore, in his highly-cited "Spatial Hearing" book, Blauert has [2] discussed the distinction between localization of a physical source and the perception of its location. The fact that a perceived auditory image belongs in a subjective auditory space, which might not necessarily match the original physical space, can translate into a disparity in the angular estimates between localization tasks and reports on perceived locations. It should be clear that it may be useful to evaluate how these psychophysical task approaches match between ATF-based and HRTF-based percepts. Indeed, such evaluations are primarily concerned with accuracy of results, and accuracy is typically much reduced when listeners' heads are immobilized (as they were in [25]). Accuracy can be quantified here as the difference between the mean angular estimates at each presented angle of incidence and the corresponding angular coordinates at which HRTFs were measured.

Although high accuracy is desirable, the present study was primarily concerned with the consistency of conveyed spatial locations for repeatedly presented virtual signals. In this case, an adequate performance measure is then the precision of the reported perceived locations, which focuses on variability of the estimates on repeated listens (standard deviation of reports). It must be noted that a properly functioning WARA application might not support high accuracy if it is more strictly required to exhibit high precision [35].

For the initial training, each listener was presented a series of spatialized virtual speech signals and used a GUI developed in MATLAB to report on the perceived incidence of the signals (using a response grid marked for lateral and elevation angles). Absolute direction judgments were made for each of seven distinct angles of incidence at which single stimuli were presented 10 times per sessions. The order of presentation of the signals was randomized throughout each session. Results of this test in terms of directional accuracy are shown for a single listener in **Figure 2**.

Comparing the distribution of lateral angle reports for the stimulus reported as lowest in elevation (the cyan-colored downward pointed triangles of **Figure 2**) to that of the stimulus rated as greatest in elevation (the yellow-colored upward pointed triangles), it is seen that only one of the reports overlap the set of reports for the stimulus heard at lower elevation. Because of this near complete dominance of one set

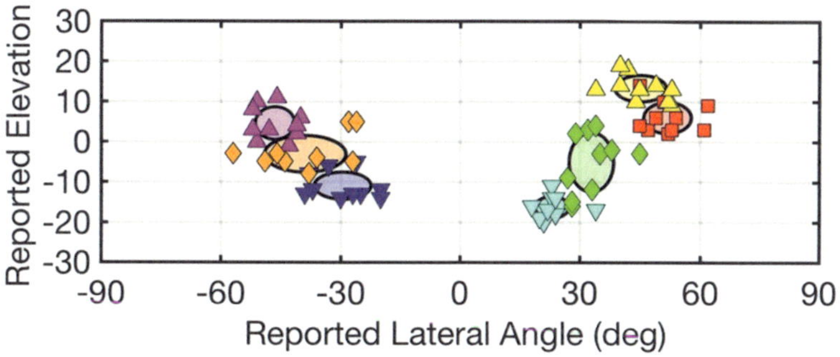

Figure 2.
A scatter plot of absolute judgments of elevation angle plotted over absolute judgments of lateral angle reported by Subject 1 for seven stimuli - each presented ten times, from directions restricted to the rear hemifield. The sets of angular judgments are plotted using downward-pointed triangles for the stimuli reported as lowest in elevation, and plotted using upward-pointed triangles for stimuli reported as highest in elevation. Behind each group of ten plotting symbols is a larger oval symbol that depicts for each stimulus the mean reported incidence angles, and also the spread of angular reports for each stimulus as measured by the standard deviation of reported angles.

of judgments over the other, a very high value of Cliff's delta for these two distributions is to be expected, and is confirmed by the obtained value of 0.99.

After completing this initial training, each of three listeners participated in an experimental test of directional precision, in which the same speech stimuli as before were successively presented in pairs in which the consecutive spatialized virtual speech signals arrived from differing angles of incidence, all restricted to the rear hemifield. In each of these pairwise comparisons, the listener had to report on the perceived offset in angle of incidence between each pair of stimuli. In effect, a complex question was to be answered regarding whether the stimulus presented second was heard to arrive from a more elevated angle, and then whether it was heard to arrive from a lateral angle to the left or right of the stimulus presented first. These judgments were collected for 84 pairwise comparisons, and the results of these for one of three listeners, Subject 1, are shown in **Figure 3**.

It is interesting to compare a measure of lateral angle dominance, based upon two sets of temporally dispersed absolute judgments for two stimuli, to the direct judgments of angular offset between the same two stimuli. Such a comparison reveals that large overlaps in absolute angular judgments are associated with smaller angular offsets reported for a given pair of stimuli (and show correspondingly small values of Cliff's delta). The right panel of **Figure 3** focusses upon responses on these two tasks given just three of the presented stimuli's seven angles of incidence. This panel shows both absolute and offset judgments plotted on reported lateral and elevation angles made by Subject 1 for those three stimuli.

In subsequent localization tests, executed with listeners' heads immobilized, stimuli were presented either by loudspeaker or earspeaker. This reproduction mode was randomly varied over trials, and listeners were required to indicate whether they could discriminate between the two reproduction modes (i.e., whether listeners heard loudspeaker or earspeaker reproduction). Confirming the similar sound character between these two modes, discrimination between trials containing loudspeaker versus earspeaker reproduction was at chance levels. It is worth noting that there was no evidence to reject the null hypothesis here, so we concluded that differences between reproduction mode were negligible. Similar localization results were obtained to those shown above in **Figures 2** and **3**, even though listeners used their own ATFs

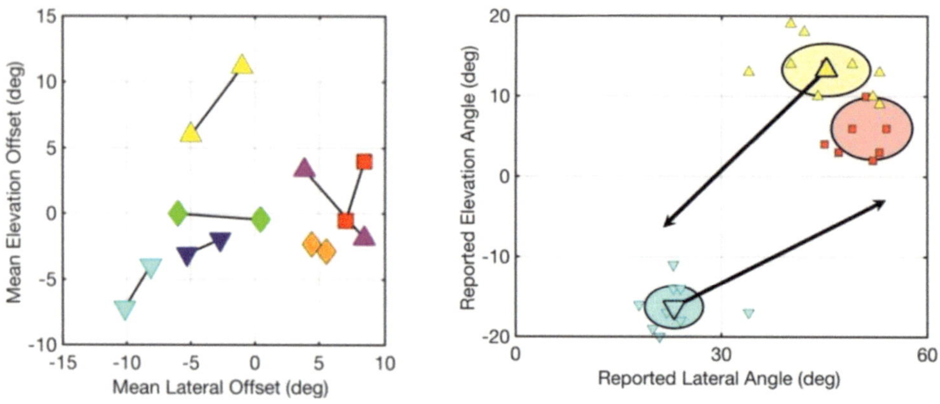

Figure 3.
The left panel shows scatter plot of absolute mean offsets in judgments of lateral angles and elevation angles made by Subject 1 for two sets of seven stimuli. Pairs of identical plotting symbols are connected by line segments to show the agreement between results for the seven stimuli when presented on either side of the listener's median plane (mean lateral offsets negated for one set to allow the plots for the two sets to be juxtaposed). The right panel shows offset judgments in terms of reported lateral and elevation angles. Arrows are drawn from the mean incidence angle for each elevated stimulus to indicate the apparent angular offset of that stimulus relative to responses given to the stimulus of lower mean elevation, and vice versa (see [25] for a more detailed discussion of these results).

on half of the trials and heard HRTF-transformed stimuli on the other half. This has been regarded as the ultimate psychophysical test in evaluating WARA system performance.

Following this test of localization performance of three listeners with restricted head movement, another HRTF-based localization test session was run in which the listeners were encouraged to move their heads in any way that aided them in making judgments with highest confidence. Recall that for the previous tests [25], listeners' heads were immobilized by having each listener bite on their own custom-fit bite bar (which was made using molded dental impression material attached to a fixed angle-iron bracket). In the subsequent earspeaker-reproduction tests in which listeners were encouraged to move their heads freely, there were two possible modes of interactive HRTF-based synthesis, enabling a comparison of 2DoF versus 3DoF head coupling of the applied HRTFs. The 2DoF head-coupling case included only changes to employed HRTFs based upon changes in head yaw and pitch. The 3DoF head-coupling case added head-roll based HRTFs changes (more than just the head yaw and head pitch employed in the 2DoF case). More detailed reporting of the results of these comparisons is beyond the scope of this chapter, but the comparison revealed a number of telling differences in user experience between these two interactive head-tracking modes. Listeners who attempted to resolve ambiguities in elevation by exploratory head rotations found an advantage in adequate 3DoF response that included head-rolling-coupled changes in HRTFs. No advantage for disambiguating front versus rear incidence was observed in the 3DoF head-coupling case relative to the 2DoF head-coupling case. No difference was expected here since front versus rear incidence is disambiguated by head-yaw-coupled HRTF changes in both cases, and no such difference was found.

In contrast to the previous tests in which directional judgments were made with heads immobilized, the subsequent tests incorporating head-tracking included direct ratings of any disorientation or disappointment for tested users under conditions of 2DoF versus 3DoF head-coupled HRTF updating. With only three listeners participating in these subsequent tests, adequate statistical tests were not supported by the quantity of data, even though the reported differences can be taken as anecdotal evidence for the superior experience enabled by 3DoF head-coupling. Suffice it to say that the three tested users gave statements during debriefing that were entirely consistent with the conclusion that 3DoF head-coupling was the preferred condition for most satisfaction with the WARA system.

3. Sensorimotor contingencies for natural interactions in AR

AR has proliferated in recent years, becoming increasingly popular across a range of industries [36]. In particular, advances in technology and reductions in acquisition costs have brought AR within reach of everyday consumers, with vendors promising ever-more realistic experiences. Major multimedia tech companies are now heavily investing in AR, and recent product developments emphasize the importance of successful implementation of WARA. The range of available forms of WARA display hardware reflects a renewed interest in unoccluding earspeaker devices — wearables that deliver sound with minimal disruption to natural hearing, through improved accommodation of human anatomical features. Not long ago, such devices were relatively difficult to source, as was found by the authors in preparation for a previous study [25], for which it was necessary to resort to lesser-known manufacturers to procure a preferred system, termed Open Guided Sound (OGS earspeaker set [18]). Similar unobstructive devices are typically positioned in the concha, leaving the ear canal unoccluded, allowing the pinna to capture sounds naturally from the environment. **Table 2** shows these audio reproduction devices that support acoustically transparent "hear-through" auditory display (i.e., that through microphones capture and then reproduce the environmental sound to the user). Such devices have been appearing commercially for the last 10 years, and are suitable for AR applications where the aptly termed "open-ear" form factor, was designed to allow the superposition of reproduced signals upon sound arriving from actual sources in the user's local environment, including the ambient and indirect sound of that environment.

While all seven of the featured devices listed in **Table 2** apply the "open-ear" design as the most common means for achieving such transparency, these devices also reflect a growing trend toward wireless convenience and support for sensorimotor coupling through tracked head movement. With the exception of the 2016 OGS example, all listed devices were announced relatively recently, and the range of available forms of the WARA display hardware reflects a renewed interest in unoccluding earspeaker devices. Recent innovations, such as in the 2024 released Apple AirPods 4, pioneered in such form factor the incorporation of head-tracking features geared toward spatial audio rendering [37], revealing a trend toward mobile WARA products—an observation supported by a report from Ericsson ConsumerLab [38]. As the technology matures, prospects supporting WARA experiences have become increasingly sophisticated. Users today anticipate experiences that are immersive, intuitive, and meaningful.

For a WARA interface, a distinction between virtual and real sound sources is made here. Whereas virtual sources are generated digitally and reproduced through a transducer device, real sound sources are instead the outcome of acoustic phenomena with origin in the physical environment. Nevertheless, the psychophysical sensation that is evoked by either type of source may give rise to identical auditory images (i.e., perceptually indistinguishably), in which case the AR phenomenon is described as realistic. An argument can be made that satisfying realistic WARA experience depends on meeting the expectation that interacting with mediated virtual content feels similar to interacting with real sound sources. In other words, for a sound source to be perceived as realistic, its acoustic cues need to create an impression consistent with a listener's everyday expectations. Empirical evidence indicates that this requirement is only viable if the multimodal AR system supports sensorimotor contingencies. Suffice it to say that users must be enabled to explore the augmented environment with their own bodily movements, much as they do in physical reality. This affordance, as suggested by Slater [39], is on the basis of the "place illusion" of virtual reality, the sensation of "being there", which in case of AR translates to the sensation of virtual content "belonging here", in the physical world. (Note that mediated content does not need to be "realistic" in the sense of excluding fantasy elements; however, to blend effectively with physical sound sources, it must adhere to certain natural and predictable patterns.)

3.1 Externalization of virtual sound sources and the perception of distance

During the course of everyday tasks, listeners are naturally and continuously moving their heads [40], thereby enabling an ongoing feedback loop between a perceived shift in position of sound sources associated with their own body movements. In addition to providing cues for sound direction discrimination, this sensorimotor predictable pattern promotes externalization of sound sources. An externalized sound source appears to have its origin out in the world, evoking a mental representation of the acoustic event, an auditory event appearing in an auditory space outside the listener's head. On the other hand, an internalized source is perceived as belonging in a subjective space within the head of the listener and poses increased effort in the formation of an auditory event coherent to an acoustic event originating out in the physical world [11].

Previous investigations demonstrated [41] that, during headphone playback, a predictable, naturalistic relationship between head movements and sound source behavior (i.e., sources remaining stable relative to the real world) is essential for creating externalized auditory images. Conversely, even if detailed binaural room transfer functions (BRTFs) are used in the rendering, failure to maintain source stability causes sensations in conflict with expectations, ultimately precluding externalization.

Indeed, prior experience suggests that a source producing no interaural differences during yaw movements ought to be located somewhere along the vertical axis passing through the head (the mid-body axis), while for roll movements, such an unresponsive source ought to be located along the front-back axis. The tendency for a sound to be perceived inside the head is exacerbated when there is no visual reference to anchor the sound source (visual-capture effect), as for sources positioned outside the listener's field of view.

Externalization is closely linked to distance perception: an externalized sound source is perceived to originate at an egocentric distance greater than zero. In this sense, the externalization is necessary for virtual sources to appear within the real world, blending seamlessly with real sound sources, potentially fusing with visible sounding objects (visual–auditory integration to create a spatially congruent perceptual experience). A clear perception of the egocentric distance of displayed virtual sound sources within an auditory environment is fundamental to the feeling of being immersed in a 3-D auditory scene. When a virtual sound source is to be rendered in a reverberant environment, it is generally accepted for adequate distance perception the inclusion of the cues inherent to the direct sound and those from reflections (indirect sound), taking into account the high-frequency spectral losses due to air absorption. However, reliability of such cues is not uniform, especially as sound level is ambiguous whenever the likely source power at the distal source is uncertain. Additionally, reverberation-related cues are harder to exploit for unfamiliar signals placed within highly damped spaces [42] (which can be an inconvenience for the reproduction of novel or fantastical sounds that lack a real-world reference). For WARA systems, the problem is compounded by the computational constraints of real-time synthesis and convolution with a BRTF matched to the real environment and for changing source-listener orientations arrangements in the room [43].

Investigating dynamic cues to auditory distance perception, Speigle and Loomis [44] showed that in addition to the environmental cues, listeners can exploit auditory motion parallax cues for distance information that emerge from source azimuthal changes during listener movements that affect the interaural axis. Kneip and Baumann [45] generalized this idea analytically, and further developed it by integrating both translational and rotational movements of the interaural axis. Implementing an analytical model, they demonstrated how, from a combined motion sequence and synchronized computation of ITDs, the information necessary to determine distance and direction of arrival of a sound source is made available.

Recent data from machine-learning modeling studies confirm the power of combining the two motion cues. In the study of Krause et al. [46], a method was presented that evidenced the significant impact on performance of combining rotation and translation cues for the task of joint distance and direction of arrival estimation for a binaural receiver.

These results further emphasize the utility of sensorimotor contingencies for the key requirement of AR to enable the perceived location of virtual sound sources in the real environment as naturally as possible, effectively mitigating perceivable qualities discriminating between virtual and physical sources. In short, by harvesting the listener's natural movements — translations enforced by locomotion and even the small spontaneous head-rotations performed to inspect a scene — an AR system can enable reliable distance perception without computation-heavy accurate BRTFs processing.

3.2 Head movement triggered by auditory events: The orienting reflex

Audition and vision are two prominent sensory modalities that cooperatively provide us with perceptual understanding of our surroundings. Humans often rely on the eyes for high-resolution spatial information, even though this capacity is best only within a relatively narrow field of view around one's line of gaze (foveal vision). In contrast, human auditory spatial acuity is relatively coarse compared to that of vision, but the spatial extent of hearing is omnidirectional, relaying spatial information for distal acoustic events that may take place in any direction around us, even those unavailable to sight (visually occluded, or viewed in darkness) [47].

Because motor actions—whether gaze-steering or hand-reaching —are typically directed to a single spatial target at any given moment, as imposed by human anatomical constraints, attentional control must dynamically allocate necessarily limited resources. This characteristic implies that the attentional resources are managed according to the behavioral relevance of incoming sensory signals—whether that relevance derives from their contribution to an ongoing task, or from their unexpectedness or salience that demands rapid reaction (for example, potential threats). Notably, an unexpected signal may seem relevant to current goals, and thus be selected for further processing and consideration [48].

3.2.1 The orientation reflex

In interacting with the environment, the auditory modality plays a critical role in directing attention. Upon detection of an acoustic event outside the current focus of attention (as an unexpected sound arriving from outside one's field of vision), the auditory system performs rapid, pre-attentive analysis of the incoming signal. Cross-modal information integration and assessment of acoustic input behavior relevance is performed, from which a motor command for a shift of attention might result [49].

This primary analysis is integral to alerting mechanisms that prompt a motor reaction causing a head-turning response to align the high-resolution optical sensors with the hearing system estimated event spatial location – an 'attention orienting reflex' that prepares subsequent actions. This overt orienting, involving coordinated movement of eyes, head, and body, manifests the need to allocate further attentional resources to a detected event, enabling finer multimodal inspection [47]. It is a natural and frequent response to sound in everyday tasks, in fact it is observable in infants shortly after birth, suggesting an innate response to sound [50, 51].

Investigating the neural phenomena of the orienting reflex, it has been suggested that saliency and mostly behaviorally relevant stimuli activate pathways to initiate the reorienting motor commands, with context, prior knowledge, and expected regularities of stimuli (predictability) modulating this process [49, 52]. Then, the stimulus-driven reorienting response may result from a wide variety of situations. For instance, it can be triggered by unexpected auditory events either related to context (a sound that does not fit the surrounding environment) or due to deviation from regularity (changes in spectro-temporal patterns), and especially so from those of behavior significance, as related to a current task (e.g., the sudden onset of a voice in a group conversation), or importantly, signaling danger (e.g., skidding tyres while crossing a road). Due to the evolutionary functional importance of sounds for the overt orienting reflex, some researchers have suggested that one primary function of the auditory spatial system is to direct one's eyes toward the auditory estimated spatial location [53].

3.2.2 Dynamic spatial information feedback advantages for audiovisual search and identification tasks

It has been aptly demonstrated that sound localization can provide an advantage in visual target search and identification tasks. Perrot et al. [54] conducted a series of experiments assessing visual search performance in conditions for which a visual target was spatially congruent with a sound source location vs. conditions of spatially incongruent visual target and sound source. Their results consistently showed a reduction of search time for the spatially congruent conditions, observing a larger effect for targets that were initially located outside the visual field. The result provides evidence for the role of the auditory modality in the regulation of gaze and its benefit for visual search tasks, even when targets are located within the visual field of view. The authors offer a supporting rationale for the observed larger advantage in the case of targets outside the visual field: in the condition of spatially uncorrelated signals, visual search is performed in a serial fashion, with successive shifts of gaze sampling potential regions until target detection. On the other hand, with the availability of auditory spatial information, gaze is promptly directed to the auditory specified location.

Interestingly, the more nuanced yet significant time reduction observed for targets within the visual field (from 20 to 80° off the fixation point) provides evidence for the persisting relevance of the acoustic information. Evaluating eye and head movements as well as eyelid closure, the authors noted that eyelids were closed for a significant portion of the duration of the head movement underlying gaze shifts. This fact suggests that continuous monitoring of a shifting image on the retina is not so important in the regulation of a shift in gaze once an eye movement has begun. The observation of a saccade suppression effect agrees with previous suggestions that localization information update is not provided during saccades [55]. In contrast, continuous auditory spatial information offers the advantage of progressively refining the required eye-head movement to bring the target to the fovea, clarifying an auditory benefit for visual target search within the visual field.

The auditory system capability to continuously update and adjust required head movement response to bring an object of interest into line of gaze was verified in a previous experiment assessing errors in a task asking subjects to orient their heads to face a target sound source [47]. A brief single pulse or a continuous pulse train was employed. For greatly lateralized targets, systematic larger errors were obtained for the single pulse condition, for which no cues to source direction during the head-turning were available. This result has been confirmed in more recent studies, with observed advantages of continuous stream of sound source localization information to motor control, not only during head-turning responses but also on hand-pointing tasks [56].

The findings have direct implications for an AR system: it is not enough for a system to comprise a binaural technique processing that places a virtual sound source at the intended location with precision and accuracy. Crucially, the evoked auditory image must also remain stable during head movements. Only under this condition can the system deliver intuitive and effective auditory display. Without such stability, the system fails to support the listener's active localization and natural reflex to orient toward unexpected sounds —undermining a fundamental aspect of embodied cognition, in which meaning-making is intimately tied to the body's actions [57]. Specifically, if we consider that a WARA technology will most likely bring in innovative (and in some cases, presumably unexpected) elements enriching the real environment, this failure would likely result in initial disorientation and perceptual discomfort, leading users to perceive the system as malfunctioning or inadequate.

3.2.3 Spatial alignment of audiovisual objects and multisensory integration

In AR systems presenting multisensory information as audiovisual objects, there are further motivations to support sensorimotor contingencies enabling auditory-stimulus-driven orienting. The head-turn response exemplifies how input from one sense—hearing—can prompt engagement of another—vision—to achieve a fuller grasp of a multisensory scene by bringing the attended item into foveal visual range while also improving auditory spatial perception (given the higher auditory resolution for the frontal region). The response effectively results in the spatial alignment of inputs in the different modalities, which has been identified as a fundamental principle for multisensory combination in tasks involving overt orienting of spatial attention [58]. Accordingly termed "the spatial rule", it postulates that maximal integration is afforded when sensory inputs are perceived as originating from the same location. For a succinct summary, the flowcharts shown in **Figure 4** presents the many factors and consequences of violations that can be involved in attempts to produce the best user experience when virtual sound sources are intended to appear as spatially stable in relation to the actual world.

Summary flowchart

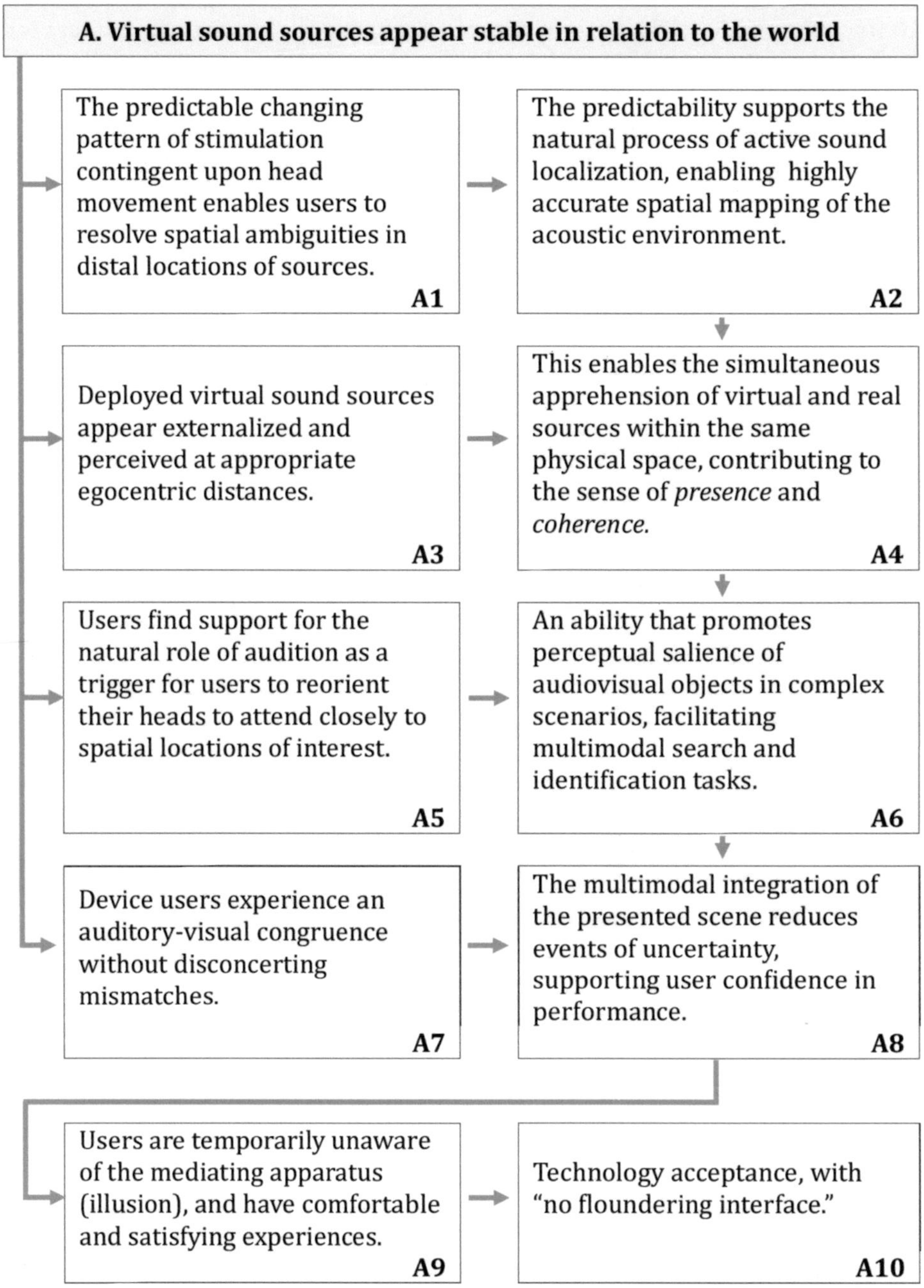

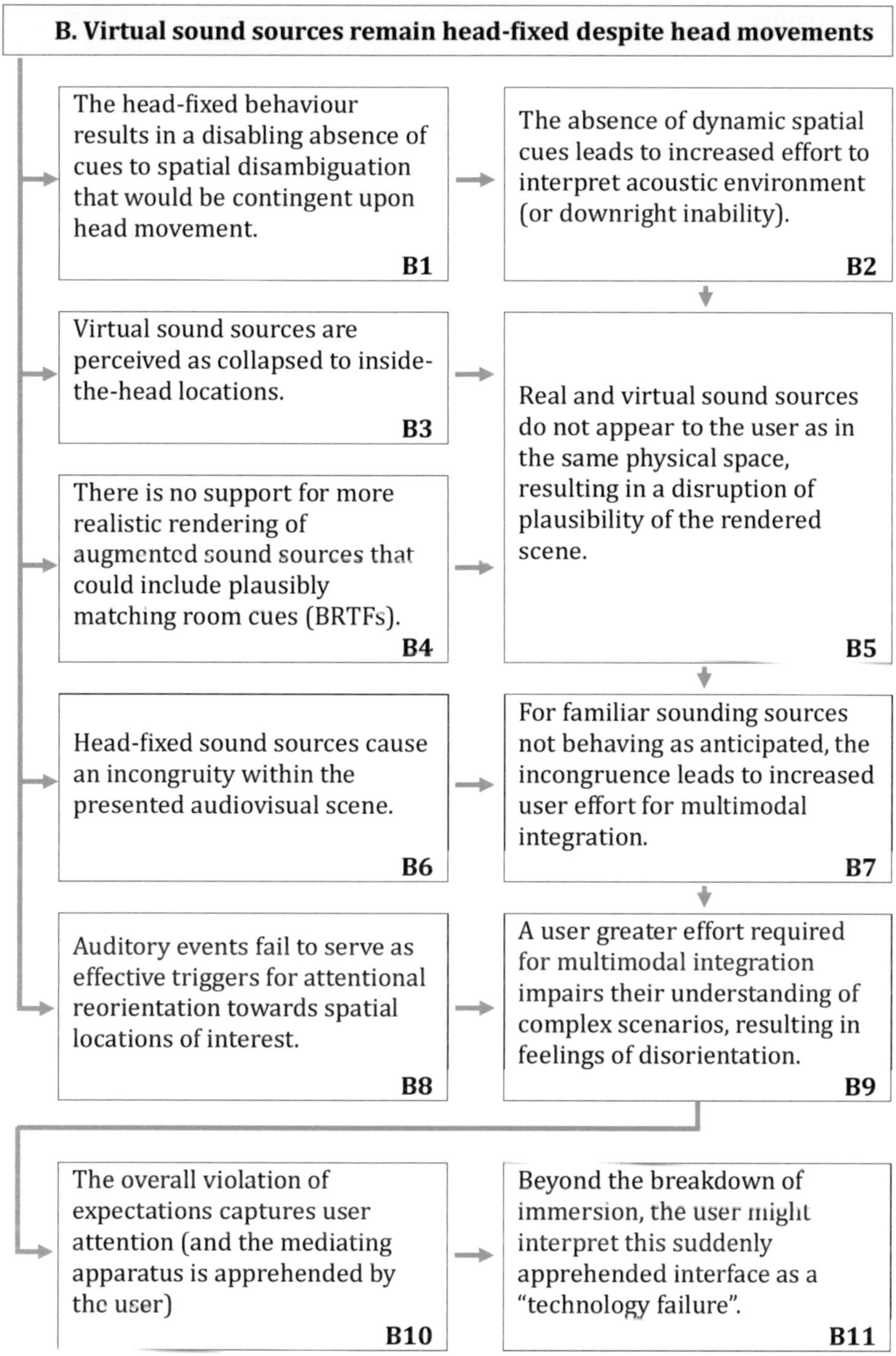

Figure 4.
Flow chart A summarizes the action and cognition that follow from the predictable and expected stable behavior of virtual sound sources for interactions in an AR environment. Conversely, flowchart B represents the negative consequences that a head-fixed behavior of virtual sound sources imparts on the perceptual expectations of natural interactions in the AR. Ultimately, the capacity of the AR system to enable expected interactions in goal-directed tasks lead to different levels of user acceptance.

4. Conclusions

Through an exposition of the many factors that influence the acceptability of auditory display technology for use in augmented reality (AR), this chapter supports the argument that naturalistic sensorimotor contingencies should be considered an essential component of successful wearable ARA system. In contrast to strong arguments that visual display technology must take precedence over ARA technology in the effort to superpose on a user's real world spatially registered interactive media, many reasons were noted here that interactive audio must be considered an essential partner to interactive 3D graphics. Indeed, when AR system users move their heads while listening to spatially stabilized sounds that are superposed on the soundscape of the real world surrounding them, directional disambiguation of virtual sounding objects is enabled in a manner that extends beyond what has been called "highly realistic" or "immersive experience" of displayed virtual sound sources. Anecdotal evidence was provided for the contention that disorientation and disappointment result for a user when virtual sound sources are not properly modulated by the contingency of the dynamic causal coupling between the user's actions and the auditory consequences of those actions. In particular, coupling ARA display with angular variation in the user's head within all three planes (i.e., full 3DoF coupling) is to be encouraged, rather than respecting only 2DoF angular variations.

Conflict of interest

The authors declare no conflict of interest. Neither of the authors is associated with the marketing or development of an augmented reality audio product.

Abbreviations

2I2AFC	2 interval, 2 alternative forced choice
2DoF	two-degrees-of-freedom
3DoF	three-degrees-of-freedom
ATF	anatomical transfer function
AR	augmented reality
ARA	augmented reality audio
BRTF	binaural room transfer function
BTE	behind the ear
DP	double polar
EETF	earspeaker to ear canal transfer function
HRTF	head-related transfer function
HTP	horizontal transverse plane
IHL	inside-the-head localization
ITC	in-the-canal
ILD	interaural level difference
ITD	interaural time delay
MSP	median sagittal (midsagittal) plane
OGS	Open Guided Sound
VAD	virtual auditory display

VLP	vertical lateral (frontal) plane
VP	vertical-polar
WARA	wearable augmented reality audio

Author details

William L. Martens[1*] and Frederico Pereira[2]

1 Faculty of Medicine, Health and Human Sciences, Macquarie University, Australia

2 CCG/ZGDV Institute, ISISE University of Minho, Guimarães, Portugal

*Address all correspondence to: william.martens@gmail.com

References

[1] Meyer K, Applewhite HL, Biocca FA. A survey of position trackers. Presence: Teleoperators & Virtual Environments. 1992;**1**(2):173-200. DOI: 10.1162/pres.1992.1.2.173

[2] Blauert J. Spatial Hearing: The Psychophysics of Human Sound Localization. Cambridge: MIT PRESS; 1996. DOI: 10.7551/mitpress/6391.001.0001. ISBN: 9780262268684

[3] Doll TJ, Gerth JM, Engelman WR, Folds DJ. Development of Simulated Directional Audio for Cockpit Applications (Report No. AAMRL-TR-86-014). Atlanta: Georgia Institute of Technology; 1986

[4] Møller H. Fundamentals of binaural technology. Applied Acoustics. 1992;**36**(3-4):171-218. DOI: 10.1016/0003-682X(92)90046-U

[5] Wallach H. The role of head movements and vestibular and visual cues in sound localization. Journal of Experimental Psychology. 1940;**27**(4): 339-368. DOI: 10.1037/h0054629

[6] Wallach H. On sound localization. The Journal of the Acoustical Society of America. 1939;**10**(4):270-274

[7] Wightman FL, Kistler DJ. Resolution of front–back ambiguity in spatial hearing by listener and source movement. The Journal of the Acoustical Society of America. 1999;**105**(5):2841-2853. DOI: 10.1121/1.426899

[8] Martens W, Cabrera D, Kim S. The 'Phantom Walker' illusion: Evidence for the dominance of dynamic interaural over spectral directional cues during walking. In: Principles and Applications of Spatial Hearing. Singapore: World Scientific; 2011. pp. 81-102. DOI: 10.1142/9789814299312_0008

[9] Martens W, Sakamoto S, Miranda L, Cabrera D. Dominance of head-motion-coupled directional cues over other cues during walking depends upon source spectrum. Proceedings of Meetings on Acoustics. 2 Jun 2013;**19**(1):050129. DOI: 10.1121/1.4800124

[10] Knudsen EI, Konishi M. Mechanisms of sound localization in the barn owl (Tyto alba). Journal of Comparative Physiology. 1979;**133**(1):13-21. DOI: 10.1007/BF00663106

[11] Martens WL, Cohen M. Spatial soundscape superposition, part I: Subject motion and scene sensibility. Acoustical Science and Technology. 2020;**41**(1):288-296. DOI: 10.1250/ast.41.288

[12] Cohen M, Martens WL. Chapter 13: Spatial soundscape superposition and multimodal interaction. In: Blauert J, Braasch J, editors. The Technology of Binaural Understanding. Berlin: Springer; 2020. pp. 351-390. Available from: https://www.springer.com/gp/book/9783030003852

[13] Martens WL. Perceptual evaluation of filters controlling source direction: Customized and generalized HRTFs for binaural synthesis. Acoustical Science and Technology. 2003;**24**(5):220-232. DOI: 0.1250/ast.24.220

[14] Härmä AH, Jakka J, Tikander M, Karjalainen M, Lokki T. Augmented reality audio for mobile and wearable appliances. Journal of the Audio Engineering Society. 2004;**52**(6):618-639

[15] Deutsch D. Grouping mechanisms in music. In: The Psychology of Music (3rd ed). Cambridge: Academic Press;

2013. pp. 183-248. DOI: 10.1016/B978-0-12-381460-9.00006-7. ISBN: 978-0-12-381460-9

[16] Møller AK, Christensen F, Hoffmann PF, Hammershøi D. Directional characteristics for different in-ear recording points. In: Audio Engineering Society Conference: 58th International Conference: Music Induced Hearing Disorders; 28-30 June 2015; Aalborg. New York: AES; 2015. pp. 5-3

[17] Middlebrooks JC, Makous JC, Green DM. Directional sensitivity of sound-pressure levels in the human ear canal. The Journal of the Acoustical Society of America. 1989;**86**(1):89-108. DOI: 10.1121/1.398224

[18] OGS - open guided sound—Open "soundfield" earphones—By ELT group. Eltgroup. n.d. Available from: https://monsieurtalbot.wixsite.com/eltgroup/ogs [Accessed: May 22, 2025]

[19] JBL Soundgear Sense | True Wireless Open-Ear Headphones. n.d. Available from: https://www.jbl.com/wireless-earbuds/SOUNDGEAR-SENSE.html [Accessed: May 22, 2025]

[20] HUAWEI. FreeClip—HUAWEI Global. n.d. Available from: https://consumer.huawei.com/en/headphones/freeclip/ [Accessed: May 22, 2025]

[21] AirPods 4. Apple (Australia). n.d. Available from: https://www.apple.com/au/airpods-4/ [Accessed: May 22, 2025]

[22] The Benefits of Open-ear Headphones | Bose. n.d. Available from: https://www.bose.com/stories/benefits-of-open-ear-headphones?srsltid=AfmBOoq0HfqjyCij Lv9gHOLLFDoEJAWaD2j89KqLXnX8dvbiKxs-6IaW [Accessed: May 22, 2025]

[23] OWS Pro. Oladance. n.d. Available from: https://www.oladanceshop.com/pages/ows-pro [Accessed: May 22, 2025]

[24] Open-ear True Wireless Earbuds | LolliClip –[Eadifier USA]. United States/English. n.d. Available from: https://www.edifier.com/us/p/true-wireless-earbuds/lolliclip [Accessed: May 22, 2025]

[25] Pereira F, Martens WL. Psychophysical validation of binaurally processed sound superimposed upon environmental sound via an unobstructed pinna and an open-ear-canal earspeaker. In: Audio Engineering Society Conference: 2018 AES International Conference on Spatial Reproduction-Aesthetics and Science; 7-9 August 2018; Tokyo. New York: AES; 2018

[26] Marentakis G, Liepins R. Evaluation of hear-through sound localization. In: Proceedings of the SIGCHI Conference on Human Factors in Computing Systems (CHI '14). New York: Association for Computing Machinery; 2014. pp. 267-270. DOI: 10.1145/2556288.2557168

[27] Tikander M. Usability issues in listening to natural sounds with an augmented reality audio headset. Journal of the Audio Engineering Society. 2009;**57**(6):430-441

[28] Hoffmann PF, Christensen F, Hammershøi D. Insert earphone calibration for hear-through options. In: AES 51st Conference on Loudspeakers and Headphones; 21-24 August 2013; Helsinki. New York: AES; 2013. pp. 3-4

[29] Huopaniemi J, Karjalainen M. Review of digital filter design and implementation methods for 3-D sound. In: Audio Engineering Society Convention 102; 22-25 March 1997; Munich. New York: AES; 1997

[30] Hiipakka M, Kinnari T, Pulkki V. Estimating head-related transfer functions of human subjects from pressure–velocity measurements. The Journal of the Acoustical Society

of America. 2012;**131**(5):4051-4061. DOI: 10.1121/1.3699230

[31] Nam J, Kolar MA, Abel JS. On the minimum-phase nature of head-related transfer functions. In: Audio Engineering Society Convention 125; 2-5 October 2008; San Francisco. New York: AES; 2008

[32] Byrne D, Sinclair S, Noble W. Open earmold fittings for improving aided auditory localization for sensorineural hearing losses with good high-frequency hearing. Ear and Hearing. 1998;**19**(1):62-71

[33] Winkler A, Latzel M, Holube I. Open versus closed hearing-aid fittings: A literature review of both fitting approaches. Trends in Hearing. 2016;**20**:233121651663174. DOI: 10.1177/2331216516631741

[34] McCloy DR, Souza PE, Wright RA, Haywood J, Gehani N, Rudolph S. The PN/NC Corpus. Version 1.0. Seattle: University of Washington; 2013. Available from: https://depts.washington.edu/phonlab/projects/uwnu.php

[35] Martens WL, Jo H, Park Y. Principal-component-based smoothing of head-related transfer functions reduces variabilty in elevation judgments for virtual sources located on a cone of confusion. In: INTER-NOISE and NOISE-CON Congress and Conference Proceedings 2011. No. 4. Osaka. Wakefield: Institute of Noise Control Engineering; 2011. pp. 3173-3181

[36] Augmented Reality Market Size, Share, Trends and Industry Growth Analysis. 2033. n.d. Available from: https://www.marketsandmarkets.com/Market-Reports/augmented-reality-market-82758548.html [Accessed: May 22, 2025]

[37] Control Spatial Audio and head tracking. Apple Support. n.d. Available from: https://support.apple.com/en-au/guide/airpods/dev00eb7e0a3/web [Accessed: May 22, 2025]

[38] Consumer Lab Extended Reality (XR) Study 2024—Ericsson. n.d. Available from: https://www.ericsson.com/en/reports-and-papers/consumerlab/reports/augmented-tomorrow-ar-experiences-beyond-smartphones-and-ar-filters [Accessed: May 22, 2025]

[39] Slater M, Banakou D, Beacco A, Gallego J, Macia-Varela F, Oliva R. A separate reality: An update on place illusion and plausibility in virtual reality. Frontiers in Virtual Reality. 2022;**3**:914392. DOI: 10.3389/frvir.2022.914392

[40] Kim C, Mason R, Brookes T. Head movements made by listeners in experimental and real-life listening activities. Journal of the Audio Engineering Society. 2013;**61**(6 Jun):425-438

[41] Brimijoin WO, Boyd AW, Akeroyd MA. The contribution of head movement to the externalization and internalization of sounds. PLoS One. 2013;**8**(12):e83068. DOI: 10.1371/journal.pone.0083068

[42] Coleman PD. Failure to localize the source distance of an unfamiliar sound. The Journal of the Acoustical Society of America. 1962;**34**(3):345-346. DOI: 10.1121/1.1928121

[43] Werner S, Klein F, Neidhardt A, Sloma U, Schneiderwind C, Brandenburg K. Creation of auditory augmented reality using a position-dynamic binaural synthesis system—Technical components, psychoacoustic needs, and perceptual evaluation. Applied Sciences. 2021;**11**(3):1150. DOI: 10.3390/app11031150

[44] Speigle JM, Loomis JM. Auditory distance perception by translating

observers. In: Proceedings of 1993 IEEE Research Properties in Virtual Reality Symposium; 25-26 October 1993; New York: IEEE; 1993. pp. 92-99. DOI: 10.1109/VRAIS.1993.378257

[45] Kneip L, Baumann C. Binaural model for artificial spatial sound localization based on interaural time delays and movements of the interaural axis. The Journal of the Acoustical Society of America. 2008;**124**(5):3108-3119. DOI: 10.1121/1.2977746

[46] Krause DA, García-Barrios G, Politis A, Mesaros A. Binaural sound source distance estimation and localization for a moving listener. IEEE/ACM Transactions on Audio, Speech, and Language Processing. 2024;**32**:996-1011. DOI: 10.1109/TASLP.2023.3346297

[47] Perrott DR, Ambarsoom H, Tucker J. Changes in head position as a measure of auditory localization performance: Auditory psychomotor coordination under monaural and binaural listening conditions. The Journal of the Acoustical Society of America. 1987;**82**(5):1637-1645. DOI: 10.1121/1.395155

[48] Macaluso E. Orienting of spatial attention and the interplay between the senses. Cortex. 2010;**46**(3):282-297. DOI: 10.1016/j.cortex.2009.05.010

[49] Cohen-Lhyver B, Argentieri S, Gas B. Audition as a trigger of head movements. In: Blauert J, Braasch J, editors. The Technology of Binaural Understanding. Modern Acoustics and Signal Processing. Cham: Springer; 2020. DOI: 10.1007/978-3-030-00386-9_23. ISBN: 978-3-030-00385-2

[50] Clarkson MG, Swain IU, Clifton RK, Cohen K. Newborns' head orientation toward trains of brief sounds. The Journal of the Acoustical Society of America. 1991;**89**(5):2411-2420. DOI: 10.1121/1.400929

[51] Muir D, Field J. Newborn infants orient to sounds. Child Development. 1979;**50**(2):431-436. DOI: 10.2307/1129419

[52] Corbetta M, Patel G, Shulman GL. The reorienting system of the human brain: From environment to theory of mind. Neuron. 2008;**58**(3):306-324. DOI: 10.1016/j.neuron.2008.04.017

[53] Heffner RS, Heffner HE. Evolution of sound localization in mammals. In: The Evolutionary Biology of Hearing. New York, NY: Springer New York; 1992. pp. 691-715. DOI: 10.1007/978-1-4612-2784-7_43. ISBN: 978-1-4612-2784-7

[54] Perrott DR, Saberi K, Brown K, Strybel TZ. Auditory psychomotor coordination and visual search performance. Perception & Psychophysics. 1990;**48**(3):214-226. DOI: 10.3758/BF03211521

[55] Davidson ML, Fox M-J, Dick AO. Effect of eye movements on backward masking and perceived location. Perception & Psychophysics. 1973;**14**(1):110-116. DOI: 10.3758/BF03198624

[56] Boyer EO, Babayan BM, Bevilacqua F, Noisternig M, Warusfel O, Roby-Brami A, et al. From ear to hand: The role of the auditory-motor loop in pointing to an auditory source. Frontiers in Computational Neuroscience. 2013;**7**:26. DOI: 10.3389/fncom.2013.00026

[57] Rocchesso D, Polotti P, Monache SD. Designing continuous sonic interaction. International Journal of Design. 2009;**3**(3):13-25

[58] Spence C. Just how important is spatial coincidence to multisensory integration? Evaluating the spatial rule. Annals of the New York Academy of Sciences. 2013;**1296**(1):31-49. DOI: 10.1111/nyas.12121

Chapter 7

Redirected Seating (RDS) in Helical Space

Michael Cohen and Alaeddin Nassani

Abstract

Redirected seating (RDS) is an adaptation of Redirected Walking (RDW) that creates the illusion of expansive virtual movement in confined spaces by virtually amplifying limited physical rotation. By applying redirected walking principles to seated experiences, RDS enables panoramic exploration using only limited chair rotation. A proof-of-concept implementation introduces amplified yaw, where perceived motion is extended through virtual azimuth gain. A swivel chair is embedded in a virtual helical scene synchronized with a coiling musical soundscape, aligning visual and auditory cues to plausibly justify restricted angular range and reinforce the azimuth-gain illusion. A pilot study confirmed the effectiveness of the approach, showing improved user experience and greater perceived virtual rotation. The RDS framework can be extended to mixed reality applications through integration of a rotary motion platform and adaptive ambient lighting systems, besides head-mounted display. When servomotor-driven chair rotation is paired with IoT-controlled lighting effects and viewed with see-through augmented reality (AR), the coherence of the azimuth-gain illusion is further strengthened. This combination blends physical constraints with enhanced virtual mobility, suggesting that seated VR can achieve perceptual benefits comparable to redirected walking within constrained physical spaces.

Keywords: device orchestration, information furniture, internet of things (IoT), redirected seating (RDS), redirected walking (RDW), rotary motion platform, virtual reality (VR), extended reality (XR)

1. Introduction

This work adapts redirected walking principles to seated VR through a helical scene and synchronized auditory cues, introducing a novel approach to azimuth gain in constrained physical spaces. Seating—including couches, stools, and benches—is one of the most widely used forms of utility furniture. Given the prevalence of seating, leveraging chairs as interactive platforms offers an accessible foundation for immersive systems. The Internet Chair [1] leverages this ubiquity as an instance of *information furniture*, determining a seated user's facing direction to adjust maps, photospherical browsers, and immersive environments including soundscapes. This chapter considers the concept of redirected seating (RDS), which adapts redirected walking (RDW) principles and techniques to seated augmented reality (AR [2]) experiences to enhance immersion and expand perceived virtual space.

1.1 Related systems

Besides extended reality (XR), this "information furniture" research is related to fields variously associated with "ubicomp" (for ubiquitous computing), outlined in **Table 1**, which organizes display and interaction systems along a continuum from fully immersive environments through handheld and wearable devices.

1.2 Redirected seating (RDS)

Humans estimate body orientation through multiple sensory inputs, including visual cues, vestibular signals, and possibly weak magnetoreception. Ability to sense the Earth's magnetic field, well documented in many animal species, may also occur in humans at a subconscious and poorly developed level, possibly via magnetite in the brain. Vision is dominant, relying on landmarks, optical flow, and vection, often overriding conflicting cues.

The vestibular system comprises semicircular canals (three in each ear), which acts like gyroscopes, and the otolithic organs (utricle and saccule) in each labyrinth (one per ear), which act like accelerometers. Together they stimulate vestibular sensation. Positional awareness involves central nervous system integration of the visual, auditory, and vestibular systems. Proprioception, awareness of the position of one's limbs as mediated by muscles, ligaments, and tendons, contributes to spatial awareness.

Redirected walking (RDW) is a VR technique to enable realistic walking within a limited tracking space, subtly manipulating the mapping between real and virtual environments to make a physical space seem larger, allowing users to explore large virtual environments from within limited physical spaces. Its adaptation to seated experiences has been little explored.

Angular excursion, the rotation around a fixed axis, can be virtually scaled. We developed [10, 11] an immersive environment that uses virtual azimuth gain [12] to compensate for limited physical rotation. A swivel chair, perhaps against a wall, might have limited rotatability, but redirected seating (RDS) can virtually amplify its rotation. By integrating a swivel chair with a virtual helical path, our prototype enables a

smart cities
smart spaces and aware environments [3]
cooperative buildings [4]
roomware [5]
media spaces
spatially immersive displays
immobots (immobile robots)
information furniture
networked appliances [6]
mobile computing (handheld, nomadic, portable)
wearable systems [7–9]
The emboldened row represents the class of device explored by the current paper.

Table 1.
Saturated: Pervasive, continuous, transparent—ubiquitous computing, a.k.a. ambient intelligence, as envisioned by Mark Weiser, Norbert Streitz, and others.

plausible situation that justifies restriction of azimuthal excursion, the yaw range through which the chair can rotate. We developed a virtual scene to justify limited excursion and excuse inability to spin indefinitely. For static standpoint (actually "sitpoint"), virtual yaw gain can be hidden in rotation, not masked by head motion as in general RDW. Assuming that complementary and coherent cues can strengthen illusions, a synchronized soundscape reinforces the coiling sensation, enhancing immersion.

In RDS, sensory coherence is subtly violated to squeeze a larger experienced space into a smaller physical space, like the "dimensionally transcendental" TARDIS from "Dr. Who." Redirected walking works because human positional sense is not absolute (unlike, for counter-example, magnetically directional sense of birds). The "cheating," or perturbation of direction, is hidden in one's head motion, masked by the uncertainty of recalibrating orientation. By subtly manipulating the user's perception of movement, RDS enables a greater sense of virtual exploration and interaction within a restricted physical space.

This allows users to experience a wider range of virtual rotation that might be physically possible, enhancing immersive potential of seated VR experiences. RDS could be particularly beneficial in applications such as VR gaming, training simulations, and virtual tourism, where users are often seated but require a sense of expansive movement.

The main objective of this work is to explore the concept of RDS, a novel approach that adapts redirected walking techniques to seated virtual reality experiences. Contributions include the development of a system that utilizes visual cues to manipulate a user's perception of rotation, enabling a wider range of virtual movement within a limited physical space, and discussion of the potential implications and applications of this technology.

2. Related research

Redirected walking (RDW) was introduced by Razzaque et al. [13], demonstrating that imperceptible rotation of a virtual environment could steer users along curved physical paths while preserving the illusion of walking straight in VR, thereby allowing users to explore virtual spaces larger than the tracked physical area. This established theoretical and physiological underpinnings of redirection, demonstrating that it can be used effectively without the user becoming aware of the manipulation or experiencing significant simulator sickness.

Jaekl et al. [14] quantified how much visual motion is tolerated during active head movement before disrupting perception of environmental stability, helping to define perceptual boundaries relevant to visually mediated redirection. Steinicke et al. [15] empirically established the detection thresholds for translation, rotation, and curvature gains in RDW, revealing the limits of redirection users can tolerate without noticing the manipulation. Suma et al. [16] leveraged change blindness to implement discrete, momentary scene redirection during visual transients, enabling abrupt layout shifts in immersive VR without user awareness. Suma et al. [17] further demonstrated a realtime system for infinite walking, dynamically planning RDW strategies to enable extended locomotion within tightly constrained tracked spaces. Langbehn and Steinicke [18] and Nilsson [19] surveyed RDW's theoretical foundations, implementation methods, and perceptual constraints, presenting a structured taxonomy and synthesis of nearly two decades of redirected walking research. Pisani et al. [20]

showed that users can intuitively navigate immersive virtual environments rendered in hyperbolic (non-Euclidean) geometry, supporting spatial interaction and exploration in topologically novel VR contexts. Yokoi et al. [21] modulated binocular disparity to allow redirected motion along a pseudo-helical path.

Multimodal integration has been another focus area in RDW research. Gao et al. [22] found that the use of incongruent visual and auditory cues can increase the detection threshold for curvature gains, making manipulations less noticeable and improving the usability of RDW techniques. This approach is supported by Nogalski and Fohl [23], who highlighted the importance of precise curvature manipulation to maintain immersion and reduce disorientation. Moriguchi and the first author [24] developed an application that modulates subjective translation and rotation, allowing users to experience larger virtual areas while physically traversing in small real-world spaces. Jeon et al. [25] developed a space-partitioning method that dynamically divides shared physical space, minimizing resets and preventing collisions using deep reinforcement learning. Azmandian et al. [26] validated simulation-based evaluations of RDW systems, showing that simulations offer accurate estimates of RDW performance, enabling extensive algorithm testing. Hirt et al. [27] examined the chaotic nature of RDW and its sensitivity to initial conditions. Recent reviews [28, 29] provide comprehensive overviews of RDW techniques, discussing taxonomy, methods, and future directions, emphasizing potential of integrating artificial intelligence (AI) to improve RDW performance. For multiuser environments, Xu et al. [30] proposed a method to coordinate multiple users in separate physical spaces, reducing reset frequencies and enhancing immersive experience in online VR applications. C. Wang et al. [12] systematically evaluated the perceptual thresholds for rotation gain in seated VR, identifying tolerable distortion limits and establishing foundational guidance for rotational redirection techniques, marking an early application of RDW principles to RDS. M. Wang et al. [31] used reinforcement learning to align virtual and physical environments, further enhancing immersive experience. Chan et al. [32] explored locomotion techniques for users seated in fixed (not rotating) chairs.

3. System

Our RDS system consists of physical setup of a swivel chair, along with a virtual setup of a VR scene featuring a helical path and helical soundscape.

3.1 Physical setup

Originally conceived to exploit the capabilities of the ${}^{S}_{c}\text{ha}_{i}\text{r}^{e}$ rotary motion platform [1], a pivoting chair with a networked servomotor—manufactured by Mechtec[1] led by Keizo Kasama, and equipped with software drivers developed in conjunction with researchers led by Zhi-Wei Luo, then at Yamagata University—featuring natural (yaw) rotatability in either direction for a generally arbitrary number of turns, our system also works fine with an ordinary office swivel chair.

In user interfaces, many rotary controllers (such as a turn knob, spin dial, or potentiometer) do not allow multiple twists, but limit such range to somewhat less than a full cycle. (It would be strange and awkward, e.g., for an audio volume knob to

[1] https://www.aizumechtec.com

DOI: http://dx.doi.org/10.5772/intechopen.1012708

have “0” and “10” superimposed or crossed.) To plausibly explain the limited excursion of our system’s experience, we arrange a virtual scene with a single-twist helical path, terminated at both ends. The user experience is no longer purely rotational, but instead a virtual orbit following a helical path with apparent vertical displacement, as the virtual helical path has vertical as well as angular dimension.

The screwed contrivance plausibly accounts for the inability to spin beyond a limited excursion such as a single revolution. A purely planar scenario would highlight the question of the rotation restrictor between 359° and 1°: A user would wonder why they could not keep rotating in the same direction. However, a helical model uses orthogonal vertical (if virtual) displacement to explain inability to “wrap-around.” Even though no significant physical vertical excursion is actually experienced (the small heaves of one’s head as expressed by ordinary head-pose being negligible), the understood scenario rationalizes the limited rotation.

For basic testing of the RDS concept, we use an ordinary office chair (as seen in **Figure 1**), positioned along a wall to physically limit its movement to a half turn (180°). The user of the system dons an HMD (Meta Quest 3 VR headset) to experience the virtual scene. A Meta Quest “Touch Plus” VR (left) controller is attached to the chair and used to track the rotation of the chair as mapped into the scene.

3.2 Virtual setup

As shown in **Figures 2** and **3**, the VR scene incorporates objects modeled in the 3D creation suite Blender,[2] which were subsequently integrated into the Unity[3] game engine. Such a scene can be populated with inner objects, closer to the virtual axis of revolution than the chair (with its separate but parallel physical axis of rotation), as

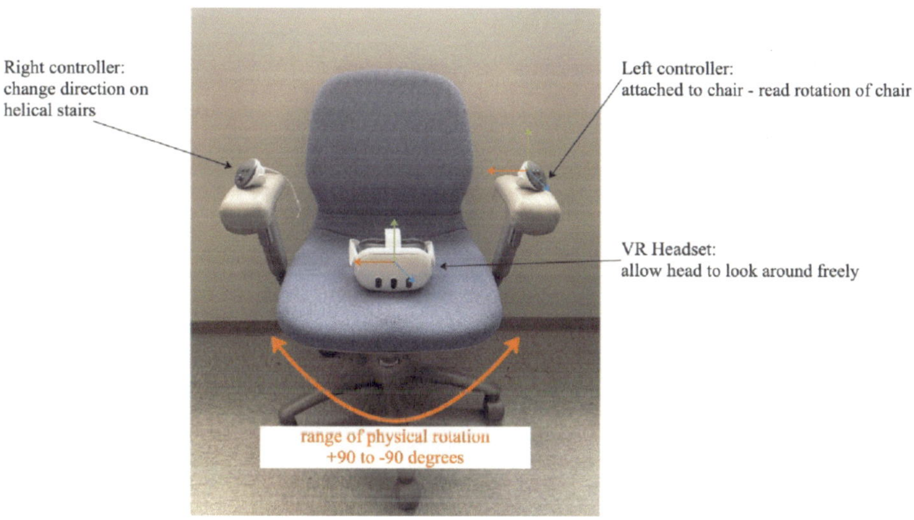

Figure 1.
*Physical setup: A chair’s rotation is tracked using a mounted VR controller (Meta Quest Touch Plus). The user might rotate through a range of only 180° in physical world (as seen in **Figure 6**), but in the virtual scene, the rotation may appear as 360° using the helical ramp.*

---

[2] https://www.blender.org

[3] https://unity.com

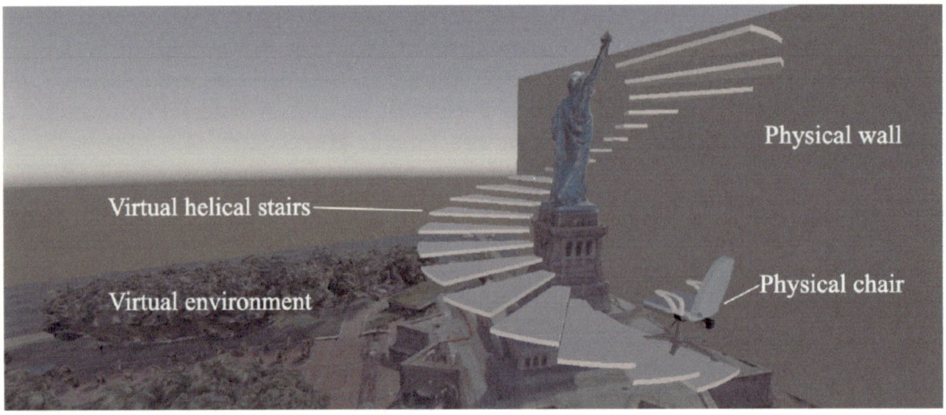

Figure 2.
Helical excursion plausibly excuses restricted rotation.

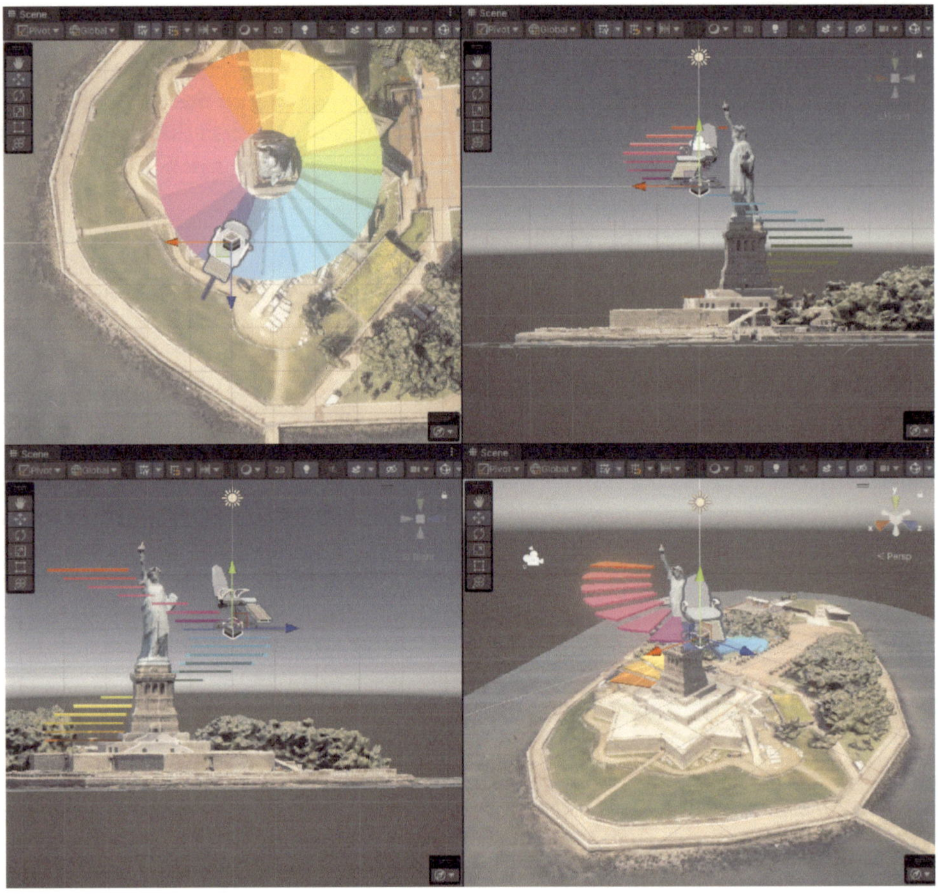

Figure 3.
Views of the helical soundscape, helicoidal ramp, and central object.

(a) C_1: outwards, facing the surrounding environment (b) C_2: upwards, facing up the helical staircase

(c) C_3: downwards, facing down the helical staircase (d) C_4: inwards, facing the center of the staircase

Figure 4.
Four principal directions of the chair on helical path, corresponding to the respective experimental conditions.

well as outer objects and scene items beyond that virtual orbit. The RDS functionality uses only chair azimuth (rotation around the vertical or gravitational axis); changing head-pose directly examines the optionally super-rotated scene. With the other, unmounted Touch Plus controller, the user may dynamically select their facing direction relative to the helical path. All the modes assume orbital phase-locked rotation and revolution, so that amplified virtual chair rotation is linked to elevation as well as virtual azimuth and yaw.

Various orbital phases are possible relative to the helical path. Principal directions (as seen in **Figure 4**) are

C_1 outwards from the helical core,

C_2 up the (left-handed) helical path,

C_3 down the helical path, and

C_4 inwards, towards the helical core.

One common convention is for the subject to face outward, away from the axis of rotation, enabling an expansive, panoramic view. Facing outward is perhaps the most natural convention, and also the most common. In rotating observation decks or

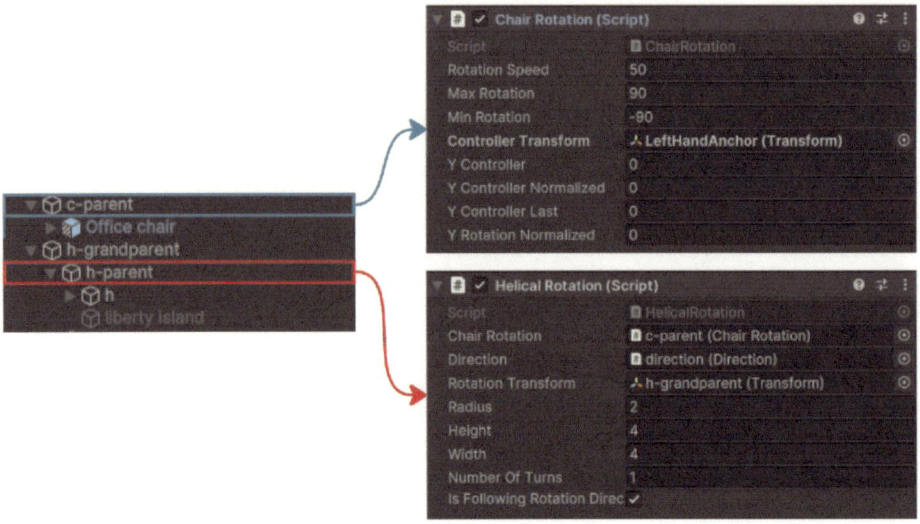

Figure 5.
Principal Unity scripts. The `Chair Rotation` *script manages the chair's limited physical rotation. The* `Helical Rotation` *script manages the virtual location and rotation of the helical ramp relative to the chair's location and rotation.*

revolving restaurants, guests face outward to enjoy panoramic vistas. Peripheral galleries of the Guggenheim Museum in New York City expect visitors to turn their back to the central atrium to engage with artworks. In a panopticon, outward-gazing observers in a central watchtower can see into peripheral cells.

Alternatively, the opposite convention, in which the subject faces an object of regard, as the near side of the Moon always faces the Earth, invites an "inspection" gesture. In amusement park centrifuge rides, riders lean back against a padded circular wall, and their gaze fixed on the ride's central hub as the structure spins. Likewise, visitors to the "Sazaedo" helical temple in Aizu-Wakamatsu[4] (and its re-creation in Tokyo[5]) ascend a coiling passage, respecting 33 statues of Kannon, the "Goddess of Mercy" *bodhisattva* of compassion, set within alcove stations around the central core.

Various strategies have been used to track chair rotation, including electromagnetically and optically [33]. As seen in **Figure 1**, we deploy the (left) Touch Plus controller as a chair tracker to track absolute azimuth, fixed to either armrest with a custom 3D-printed PLA cradle to be visible to the headset, which uses "inside-out" tracking as the HMD's infrared cameras detect LEDs on the controllers. Such continuous measurement is used to displace (especially horizontally rotate and vertically heave) the immersive scene (including whatever scale factor) and determine which musical note to play. The other (right) Touch Plus controller is used for player controls, including indexing through the four principal directions.

The core gameplay scripts in Unity (diagrammed in **Figure 5**) are: (1) `Chair Rotation` script, which monitors and manages the physical rotation of the chair, and (2) `Helical Rotation` script, which manages changing position of the virtual environment, including the helical ramp relative to the chair.

---

4 https://samurai-city.jp/en/sightseeing/2116

5 https://www.hiroshisenju.com/ja/kokodejian-remasu/da-zheng-da-xue-sazaetang

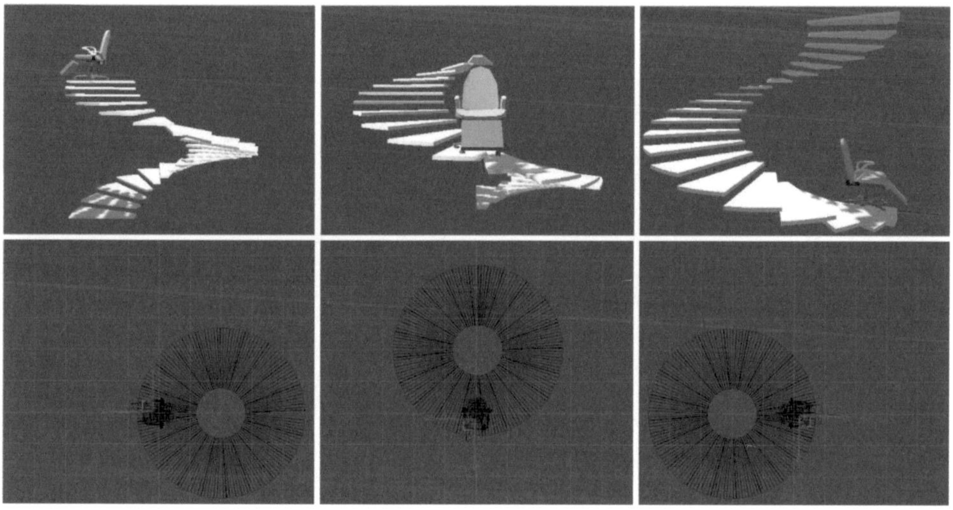

Figure 6.
Location and rotation of the chair relative to the helical ramp. Top row is sequence of elevation views showing the dilated virtual orbit; bottom row is a plan view showing the corresponding physical rotation.

The position (x, y, z) of the virtual environment (**Figure 6**) relative to the rotation of the chair is determined by the following formula, where t is the orbital parameter, θ tracks the real-world chair orientation $(-90^{\circ} \leq \theta \leq 90^{\circ})$, N is the number of helical turns (1 for the prototype), r is radius of the staircase helix, and h is its total height:

$$t = \frac{\theta + 90}{180} \times 2\pi \times \mathrm{N}$$

$$x = \mathrm{r}\cos(t)$$
$$y = \mathrm{r}\sin(t)$$
$$z = \frac{\mathrm{h}}{2\pi \times \mathrm{N}} \times t$$

The soundscape comprises a musical scale [34, 35], since it features attractive qualities of cyclic nature and closure (both because of pitch class equivalence), direct (basically logarithmic) correspondence with the vertical dimension, and natural limitability, namely an 8-note, major scale, comprising a heptatonic (7-note) scale, and the octave note above the corresponding tonic to provide a sense of completion. We use the major scale because of its familiarity, but could alternately have used a chromatic scale or any 8^{ve}-spanning scale. Scale notes are triggered as the chair turns, virtually scaled or not.

4. Experience

At run time, the user selects a chair orientation corresponding to one of the four principal directions: inwards facing the inner core (featuring a model of the Statue of Liberty in our prototype), down the (left-handed) helical path, outwards, or up the

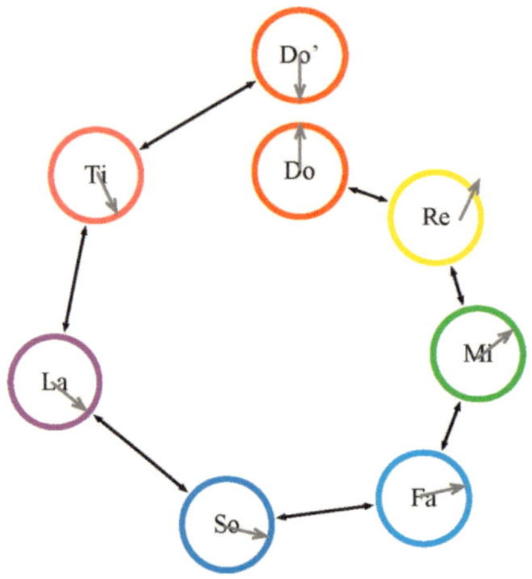

Figure 7.
Physical rotation, indicated by embedded arrows (0°↔180°), and gain-amplified virtual revolution, indicated by azimuth of note-labeled circles (0°↔360°), encoded by major scale notes and color wheel hues.

helical path. Such orientation may be changed during the excursion, which adjustment is animated by virtual rotation of the platform and with it one's own virtual direction. Since foot-shuffling to spin a swivel chair is necessarily circumferential, and physical rotation is around the pivot axis of the chair—which is slightly in front of the sitter's vertical axis (which is along the spine)—perhaps the most natural relative direction is outward (C_1), with one's back to the axial core, since the helical musical scale is projected into egocentric space, redundantly encoded with both tone (8-note major scale) and direction. The closure represented by the 8th note of the scale spanned by the octave establishes a "bracketing" context, like a closing delimiter such as a right parenthesis, reinforcing the boundaries of the experience. Since the notes of the major scale are uniformly spaced along the helix [36], as diagrammed by **Figure 7**, the effect of continuous chair rotation across a physical half-turn with virtual azimuth overdrive 2:1 is like a *glissando* through an octave across the white keys of a piano **Figure 8**.

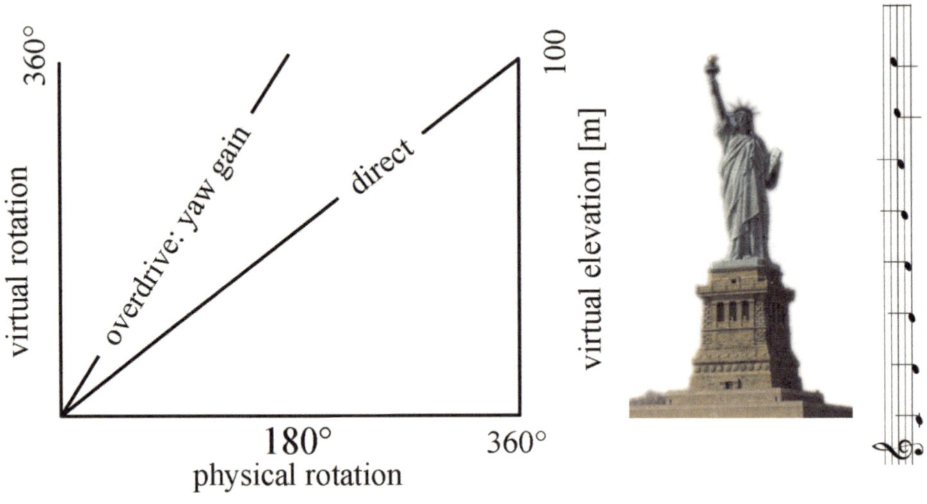

Figure 8.
Unwrapped helix for direct and RDS with musical cues.

Visible spheres representing the point-sourced scale notes are arranged at the same elevation and with the same sloped pitch as the helicoidal ramp, but with variably adjustable radius. Grand piano notes rendered as the rotating chair enters each sector have sustained duration, so their acoustic tail can be heard even as new notes are triggered.

4.1 Video

The accompanying video[6] shows a typical session. Using split-screen display, two perspectives are juxtaposed:

- Exocentric ("3rd-person") view of exterior scene
- Endocentric ("1st-person") view (half of immersive stereographic display) of virtual scene

5. Subjective validation: Pilot study

For initial validation of psychophysical sensation of the RDS effect, we recruited (n = 5, all male) participants aged 20–49 (mean = 27.2, SD = 12.3) from our university campus to try the system and provide feedback. Three of them (60%) were previously familiar with VR. Informed consent was obtained from all subjects involved in the study, which did not require research ethics examination under the University of Aizu research ethics policy. Data and scripts are available upon request.

5.1 Experiment

The experimental task involved participants navigating a virtual left-handed helical ramp coiled around a model of the Statue of Liberty and its surroundings, including helical musical soundscape, using a VR headset (Meta Quest 3) and its controllers. Participants were instructed to actively ascend and descend the ramp twice, physically twisting the chair (through a physical half-turn but virtual whole-turn) by shuffling feet on the floor, adjusting virtual chair direction with hand-held controller to experience the scene through four orientations (principal directions) relative to the virtual helical ramp, accompanied by natural visual scanning through head and eye movement. The four conditions were presented in randomized order using Latin square design (not fully balanced).

Prior to the experiment, participants provided demographic information and indicated their familiarity with VR. After each condition, they rated ease of use using a seven-point Likert scale "*Overall, how easy or difficult was it to perform this task? (1: very difficult, 7: very easy)*" as Single Ease Question (SEQ) [37], described their emotional experience using an Emoji Grid [38], and estimated the perceived range of virtual rotation "*What is the range of virtual rotation you experienced? (90°, 180°, 270°, 360°).*" Following completion of all four conditions, participants ranked their preferred orientations and provided free-form feedback on their experience.

---

[6] https://cdnintech.com/public/videos/Redirected%20Seating%20RDS%20in%20Helical%20Space.zip

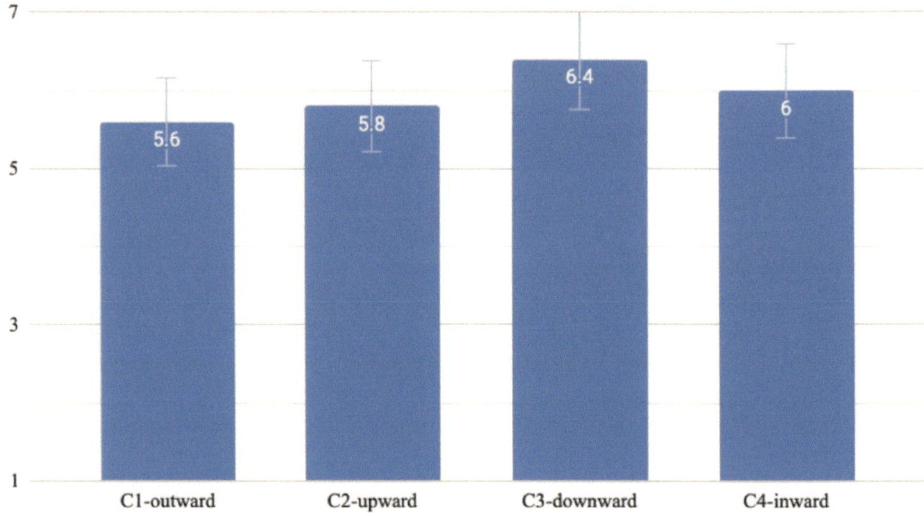

Figure 9.
Post-condition data for Single Ease Question (SEQ). For each condition (principal direction), participants were requested to rate their experience regarding ease of use [37].

5.2 Results

Results of the per-condition questions (**Figure 9**) show similar evaluations for all four conditions. For the Single Ease Question, principal direction C_3-downward had the highest average score of 6.4, while C_1-outward had the lowest average score of 5.6.

Regarding experienced and perceived emotion (**Figure 10**), results from the Emoji Grid rated all conditions as slightly positive (valence = 3.7) and slightly excited (arousal = 3.5). Principal direction C_2-upward had the highest valence score (4), while C_1-outward had the highest arousal score (3.6).

Figure 10.
Experienced emotion: For each condition (principal direction with respect to the helical ramp), participants were asked to rate experienced emotion [38] regarding both valence (horizontal axis) and arousal (vertical axis).

DOI: http://dx.doi.org/10.5772/intechopen.1012708

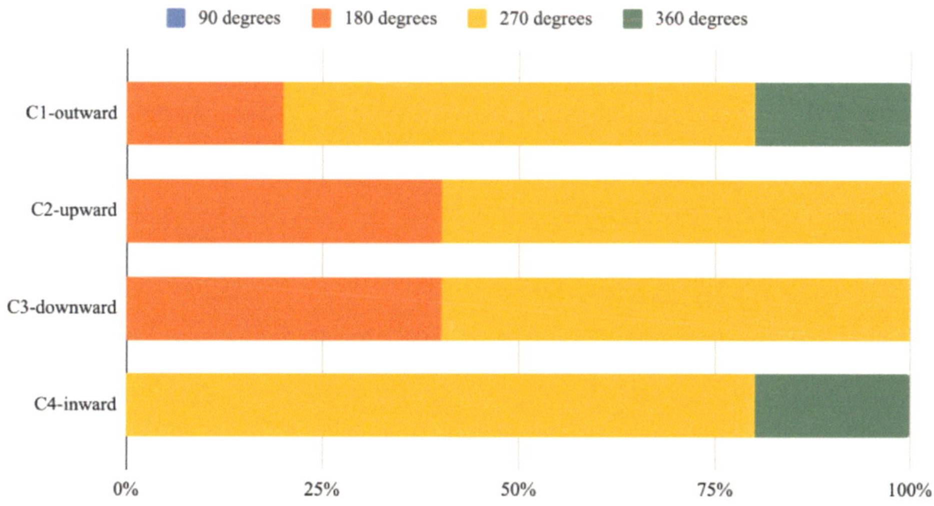

Figure 11.
Rotation Felt: For each condition (principal direction), participants were asked to rate their experience regarding range of virtual rotation felt during the experience.

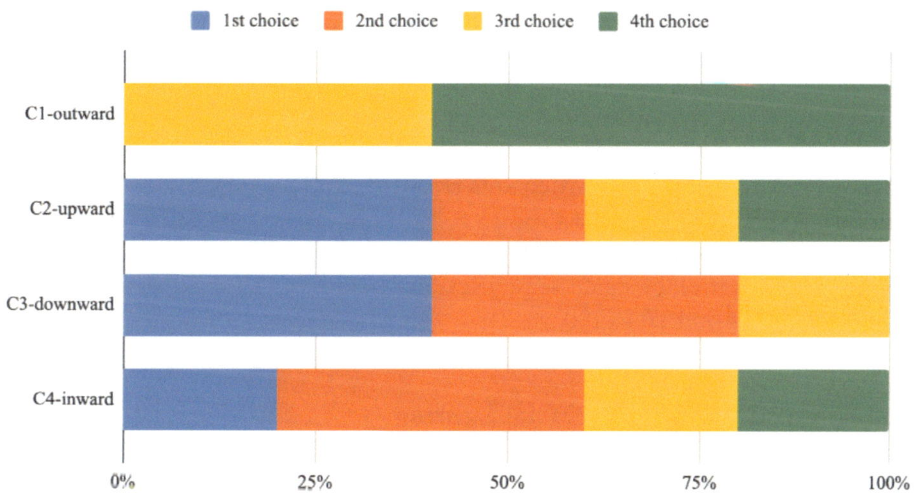

Figure 12.
Direction preference.

For the range-of-rotation question (**Figure 11**), only two conditions—C_1-outward and C_4-inward—elicited the reports of perceived 360° rotation. All conditions showed a majority of 270° responses, with C_4-inward yielding the highest number. No 90° reports were observed in any condition.

For the post-experiment questions (**Figure 12**), two conditions, C_2-upward and C_3-downward, were reported as the first choice in terms of preference, followed by C_4-inward as third choice, while C_1-outward was most often reported as the fourth choice and least preferred condition.

For the free-form questions, subjects reported positive impressions for C_2-upward (e.g., *P3*: "*Upward felt more indulging in a way that you could see the statue from a proper angle and also see the nature around.*") and C_3-downward (e.g., *P4*: "*The downward direction felt the most natural to me when I was walking up or down the stairs. It felt the easiest.*"). Subjects reported negative responses for C_1-outward (e.g., *P1*: "*It gave me vertigo,*" *P3*: "*Outward felt a bit weird,*" and *P2*: "*Not having the stairs in front of me felt a little disorienting.*").

5.3 Summary of results

While all conditions were rated as relatively easy to use, there was a slight preference (seen in **Figure 9**) for the C_3-downward condition, suggesting that it felt the most natural or intuitive for users. This could be due to the alignment of the virtual movement with the user's natural head movement when walking up or down stairs. The C_1-outward condition was the least preferred, despite its "natural" popularity, with some users reporting feelings of vertigo or disorientation. This could be attributed to the lack of visibility of a fixed reference point in the center of the helical ramp when facing outward. In the other conditions (C_2-upward, C_3-downward, C_4-inward), the central axis of the helix is visible, centrally or peripherally, providing a more stable visual reference. In contrast, the outward condition directs the user's gaze away from this central axis, potentially leading to a sense of instability and disorientation.

The emotional responses (**Figure 10**) were generally positive across all conditions, indicating that the RDS system was successful in creating an engaging and enjoyable experience. The C_2-upward condition elicited the highest valence ratings, suggesting that users found it the most pleasant and enjoyable. This could be due to the sense of anticipation and excitement associated with ascending the path.

The results for the perceived range of rotation (**Figure 11**) were somewhat surprising. While the majority of participants reported experiencing 270° of rotation in all conditions, some reported experiencing a full 360° in the C_1-outward and C_4-inward conditions. This suggests that the RDS system was successful in extending the perceived range of rotation beyond the physical limitations of the chair, even though the actual rotation was limited to 180°.

6. IoT-controlled pseudo-fiducial lighting

Magnified sensation of rotation like that enabled by RDS can be heightened by exploiting IoT lighting in a kind of relaxed rotational vection, the illusion of self-motion typically induced by large-scale visual motion. A ring of eight networked lights uniformly spaced around a spinning chair can display a pattern of colors which the seated user uses for orientation, as seen in **Figure 13**. We use the Philips Hue lighting system,[7] wirelessly controlled for convenience. In typical settings, static ambient fiducial lights function as fixed spatial reference points, providing reliable landmarks that help users maintain orientation within the environment. In our design, the fiducial lighting is deliberately programmed to rotate in the direction opposite to the user's physical rotation, producing a deceptive cue that can disrupt the user's spatial perception and orientation. Mapping of directions to colors is somewhat

[7] https://www.philips-hue.com

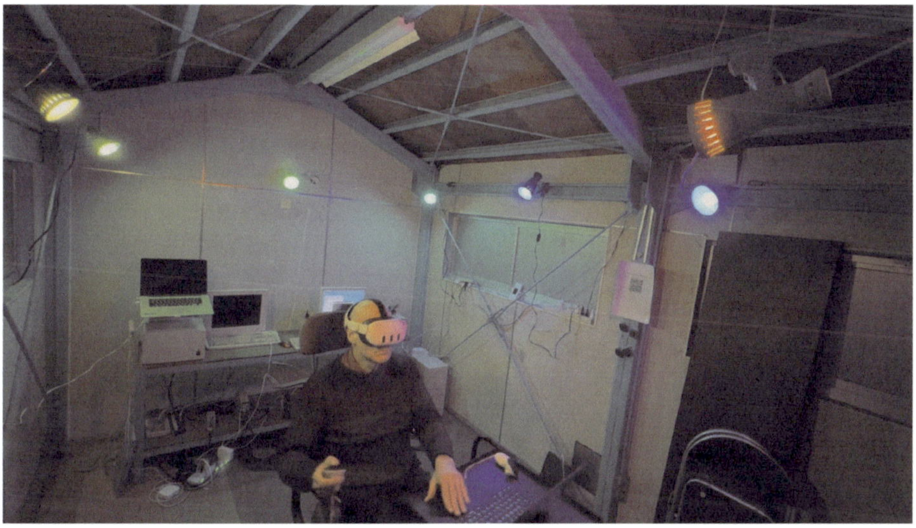

Figure 13.
Pseudo-fiducial lighting, showing eight networked lights around the chair.

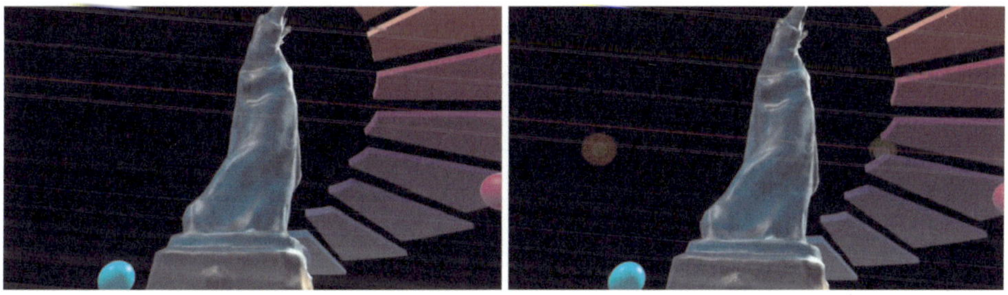

(a) (b)

Figure 14.
Pseudo-fiducial lighting exposed by video pass-through AR. (a) Pass-through disabled, and (b) Pass-through enabled.

arbitrary, but we used uniformly spaced samples from the color wheel. Such lighting represents a simple dynamic display, a low resolution version of interactive projection mapping, as popularized by location-based entertainment (LBE) attractions, such as those produced by TeamLab[8] and Meow Wolf.[9]

In a dimly lit setting, a user wearing an HMD with barely translucent video pass-through sees only illuminated elements, while the rest of the room remains in near darkness. The effect is of lights suspended in an ambiguous, almost ethereal space, "through a glass darkly," as seen in **Figure 14**. Rather than presenting a static scene, the system subtly counter-rotates a color pattern in opposition to the user's virtually amplified rotation. This covert visual manipulation causes the user to overestimate their own rotational motion, producing an exaggerated sensation of yaw displacement. With eight lights arranged in a circular pattern, the counter-rotation of the

8 https://www.teamlab.art
9 https://meowwolf.com

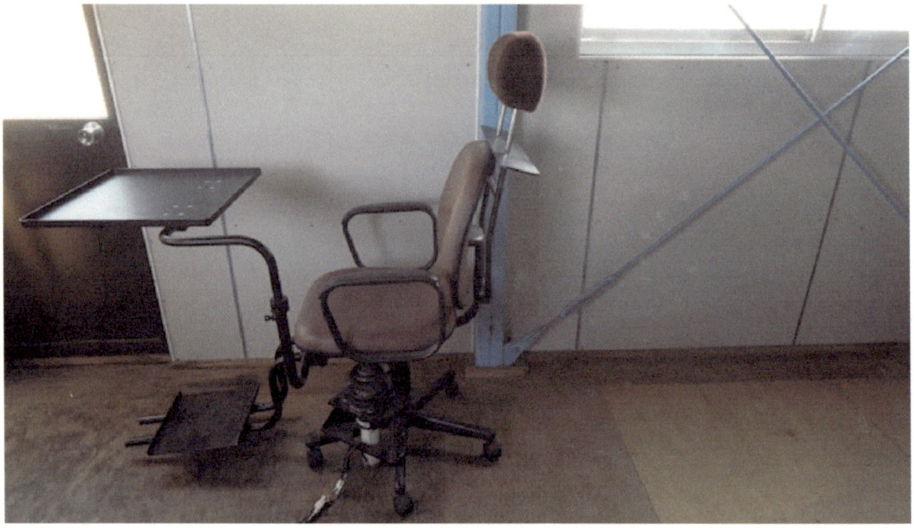

Figure 15.
${}^{S}_{c}ha_{i}r^{e}$ rotary motion platform arranged with the restricted swivel range inhibiting full and indefinite rotation, especially with projecting desktop (computer tray) and footrest. For instance, if the ${}^{S}_{c}ha_{i}r^{e}$ were against a wall (or close to a similar chair), it could rotate only a half-turn (about 180°), since its footrest protrudes beyond the chair's footprint and would collide with nearby objects. RDS can virtually dilate this limited range to simulate a single full 360° turn.

colored light projection is synchronized with an RDS gain of 2:1, so that a physical rotation of 22.5° (the actual spacing between the lighting fixtures) yields a corresponding virtual rotation of 45°, congruently integrating the immersive virtual environment and the ambient lighting display.

The fiducial lighting system with deceptive adaptive behavior leverages spatial psychological effects. Instead of an ordinary pivot chair, we use the ${}^{S}_{c}ha_{i}r^{e}$, shown in **Figure 15**. Absence of direct contact with ground because of the chair's footrest, along with its motor-driven rotation, complementing fuzzy estimation of yaw, and the rotating lighting color assignments deceive the user's sense of orientation, exploiting one's tendency to rely upon the ambient features as fixed reference points.

7. Limitations

The current implementation of RDS has several limitations. Some practical issues can be mentioned.

The system is basically designed for a single user and may not be easily adaptable to multiuser VR environments. Additionally, the system's effectiveness may be limited by individual differences in proprioception and susceptibility to motion sickness.

There is some tension between the illumination needed for the XR tracking and the low light levels needed to obscure the room environment. Our experiments used a low-level intensity setting for the IoT lighting (using the Philips Hue API, 10/254), which does not leak too much light to expose room features. Lighting fixtures are further focused with shading hoods around each bulb. Because of literally obscure conditions (dim light, shaded from ambient environment, barely translucent video pass-through), it is difficult to estimate distance of the light source, so the circumstances are forgiving regarding somewhat variable arrangement. The lights should ideally be positioned at some distance from the seat. In the proof-of-concept prototype, however, the limited space in our small workshop required placing them somewhat closer to the chair, causing their see-through display to intrude into the virtual space.

In practical scenarios, physical constraints of a user's environment must be taken into account. The $\pm 90^{\circ}$ range assumed in this work might not always be applicable. For instance, a chair in a corner might permit only a quarter turn ($\pm 45^{\circ}$). Because different environments impose different limits on chair rotation, a general RDS system should remain adaptable, with the parameters configurable to the available space. In addition, limits of plausible azimuth gain establish perceptual thresholds beyond which virtual rotation becomes noticeable or uncomfortable. Further research is needed to determine these thresholds and to develop methods for mitigating their effects.

The design of the physical setup, particularly the chair, needs to prioritize user comfort and safety while allowing for the necessary range of movement. The virtual environment should be designed to minimize potential for motion sickness or disorientation. Additionally, calibration of the system to accurately track and translate a user's physical movement into the virtual environment is crucial for seamless and immersive experience.

While the concept of RDS shows promise, we note that the system has not been fully tested on a large scale with human subjects. The current findings are based on pilot tests and theoretical models, and further study is needed to validate the effectiveness and usability of RDS in real-world scenarios.

8. Future work

Future work on RDS could focus on several areas. Firstly, expanding the system to accommodate multiple users would enhance its applicability to social VR experiences and collaborative settings. Secondly, integrating other sensory modalities, such as haptic feedback, could further enhance the sense of immersion and realism, especially in deployments on the $^{S}_{c}ha_{i}r^{e}$ platform. Furthermore, exploring the use of AI and machine learning algorithms could lead to personalized RDS experiences that adapt to individual users' preferences and physiological responses. Finally, conducting more extensive user studies, including consideration of cybersickness (typically experienced in simulators hobbled by sensory modality incoherence), perhaps through administration of Simulator Sickness Questionnaire (SSQ) focused on such VR discomfort [39], is crucial to validate the long-term effectiveness and comfort of RDS, and to identify the potential negative side effects.

9. Conclusion

Redirected seating extends the principles of redirected walking to seated VR experiences. By manipulating a user's perception of rotation and providing a plausible explanation for restriction of angular excursion, RDS can enhance immersion and usability of seated VR experiences. Servomotor-driven chair rotation combined with coherently coordinated adaptive lighting effects controlled by IoT protocol and device orchestration [40] reinforces the RDS and azimuth gain illusion. HMDs with optical see-through as in Microsoft HoloLens or Magic Leap would presumably work as well as the video pass-through currently prototyped. While the current implementation has some limitations, future research directions—such as multi-user support, integration of other sensory modalities, and personalized experiences—offer promising avenues for further development. With continued consideration of practical factors including user comfort, safety, and adaptability to various physical spaces, RDS could enhance various applications, including gaming, training simulations, virtual tourism, healthcare, and education.

Acknowledgements

We thank Rintarō Satō for his invaluable contribution on this research project including part of the prototype development, 3D printing, pilot testing, and video editing.

Abbreviations

AI	artificial intelligence
API	application programming interface
AR	augmented reality
HMD	head-mounted display
IoT	internet of things
LBE	location-based entertainment
MR	mixed reality
RDS	redirected seating
RDW	redirected walking
SEQ	Single Ease Question
SSQ	Simulator Sickness Questionnaire
VR	virtual reality
XR	extended reality

Author details

Michael Cohen[1,2]* and Alaeddin Nassani[1]

1 University of Aizu, Aizu-Wakamatsu, Fukushima, Japan

2 Higashi Nippon International University, Iwaki, Fukushima, Japan

*Address all correspondence to: xilehence@mac.com

References

[1] Cohen M. The internet chair. IJHCI: Int. Journal of Human-Computer Interaction. 2003;**15**(2):297-311. DOI: 10.1207/S15327590IJHC1502_7

[2] Feiner SK. Augmented reality: A new way of seeing. Scientific American. 2002;**286**(4):48-55. DOI: 10.1038/scientificamerican0402-48

[3] Cooperstock JR, Fels SS, Buxton W, Smith KC. Reactive environments: Throwing away your keyboard and mouse. Communications of the ACM. 1997;**40**(9):65-73. DOI: 10.1145/260750.260774

[4] Streitz N, Konomi S, Burkhardt H-J, editors. Cooperative Buildings: Integrating Information, Organization, and Architecture. Berlin: Springer; 2014. DOI: 10.1007/978-3-540-72727-9

[5] Brooks RA. The intelligent room project. In: Marsh JP, Nehaniv CL, Gorayska B, editors. CT: Proc. Second Int. Conf. on Cognitive Technology Humanizing the Information Age. Aizu-Wakamatsu, Japan: IEEE; 1997. pp. 271-278. DOI: 10.1109/CT.1997.617707

[6] Lewis T. Information appliances: Gadget netopia. IEEE Computer. 1998;**31**(1):59-68. DOI: 10.1109/2.641978

[7] Billinghurst M, Starner T. Wearable devices: New ways to manage information. Computer. 1999;**32**(1):57-64. DOI: 10.1109/2.738305

[8] Mann S. Smart clothing: The wearable computer and wearcam. Personal Technologies: Personal and Ubiquitous Computing. 1997;**1**(1):21-27. DOI: 10.1007/BF01317885

[9] Starner T, Mann S, Rhodes B, Levine J, Healey J, Kirsch D, et al. Augmented reality through wearable computing. Presence: Teleoperators and Virtual Environments. 1997;**6**(4):386-398. DOI: 10.1162/pres.1997.6.4.386

[10] Cohen M, Nassani A, Satō R. Helical soundscape reinforcing azimuth gain for redirected seating. In: Tanabe T, Yem V, editors. ICAT-EGVE: Proc. Int. Conf. On Artificial Reality and Telexistence, Eurographics Symp. on Virtual Environments — Posters and Demos. Tsukuba, Japan: The Eurographics Association; 2024. DOI: 10.2312/egve.20241406

[11] Nassani A, Satō R, Cohen M. Redirected seating: The helical illusion for seated VR experiences. In: Zielasko D, Weissker T, editors. LocXR: Proc. Workshop on Locomotion and Wayfinding in XR (ISMAR: IEEE Int. Symp. on Mixed and Augmented Reality Adjunct). Bellevue, Washington: IEEE; 2024. pp. 96-101. DOI: 10.1109/ISMAR-Adjunct64951.2024.00030

[12] Wang C, Zhang S-H, Zhang Y, Zollmann S, Hu S-M. On rotation gains within and beyond perceptual limitations for seated VR. IEEE Transactions on Visualization and Computer Graphics. 2023;**29**(7):3380-3391. DOI: 10.1109/TVCG.2022.3159799

[13] Razzaque S, Swapp D, Slater M, Whitton MC, Steed A. Redirected walking in place. In: EGVE: Proc. Eurographics Wkshp. on Virtual Environments. Eindhoven, Netherlands: Eurographics Assoc.; 2002. pp. 123-130. DOI: 10.5555/509709.509729

[14] Jackl P, Jenkin M, Harris L. Perceiving a stable world during active rotational and translational head movements. Experimental Brain Research. 2005;**163**(3):388-399. DOI: 10.1007/s00221-004-2191-8

[15] Steinicke F, Bruder G, Hinrichs K, Lappe M. Real walking through virtual environments by redirection techniques. JVRB: Journal of Virtual Reality and Broadcasting. 2010;**6**(2):1-9. DOI: 10.20385/1860-2037/6.2010.2

[16] Suma EA, Lipps Z, Finkelstein S, Krum DM, Bolas M. Imposing spatial structure on immersive virtual environments via redirected walking. In: Proc. IEEE Virtual Reality Conference (VR). Piscataway, NJ, USA: IEEE; 2012. pp. 179-180. DOI: 10.1109/VR.2012.6180908

[17] Suma EA, Azmandian M, Grechkin T, Phan T, Bolas M. Making small spaces feel large: Infinite walking in virtual reality. In: ACM SIGGRAPH Emerging Technologies. New York, NY, USA: ACM; 2015. p. 16:1. DOI: 10.1145/2782782.2792496

[18] Langbehn E, Steinicke F. Redirected walking in virtual reality. In: Lee N, editor. Encyclopedia of Computer Graphics and Games. Cham: Springer International Publishing; 2018. pp. 1-11. DOI: 10.1007/978-3-319-08234-9_253-1

[19] Nilsson NC, Peck T, Bruder G, Hodgson E, Serafin S, Whitton M, et al. 15 years of research on redirected walking in immersive virtual environments. CG&A: IEEE Computer Graphics and Applications. 2018;**38**(2): 44-56. DOI: 10.1109/MCG.2018.111125628

[20] Pisani VA, Hurd O, Hawthorne N, Kurniawan S. Navigation by walking in hyperbolic space using virtual reality. In: CHI PLAY— Extended Abstracts of Annual Symp. on Computer-Human Interaction in Play. New York, NY, USA: ACM; 2019. pp. 611-618. DOI: 10.1145/3341215.3356287

[21] Yokoi S, Yoshida T, Matsumoto K, Narumi T. Interactive impossible objects: Designing physical interaction with impossible objects using binocular disparity adjustment and redirection. In: ACM SIGGRAPH Emerging Technologies. New York, NY, USA: Association for Computing Machinery; 2025. DOI: 10.1145/3721257.3734030

[22] Gao P, Matsumoto K, Narumi T, Hirose M. Visual-auditory redirection: Multimodal integration of incongruent visual and auditory cues for redirected walking. In: ISMAR: Proc. Int. Symp. on Mixed and Augmented Reality. Piscataway, NJ, USA: IEEE; 2020. pp. 639-648. DOI: 10.1109/ISMAR50242.2020.00092

[23] Nogalski M, Fohl W. Curvature gains in redirected walking: A closer look. In: Proc. IEEE Virtual Reality (VR). Los Angeles: IEEE; 2017. pp. 267-268. DOI: 10.1109/VR.2017.7892279

[24] Moriguchi T, Cohen M. Redirected walking for virtually expanded play area. In: Roy D, Fragulis GF, Campos HC, editors. ETLTC: Proc. ACM Chapter Conf. on Educational Technology, Language and Technical Communication. Vol. 102. Les Ulis Cedex, France: EDP Sciences; 2021. p. 04008. DOI: 10.1051/shsconf/202110204008

[25] Jeon SB, Kwon SU, Hwang JY, Cho YH, Kim H, Park J, et al. Dynamic optimal space partitioning for redirected walking in multi-user environment. ACM Transactions on Graphics. 2022;**41**: 7. DOI: 10.1145/3528223.3530113

[26] Azmandian M, Yahata R, Grechkin T, Thomas J, Rosenberg ES. Validating simulation-based evaluation of redirected walking systems. IEEE Transactions on Visualization and Computer Graphics. 2022;**28**:2288-2298. DOI: 10.1109/TVCG.2022.3150466

[27] Hirt C, Kompis Y, Holz C, Kunz A. The chaotic behavior of redirection - revisiting simulations in redirected walking. In: IEEE VR: Proc. Int. Conf. on Virtual Reality and 3D User Interfaces. Piscataway, NJ, USA: IEEE; 2022. pp. 524-533. DOI: 10.1109/VR51125.2022.00072

[28] Fan L, Li H, Shi M. Redirected walking for exploring immersive virtual spaces with HMD: A comprehensive review and recent advances. IEEE Transactions on Visualization and Computer Graphics. 2023;**29**:4104-4123. DOI: 10.1109/TVCG.2022.3179269

[29] Li YJ, Steinicke F, Wang M. A comprehensive review of redirected walking techniques: Taxonomy, methods, and future directions. Journal of Computer Science and Technology. 2022;**37**:561-583. DOI: 10.1007/s11390-022-2266-7

[30] Xu SZ, Liu JH, Wang M, Zhang FL, Zhang SH. Multi-user redirected walking in separate physical spaces for online vr scenarios. IEEE Transactions on Visualization and Computer Graphics. 2024;**30**:1916-1926. DOI: 10.1109/TVCG.2023.3251648

[31] Wang M, Chen ZY, Cai WC, Steinicke F. Transferable virtual-physical environmental alignment with redirected walking. IEEE Transactions on Visualization and Computer Graphics. 2024;**30**:1696-1709. DOI: 10.1109/TVCG.2022.3224073

[32] Chan L, Mi T-W, Hsueh ZH, Huang Y-C, Hsu MY. Seated-WIP: Enabling walking in-place locomotion for stationary chairs in confined spaces. In: Proc. CHI Conf. on Human Factors in Computing Systems. New York, NY, USA: Association for Computing Machinery; 2024. DOI: 10.1145/3613904.3642395

[33] Cohen M, Doi K, Hattori T, Mine Y. Control of navigable panoramic imagery with information furniture: Chair-driven 2.5D steering through multistandpoint QTVR panoramas with automatic window dilation. In: Miyazaki T, Paik I, Wei D, editors. CIT: Proc. 7th Int. Conf. on Computer and Information Technology. Los Alamitos, CA, USA: IEEE Computer Society; 2007. pp. 517-522. DOI: 10.1109/CIT.2007.140

[34] Herder J, Cohen M. The helical keyboard: Perspectives for spatial auditory displays and visual music. Journal of New Music Research. 2002;**31**(3):269-281. DOI: 10.1076/jnmr.31.3.269.14180

[35] Villegas J, Cohen M. Mapping musical scales onto virtual 3D spaces. In: Suzuki Y, Brungart D, Iwaya Y, Iida K, Cabrera D, Kato H, editors. Principles and Applications of Spatial Hearing. Singapore: World Scientific; 2011. pp. 463-472. DOI: 10.1142/9789814299312_0036

[36] Hook J. Exploring musical spaces: A synthesis of mathematical approaches. In: Oxford Studies in Music Theory. New York, NY, USA: Oxford University Press; 2022

[37] Sauro J, Dumas JS. Comparison of three one-question, post-task usability questionnaires. In: CHI: Proc. SIGCHI Conf. on Human Factors in Computing Systems. New York, NY, USA: ACM; 2009. pp. 1599-1608. DOI: 10.1145/1518701.1518946

[38] Toet A, van Erp JB. The emojigrid as a tool to assess experienced and perceived emotions. The Psychiatrist. 2019;**1**(1):469-481. DOI: 10.3390/psych1010036

[39] Kennedy RS, Lane NE, Berbaum KS, Lilienthal MG. Simulator sickness

questionnaire: An enhanced method for quantifying simulator sickness. The International Journal of Aviation Psychology. 1993;**3**(3):203-220. DOI: 10.1207/s15327108ijap0303_3. ISSN (print): 1050-8414, ISSN (online): 1532-7108

[40] Francombe J, Woodcock J, Hughes RJ, Mason R, Franck A, Pike C, et al. Qualitative evaluation of media device orchestration for immersive spatial audio reproduction. Journal of the Audio Engineering Society. 2018;**66**(6):414-429. DOI: 10.17743/jaes.2018.0027

Section 3

Applications: Professional and Design Practice

Chapter 8

Transforming Neurosurgery with Augmented Reality

Chih-Wei Huang, Chi-Ruei Li, Mao-Shih Lin, Chiu-Chun Chen and Hsi-Kai Tsou

Abstract

Augmented reality (AR) technology is revolutionising neurosurgery, with significant applications in intraoperative navigation, patient education, and medical training. AR enables real-time three-dimensional (3D) image projection into the surgical field, allowing surgeons to localise lesions precisely and avoid critical structures. This reduces intraoperative errors and enhances surgical safety. AR also offers intuitive 3D models that help patients understand disease mechanisms and surgical plans, thereby improving patient education, communication, and engagement. In medical training, AR simulations provide safe and interactive environments for medical students and residents to practice procedures, shortening their learning curve and improving their surgical skills. Despite these advancements, AR in neurosurgery still faces challenges such as image registration errors, hardware compatibility issues, and intraoperative latency. The integration of emerging technologies—such as artificial intelligence, 5G networks, and mixed reality—is expected to overcome these challenges and ensure more accurate and efficient AR systems. As these innovations progress, the role of AR in neurosurgery will expand. This will lead to safer, more precise surgical procedures and transform the landscape of surgical visualisation and education.

Keywords: augmented reality, surgical navigation, image guided surgery, learning curve, medical training, patient education, health communication

1. Introduction

Neurosurgery has a long and distinguished history. Ongoing advancements in imaging technology are continuously transforming surgical visualisation techniques. From the inception of direct visual inspection to the introduction of microsurgery, clarity and precision have significantly improved in this surgical field. Surgical imaging has evolved from X-rays to computed tomography (CT) and magnetic resonance imaging (MRI), eventually integrating with image-guided navigation systems. AR technology has emerged in recent years, resulting in revolutionary changes in neurosurgery. Imaging-assisted technologies have advanced from basic surface anatomy and craniometry to two-dimensional (2D) imaging such as X-rays, 3D imaging such as CT and MRI, and even functional imaging for advanced brain mapping such as diffusion tensor image for visualisation of white fibre tracts.

IntechOpen

User interfaces have also progressed significantly from simple screen displays to navigation systems capable of spatial registration. These advancements allow real-time alignment of imaging data with patient anatomy. Today, AR represents a major technological advancement. Medical images can be directly and dynamically projected into the surgeon's field of view, adapting to changes in perspective. This provides an intuitive and immersive user experience that enhances precision in the planning, navigation, and execution of complex surgical procedures.

From the 1990s, there has been increased deployment of AR technology in neurosurgery [1]. Studies [2] demonstrate that AR navigation improves surgical team communication, shortens operative times, enhances placement accuracy [3, 4], and reduces surgery-related complications [5–10].

Intraoperative AR technology offers real-time 3D imaging, allowing surgeons to identify critical anatomical structures without diverting attention from the surgical site [11]. AR-based 3D models provide intuitive representations of disease mechanisms and surgical plans, thereby improving patient education, comprehension, and engagement [5, 6, 9, 10, 12, 13]. In medical training, AR simulations create safe, interactive learning environments for residents and medical students. This helps shorten their learning curves and improve their surgical skills [8, 9, 14–16].

Despite these advancements, AR technology still faces challenges such as image registration errors, hardware compatibility issues, and intraoperative latency. These challenges necessitate the integration of artificial intelligence (AI) for automated image calibration, development of standardised device interfaces, and application of 5G networks to ensure efficient real-time image transmission.

In the future, integration of AI-assisted navigation, remote surgical guidance, mixed reality (MR), and digital twin technology is anticipated to drive the development in the field of neurosurgery and enhance surgical safety and precision.

The subsequent sections of this chapter address the following topics:

1. AR in intraoperative navigation

2. AR in patient education

3. AR in medical training

4. AR challenges, solutions, and future trends

2. AR in intraoperative navigation

Neurosurgery has evolved alongside advances in imaging technology, making it a pioneering specialty for utilising intraoperative imaging to assist in surgical procedures. Structural imaging modalities such as CT and MRI have significantly enhanced the precision of lesion localisation. However, because of its deep-seated and delicate nature, the nervous system cannot be easily exposed. As observed in other surgical fields, there is a longstanding need for more advanced guidance systems. This contributed to early adoption of navigation systems in neurosurgery. Given their extensive experience with image-assisted procedures, neurosurgeons are generally open to new imaging technologies such as AR and advanced endovascular interventional imaging. These innovations continue to improve surgical accuracy, safety, and outcomes, further solidifying imaging as an integral part of neurosurgical practice.

2.1 Importance of intraoperative navigation

Accurate intraoperative navigation is critical in neurosurgery. Even minor errors can lead to severe neurological damage or surgical failure [13, 17–19]. Research indicates that AR technology can effectively reduce intraoperative errors by providing real-time 3D imaging to help surgeons identify targets and avoid critical structures. In doing so, surgical efficiency and safety are improved [5, 8, 13, 16, 20].

AR projection accuracy is related to the stability and precision of the spatial coordinate system [21], which serves as the framework for neurosurgical navigation. Navigation systems that are currently used in practice, whether based on optical recognition or electromagnetic tracking [1], have been extensively validated. Integrating AR with these well-established navigation systems allows the technology to “stand on the shoulders of giants” by building on this established foundation.

Intraoperative misalignment, such as unnoticed translational or rotational shifts, is a persistent challenge in traditional navigation and can compromise accuracy. These issues are detected more easily by using AR-assisted systems. By projecting an external frame around the target object, any deviations or misalignments are immediately apparent.

This enables surgeons to promptly adjust or revalidate the intraoperative imaging. This proactive approach not only enhances surgical precision but also adds an additional layer of safety to complex neurosurgical procedures.

2.2 AR navigation system and workflow

Azuma [22] identified three essential elements of AR:

1. Combines real and virtual: AR simultaneously integrates real world and virtual objects.

2. Interactive in real time: Users can interact with virtual objects in real time.

3. Registered in three dimensions: Virtual content is accurately aligned within the 3D space of the real world.

These principles emphasise that AR offers real-time fusion of the physical and virtual worlds, enabling seamless interactions and enhancing perception. To integrate AR with intraoperative navigation systems, Azuma’s three AR elements [22] can be applied as follows:

Step 1. Virtual image generation (Element 1)

- Extract and reconstruct 3D anatomical models from patient structural imaging data (e.g. CT or MRI) for AR projection.

Step 2. Image registration (elements 1 and 3)

- Align virtual images with the patient’s anatomical structures—a process known as registration, which ensures that digital overlays match the actual position of anatomical features during surgery.

- Common registration methods:

o Fiducial markers: Small fixed objects (such as screws or adhesive markers) placed on the patient's skin or bone to serve as precise reference points for aligning virtual images to real anatomy.

o Surface matching: A technique where 3D scanners capture the patient's facial [23] or anatomical contours and align them with imaging data for accurate registration.

Step 3. Real-time tracking (Element 2)

- Continuously track the spatial positions of the patient, surgical instruments, and AR display devices—a technique referred to as tracking, which maintains the alignment between the real world and virtual images during surgical movements.

- Tracking technologies:

o Optical tracking system: Infrared cameras and reflective markers are used for precise spatial tracking.

o Electromagnetic tracking: This technology is ideal for scenarios in which direct line-of-sight tracking is obstructed (e.g., endoscopic procedures).

Step 4. Display and projection

- Select appropriate AR display devices based on surgical needs.

o *Wearable AR devices*

Surgeons can use hand gestures and voice commands to adjust the image view, enhancing operational flexibility and supporting multiuser collaboration [20, 24].

- HoloLens 2 (USA, Microsoft) offers high-precision spatial mapping and gesture control, which are widely used in medical applications.

o Magic Leap 2 (USA, Magic Leap) functional surgery simulators that enhanced 3D rendering. It is suitable for surgical guidance and medical training.

o Epson Moverio BT-45CS (Japan, Epson) is equipped with transparent optical display technology, which is ideal for high-precision medical applications.

o *Microscope-based AR systems*

Virtual overlays are integrated directly into the field of view of a surgical microscope, enhancing precision during neurosurgical procedures.

o Carl Zeiss Meditec AG (Germany, ZEISS)

o Leica Microsystems GmbH (Germany, Leica)

o Olympus Corporation (Japan, Olympus))

2.3 Comparing microscope AR projection and wearable AR devices

AR navigation systems in neurosurgery primarily incorporate two types of devices [1, 2, 20, 24]: surgical microscopes and wearable AR devices. Each approach presents unique advantages and inherent limitations, rendering them suitable for different surgical scenarios.

Microscope-based AR systems are purpose-built for surgical applications, designed specifically to meet the visual and ergonomic demands of complex operations such as neurosurgery. Unlike wearable AR devices that prioritise portability and flexibility, microscope-integrated AR systems focus on delivering high-fidelity, real-time imaging tailored for microsurgical precision.

In these systems, virtual anatomical overlays are directly incorporated into the optical pathway of surgical microscopes. This enables surgeons to visualise 3D reconstructions of anatomical structures—such as tumour boundaries, vascular networks, and bony landmarks—superimposed precisely within the microscope's native field of view without disrupting focus or workflow.

One key advantage of microscope-based AR is its capacity to support true stereoscopic (binocular) viewing, enabling natural and accurate depth perception. Moreover, the 3D virtual overlay dynamically adjusts with the microscope's focal depth, enabling a layered "see-through" effect where deeper and superficial anatomical structures can be visualised separately depending on the surgeon's focus. For example, as illustrated in **Figure 1C**, transparent overlays of the vertebral artery and bone anatomy shift perspective in accordance with the microscope's focal plane, enhancing intraoperative depth orientation.

Because they are engineered for surgical use, microscope-based AR systems offer several key advantages:

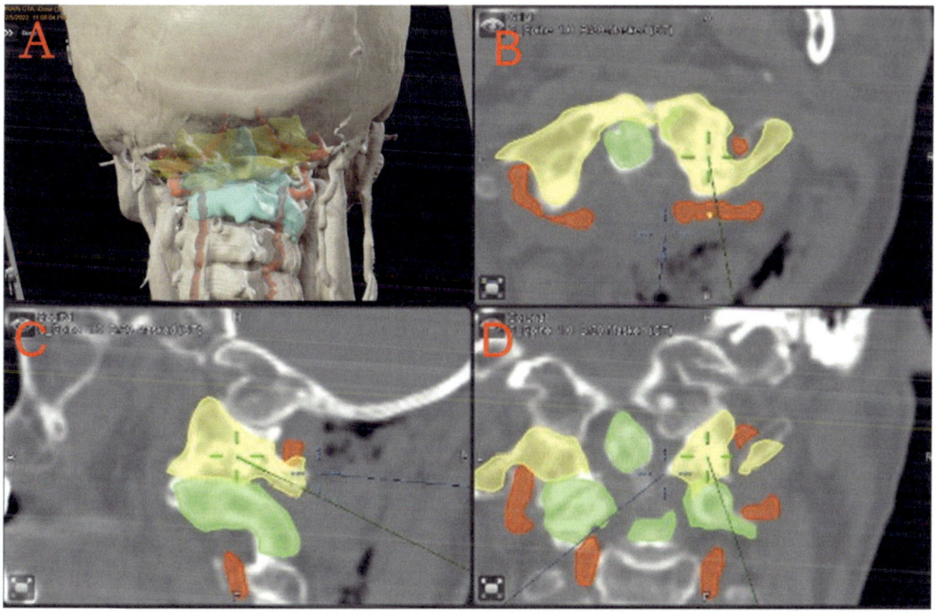

Figure 1.
Visualisation of vertebral bodies and vertebral arteries in navigation software and surgical field.

- Optical zoom and high-resolution magnification for visualising deep or minute structures.
- Manual or autofocus control that synchronises with 3D overlays for precise depth targeting.
- Built-in coaxial lighting for clear illumination without external sources.
- Stereoscopic depth perception enhancing hand-eye coordination during delicate dissection.
- Dynamic 3D overlay adaptation with focus changes, supporting layer-by-layer anatomical navigation.
- Ergonomic viewing posture and foot-pedal control, reducing surgeon fatigue during prolonged operations.

Collectively, these characteristics make microscope-based AR systems especially suitable for procedures requiring high spatial accuracy and visual clarity, such as tumour resections near critical brain areas, arteriovenous malformation dissections, and complex spinal instrumentation (**Table 1**).

Wearable AR devices and microscope-based AR systems offer unique advantages and can coexist in neurosurgical procedures to enhance surgical accuracy and efficiency.

- *Macroscopic phase—ideal for wearable AR devices:*

  During the initial stages of surgery, such as *craniotomy* (a surgical procedure where a bone flap is temporarily removed from the skull to access the brain) for scalp flap and bone flap design, a broader and more flexible view is essential. Wearable AR devices project imaging data directly into the surgeon's field of view, minimising the need to look away from the operative field and enhancing surgical workflow.

Feature	Microscope AR projection	Wearable AR devices
Magnification	High optical magnification for fine structures	Digital magnification with resolution limitations
Focusing	Automatic and manual focusing options	Limited focusing capability
Lighting Integration	Built-in lighting for clear visualisation	Requires external lighting assistance
Flexibility	Fixed orientation based on microscope position	Flexible viewpoint with head-mounted display
User Interaction	Operated *via* microscope controls	Intuitive control using hand gestures and voice
Collaboration	Single-user viewing through an eyepiece	Multi-user collaboration supported
Hardware Requirements	Specialised hardware integration required	Operates with standard wireless devices

Table 1.
Comparison of microscope-based AR projection and wearable AR devices in neurosurgical procedures.

- *Microscopic phase—ideal for microscope-based AR systems:*

  As surgery advances to detailed tasks, such as tumour resection or vascular lesions, precise angle adjustments, variable focusing, and high magnification become critical. Microscope-integrated AR systems provide high-resolution imaging with an accurate overlay of the preoperative data, thereby supporting delicate procedures. Additionally, the ergonomic design of surgical microscopes helps reduce the surgeon's visual fatigue during prolonged operations.

2.4 Clinical case studies

2.4.1 Case 1: C1-C2 atlantoaxial joint fixation surgery

Atlantoaxial instability, which involves excessive movement between the first two cervical vertebrae (C1 and C2), is considered one of the most anatomically complex and high-risk conditions in spinal surgery. Surgical stabilisation requires placing screws through narrow, deeply seated bony channels while avoiding critical vascular structures, such as the vertebral arteries. Precision is essential to avoid neurological or vascular injury and to restore cervical spine stability (**Figures 2** and **3**).

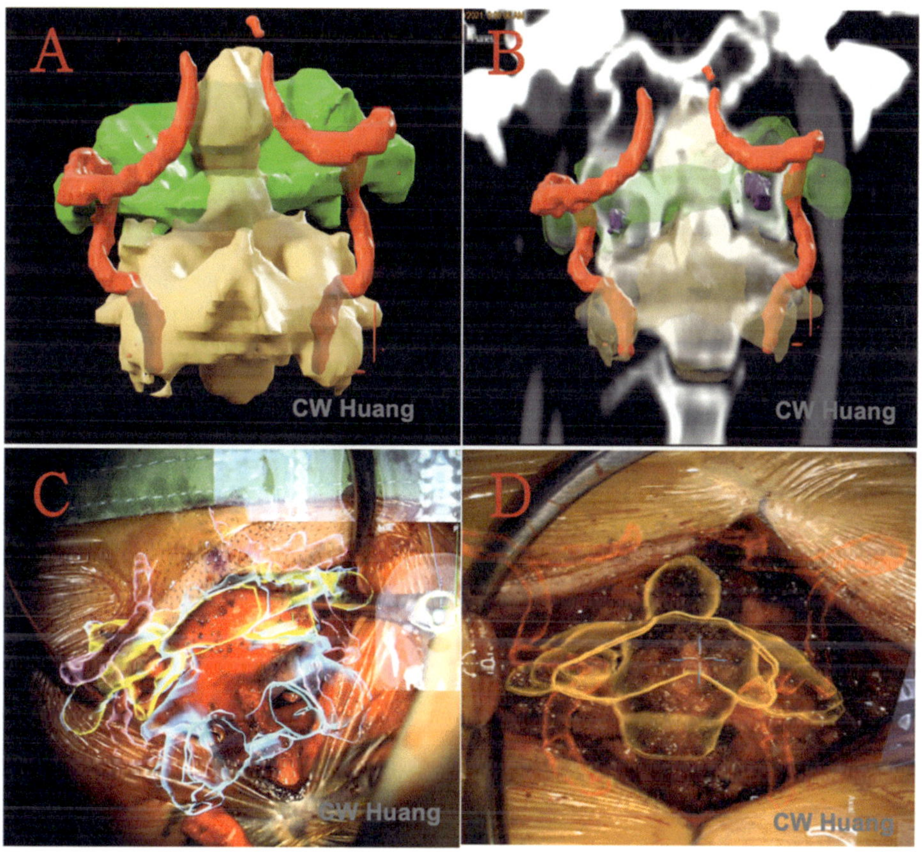

Figure 2.
3D reconstruction of cervical spine anatomy with surrounding vascular structures.

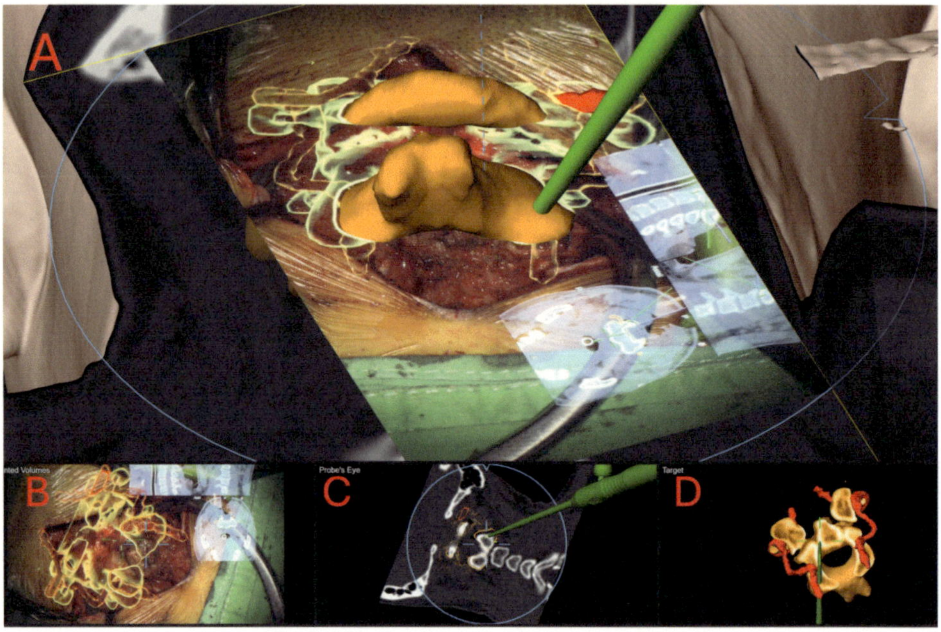

Figure 3.
Real-time navigation information displayed in the surgical field via *microscope.*

In a case [25] the surgical team utilised an AR navigation system to generate 3D anatomical models and project them into the operative field. This technology helped the surgical team identify the path of the vertebral artery, thereby preventing vascular injury and improving spatial understanding during this complex spinal surgery. Postoperative imaging confirmed the accurate screw placement without complications, demonstrating the effectiveness of AR in enhancing surgical precision and safety.

In such cases, AR provides an intuitive visualisation of the spinal pedicle screw trajectory. It allows the overall skeletal framework to be used as a reference to detect deviations, especially when deep anatomical structures cannot be directly exposed [25–27].

A pedicle cannulation (screw insertion into the spine for stabilisation) study [3] revealed that the clinical accuracy of an AR-guided insertion was 97.4% compared with 89.3% for freehand insertion. Navigation accuracy had a mean registration error of approximately 1 mm when referring to intraoperative CT scans [4].

A comprehensive 3D model of the patient's cervical spine highlights the bony structures and angioarchitecture.

- Yellow: First cervical vertebra (atlas)
- Green: Second cervical vertebra (axis)
- Red: Vertebral artery (VA)

Viewpoints:

- A: 3D perspective view illustrating spatial relationships between the vertebrae and VA.

- B: Axial view for cross-sectional visualisation of the vertebrae and VA.
- C: Sagittal view illustrating the vertical alignment and depth of anatomical structures.
- D: Coronal view for frontal analysis of the vertebral and vascular structures.

This multi-view reconstruction enhances preoperative planning by providing a precise spatial orientation of critical anatomical landmarks, which is crucial for surgical navigation and avoiding vascular injury.

This figure demonstrates the integration of 3D anatomical models with surgical navigation systems, enhancing intraoperative visualisation and precision. This multimodal visualisation bridges the divide between preoperative planning and intraoperative execution. In doing so, it improves accuracy and safety in complex cervical spine procedures.

- A: 3D reconstruction of the C1 and C2 vertebral bodies along with the bilateral VA generated from CT scans, highlighting their spatial relationships.
- B: Fusion of 3D models with the original CT images, providing enhanced anatomical context and accurate localisation.
- C: Application of fused images during surgical procedures (or cadaver dissection) to enable real-time anatomical guidance in the surgical field.
- D: Translucent view of the C2 vertebral body revealing the course of the vertebral arteries to prevent vascular injury during surgery.

This figure demonstrates integration of real-time navigation data with the surgical microscope, enhancing intraoperative precision. This integration enhances visualisation, facilitates precise targeting, and reduces the risk of injury to critical structures such as the VA.

- A: Projection of 3D anatomical structures into the microscope view. The probe (green) is directed toward the pedicle of the C2 vertebral body (yellow). The VA is highlighted in red, allowing precise navigation.
- B: Translucent 3D structures are overlaid in the field of view of the microscope and dynamically aligned with the focal point as the microscope moves, thereby maintaining an accurate spatial orientation.
- C: Navigation system interface showing real-time localisation and alignment assisting in the accurate placement of surgical instruments.
- D: Isolated 3D model displaying the C2 vertebral body and probe, highlighting their spatial relationship for detailed preoperative and/or intraoperative planning.

2.4.2 Case 2: Brain arteriovenous malformation

Arteriovenous malformations (AVMs) are abnormal tangles of arteries and veins that bypass normal brain tissue, disrupting blood flow and oxygen delivery. They are considered among the most complex and challenging conditions in neurosurgery due to their delicate, variable vascular structure and high risk of rupture. Successful treatment often requires meticulous preoperative planning and precise intraoperative navigation (**Figures 4** and **5**).

In this case, a left temporal lobe AVM was identified, AR was applied during the preoperative stage to reconstruct the vascular architecture. The system projects the feeding arteries (inflow) and drainage veins (outflow) into the field of view in real time during surgery, guiding the surgical team to selectively occlude abnormal vessels. The AVM was successfully resected, and the patient experienced a marked reduction in postoperative seizure frequency, demonstrating the utility of AR in cerebrovascular surgery.

In such cases, AR allows surgeons to easily identify anatomical locations even in complex vascular structures such as AVMs. Therefore, in vascular malformations,

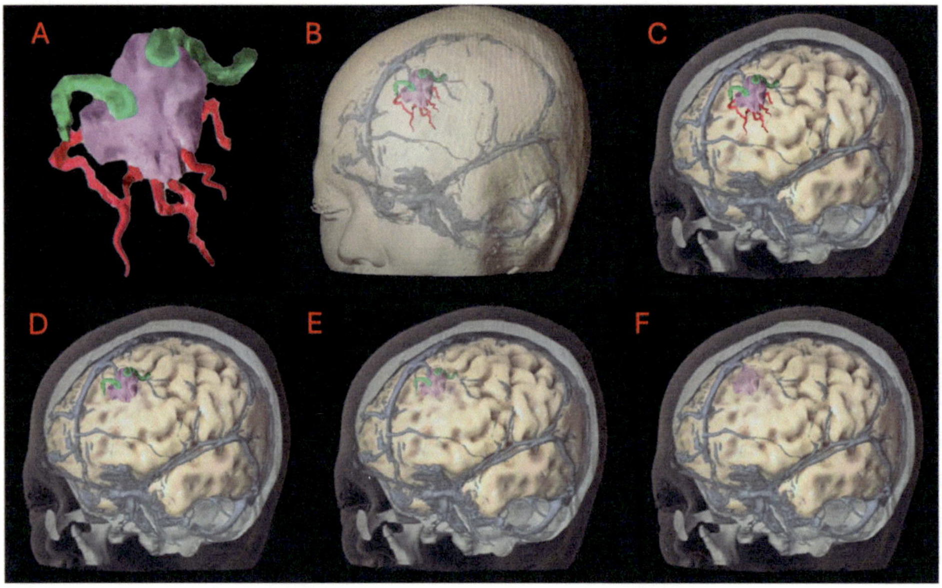

Figure 4.
Visualisation of brain arteriovenous malformation (bAVM) as a 3D object in navigation software.

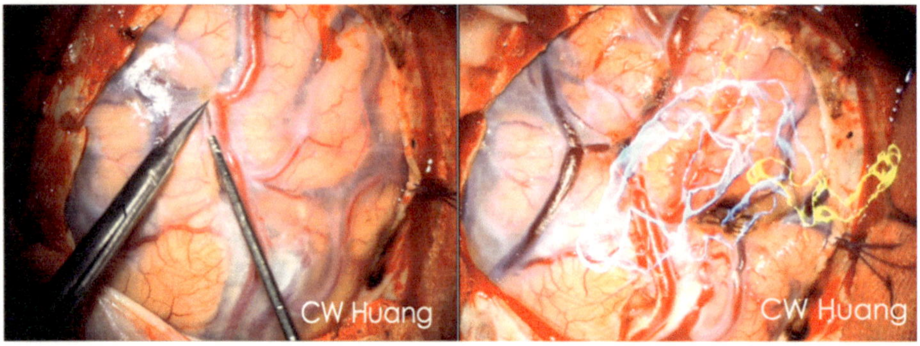

Figure 5.
Comparing traditional microscopic view and AR-enhanced projection in bAVM surgery.

applying AR during surgery provides valuable information that aids in achieving surgical objectives.

This figure illustrates the integration of bAVM AR imaging with brain MRI using the Brainlab navigation system (Brainlab AG, Munich, Germany). It demonstrates a simulated surgical workflow for a bAVM. Fusing 3D AR imaging with traditional MRI enhances surgical planning and intraoperative navigation. In doing so, it improves a surgeon's ability to assess spatial relationships and execute precise resections of complex bAVMs.

- A: 3D reconstruction of the bAVM with distinct colour coding for anatomical clarity: feeding arteries (pink), drainage veins (green), and the nidus (abnormal tangle of blood vessels) (purple).

- B & C: Fused images combining AR-based bAVM mapping with MRI data, providing intuitive visualisation of the spatial relationships among the bAVM, scalp, skull, cerebral vessels, and brain tissue.

- D & E: Surgical simulation showing the gradual obliteration process, starting with complete occlusion of the feeding arteries and leading to progressive shrinkage of the nidus and drainage veins.

- F: Final surgical step, where the drainage veins were coagulated, and the nidus was safely resected.

This figure highlights the differences between conventional microscopy and AR-assisted visualisation during bAVM surgery.

- Left: Traditional microscopic view, providing a clear image of the surgical field but lacking enhanced visualisation of critical vascular structures.

- Right: AR-enhanced microscopic view with overlaid anatomical structures. The feeding artery is highlighted in yellow, and the AVM nidus is shown in blue, enabling the precise identification of key vascular components.

- Integrating AR projections into the surgical field enhances spatial awareness and assists in the safe and accurate resection of bAVMs.

2.4.3 Case 3: Brain tumour resection

Brain tumour surgery requires extremely precise planning and execution, as even small errors can affect critical brain functions such as speech, vision, or movement. Before surgery, doctors must identify the exact location and size of the tumour, as well as its relationship to nearby structures such as nerves and blood vessels. Traditionally, this planning was based on 2D images from MRI or CT scans, which could be hard to visualise during the actual operation. AR now allows surgeons to see a 3D model of the tumour overlaid directly onto the patient's head in the operating room. This helps guide the surgical approach and ensures the tumour is removed safely and completely (**Figure 6**).

In a right temporal lobe tumour resection, AR technology was used to create patient-specific 3D models highlighting the tumour, optic nerve, and middle cerebral artery. These models were projected onto the surgical field to assist with incision

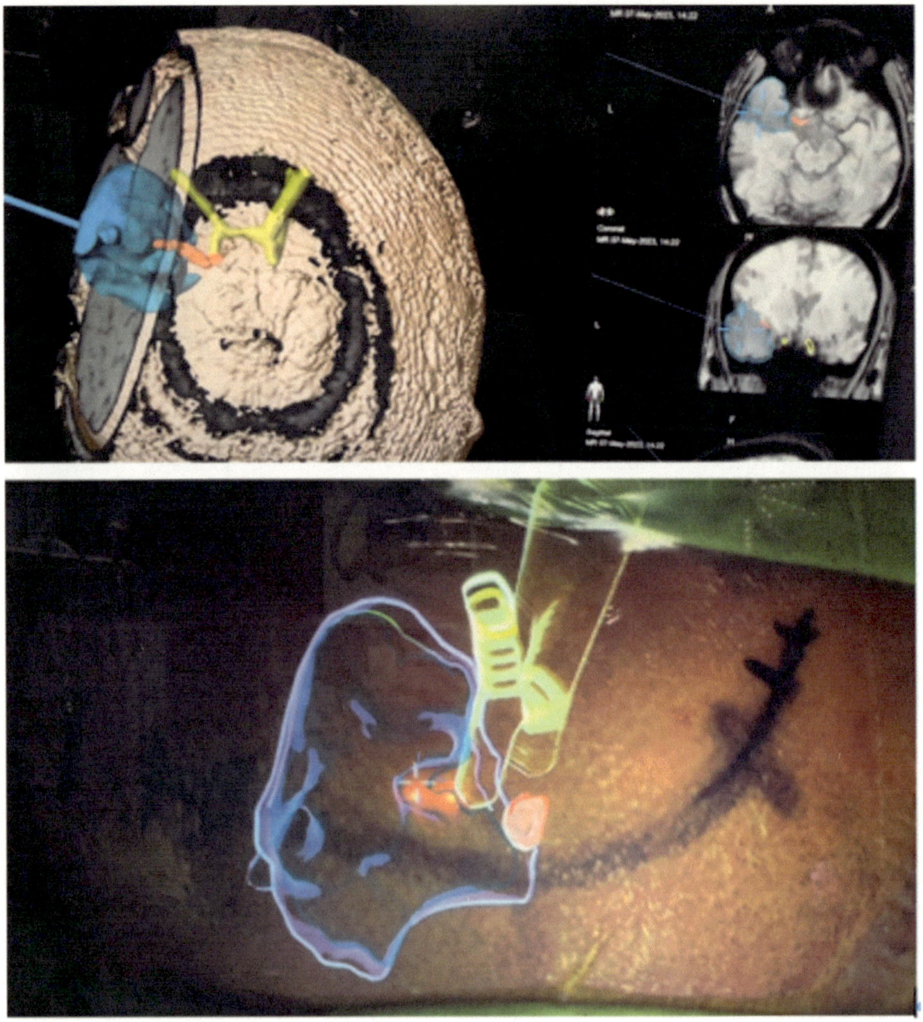

Figure 6.
Applying AR in brain tumour surgery.

planning and tumour boundary identification. The surgery resulted in a complete tumour resection without complications. This illustrates the role of AR in enhancing preoperative planning and intraoperative navigation.

The AR system accurately and reliably projected images onto the patient's head, skull, and brain surface during the procedure. Its ergonomic advantages improved neurosurgical planning and enabled surgeons to perform image-guided neurosurgery with direct visualisation [21, 26, 28].

This figure illustrates the use of AR technology for preoperative planning and intraoperative navigation during brain tumour surgery. By integrating AR into brain tumour surgery, surgeons can enhance spatial orientation, reduce surgical risks, and improve overall procedural accuracy.

- *The upper pane displays a 3D-reconstructed model overlaid with navigation information.* In this model, the tumour is highlighted in blue, the optic nerve is marked in yellow, and the middle cerebral artery is shown in orange. This layered visualisation assists surgeons in accurately perceiving the spatial relationships between the tumour and adjacent critical neurovascular structures.

- *The lower pane presents the AR overlay projected onto the patient's scalp during the pre-incision planning stage.* This overlay delineates the tumour and adjacent anatomical structures, thereby facilitating precise surgical planning and optimised incision placement.

3. AR in patient education

In modern healthcare, effective communication among healthcare professionals, patients, and their families is crucial. As medical procedures become increasingly complex, understanding the diagnosis, surgical plans, and associated risks can be challenging for individuals without a medical background. AR and virtual reality (VR) provide immersive, interactive, and visually intuitive educational tools that empower patients and their families to actively engage in decision-making processes.

3.1 Using AR and VR to understand anatomical structures

Traditional anatomical explanations often rely on verbal descriptions or static 2D images, making it difficult for patients to grasp intricate anatomical details. AR and VR transform these abstract concepts into interactive 3D models (**Figures 2** and **1A** and **B** show a representative AR visualisation of anatomical structures), allowing patients to visualise the affected structures and surrounding anatomy in real time. For example, AR applications can display a 3D spinal model, helping patients and their families understand the affected areas and planned surgical approach.

In addition, because 3D models are already generated during AR workflows, these data can be seamlessly converted to VR environments. VR simulations provide an immersive educational experience [29, 30], allowing patients and their families to explore the anatomical structures and surgical approach from different perspectives. In doing so, patient comprehension and engagement is enhanced.

Surgical procedures are often anxiety-inducing for patients and their families. AR and VR technology enables medical professionals to review step-by-step surgical simulations (**Figure 6**). This demonstrates each surgical phase from the incision to tissue manipulation and structural stabilisation. Interactive models can highlight high-risk areas such as nerves or blood vessels, offering a clear and comprehensible explanation of potential complications and risk mitigation strategies.

3.2 Family education and support

Family members are often deeply involved in treatment decisions and postoperative care. AR and VR tools facilitate understanding of their relative's condition [31, 32] and the rationale behind the chosen treatment. By engaging families with interactive educational content, AR and VR help create a unified, informed support system that improves patient care outcomes.

AR and VR technology has revolutionised patient education by simplifying complex medical information into accessible, interactive formats. By clearly illustrating anatomical structures, surgical steps, and potential risks, these tools reduce anxiety, build trust, and enhance communication among patients, families, and medical professionals.

4. AR in medical training

With the advancements in medical technology, demands and challenges of medical training continue to increase. Traditional methods, such as lectures, diagrams, and cadaver dissection, can no longer prepare learners to meet the needs of modern medicine in terms of precision and clinical skills. AR and VR provide a new medical education model that overlays real-time images on interactive 3D models.

4.1 Applications of AR and VR in medical education

AR technology is increasingly being applied in medical education. Using neurosurgery as example, these applications include:

- *Anatomy education*
    - AR technology allows learners to interact with 3D anatomical models to understand complex structures without relying solely on limited cadaver resources [29, 30, 33–36].
- *Surgical simulation training*
    - AR systems enable the practise of core skills in a risk-free environment, including anatomical structure recognition, spatial localisation, and understanding the relationship between patient positioning and surgical approach. For instance, AR-guided ventricular puncture and external ventricular drain placement training (a catheter placed into brain ventricles to relieve pressure) uses 3D images to help beginners understand anatomical landmarks and practise techniques repeatedly [29, 37, 38].
- *Brain surgery and AVM resection training*
    - Hybrid AR and VR systems allow learners to perform craniotomies, tumour resections, and vascular procedures using interactive 3D models [6, 39].
- *Spinal surgery training (***Figure** *7)*
    - In spinal neurosurgery, AR assists in pedicle screw placement by visualising trajectories and understanding the bone structures and surrounding nerve anatomy [27, 40].

This figure illustrates the integration of AR technology with minimally invasive lumbar surgery training for enhancing spatial awareness and precision. This AR-integrated training model provides a realistic simulation to improve surgical accuracy, procedural confidence, and trainee skill development in minimally invasive spinal surgeries.

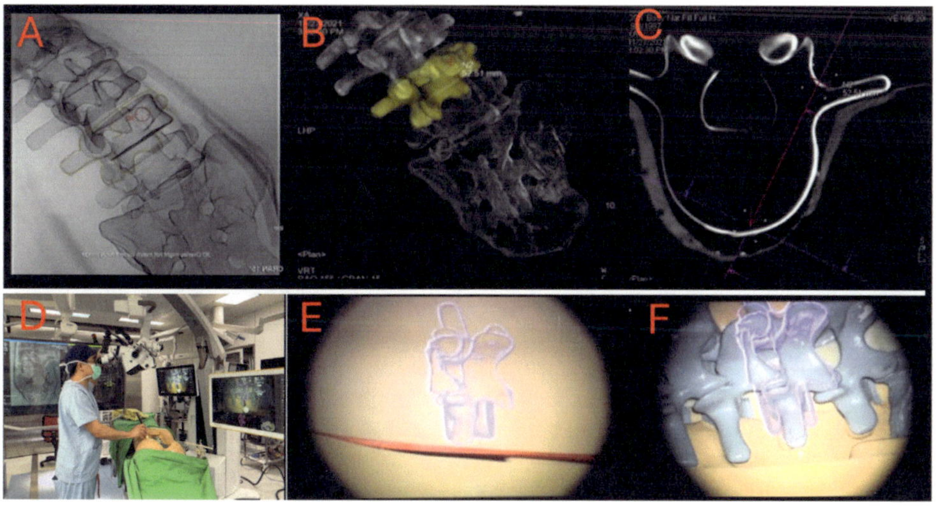

Figure 7.
Augmented reality for minimally invasive lumbar surgery training.

- A: Acquisition *of CT imaging from the training phantom*
- *(an anatomical model used for imaging practice).*
- *B: Generation of 3D visualisation of the target spinal segment, fused, and registered with the navigation and AR systems.*
- *C: Preoperatively planned pedicle screw trajectory, displayed for reference.*
- *D: Microscope-based AR projection simulating the surgical environment and instrument positioning.*
- *E: Surface projection of the target anatomy and planned incision site, assisting in precise localisation.*
- *F: AR projection after removing the overlay, demonstrating the alignment between the AR model and the physi*cal phantom.

4.2 Development and advantages of AR simulators

AR simulators are increasingly replacing traditional training models with realistic and interactive learning experiences. By overlaying virtual information on physical models, learners can practise medical procedures repeatedly and review their performance using real-time feedback. Although the initial setup cost is higher for this training approach, the high reusability and broad application potential reduce long-term costs. This makes AR simulators particularly suitable for resource-constrained regions.

Other advantages include:

- Immersive learning: AR systems provide virtual surgical environments that mimic real-world scenarios [29].

- Real-time feedback: AR, with haptic feedback systems [41, 42], enhances training realism, enabling trainees to experience tactile sensations closely resembling real surgical procedures.

- Remote training: AR facilitates synchronised training sessions across different locations.

- AR-VR mode switching: The generated 3D models can be easily switched to VR for preoperative planning.

In recent years, an increasing number of training modules that combine physical models with AR projections have become available. These companies have extensive experience in developing AR neurosurgical training modules and offer advanced solutions for neurosurgical medical education and surgical skill development.

- NeuroVR is a well-known VR and AR neurosurgical simulation platform that provides various surgical training programmes, allowing trainees to practise procedures using interactive tools. Website: www.surgicalscience.com/simbionix

- ImmersiveTouch developed the ImmersiveView™ 5 platform, integrating AR technology to offer neurosurgeons a virtual environment for surgical planning and hands-on training.

- Website: www.immersivetouch.com

- Mentice provides AR-based vascular interventional surgery simulators that are also applicable for neurosurgical training. Website: www.mentice.com

4.3 Future directions

- AI-assisted learning: Integrating AI to adapt content based on learner performance.

- Integration with VR: Merging AR and VR for more comprehensive training.

- Personalised learning: Tailoring content based on individual needs.

AR technology is transforming medical training by creating a safe, efficient, and realistic learning environment. This allows learners to practise their skills, receive feedback, and build expertise. Considering ongoing research and technological advancements, the application of AR in medical training is expected to expand and improve educational outcomes.

5. AR challenges, solutions, and future trends

AR-assisted surgery presents various technical challenges alongside significant opportunities for future advancements.

5.1 Technical challenges and solutions

- *Image registration drift*: One of the biggest challenges of integrating AR into surgical assistance is image registration drift [43]. Brain shifts during neurosurgical procedures or spinal motion can cause misalignment between projected images and actual anatomy. While rigid head clamps or stable spinal structures help maintain accuracy, tissue shifts continue to pose problems.

  - Potential solutions: Future solutions may involve AI-assisted surface-tracking algorithms, intraoperative ultrasound [44, 45], MRI, and CT to dynamically adjust the image overlays [43]. These innovations will enable the real-time data acquisition, internal transmission within surgical systems, and immediate analysis of visual information to maintain image alignment accuracy during surgical procedures.

- *Device compatibility:* AR hardware and software from different manufacturers often lack interoperability, which complicates data sharing and integration.

  - Image guided therapy (IGT) [46] standards are expected to standardise interfaces and protocols, ensuring seamless communication across systems.

- *Projection lag:* This is a critical challenge in real-time 3D imaging, particularly in high-precision applications such as surgical navigation.

  - To maintain synchronisation between the virtual overlays and real-world anatomy, total delay from target detection to image projection should be kept under 10 milliseconds, with a minimum 120 Hz refresh rate [47, 48].

  - Optimised Projection Workflow and Timing:

  - Target Detection →Graphic Analysis →Projection Update →Relative Position Recognition →Image Projection

  - Impact of refresh rate [47, 48]:

  - *Low refresh rate (<90 Hz):*

  - May cause noticeable lag, ghosting, and screen tearing, which increase the risk of eye strain and motion sickness.

  - *High refresh rate (≥120 Hz):*

  - Ensures smooth and fluid visuals with minimal perceived latency. Crucial for real-time feedback in applications like surgical navigation.

  - Human eye latency perception [48]:

  - <30 ms: Generally imperceptible.

  - 15–20 ms: Target range for real-time interaction.

  - <10 ms: Required for high-end applications (e.g., surgery).

5.2 Future trends and innovations

- *Remote surgical assistance* [49–51]: Although HMDs are commonly connected via Wi-Fi or Bluetooth, these local wireless protocols may be limited by latency, bandwidth, and environmental stability. In contrast, 5G technology provides ultra-low latency and high data throughput, enabling seamless real-time AR rendering and communication. These features are particularly critical for remote surgical assistance, where expert surgeons can guide procedures in under-resourced or geographically isolated settings without interruption or delay.

- *Microscope-based AR projection advancements:* Head-up display goggles are currently mainstream in AR-assisted surgeries. Despite being bulky and having several limitations, microscope-based AR projection offers unique advantages in specific surgical scenarios. It excels in cases that require high magnification, precise depth of field, and better fatigue management for prolonged use. In addition, it supports hands-free operations through features such as foot pedal control, enabling surgeons to maintain focus while adjusting the view. These strengths highlight the potential areas for future development and improvement of microscope-integrated AR systems.

- *MR and multisensory integration:* AR's convergence with MR will enable simultaneous integration of touch [41, 42], sight, and sound to enhance surgical precision. Future systems may simulate tissue texture and elasticity, thereby offering immersive preoperative planning and intraoperative navigation.

- *AI-driven image analysis and calibration:* Machine learning algorithms are being developed to track tissue shifts, identify critical structures, and dynamically recalibrate images.

- *AR navigation surgery:* This technical field is a critical milestone toward future innovations, such as robotics surgery in MR [52, 53] and data-driven outcome predictions [53]. The quantification of surgical procedures enables the collection of meaningful data that are essential for advancing automated surgery.

- *Digital twin technology* [54]: Preoperative imaging data can be transformed into digital twins (virtual replicas of patient's anatomy) to simulate procedures, predict outcomes, and guide clinical decision-making.

6. Conclusion

AR is transforming the field of neurosurgery owing to its applications in intraoperative navigation, patient education, and medical training. By projecting real-time 3D images into the surgical field, AR enhances accuracy and safety. A systematic review [55] of 116 studies found that 82% of MR applications in neurosurgery focused on cranial procedures. Among these, approximately 34% reported improved tumour resection rates and better patient outcomes. This evidence further supports the clinical utility of MR technologies in enhancing surgical performance. In addition to supporting surgeons, AR improves patient and family understanding of complex conditions by turning medical images into intuitive visual explanations. For medical trainees, AR-based simulations create a safe, immersive environment for practicing procedures and building skills without risk to patients. Nevertheless, technical challenges such as image registration drift, device compatibility, and projection lag persist; however, advancements in AI, 5G, and MR are poised to overcome these hurdles. As AR and VR technologies continue to evolve, their integration with intraoperative imaging, digital twin simulations, and remote surgical support will revolutionise surgical visualisation and education, paving the way for a safer and more intelligent future of neurosurgery.

Acknowledgements

The authors express their gratitude to the neurosurgical radiology technicians, including Zhe-Hao Lin, Meng-Ru Li, Hong-Xin Lin, Shi-Rui Huang, and Pei-Yu Wang, for their invaluable contributions throughout the development of the AR system. Their expertise, creativity, and technical support played a crucial role in every stage of this study, from image acquisition to AR model integration and surgical navigation refinement.

Conflict of interest

The authors declare no conflict of interest.

Abbreviation

2D	two-dimensional
3D	three-dimensional
5G	fifth-generation mobile network
AI	artificial intelligence
AR	augmented reality
AVM	arteriovenous malformation
bAVM	brain arteriovenous malformation
C1	first cervical vertebra
C2	second cervical vertebra
CT	computed tomography
DSA	digital subtraction angiography
DTI	diffusion tensor imaging
fMRI	functional magnetic resonance imaging
HUD	head-up display
IGS	image-guided surgery
MCA	middle cerebral artery
MR	mixed reality
MRI	magnetic resonance imaging
VA	vertebral artery
VR	virtual reality

Author details

Chih-Wei Huang[1,2], Chi-Ruei Li[1,2], Mao-Shih Lin[2], Chiu-Chun Chen[2] and Hsi-Kai Tsou[3,4,5,6]*

1 Institute of Medicine, Chung Shan Medical University, Taichung, Taiwan

2 Department of Neurosurgery, Neurological Institute, Taichung Veterans General Hospital, Taichung, Taiwan

3 Functional Neurosurgery Division, Neurological Institute, Taichung Veterans General Hospital, Taichung, Taiwan

4 Department of Post-Baccalaureate Medicine, College of Medicine, National Chung Hsing University, Taichung, Taiwan

5 Department of Rehabilitation, Jen-Teh Junior College of Medicine, Nursing and Management, Miaoli, Taiwan

6 College of Health, National Taichung University of Science and Technology, Taichung, Taiwan

*Address all correspondence to: tsouhsikai@gmail.com

References

[1] Meola A, Cutolo F, Carbone M, Cagnazzo F, Ferrari M, Ferrari V. Augmented reality in neurosurgery: A systematic review. Neurosurgical Review. 2017;**40**:537-548. DOI: 10.1007/s10143-016-0732-9

[2] Guha D, Alotaibi NM, Nguyen N, Gupta S, McFaul C, Yang VXD. Augmented reality in neurosurgery: A review of current concepts and emerging applications. The Canadian Journal of Neurological Sciences. 2017;**44**(3):235-245. DOI: 10.1017/cjn.2016.443

[3] Burström G, Nachabe R, Persson O, Edström E, Terander AE. Augmented and virtual reality instrument tracking for minimally invasive spine surgery: A feasibility and accuracy study. Spine. 2019;**44**(15):1097-1104. DOI: 10.1097/BRS.0000000000003006

[4] Carl B, Bopp M, Saß B, Voellger B, Nimsky C. Implementation of augmented reality support in spine surgery. European Spine Journal. 2019;**28**(7): 1697-1711. DOI: 10.1007/s00586-019-05969-4

[5] van Doormaal JA, van Doormaal TP. Augmented reality in neurosurgery. Advances in Experimental Medicine and Biology. 2024;**1462**:351-374. DOI: 10.1007/978-3-031-64892-2_21

[6] Isikay I, Cekic E, Baylarov B, Tunc O, Hanalioglu S. Narrative review of patient-specific 3D visualization and reality technologies in skull base neurosurgery: Enhancements in surgical training, planning, and navigation. Frontiers in Surgery. 2024;**11**:1427844

[7] Kashif M, Muthana A, Al-Qudah AM, Hoz SS. The influence of artificial intelligence on neurological surgery and patient outcome. Surgical Neurology International. 2024;**15**:211. DOI: 10.25259/SNI_321_2024

[8] Hey G, Guyot M, Carter A, Lucke-Wold B. Augmented reality in neurosurgery: A new paradigm for training. Medicina (Kaunas, Lithuania). 2023;**59**(10):1721. DOI: 10.3390/medicina59101721

[9] Sharma N, Mallela AN, Khan T, Canton SP, Kass NM, Steuer F, et al. Evolution of the meta-neurosurgeon: A systematic review of the current technical capabilities, limitations, and applications of augmented reality in neurosurgery. Surgical Neurology International. 2024;**15**:146. DOI: 10.25259/SNI_167_2024

[10] Kolluru V, Mungara S, Chintakunta AN, Telaganeni CS, Kolluru L. Surgical data science and associated techniques facilitate the development of contemporary equipment like Apple's vision pro. The International Journal of Preventive Medicine and Health (IJPMH). 2024;**5**(1):1-9. DOI: 10.54105/ijpmh.D3648.0501124

[11] Li C-R, Shen C-C, Yang M-Y, Tsuei Y-S, Lee C-H. Intraoperative augmented reality in microsurgery for intracranial arteriovenous malformation: A case report and literature review. Brain Sciences. 2023;**13**(4):653. DOI: 10.3390/brainsci13040653

[12] Khizar A. Artificial intelligence and neurosurgery: A revolution in the field. Pakistan Journal of Neurological Sciences. 2023;**18**(4):Article 2. DOI: 10.56310/pjns.v18i04.244

[13] Satoh M, Nakajima T, Yamaguchi T, Watanabe E, Kawai K. Evaluation of

augmented-reality based navigation for brain tumor surgery. Journal of Clinical Neuroscience. 2021;**94**:305-314. DOI: 10.1016/j.jocn.2021.10.033

[14] Park JJ, Tiefenbach J, Demetriades AK. The role of artificial intelligence in surgical simulation. Frontiers in Medical Technology. 2022;**4**:1076755. DOI: 10.3389/fmedt.2022.1076755

[15] Cai S, Zhou Y, Shen J, Guo J, Xiong X, Jiang X. Augmented reality based surgical training and education system for neurosurgery. In: 2022 International Conference on Advanced Robotics and Mechatronics (ICARM). Piscataway, NJ, USA: IEEE; 2022

[16] Java MI, Hidayati SC, Sarno R, Anistyasari Y, Ali K, editors. Assisting neurosurgeons: Advancing brain tumor surgery with smartphone augmented reality navigation. In: 2024 International Conference on Innovation and Intelligence for Informatics, Computing, and Technologies (3ICT). Sakhir, Bahrain: IEEE; 2024

[17] Mezger U, Jendrewski C, Bartels M. Navigation in surgery. Langenbeck's Archives of Surgery. 2013;**398**(4):501-514. DOI: 10.1007/s00423-013-1059-4

[18] Solís ST, de Quintana SC, Sánchez JG, Portales IF, de Pedro MÁ, Berrocal VR, et al. Intraoperative imaging in the neurosurgery operating theatre: A review of the most commonly used techniques for brain tumour surgery. Neurocirugía (English Edition). 2020;**31**(4):184-194. DOI: 10.1016/j.neucir.2019.08.007

[19] Wirtz CR. Intraoperative navigation mit Fokus auf der Schädelbasis [intraoperative navigation, with focus on the skull base]. HNO. 2016;**64**(9):635-640. DOI: 10.1007/s00106-016-0215-x

[20] Van Gestel F, Frantz T, Buyck F, Geens W, Neuville Q, Bruneau M, et al. Neuro-oncological augmented reality planning for intracranial tumor resection. Frontiers in Neurology. 2023;**14**:1104571. DOI: 10.3389/fneur.2023.1104571

[21] Edwards PE, Chand M, Birlo M, Stoyanov D. The challenge of augmented reality in surgery. In: Digital Surgery. 2021. pp. 121-135. DOI: 10.1007/978-3-030-49100-0_10

[22] Azuma RT. A survey of augmented reality. Presence: Teleoperators and Virtual Environments. 1997;**6**(4):355-385. DOI: 10.1162/pres.1997.6.4.355

[23] Grimson WEL, Kikinis R, Jolesz FA, Black PM. Image-guided surgery. Scientific American. 1999;**280**(6):62-69. DOI: 10.1038/scientificamerican0699-62

[24] Incekara F, Smits M, Dirven C, Vincent A. Clinical feasibility of a wearable mixed-reality device in neurosurgery. World Neurosurgery. 2018;**118**:e422-e4e7. DOI: 10.1016/j.wneu.2018.06.208

[25] Li C-R, Chang Y-J, Lin M-S, Tsou H-K. Augmented reality in spine surgery: A case study of atlantoaxial instrumentation in Os odontoideum. Medicina (Kaunas, Lithuania). 2024;**60**(6):874. DOI: 10.3390/medicina60060874

[26] Tabrizi LB, Mahvash M. Augmented reality–guided neurosurgery: Accuracy and intraoperative application of an image projection technique. Journal of Neurosurgery. 2015;**123**(1):206-211. DOI: 10.3171/2014.9.JNS141001

[27] Huang CW, Lin MS, Tzeng CY, Chen TY, Tsou HK. The need for precise and accurate imaging navigation in cervical spine surgery for rheumatoid arthritis. International Journal of

Rheumatic Diseases. 2024;**27**(2):e15084. DOI: 10.1111/1756-185X.15084

[28] López WOC, Navarro PA, Crispin S. Intraoperative clinical application of augmented reality in neurosurgery: A systematic review. Clinical Neurology and Neurosurgery. 2019;**177**:6-11. DOI: 10.1016/j.clineuro.2018.11.018

[29] Yamazaki A, Ito T, Sugimoto M, Yoshida S, Honda K, Kawashima Y, et al. Patient-specific virtual and mixed reality for immersive, experiential anatomy education and for surgical planning in temporal bone surgery. Auris, Nasus, Larynx. 2021;**48**(6):1081-1091. DOI: 10.1016/j.anl.2021.03.009

[30] Moro C, Štromberga Z, Raikos A, Stirling A. The effectiveness of virtual and augmented reality in health sciences and medical anatomy. Anatomical Sciences Education. 2017;**10**(6):549-559. DOI: 10.1002/ase.1696

[31] Moawad GN, Elkhalil J, Klebanoff JS, Rahman S, Habib N, Alkatout I. Augmented realities, artificial intelligence, and machine learning: Clinical implications and how technology is shaping the future of medicine. Journal of Clinical Medicine. 2020;**9**(12):3811. DOI: 10.3390/jcm9123811

[32] Prabha N, Prasad N, Ziyad N, Abraham JP, Paul RT. Enhanced Medical Image Analysis: Leveraging 3D Visualization and VR-AR Technology. 2024. DOI: 10.21203/rs.3.rs-4219592/v1

[33] Neyem A, Cadile M, Burgos-Martínez SA, Farfán Cabello E, Inzunza O, Alvarado MS, et al. Enhancing medical anatomy education with the integration of virtual reality into traditional lab settings. Clinical Anatomy. 2024;**38**(3):249-268. DOI: 10.1002/ca.24213

[34] Lungu AJ, Swinkels W, Claesen L, Tu P, Egger J, Chen X. A review on the applications of virtual reality, augmented reality and mixed reality in surgical simulation: An extension to different kinds of surgery. Expert Review of Medical Devices. 2021;**18**(1):47-62. DOI: 10.1080/17434440.2021.1860750

[35] Elumalai G, Zainuddin FF, Abdullah NF, Sankaravel M, Abadi FH. Effectiveness of learning human anatomy using threedimensional augmented reality application. Fizjoterapia Polska. 2024;**24**(4):351-355. DOI: 10.56984/8zg01a8e6g2

[36] Murakami T, Tajika Y, Ueno H, Awata S, Hirasawa S, Sugimoto M, et al. An integrated teaching method of gross anatomy and computed tomography radiology. Anatomical Sciences Education. 2014;**7**(6):438-449. DOI: 10.1002/ase.1430

[37] Aloul Z, Colman S, El-Bahnasawi M, Abdulkader N, Rawaf D, Khalil M. SP1.14-advancing surgical education: A pilot study evaluating the impact of augmented reality in post-graduate surgical skill training. British Journal of Surgery. 2024;**111**(Suppl. 8): znae197.021. DOI: 10.1093/bjs/znae197.021

[38] Shahrezaei A, Sohani M, Taherkhani S, Zarghami SY. The impact of surgical simulation and training technologies on general surgery education. BMC Medical Education. 2024;**24**(1):1297. DOI: 10.1186/s12909-024-06299-w

[39] Huang C-W, Lee C-H, Chung K C, Tsuei Y-S. Feasibility and workflow analysis of IV-DSA-based augmented reality-guided brain arteriovenous malformation resection in a hybrid operating room: i-flow tailored method. Journal of NeuroInterventional

Surgery. 2025;**17**(3):332. DOI: 10.1136/jnis-2023-020797

[40] Costa F, Mazzapicchi E, Restelli F, Sebastiano DR, Cojazzi V, Innocenti N, et al. Sharpening skills: The role of virtual simulation in enhancing spinal neurosurgical proficiency. Preprint. 2024. DOI: 10.20944/preprints202409.0735.v1

[41] Kudry P, Cohen M. Enhanced wearable force-feedback mechanism for free-range haptic experience extended by pass-through mixed reality. Electronics. 2023;**12**(17):3659. DOI: 10.3390/electronics12173659

[42] Kudry P, Cohen M. Development of a wearable force-feedback mechanism for free-range haptic immersive experience. Frontiers in Virtual Reality. 2022;**3**:824886. DOI: 10.3389/frvir.2022.824886

[43] Tonutti M, Gras G, Yang G-Z. A machine learning approach for real-time modelling of tissue deformation in image-guided neurosurgery. Artificial Intelligence in Medicine. 2017;**80**:39-47. DOI: 10.1016/j.artmed.2017.07.004

[44] Tenajas R, Miraut D, Illana CI, Alonso-Gonzalez R, Arias-Valcayo F, Herraiz JL. Recent advances in artificial intelligence-assisted ultrasound scanning. Applied Sciences. 2023;**13**(6):3693

[45] Huang Q, Zeng Z. A review on real-time 3D ultrasound imaging technology. BioMed Research International. 2017;**2017**:6027029. DOI: 10.1155/2017/6027029

[46] Tokuda J, Fischer GS, Papademetris X, Yaniv Z, Ibanez L, Cheng P, et al. OpenIGTLink: An open network protocol for image-guided therapy environment. The International Journal of Medical Robotics and Computer Assisted Surgery. 2009;**5**(4):423-434. DOI: 10.1002/rcs.274

[47] Wang J, Shi R, Zheng W, Xie W, Kao D, Liang H-N. Effect of frame rate on user experience, performance, and simulator sickness in virtual reality. IEEE Transactions on Visualization and Computer Graphics. 2023;**29**(5):2478-2488. DOI: 10.1109/TVCG.2023.3247057

[48] Stein N, Niehorster DC, Watson T, Steinicke F, Rifai K, Wahl S, et al. A comparison of eye tracking latencies among several commercial head-mounted displays. Perception. 2021;**12**(1):2041669520983338. DOI: 10.1177/2041669520983

[49] Wisotzky EL, Rosenthal J-C, Meij S, van den Dobblesteen J, Arens P, Hilsmann A, et al. Telepresence for surgical assistance and training using eXtended reality during and after pandemic periods. Journal of Telemedicine and Telecare. 2025;**31**(1):14-28. DOI: 10.1177/1357633X231166226

[50] Cofano F, Di Perna G, Bozzaro M, Longo A, Marengo N, Zenga F, et al. Augmented reality in medical practice: From spine surgery to remote assistance. Frontiers in Surgery. 2021;**8**:657901. DOI: 10.3389/fsurg.2021.657901

[51] Wang P, Bai X, Billinghurst M, Zhang S, Zhang X, Wang S, et al. AR/MR remote collaboration on physical tasks: A review. Robotics and Computer-Integrated Manufacturing. 2021;**72**:102071. DOI: 10.1016/j.rcim.2020.102071

[52] Nathoo N, Çavuşoğlu MC, Vogelbaum MA, Barnett GH. In touch with robotics: Neurosurgery for the future. Neurosurgery.

2005;**56**(3):421-433. DOI: 10.1227/01.Neu.0000153929.68024.Cf

[53] Wagner CR, Phillips T, Roux S, Corrigan JP. Future directions in robotic neurosurgery. Operative Neurosurgery. 2021;**21**(4):173-180. DOI: 10.1093/ons/opab135

[54] Geng R, Li M, Hu Z, Han Z, Zheng R. Digital twin in smart manufacturing: Remote control and virtual machining using VR and AR technologies. Structural and Multidisciplinary Optimization. 2022;**65**(11). DOI: 10.1007/s00158-022-03426-3

[55] Dadario NB, Quinoa T, Khatri D, Boockvar J, Langer D, D'Amico RS. Examining the benefits of extended reality in neurosurgery: A systematic review. Journal of Clinical Neuroscience. 2021;**94**:41-53. DOI: 10.1016/j.jocn.2021.09.037

Chapter 9

Augmented Reality as a Tool for Improving Energy Efficiency in the Conservation of Heritage Buildings

Mihrimah Şenalp, Erdem Köymen and Enes Yaşa

Abstract

Conserving historic buildings is essential for transmitting cultural heritage to future generations, but achieving energy efficiency remains a significant challenge. Augmented Reality (AR) offers an innovative approach to conserving historic buildings by integrating energy efficiency improvements into building physics and restoration. AR supports decision-making by overlaying virtual elements onto physical environments, allowing real-time visualization of energy interventions and their impacts. In Human-Computer Interaction (HCI), AR aligns energy performance metrics with the physical realities of historical buildings, enabling pre-analysis of energy strategies to optimize performance while conserving building authenticity. This chapter systematically examines the role of AR in the energy performance and retrofit processes of historical buildings, using research from major databases. Additionally, analyses were interpreted and future studies suggested by Artificial Intelligence (AI). It highlights AR's potential to contribute to energy efficiency, offering a novel approach to the sustainable conservation of cultural heritage.

Keywords: augmented reality technology, energy efficiency, heritage building, integration of augmented reality, HBIM

1. Introduction

Rapid advances in modern information technology have created a strong demand for innovative human-computer interfaces. Unlike Virtual Reality (VR), which places users entirely within a digital world [1], Augmented Reality (AR) overlays digital elements onto the real environment, enhancing perception without isolating users from their surroundings [2]. Since the 2010s, AR's combination with VR and 3D reconstruction technologies has significantly broadened its applications. Despite these developments, substantial challenges remain, particularly in accurately modeling complex environments and achieving real-time mapping [3], technical implementation, screen-time management, and ensuring intuitive usability, all crucial for AR's long-term sustainability [4].

AR, accessed primarily through mobile apps or specialized glasses, has become widely adopted in presenting historical monuments to broader audiences [5].

IntechOpen

It promotes deeper engagement with architectural heritage by providing immersive, multisensory experiences involving sight, hearing, and touch [6]. Moreover, AR supports Building Information Modelling (BIM) by visually overlaying digitally stored building information directly onto physical settings [7]. Development of VR and AR technologies is necessary to utilize BIM models and datasets in areas such as operational training, technical tool development, and entertainment [8]. Importantly, AR and VR have been identified as highly beneficial tools for promoting public awareness and enhancing understanding of cultural heritage [9, 10]. These technologies effectively illustrate historical functions, architectural details, structural features, and traditional construction methods, thereby supporting informed restoration and conservation decisions [11].

Visitors can interact dynamically with historical buildings via AR's engaging and informative content, providing valuable context that enriches the visitor experience [12]. This interactivity especially benefits lesser-known heritage sites [13], creating emotional connections between visitors and cultural heritage [4, 14–16]. Furthermore, converting heritage data into Historical Building Information Modelling (HBIM) systems facilitates dynamic and extensive data collection. When made accessible as open-source platforms under appropriate legal frameworks, HBIM promotes wider use and collaboration among researchers and professionals [17]. AR plays a pivotal role in heritage conservation by improving maintenance processes and enabling more effective data sharing [18]. For instance, an AR system developed by Jalilzadehazhari and Kurkinen [19] revealed hidden structural elements, significantly reducing costs and time during energy renovation processes.

Additionally, AR enriches digital models with environmental data, supporting designers in optimizing building energy performance. By visualizing HBIM-derived energy data, AR raises awareness of historical buildings' energy performance and provides critical insights necessary for targeted improvements, ultimately promoting energy efficiency and sustainable environmental management [20]. Thus, AR uniquely bridges cultural heritage conservation with energy efficiency objectives, facilitating innovative solutions that respect historical authenticity. The following subsection outlines the objectives and scope of this study, defining the research questions and methodological approach guiding subsequent analyses.

1.1 Objectives and scope of the study

This subsection defines the role of AR technologies in improving energy efficiency in historical buildings while simultaneously preserving their cultural value. Specifically, it outlines how AR can practically contribute to reducing energy consumption and describes the methodologies that support these contributions. Energy consumption remains a critical challenge in buildings, particularly within historical structures where interventions must respect heritage authenticity. Monitoring energy usage, enhancing efficiency, and developing tailored energy-saving strategies are thus essential. However, historical buildings present unique constraints, often restricting interventions to non-destructive methods. Digital technologies, including AR and VR, are increasingly utilized as effective, non-invasive tools to address these limitations. This chapter systematically examines AR's potential for improving energy efficiency in historical buildings, exploring how AR technologies can be effectively applied to heritage contexts. It further highlights practical opportunities, identifies limitations, and provides detailed recommendations for future research directions. By defining theoretical objectives, practical applications, and methodological boundaries, this subsection establishes a framework that guides subsequent analyses. Following this clarification of the study's objectives, the next section will explore how AR technologies are specifically utilized within historical buildings, providing concrete examples of their practical implementation in cultural heritage contexts.

1.2 AR technologies in heritage buildings

AR technologies are increasingly being utilized in applications aimed at conserving and promoting cultural heritage. This subsection outlines AR's contributions to archival documentation, restoration processes, and interactive presentations of historical buildings, providing relevant examples and practical frameworks. AR's realistic visualization capabilities and user-friendly interfaces make it an especially valuable tool for effectively conserving and disseminating cultural heritage [21–23]. By overlaying virtual information onto physical environments, AR creates interactive experiences that surpass traditional static digital documentation methods [24]. This immersive quality is particularly valuable in interpreting architectural details, historical contexts, and spatial relationships within heritage sites [25].

AR integrates modern technological advances with historical contexts by overlaying cultural and architectural information onto real-world settings. Consequently, users can explore cities, neighborhoods, and individual historical buildings interactively and comprehensively [26–28]. Recent developments in wireless connectivity, sensor technology, and cloud computing have significantly popularized mobile AR, making it accessible and practical for educational purposes, digital preservation [29], and tourism activities [30, 31]. For instance, museum visitors' experiences are greatly enriched through AR's combination of historical data, architectural features, and past social contexts presented through engaging storytelling methods [32]. Moreover, AR uncovers structural details typically inaccessible during conventional visits, adding significant value to the visitor experience (**Figure 1**) [33, 34]. In sensitive historical areas, AR effectively helps manage visual impacts and public perception [35], while also expanding opportunities for cultural heritage promotion and related creative industries, such as gaming and educational platforms [36].

Figure 1.
Potential applications of AR [32].

Furthermore, AR can digitally reconstruct structures affected by natural disasters, fires, or wars [6, 37]. A notable example is the virtual tour created for Notre Dame Cathedral following a major fire, which provided visitors a meaningful experience while promoting energy conservation and reducing environmental impacts (**Figure 2**) [39]. AR-based solutions also maintain public access during situations such as pandemics, allowing continued engagement with heritage sites through digital means [40].

AR and VR technologies also significantly improve accessibility to cultural heritage, particularly for individuals with disabilities, elderly visitors [15], and younger audiences [41, 42]. Gamified AR scenarios and educational projects enable exploration of tangible and intangible heritage dimensions, creating engaging and meaningful learning pathways (**Figure 3**) [44]. Although some research notes hesitation among older users [45], broader evidence shows that connecting AR with VR creates effective ways to make heritage accessible, engaging, and comprehensible to diverse audiences [46]. AR cannot fully replace physical visits or direct human interactions, but it effectively enhances these experiences by seamlessly presenting digital information within the actual environment (**Figure 4**).

To summarize, AR enhances cultural heritage through interactive experiences and supports maintenance and restoration processes. The next subsection will explore its role in improving energy efficiency in historical buildings and its impact on energy conservation and sustainability. It should be emphasized that AR technology is not confined solely to visual elements but can also integrate auditory and multimodal layers (e.g., auralization), thereby offering a more immersive experience. This capability enables both the in-depth analysis of acoustic performance in historic buildings and the digital recreation of original auditory features, thus enhancing the overall heritage experience.

Figure 2.
Images from the Notre Dame virtual tour [38].

a) Learning from the audio
b) Storytelling
c) Landmarks details in town map

Figure 3.
Images related to the application developed by Dionisio and Nisi [43].

DOI: http://dx.doi.org/10.5772/intechopen.1011151

ealtime visualization

Questions about site

Figure 4.
Enhancing physical visits via AR [47].

1.3 Energy efficiency in heritage buildings

Historical buildings often cannot fully benefit from modern energy-saving solutions due to the critical need to conserve their original architectural character. This section evaluates both passive and active energy efficiency strategies, examining how these methods align with international standards and conservation principles. Energy performance in buildings involves optimizing energy use while minimizing environmental impacts (**Figure 5**). In historical structures, lower energy efficiency primarily results from poor insulation properties of traditional building materials and reliance on outdated mechanical systems. These issues not only elevate energy consumption but also create challenges in maintaining comfortable indoor temperatures. Given the necessity of preserving authenticity, energy efficiency measures must be carefully planned and implemented through non-invasive interventions.

Energy calculations with this system are performed according to the following equation system [48]:

Q_BSL= Q_Loss- Q_Gain

Q_Loss= Q_Component+ Q_Ventilation

Q_BSL= Building load

Q_Loss=Total heat loss rate

Q_Gain= Total heat gains excluding those from the HVAC system

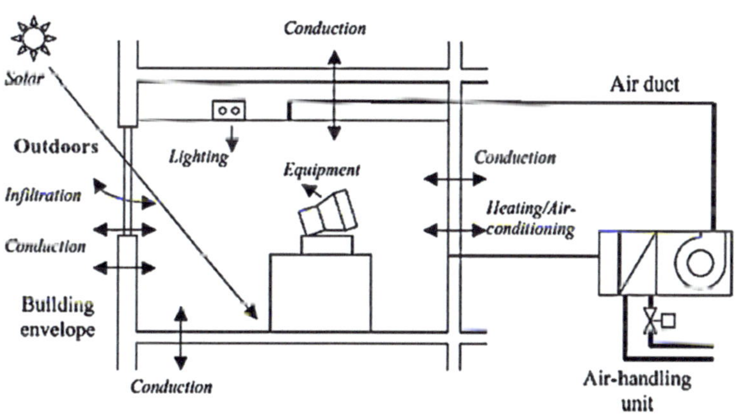

Figure 5.
Energy transmission process in HVAC-equipped buildings [48].

Q_Component= Heat loss due to building components (e.g.,walls,roof,etc.)
Q_Ventilation= Heat loss caused by the ventilation system

Energy improvements in historical buildings are guided by recognized international standards and frameworks (**Table 1**). Notably, EN 16883 [54] provides comprehensive guidelines for enhancing energy performance specifically in historic structures, while ASHRAE Guideline 34 [51] outlines essential technical criteria for balancing effective energy management with heritage conservation.

Improving energy efficiency usually begins with careful assessments of insulation strategies. Internal insulation methods, when meticulously applied with consideration to moisture management, significantly reduce heat loss [59].

In addition to insulation, passive design approaches play a critical role. Utilizing the inherent thermal mass of historic building material [60], improving natural ventilation [61], employing low-reflectivity glazing, using customizable panel colors [62], and applying shading techniques all contribute to stable indoor temperatures and reduced energy demands. These passive strategies complement active energy solutions, including advanced HVAC systems and renewable technologies like photovoltaic [63] and geothermal energy systems [64]. Accurate energy performance simulations using software tools such as EnergyPlus [65], DesignBuilder [48], and Computational Fluid Dynamics (CFD) models [66] facilitate precise predictions and optimization of energy strategies. Historical buildings, however, typically exhibit greater energy losses and air leakages compared to contemporary constructions, highlighting the necessity of targeted interventions.

Considering these challenges, digital modeling tools like HBIM and AR emerge as essential instruments to support and effectively implement energy improvements. The next subsection examines how HBIM and AR are utilized together, creating solutions that enhance cultural heritage conservation while achieving sustainable energy management.

1.4 Historical building information modelling (HBIM) enhanced by augmented reality (AR)

Historical Building Information Modelling (HBIM) involves digitizing historical buildings into detailed databases, whereas AR projects this digital data directly in the

Standard	Content
ASHRAE 90.1 [49]	Baseline energy-efficiency requirements for buildings
ASHRAE 100 [50]	Comprehensive criteria for enhancing energy efficiency in existing buildings, including historical buildings
ASHRAE Guideline 34 [51]	Technical framework for energy retrofitting of historic buildings, balancing comfort, efficiency, and heritage authenticity
ISO 16813 [52]	Principles for healthy indoor environments and energy-efficient design
ISO 52016-1 [53]	Calculation methods for assessing building energy performance
EN 16883 [54]	Guidance for indoor health and energy efficiency in heritage contexts
EN 16247 [55]	Procedures for conducting building energy audits
BS 7913 [56]	Guidelines for energy upgrades without compromising heritage values
EN 16798-2 [57]	Performance and comfort optimization in naturally ventilated historic buildings
EN 15217 [58]	Methodology for energy-performance certification systems

Table 1.
Standards related to energy performance in historical buildings.

field to support decision-making processes. This section explores how combining HBIM and AR technologies enhances efforts in heritage conservation and energy efficiency. Building Information Modelling (BIM) effectively manages all stages of building lifecycle processes from initial planning and operation to ongoing maintenance and restoration [67]. BIM further provides sophisticated simulation and analysis tools for informed decision-making regarding building performance, sustainability, and energy efficiency.

When combined with BIM, Common Data Environments (CDE) centralize data storage, ensuring coordinated management of extensive model-based information and improving data quality [68]. HBIM specifically adapts standard BIM methodologies to historical buildings, creating detailed digital models derived from point cloud data, centralizing cultural heritage documentation, and facilitating interdisciplinary collaboration [69]. Since its introduction in 2009, HBIM has significantly advanced heritage documentation by merging traditional paper-based data with modern digital approaches, becoming an indispensable tool in heritage conservation practices (**Figure 6**) [71]. However, complex geometries, limited accessibility, and large volumes of heterogeneous data characteristic of historical structures pose significant challenges for precise measurement and digital representation. Although laser scanning and photogrammetry provide detailed documentation [72], harmonizing parametric objects into HBIM remains challenging, often necessitating middleware platforms, possibly enhanced by artificial intelligence (AI), to accelerate accurate model creation and customization [73, 74].

Given the unique features of historical buildings, HBIM models must include customized parametric elements and function as digital twins, storing semantic data on accessible digital platforms [71]. Such comprehensive digitalization enables widespread access and utilization among heritage professionals, accelerating documentation and analysis processes. Digital twin (DT) methodology involves constructing a continuously updated virtual counterpart of a physical structure, enabling real-time monitoring, analysis, and predictive simulation in virtual environments (**Figures 7** and **8**). Urban digital twin (UDT) technology extends this concept to entire urban areas, providing harmonized models for analyzing and managing urban heritage contexts.

Beyond restoration, HBIM supports heritage management through digital documentation, planning [77], pathology analysis, scenario simulations, and archaeological site digitization. Connecting HBIM with Geographic Information Systems (GIS), VR/AR, and academic research further enhances heritage conservation and public awareness [73, 78]. Additionally, AR-integrated drone systems enhance BIM model creation by capturing accurate structural data from difficult-to-access areas (**Figure 9**). HBIM also enables detailed energy analyses and thematic evaluations [80], such as integrating photovoltaic systems into historical contexts (**Figure 10**) [81].

Although visualization is not HBIM's primary function, connecting its detailed 3D models with VR, Mixed Reality (MR), and AR enables immersive virtual tours and efficient information dissemination (**Figure 11**) [82, 83]. The HBIM–AR combination

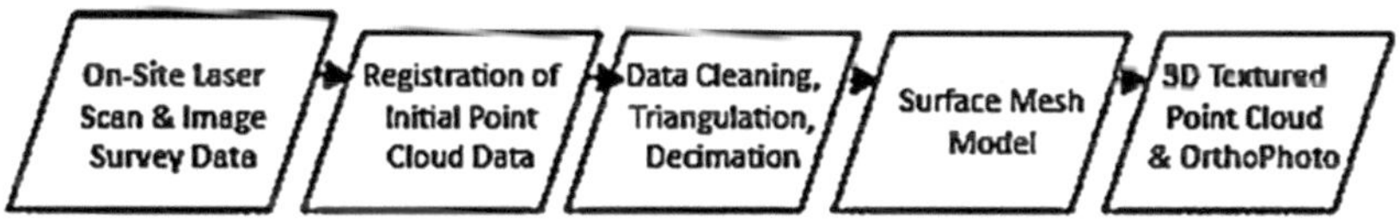

Figure 6.
HBIM creation process [70].

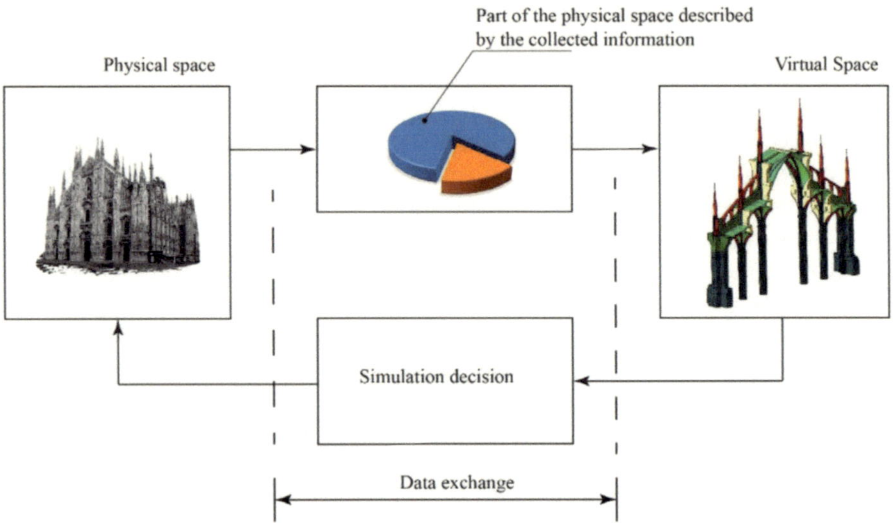

Figure 7.
Schematic representation of digital twin application [75].

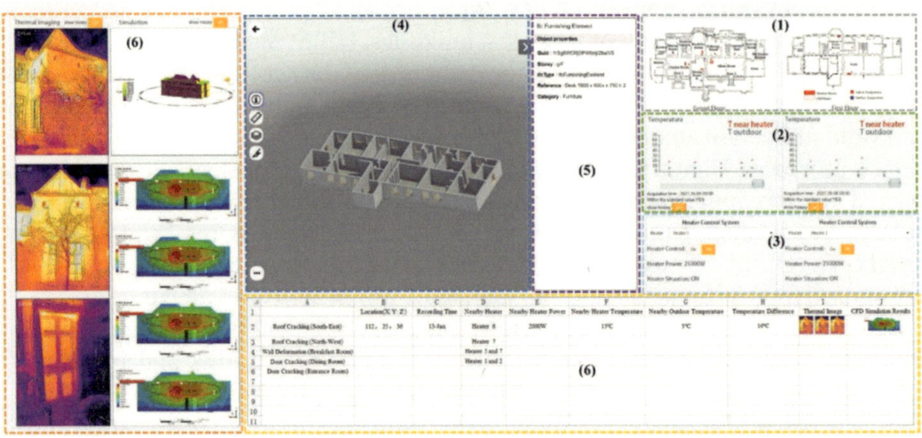

Figure 8.
The digital twin platform developed for improving thermal performance serves as an example [76].

notably improves cultural heritage accessibility [84, 85], facilitating temporal visualizations and incorporating realistic environmental factors such as sun position and shadows for enhanced realism (**Figure 12**) [87].

AR proves especially valuable for digitizing artwork [88], archaeological documentation through photogrammetry [86, 89], and remote visualization of structural deteriorations, greatly benefiting research and conservation [47, 90, 91]. Overlaying digital models onto physical structures, AR identifies problematic areas, suggests restoration solutions [92], and allows users to virtually experience partially destroyed or intangible heritage elements, thereby enriching the understanding of historical contexts [93–95]. AR also supports investigating and reviving acoustic heritage, as demonstrated in Notre Dame Cathedral, combining visual aesthetics with historically accurate soundscapes to enhance cultural heritage dissemination [96].

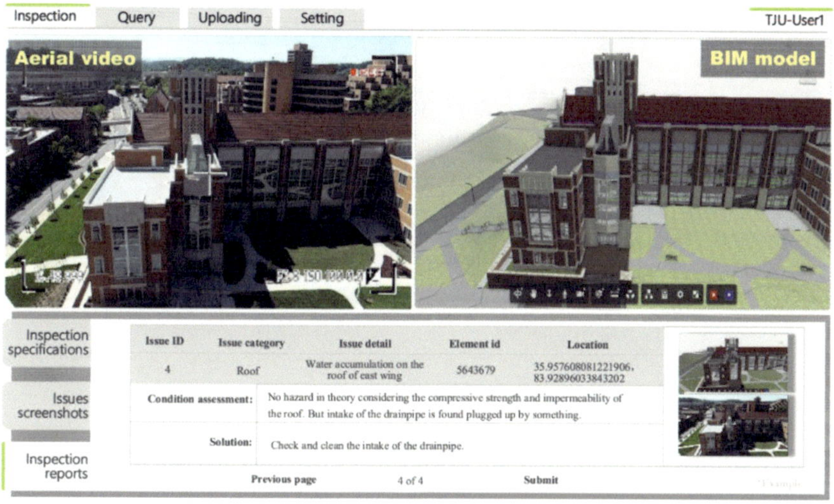

Figure 9.
An example of an AR-integrated drone system [79].

Figure 10.
HBIM model developed for building-integrated photovoltaics (BIPV) [81].

Figure 11.
The AR browsing application captures the scene, identifies artifacts, and adds an interaction button to each [16].

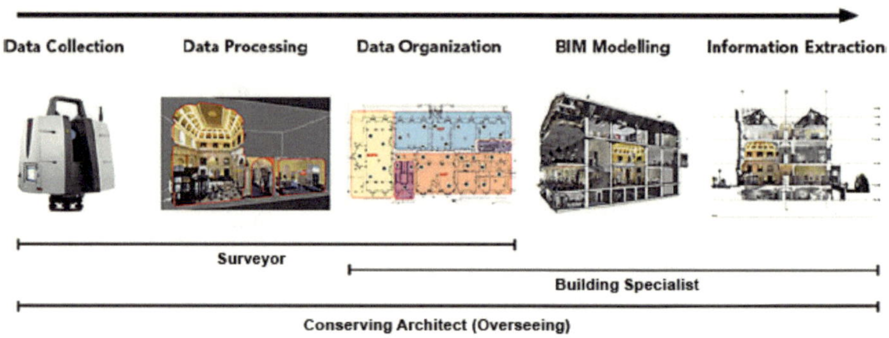

Figure 12.
AR implementation process for historical buildings [86].

Despite these advancements, challenges remain regarding accurately capturing complex geometries, synthesizing semantic data, and managing extensive datasets (**Figure 13**). Addressing these issues requires interdisciplinary collaboration, standardized HBIM methodologies, AI-supported middleware solutions, and improved data-sharing mechanisms.

By combining detailed digital documentation with immersive AR visualization, the HBIM–AR connection provides innovative, efficient, and engaging heritage conservation solutions that balance authenticity and contemporary needs (**Figures 14–16**). Thus, harmonizing HBIM and AR establishes a comprehensive framework for conserving historical buildings and optimizing their energy performance.

Digital technologies increasingly support energy efficiency strategies (e.g., insulation, natural ventilation, HVAC, and renewable energy) in historical buildings. HBIM and AR simplify data collection, analysis, and interventions in buildings with complex geometries and strict conservation requirements. Real-time monitoring

Figure 13.
A screenshot of the application running on a tablet with IR (infrared) thermography, as viewed by users [97].

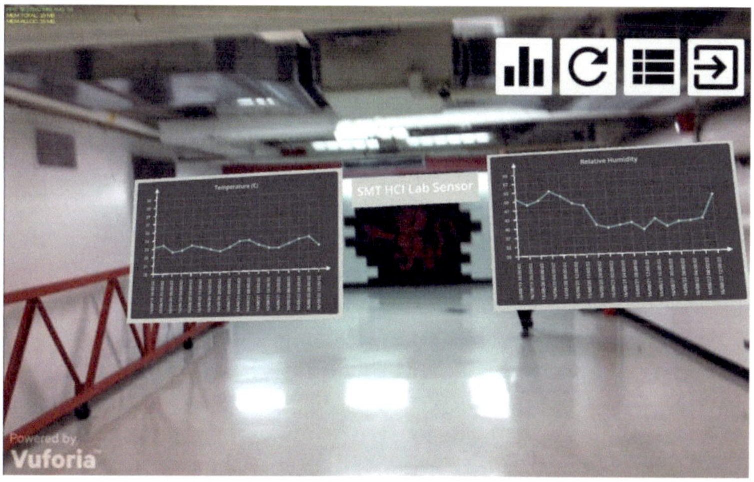

Figure 14.
Temperature and relative humidity AR image for modern building [98].

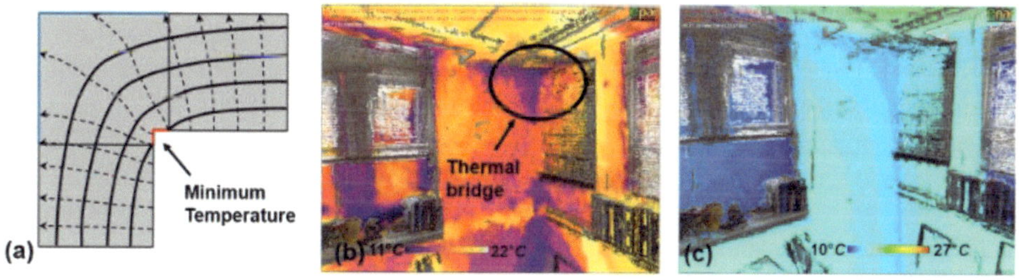

Figure 15.
Image of developed energy performance augmented reality (EPAR) environment: (a) Schematic representation of a thermal bridge at an interior corner of the building environment, (b) Visualization of the thermal bridge in the 3D thermal mesh model, and (c) VRML-based (virtual reality modelling language) CFD model of the same area [99].

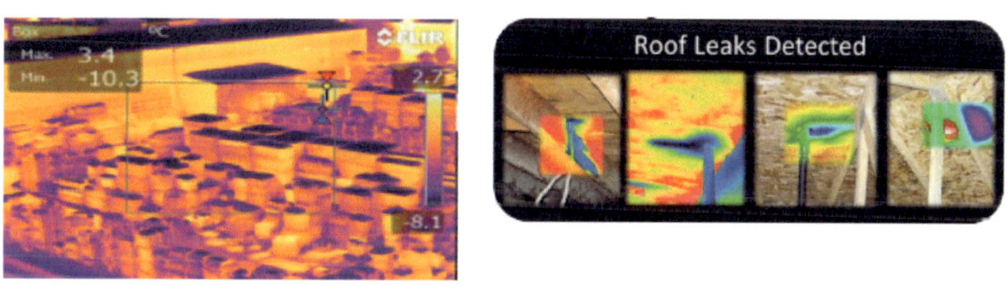

Example of temperature visualization

Example of leak visualization

Figure 16.
AR-integrated IR technology [100]

using digital twins enables the simultaneous achievement of heritage conservation and energy efficiency goals. The following sections will explore case studies to demonstrate the effectiveness of the HBIM and AR combination, guiding future research and establishing best practices.

2. Research methodology

This chapter reviews applications of AR for enhancing energy performance in historical buildings and employs bibliometric analysis to identify key trends and research gaps. The research methodology comprises three primary components: bibliometric analysis, a detailed literature review, and AI-supported identification of interdisciplinary connections. Initially, a comprehensive search was conducted across scientific databases—including Springer, ScienceDirect, Web of Science, and Scopus—for publications containing relevant terms such as "Historic Building," "Historical Building," "Built Heritage," "Energy Efficiency," "Augmented Reality (AR)," and "Human Computer Interaction (HCI)" in titles, abstracts, or keywords. These keywords represent core aspects of this research, specifically addressing historical buildings, energy efficiency, and AR technology applications. Although no time restrictions were applied, the majority of relevant studies date from 2010 onwards, reflecting the novelty of the research topic. All identified studies underwent thorough analysis, and irrelevant or duplicate studies were systematically excluded.

The research process began with a bibliometric analysis using VOSviewer software. This analysis visualized keyword co-occurrences to identify frequently studied topics, emerging research themes, and existing gaps. Findings from this step provided an overview of current research dynamics, clarifying areas that require further investigation. The subsequent literature review phase involved an in-depth evaluation of selected publications, examining AR techniques, simulation methodologies, and their specific applications within historical building contexts. This stage critically assessed how AR has been implemented in heritage conservation, energy efficiency assessments, and restoration processes. Additionally, it identified the technical and practical challenges associated with AR adoption, including data accuracy issues, compatibility with existing BIM systems, and other technological constraints.

Considering the emerging nature of this field, an AI-supported analysis further refined the review. Advanced analytical methods identified interdisciplinary connections, highlighted overlapping research contexts, and uncovered additional perspectives. AI analysis particularly helped understand interactions between AR applications, HBIM, energy simulation tools, and sustainability assessments. This step was crucial for recognizing potential synergies between AR technology and energy optimization strategies, providing new perspectives into understudied areas, and highlighting potential directions for future research.

Throughout this structured methodological approach, perspectives extracted from literature review, bibliometric analysis, and AI-supported analyses were systematically documented. These insights informed the subsequent discussion section (Subsection 3.3), structuring a connected narrative on the role and potential of AR within heritage conservation and energy efficiency strategies. By adopting this rigorous and structured research methodology, the chapter assesses existing literature, defines research objectives, and establishes robust suggestions for future investigations.

3. Literature review

3.1 Bibliometric analysis

Initially, a total of 433 papers were identified. After a careful screening process, 420 were excluded due to duplication, methodological limitations, or irrelevance.

Among the 13 studies remaining, three directly addressed AR applications in energy analysis within historical buildings. The other ten provided energy-related discussions and recommendations without direct analytical content. These studies, including nine journal articles, three conference papers, and one book chapter, formed the basis for the literature review.

The co-occurrence of keywords in publications was analyzed using the VOSviewer tool (**Figure 17**). A total of 88 keywords were identified based on indexed keywords. The network graph was created considering keywords that appeared at least once and those with a minimum of two occurrences: frequently used keywords are represented by larger circles, and connection strength is indicated by line thickness. The analysis revealed a high frequency of terms such as "point cloud," "augmented reality," and "BIM" alongside keywords like "energy assessment," "3D data processing," "artificial intelligence," "heritage building," and "laser scanning." Studies have primarily been conducted since 2018, with most research originating in Italy, followed by China. A co-authorship analysis using VOSviewer identified 55 authors mentioned in articles, with 16 connections detected when a minimum of one article per author was set.

In summary, the bibliometric analysis indicates that the use of AR in the context of energy performance in historical buildings is still a nascent field, yet research in this area has begun. The findings of this analysis reveal that studies in this domain are often conducted in conjunction with HBIM, incorporating laser scanning and AI technologies. Bibliometric analyses have highlighted trends and identified gaps, showing that AR-based energy efficiency research in historical buildings remains limited. Accordingly, the next section will relate the findings derived from the literature to the primary objective of this study, providing an evaluation of the potential of AR technology to enhance energy performance in historical buildings.

3.2 AR in historical buildings according to energy efficiency

Integrating digital technologies, especially AR, is effective for visualizing thermal optimization outcomes, enabling informed decisions in design and heritage

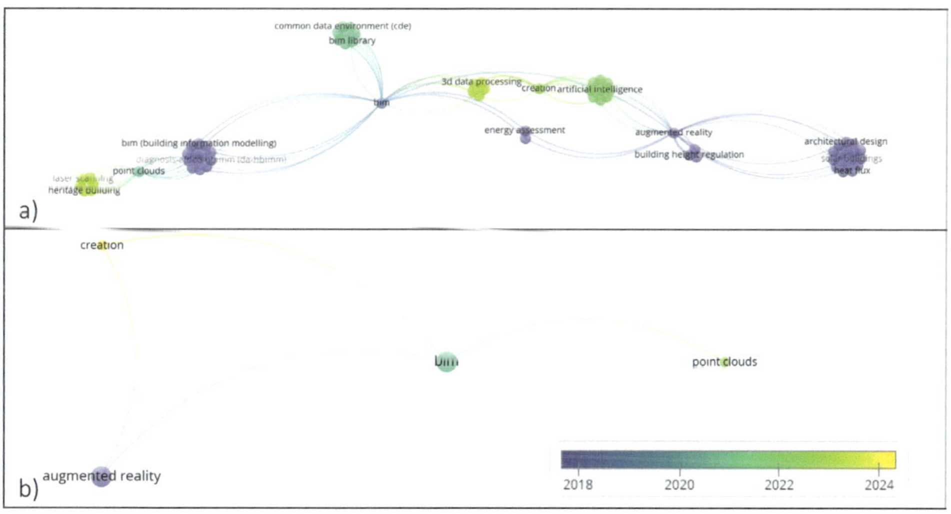

Figure 17.
Keyword analysis (a) Co-occurrence count = 1 (b) Co-occurrence count = 2.

conservation [101]. Creating digital twins of historical sites combined with AR enhances user engagement and comprehension [102], notably when visualizing energy simulations and resource efficiency measures through connected HBIM–AR models [39, 101]. Such technologies offer real-time insights into building conditions, significantly aiding sustainability and long-term heritage conservation goals [8].

Beyond analyzing energy interventions, AR offers a highly interactive way to communicate how proposed construction or infrastructure projects may affect historical sites [103]. Its capability to visualize sensor-generated data simplifies building performance assessments and enhances sustainability training [98]. Combined BIM-based platforms with real-time sensor data support AR applications across scales, from individual buildings to extensive archaeological sites, ensuring effective monitoring and energy management (**Figure 18**) [104].

AR significantly contributes to energy performance analysis in historical buildings, particularly through integrating renewable energy systems and increasing user awareness of sustainability, aligning heritage conservation with digitalization. Several studies exemplify these capabilities. Adán et al. [105] explored AR combination with thermal point cloud technologies, while Alazmi and Seo [106] examined AR's visualization potential for temperature analysis in historic contexts. Alva et al. [107] developed urban-scale AR applications that facilitate significant energy savings through optimized LED lighting and solar panel integration, modernizing the energy systems of historical buildings without compromising their heritage value. Additionally, Digital Twin (DT) and Urban Digital Twin (UDT) methods enable the identification of buildings with high carbon emissions, optimizing maintenance cycles, and supporting energy system upgrades while preserving cultural heritage (**Figure 19**).

Osello et al. [108] combined integrated multiple models (architectural, structural, mechanical, electrical, and HVAC) using Autodesk Revit, complete with sensor modules for real-time monitoring of temperature, humidity, and lighting. Exporting the model in FBX due to geometric complexity, they created a virtual environment

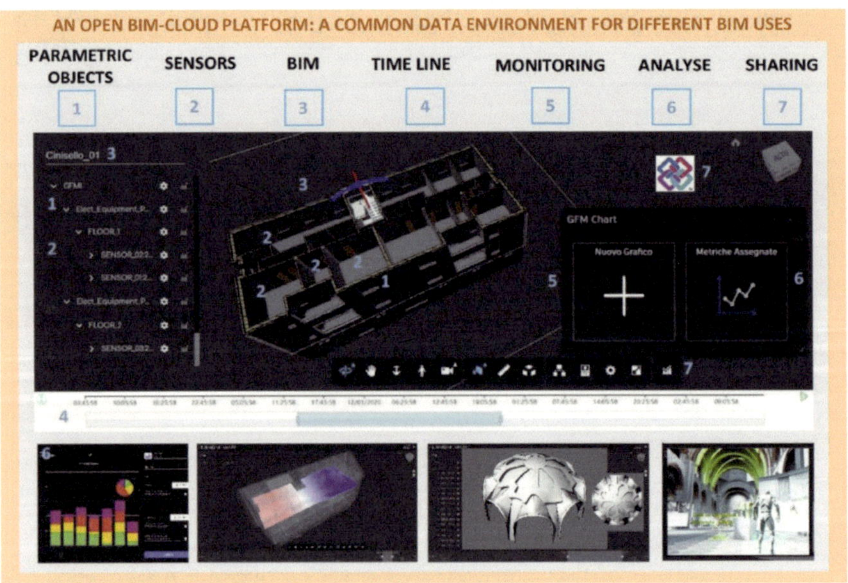

Figure 18.
Methodologic workflow from Brumana, Stanga, and Banfi [104].

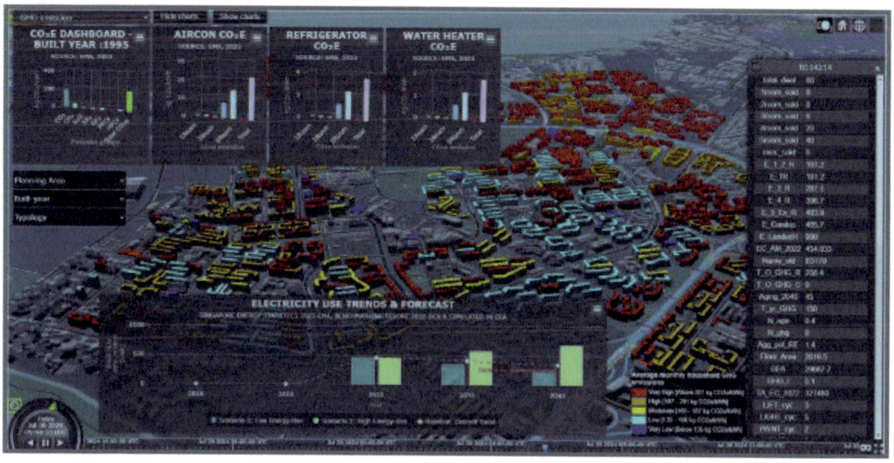

Figure 19.
Data visualizations from Alva et al. [107].

accessible via an AR-enabled Android app: scanning a simple QR code allowed users to navigate 3D data effectively (**Figure 20**). Antonelli et al. [109] conducted experiments and introduced a 5G-based AR system at L'Aquila University, optimizing energy consumption and improving structural monitoring alongside disaster management in heritage contexts.

Upon examining these case studies, considerable variations emerge in methodologies, software tools, and evaluated parameters (**Table 2**). Despite these differences, each case highlights AR's adaptability and significant potential to connect energy efficiency strategies effectively within heritage conservation practices. **Table 2**

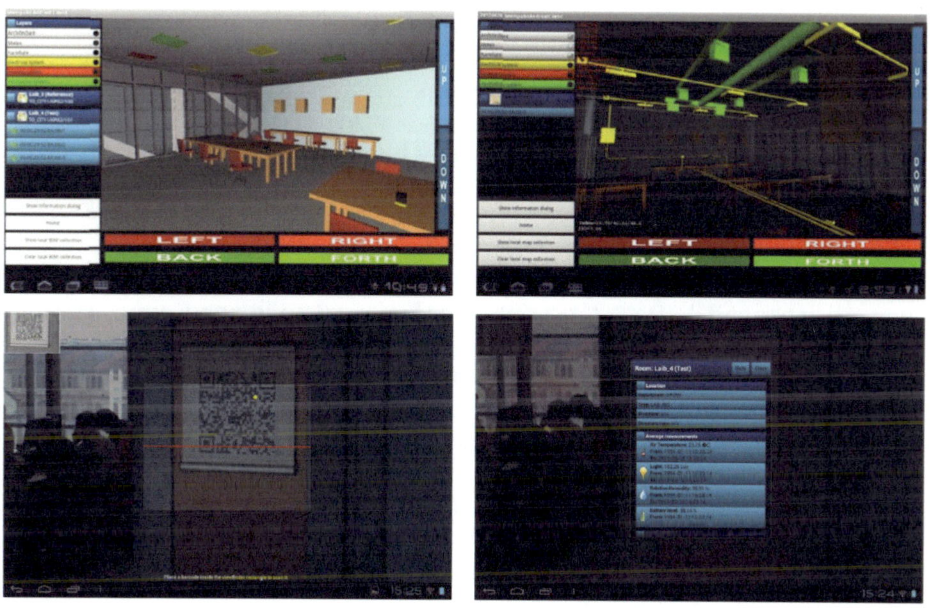

Figure 20.
Images from the application developed by Osello et al. [108].

	Evaluation standard	Parameters	Software	Country	Subject
Alva et al. [107]	CIBSE tm65	GHG Emissions, Energy Usage	City Energy Analyst (CEA), QGIS	Singapore	Urban Digital Twins (UDT)
Osello et al. [108]	COBIE (Construction Operations Building Information Exchange)	Disaster Management, Energy Optimization, Facility Management, Seismic	Autodesk Revit, EnergyPlus, Green Building Studio, Design Builder, Navisworks, MS Project, and SQL Server	Italy	Multifaceted Approach to Historical Buildings
Antonelli et al. [109]	3GPP, ITU, IEEE, QoS	Structural Monitoring of Buildings, Building Automation, Information and Communication Technologies	MATLAB, NS-3 (Network Simulator 3), OpenAirInterface (OAI), FlexRAN,	Italy	Multifaceted Approach to Historical Buildings

Table 2.
Analysis of review articles.

summarizes these diverse approaches, indicating measured parameters and employed software platforms. This analysis provides a foundation for identifying best practices and outlining future research directions. The next subsection further develops research suggestions derived from insights gathered through reviewing existing studies in this evolving field.

3.3 Exploring the interconnections between studies in the context of research

This subsection details the significant suggestions identified in the literature, emphasizing AR technology's potential for improving energy performance in historical buildings. Using AI-supported analyses, key interdisciplinary intersections, trends, and methodological overlaps in existing literature have been summarized. The resulting research suggestions provide practical strategies and illustrative scenarios, beneficial for both technical teams and restoration specialists involved in heritage conservation and energy performance optimization (**Table 3**).

These suggestions demonstrate AR technology's substantial potential to enhance energy efficiency and heritage conservation in historical buildings. Connecting AR with BIM and digital twin methodologies enables real-time collaboration, remote operation capabilities, and efficient data sharing, supported by platforms like Autodesk BIM 360, Microsoft HoloLens, and Unity Reflect. Specifically, AR visualization capabilities enhance rapid identification of energy inefficiencies, enabling targeted interventions and informed decision-making [105, 108].

Digital twin and HBIM connections within AR environments allow virtual evaluation of potential improvements, optimizing strategies for heritage conservation and energy efficiency [85, 107]. Similarly, passive and active energy solutions benefit significantly from AR simulations, facilitating informed planning decisions for strategies such as natural ventilation, insulation improvements, solar panel installation, and geothermal systems connection [60, 61]. Similarly, in active energy solutions,

Topic	Description	Proposed method	Example application scenarios	Ref.
Visualization and decision support	AR visualization of energy losses (heat, humidity, temperature)	AR-based sensor data visualization and pre-assessment of energy strategies	Thermal imagery overlays on façades highlighting insulation deficiencies	[105, 108]
Digital twin and HBIM connections	Virtual models enabling energy simulations via digital twins and HBIM	Integration of digital twins with AR for virtual performance testing	Virtual testing of double-glazed windows and insulation in AR environments to identify optimal energy efficiency solutions	[85, 107]
Passive energy solutions	Natural ventilation, thermal mass, and optimized sunlight utilization	AR simulations visualizing the effects of passive design strategies	AR testing of window positioning, shading, and ventilation strategies for comfort	[60, 61]
Active energy solutions	Renewable energy systems and efficient HVAC technologies	AR-supported simulations optimizing renewable and active energy systems	AR simulation of solar panel and geothermal system placement on heritage roofs	[62, 63]
Data collection and analysis	Real-time sensor data collection and AR visualization	AR-based interactive visualization integrated with energy management algorithms	Interactive AR display of temperature, humidity, and CO_2 levels for adaptive control	[108, 109]
simulation and testing	Pre-restoration AR simulations of energy improvement strategies	AR-based evaluation of insulation and retrofitting interventions	Virtual restoration planning tests insulation types without heritage damage	[14, 106]
Education and awareness	AR modules illustrating sustainable practices for teams and visitors	Interactive AR storytelling highlighting energy efficiency solutions	Heritage site AR tours enhancing understanding of sustainable practices	[2, 110]
Cultural heritage and restoration support	AR-supported planning of energy enhancements preserving architectural integrity	AR simulations for discrete insulation solutions	Restoration teams using AR to plan low-impact insulation on heritage structures	[85, 86]
Renewable energy integration	Optimization of renewable energy integration (solar, geothermal)	AR-based simulation balancing renewable integration with aesthetic conservation	AR virtual placement of solar panels on heritage roofs, optimizing energy yield	[63, 107]
Visitor experience and education	AR-enhanced experiences to learn about historical building energy systems	AR-supported interactive storytelling and educational modules	Visitors exploring energy consumption and sustainability via AR tours	[6, 29]
Social potential	Real-time collaboration via AR combined with BIM and digital twins	AR applications enabling stakeholder visualization of interventions	Stakeholders using AR HBIM overlays for collaborative restoration planning	[26, 102]

Table 3.
Research topics for energy solutions with AR in historical buildings.

AR-supported simulations facilitate evaluation of renewable energy systems and HVAC configurations; for example, by virtually testing various solar panel layouts to assess both energy production and architectural compatibility [62, 63]. In data collection and analysis, AR significantly simplifies real-time visualization of sensor measurements, facilitating immediate response and adaptive energy management [108, 109]. Furthermore, AR-based simulation tools enable the pre-assessment of different insulation or retrofitting scenarios to ensure optimal intervention strategies [14, 106].

AR also enhances education and public awareness by providing interactive educational experiences on sustainability within historical contexts [2, 110]. Moreover, AR applications effectively support restoration efforts by allowing non-invasive visualization of energy efficiency measures, ensuring heritage unity and aesthetic compatibility [85, 86]. AR-based simulations also help assess the suitability of renewable energy systems, such as solar panels, ensuring their combination does not detract from the building's historic appearance [63, 107].

Finally, AR significantly enriches visitor experiences, improving public understanding of historical building sustainability through engaging storytelling, interactive scenarios, and detailed energy simulations [6, 29]. Additionally, AR connection with BIM and digital twins promotes effective stakeholder collaboration and broader community engagement with cultural heritage conservation [26, 102]. These expanded suggestions thus provide a detailed framework for future research and practical implementation, maximizing AR's potential in conserving historical authenticity and promoting sustainable energy management.

4. Conclusion

AR technology is increasingly recognized as a valuable tool for digital documentation and the conservation of historical buildings. Although AR applications in building physics and detailed implementation strategies are still evolving, current capabilities already extend beyond basic visualization. Specifically, AR can display real-time thermal performance maps, air quality indicators, and energy consumption data. These features facilitate pre-evaluation of energy-saving interventions, such as insulation improvements or window retrofitting, thereby supporting sustainable energy optimization while conserving architectural authenticity. Combining AR with digital twins and HBIM further improves the accuracy of historical building analysis and restoration processes. Using AR alongside thermal imaging and sensors helps precisely detect energy losses and monitor environmental conditions within heritage structures. Additionally, AR-equipped drone systems effectively map thermal data onto 3D building models, enhancing the accessibility and comprehensiveness of energy assessments.

Within the scope of this study, the relationship between AR and historical buildings is defined, focusing specifically on research evaluating and enhancing energy performance—an area currently underexplored yet holding significant potential for both research and practical applications. Subsequently, all reviewed studies are analyzed to identify their connections with AI, from which research topics are developed, and suggestions for future studies are proposed.

Despite promising developments, the use of AR to enhance energy efficiency in historical buildings remains limited in existing research. Digital methods allowing minimally invasive data collection are essential for identifying optimal energy strategies compatible with heritage conservation. Moreover, AR-based visualizations can significantly improve the aesthetic compatibility of renewable energy solutions, aligning conservation objectives with sustainability standards, such as Net Zero Energy Building (NZEB) guidelines. Advances in mobile and pervasive computing have expanded AR's applications in cultural heritage. Yet, research into lightweight, energy-efficient AR solutions remains underexplored. Future research should emphasize developing energy-conscious AR applications, advanced sensor-fusion techniques, and AI-supported analytics capable of automatically detecting issues and suggesting improvements, for instance, recommending insulation when detecting heat loss. Standardizing AR data-sharing practices across interdisciplinary teams would further streamline workflows. Additionally, creating engaging AR experiences dedicated to sustainability education could effectively enhance public awareness of energy-efficient heritage conservation practices.

In summary, AR technology holds considerable promise for improving energy efficiency and ensuring the sustainable management of historical buildings while maintaining cultural authenticity. Continued research, especially into AR's connections with digital twins, HBIM, and artificial intelligence, will yield deeper insights, strengthening heritage conservation efforts and expanding the impact of sustainability within cultural heritage management.

Acknowledgements

In preparing this work, the authors utilized OpenAI's ChatGPT-4 to review the text, perform literature searches, and enhance its structure. The final version of the publication was reviewed and edited by the authors, who assumed full responsibility for its content.

A.Appendix

AI	artificial intelligence
AR	augmented reality
BIM	building information modeling
BIPV	building-integrated photovoltaics
CDE	common data environment
CFD	computational fluid dynamics
DT	digital twin
GHG	greenhouse gas
GIS	geographic information system
HBIM	historic building information modelling
HCI	human-computer interaction
HVAC	heating, ventilation, and air-conditioning
IR	infrared
MR	mixed reality
NZEB	net zero energy building
UDT	urban digital twin
VR	virtual reality

Author details

Mihrimah Şenalp[1*], Erdem Köymen[2] and Enes Yaşa[3]

1 Faculty of Design and Architecture, Konya Technical University, Konya, Turkiye

2 Faculty of Engineering and Natural Sciences, Istanbul Sabahattin Zaim University, Istanbul, Turkiye

3 Faculty of Architecture, Istanbul Technical University, Istanbul, Turkiye

*Address all correspondence to: msenalp@ktun.edu.tr

References

[1] van Lopik K, Sinclair M, Sharpe R, Conway P, West A. Developing augmented reality capabilities for industry 4.0 small enterprises: Lessons learnt from a content authoring case study. Computers in Industry. 2020;**117**:103208. DOI: 10.1016/j.compind.2020.103208

[2] Li X, Yi W, Chi H-L, Wang X, Chan AP. A critical review of virtual and augmented reality (VR/AR) applications in construction safety. Automation in Construction. 2018;**86**:150-162. DOI: 10.1016/j.autcon.2017.11.003

[3] Lu Y, Wang S, Fan S, Lu J, Li P, Tang P. Image-based 3D reconstruction for Multi-Scale civil and infrastructure Projects: A review from 2012 to 2022 with new perspective from deep learning methods. Advanced Engineering Informatics. 2024;**59**:102268. DOI: 10.1016/j.aei.2023.102268

[4] Ramtohul A, Khedo KK. Augmented reality systems in the cultural heritage domains: A systematic review. Digital Applications in Archaeology and Cultural Heritage. 2024;**32**:1-23. DOI: 10.1016/j.daach.2024.e00317

[5] Tira Y, Türkoğlu H. Circularity-based decision-making framework for the integrated conservation of built heritage: the case of the Medina of Tunis. Built Heritage. 2023;**7**(1):16. DOI: 10.1186/s43238-023-00093-1

[6] Li Y, Du Y, Yang M, Liang J, Bai H, Li R, et al. A review of the tools and techniques used in the digital preservation of architectural heritage within disaster cycles. Heritage Science. 2023;**11**(1):199. DOI: 10.1186/s40494-023-01035-x

[7] Dinis FM, Poças Martins J, Rangel B, Guimarães AS, Soeiro A. Extending access to BIM information: Merging augmented reality interfaces and semantic enrichment. In: New Advances in Building Information Modeling and Engineering Management. Cham: Springer; 2023. pp. 17-29. DOI: 10.1007/978-3-031-30247-3_2

[8] Bruno S, De Fino M, Fatiguso F. Historic Building Information Modelling: performance assessment for diagnosis-aided information modelling and management. Automation in Construction. 2018;**86**:256-276. DOI: 10.1016/j.autcon.2017.11.009

[9] Yan W, Culp C, Graf R. Integrating BIM and gaming for real-time interactive architectural visualization. Automation in Construction. 2011;**20**(4):446-458. DOI: 10.1016/j.autcon.2010.11.013

[10] Zarrabi M, Valibeig N. 3D modelling of an Asbad (Persian windmill): a link between vernacular architecture and mechanical system with a focus on Nehbandan windmill. Heritage Science. 2021;**9**:1-11. DOI: 10.1186/s40494-021-00587-0

[11] Masini N, Sileo M, Leucci G, Soldovieri F, D'Antonio A, de Giorgi L, et al. Integrated in situ investigations for the restoration: the case of regio VIII in Pompeii. In: Sensing the Past: From Artifact to Historical Site. 2017. pp. 557-586. DOI: 10.1007/978-3-319-50518-3_29

[12] Meriem K, Makram M, Farah IR. Virtual and augmented reality in the valuation of the Tunisian cultural heritage: Application to Thysdrus (ElJem) Amphitheater. In: 2018 International Conference on Intelligent

Systems (IS). Portugal: IEEE; 2018. DOI: 10.1109/IS.2018.8710529

[13] Cigola M, Gallozzi A, Gargaro S, Paris L, Strollo RM. Information and communication technology (ICT) for built cultural heritage. In: Handbook of Cultural Heritage Analysis. Cham: Springer; 2022. pp. 1329-1349. DOI: 10.1007/978-3-030-60016-7_45

[14] Salimullah A, Nabi R. Protection of sacred tourism sites, festivals and events in Bangladesh over augmented reality: An experience of cultural heritage based tourism. In: Technology Application in Tourism Fairs, Festivals and Events in Asia. Cham: Springer; 2022. pp. 99-118. DOI: 10.1007/978-981-16-8070-0_6

[15] Doulamis N, Doulamis A, Ioannidis C, Klein M, Ioannides M. Modelling of static and moving objects: digitizing tangible and intangible cultural heritage. In: Ioannides M, Magnenat-Thalmann N, Papagiannakis G, editors. Mixed Reality and Gamification for Cultural Heritage. Springer; 2017. pp. 567-589. DOI: 10.1007/978-3-319-49607-8_23

[16] Gigliarelli E, Quattrone G, editors. Shared solutions to tackle restoration restrictions and requirements for cultural landscape and the sustainable conservation of cultural heritage. In: Digital Heritage Progress in Cultural Heritage: Documentation, Preservation, and Protection: 5th International Conference, EuroMed 2014, Limassol, Cyprus, November 3-8, 2014 Proceedings 5. Cham: Springer; 2014. DOI: 10.1007/978-3-319-13695-0_31

[17] Yıldız NB, Kalpaklı Z, Özkaraca N. Creation of historical building information modelling (HBIM) library, A case study of registered house (No: 56), Akçakoca. Düzce Üniversitesi Bilim ve Teknoloji Dergisi. 2024;**12**(2):901-914. DOI: 10.29130/dubited.1241508

[18] Sánchez-Aparicio LJ, Masciotta M-G, Garcia-Alvarez J, Ramos LF, Oliveira DV, Martín-Jiménez JA, et al. Web-GIS approach to preventive conservation of heritage buildings. Automation in Construction. 2020;**118**:103304. DOI: 10.1016/j.autcon.2020.103304

[19] Jalilzadehazhari E, Kurkinen E-L. Development and application of a novel AR-tool being used in energy renovations. In: IOP Conference Series: Earth and Environmental Science. India: IOP Publishing; 2022. DOI: 10.1088/1755-1315/1085/1/012059

[20] Brumana R, Tucci G, Zlatanova S. Special issue "GEORES: HBIM as part of a co-working geospatial ecosystem". Applied Geomatics. 2022;**14**(Suppl 1):1-3. DOI: 10.1007/s12518-021-00408-w

[21] Cuperschmid ARM, Dias MS. Valuing and sharing contemporary architectural heritage: Exploring the scan-to-HBIM-to-XR process with Veneza farm chapel. In: Contemporary Heritage Lexicon. Vol. 1. Cham: Springer; 2024. pp. 109-127. DOI: 10.1007/978-3-031-65104-5_6

[22] Dang X, Liu W, Hong Q, Wang Y, Chen X. Digital twin applications on cultural world heritage sites in China: A state-of-the-art overview. Journal of Cultural Heritage. 2023;**64**:228-243. DOI: 10.1016/j.culher.2023.10.005

[23] Aburamadan R, Trillo C, Udeaja C, Moustaka A, Awuah KG, Makore BC. Heritage conservation and digital technologies in Jordan. Digital Applications in Archaeology and Cultural Heritage. 2021;**22**:e00197. DOI: 10.1016/j.daach.2021.e00197

[24] Münster S, Prechtel N. Beyond software. Design implications for

virtual libraries and platforms for cultural heritage from practical findings. In: Digital Heritage Progress in Cultural Heritage: Documentation, Preservation, and Protection: 5th International Conference, EuroMed 2014, Limassol, Cyprus, November 3-8, 2014 Proc 5. Cham: Springer; 2014. DOI: 10.1007/978-3-319-13695-0_13

[25] Ocón D. Digitalisation and cultural heritage tourism in Asia: Stepping in without stepping out. In: Cultural Leadership in Transition Tourism: Developing Innovative and Sustainable Models. Cham: Springer; 2022. pp. 157-81. DOI:10.1007/978-3-031-14121-8_9

[26] Pan S-Y, Gao M, Kim H, Shah KJ, Pei S-L, Chiang P-C. Advances and challenges in sustainable tourism toward a green economy. Science of the Total Environment. 2018;**635**:452-469. DOI: 10.1016/j.scitotenv.2018.04.134

[27] Boeri A, Longo D, Massari M, Sabatini F, Turillazzi B. The role of historical city centers in the climate-neutral transition of cities: The digital twin as a tool for dynamic and participatory planning. In: ETHICS: Endorse Technologies for Heritage Innovation: Cross-Disciplinary Strategies. Cham: Springer; 2024. pp. 9-19. DOI: 10.1007/978-3-031-50121-0_2

[28] Di Ludovico D. Cities in transformation: Smarter reconstruction in historic city centres. In: Historic Cities in the Face of Disasters: Reconstruction, Recovery and Resilience of Societies. 2021. pp. 493-507. DOI: 10.1007/978-3-030-77356-4_29

[29] Ha T, Woo W. Design considerations for implementing an interactive DigiLog book. In: Digital Heritage Progress in Cultural Heritage: Documentation, Preservation, and Protection: 5th International Conference, EuroMed 2014, Limassol, Cyprus, November 3-8, 2014 Proc 5. Cham: Springer; 2014. DOI: 10.1007/978-3-319-13695-0_75

[30] Berrett BE, Vernon CA, Beckstrand H, Pollei M, Markert K, Franke KW, et al. Large-scale reality modeling of a university campus using combined UAV and terrestrial photogrammetry for historical preservation and practical use. Drones. 2021;**5**(4):136. DOI: 10.3390/drones5040136

[31] Guidi G, Frischer BD. 3D digitization of cultural heritage. In: 3D imaging, Analysis and Applications. 2020. pp. 631-697. DOI: 10.1007/978-3-030-44070-1_13

[32] Li J, Zheng X, Watanabe I, Ochiai Y. A systematic review of digital transformation technologies in museum exhibition. Computers in Human Behavior. 2024;**161**:1-30. DOI: 10.1016/j.chb.2024.108407

[33] Li W, Xiao JX. User experience in digital museums: a case study of the palace museum in Beijing. In: International Conference on Human-Computer Interaction. Cham: Springer; 2021. DOI: 10.1007/978-3-030-77411-0_28

[34] Park H, Heo J, Kim J. Before you visit: New opportunities for the digital transformation of museums. In: International Conference on Human-Computer Interaction. Cham: Springer; 2021. DOI: 10.1007/978-3-030-77411-0_29

[35] Caporale D, Sangiorgio V, De Lucia C. Extended reality-based choice experiment to assess the impact of offshore wind turbines in historic center: The case of Manfredonia.

Journal of Environmental Management. 2024;**349**:119454. DOI: 10.1016/j.jenvman.2023.119454

[36] Ioannides M, Davies R, Chatzigrigoriou P, Papageorgiou E, Leventis G, Nikolakopoulou V, et al. 3D digital libraries and their contribution in the documentation of the past. In: Ioannides M, Magnenat-Thalmann N, Papagiannakis G, editors. Mixed Reality and Gamification for Cultural Heritage. 2017. pp. 161-199. DOI: 10.1007/978-3-319-49607-8_6

[37] Walters LC, Michlowitz RA, Adams MJ. Using laser scans and 'life history'to remember heritage in virtual environments. In: Virtual, Augmented and Mixed Reality Industrial and Everyday Life Applications: 12th International Conference, VAMR 2020, Held as Part of the 22nd HCI International Conference, 2020, Copenhagen, Denmark, July 19-24, 2020, Proceedings, Part II 22. Springer; 2020. DOI: 10.1016/j.techfore.2022.121604

[38] Virtual tour of Notre-Dame Cathedral. Available from: https://www.friendsofnotredamedeparis.org/virtual-tour-notre-dame/ [Accessed: January 19, 2025]

[39] Allal-Chérif O. Intelligent cathedrals: Using augmented reality, virtual reality, and artificial intelligence to provide an intense cultural, historical, and religious visitor experience. Technological Forecasting and Social Change. 2022;**178**:121604. DOI: 10.1016/j.techfore.2022.121604

[40] Fang T, Zhao F. Research on digital dissemination of Chinese classical garden culture. In: International Conference on Human-Computer Interaction. Cham: Springer; 2021. DOI: 10.1007/978-3-030-77411-0_5

[41] Elbelkasy MI. Sustainability of heritage buildings reuse between competition and integration case study (Fuwwah and Rosetta). Journal of Umm Al-Qura University for Engineering and Architecture. 2024;**15**(3):327-339. DOI: 10.1007/s43995-024-00061-5

[42] Liarokapis F, Petridis P, Andrews D, de Freitas S. Multimodal serious games technologies for cultural heritage. In: Ioannides M, Magnenat-Thalmann N, Papagiannakis G, editors. Mixed Reality and Gamification for Cultural Heritage. 2017. pp. 371-392. DOI: 10.1007/978-3-319-49607-8_15

[43] Dionisio M, Nisi V. Leveraging Transmedia storytelling to engage tourists in the understanding of the destination's local heritage. In: Multimedia Tools and Applications. 2021. pp. 34813-34841. DOI: 10.1007/s11042-021-10949-2

[44] Papaefthymiou M, Kateros S, Georgiou S, Lydatakis N, Zikas P, Bachlitzanakis V, et al. Gamified AR/VR character rendering and animation-enabling technologies. In: Ioannides M, Magnenat-Thalmann N, Papagiannakis G, editors. Mixed Reality and Gamification for Cultural Heritage. 2017. pp. 333-357. DOI: 10.1007/978-3-319-49607-8_13

[45] Ardekani AM, Labadi S, von Jungenfeld R. Evaluating visitors' experiences at St. Augustine's Abbey, Canterbury. In: Historic Cities in the Face of Disasters: Reconstruction, Recovery and Resilience of Societies. 2021. pp. 509-521. DOI: 10.1007/978-3-030-77356-4_30

[46] Nofal E, Stevens R, Coomans T, Moere AV. Communicating the spatiotemporal transformation of architectural heritage via an in-situ projection mapping installation. Digital Applications in Archaeology and

Cultural Heritage. 2018;**11**:e00083. DOI: 10.1016/j.daach.2018.e00083

[47] Liestøl G. Along the Appian Way. Storytelling and memory across time and space in mobile augmented reality. In: Digital Heritage Progress in Cultural Heritage: Documentation, Preservation, and Protection: 5th International Conference, EuroMed 2014, Limassol, Cyprus, November 3-8, 2014 Proceedings 5. Cham: Springer; 2014. DOI: 10.1007/978-3-319-13695-0_24

[48] Harish V, Kumar A. A review on modeling and simulation of building energy systems. Renewable and Sustainable Energy Reviews. 2016;**56**:1272-1292. DOI: 10.1016/j.rser.2015.12.040

[49] ASHRAE90.1. Energy Standard for Buildings Except Low-Rise Residential Buildings. USA: American Society of Heating, Refrigerating and Air-Conditioning Engineers (ASHRAE); 2022

[50] ASHRAE100. Energy Efficiency in Existing Buildings. USA: American Society of Heating, Refrigerating and Air-Conditioning Engineers (ASHRAE); 2018

[51] ASHRAEGuideline34. Energy Guideline for Historic Buildings. USA: American Society of Heating, Refrigerating and Air-Conditioning Engineers (ASHRAE); 2019

[52] ISO16813. Building Environment Design—Indoor Environment—General Principles. Switzerland: International Organization for Standardization (ISO); 2006

[53] ISO52016-1. Energy Performance of Buildings—Energy Needs for Heating and Cooling, Internal Temperatures and Sensible and Latent Heat Loads—Part 1: Calculation Procedures. Switzerland: International Organization for Standardization (ISO); 2017

[54] EN16883. Conservation of Cultural Heritage—Guidelines for Improving the Energy Performance of Historic Buildings. Belgium European Committee for Standardization (CEN); 2017

[55] EN16247. Energy Audits. Belgium: European Committee for Standardization (CEN);

[56] BS7913. Guide to the Conservation of Historic Buildings. United Kingdom: British Standards Institution (BSI); 2013

[57] EN16798-2. Energy Performance of Buildings. Belgium European Committee for Standardization (CEN); 2019

[58] EN15217. Belgium European Committee for Standardization (CEN)

[59] De Vita M, Massari G, De Berardinis P. Retrofit methodology based on energy simulation modeling applied for the enhancement of a historical building in L'Aquila. Energies. 2020;**13**(12):3289. DOI: 10.3390/en13123289

[60] Ariyarathna IS, Kariyakarawana M, Abeyrathna WP, Danilina N, Halwatura RU. Analysis of operational energy between adaptive reuse historic buildings (ARHB) and modern office buildings: A case study in Sri Lanka. Architecture. 2023;**3**(3):344-357. DOI: 10.3390/architecture3030019

[61] Thravalou S, Philokyprou M, Michael A. The impact of window control on thermal performance. Investigating adaptable interventions in vernacular Mediterranean heritage. Journal of Architectural Conservation. 2018;**24**(1):41-59. DOI: 10.1080/13556207.2018.1456058

[62] Polo López CS, Lucchi E, Leonardi E, Durante A, Schmidt A, Curtis R. Risk-benefit assessment scheme for renewable solar solutions in traditional and historic buildings. Sustainability. 2021;**13**(9):5246. DOI: 10.3390/su13095246

[63] De Berardinis P, Rotilio M, Capannolo L. Energy and sustainable strategies in the renovation of existing buildings: An Italian case study. Sustainability. 2017;**9**(8):1472. DOI: 10.3390/su9081472

[64] Cadelano G, Cicolin F, Emmi G, Mezzasalma G, Poletto D, Galgaro A, et al. Improving the energy efficiency, limiting costs and reducing CO2 emissions of a museum using geothermal energy and energy management policies. Energies. 2019;**12**(16):3192. DOI: 10.3390/en12163192

[65] U.S. Department of Energy. EnergyPlus; 2014. Available from: https://www.energy.gov/eere/buildings/articles/energyplus [Accessed: April 10, 2025]

[66] Zhu Y, Duan W. Indoor thermal energy optimization and 3D visualization based on ambient light sensing in the protection of historical architectural landscapes. Thermal Science and Engineering Progress. 2024;**54**:102819. DOI: 10.1016/j.tsep.2024.102819

[67] Dore C, Murphy M, McCarthy S, Brechin F, Casidy C, Dirix E. Structural simulations and conservation analysis-historic building information model (HBIM). The International Archives of the Photogrammetry, Remote Sensing and Spatial Information Sciences. 2015;**40**:351-357. DOI: 10.5194/isprsarchives-XL-5-W4-351-2015

[68] Preidel C, Borrmann A, Mattern H, König M, Schapke S-E. Common Data Environment. Building Information Modeling: Technology Foundations and Industry Practice. Cham: Springer; 2018. pp. 279-291. DOI: 10.1007/978-3-319-92862-3_15

[69] Murphy M. Historic Building Information Modelling. Dublin: Dublin Institute Technology; 2012

[70] Murphy M, McGovern E, Pavia S. Historic building information modelling (HBIM). Structural Survey. 2009;**27**(4):311-327. DOI: 10.1108/02630800910985108

[71] Diara F. HBIM open source: A review. ISPRS International Journal of Geo-Information. 2022;**11**(9):472. DOI: 10.3390/ijgi11090472

[72] Bruno N, Roncella R. HBIM for conservation: A new proposal for information modeling. Remote Sensing. 2019;**11**(15):1751. DOI: 10.3390/rs11151751

[73] Cotella VA. From 3D point clouds to HBIM: application of artificial intelligence in cultural heritage. Automation in Construction. 2023;**152**:104936. DOI: 10.1016/j.autcon.2023.104936

[74] Alshawabkeh Y, Baik A, Miky Y. HBIM for conservation of built heritage. ISPRS International Journal of Geo-Information. 2024;**13**(7):231. DOI: 10.3390/ijgi13070231

[75] Angjeliu G, Coronelli D, Cardani G. Development of the simulation model for Digital Twin applications in historical masonry buildings: The integration between numerical and experimental reality. Computers and Structures. 2020;**238**:106282. DOI: 10.1016/j.compstruc.2020.106282

[76] Cheng JC, Zhang J, Kwok HH, Tong JC. Thermal performance

improvement for residential heritage building preservation based on digital twins. Journal of Building Engineering. 2024;**82**:1-20. DOI: 10.1016/j.jobe.2023.108283

[77] Moyano J, Carreño E, Nieto-Julián JE, Gil-Arizón I, Bruno S. Systematic approach to generate Historical Building Information Modelling (HBIM) in architectural restoration project. Automation in Construction. 2022;**143**:104551. DOI: 10.1016/j.autcon.2022.104551

[78] Lovell LJ, Davies RJ, Hunt DV. The application of historic building information modelling (HBIM) to cultural heritage: a review. Heritage. 2023;**6**(10):6691-6717. DOI: 10.3390/heritage6100350

[79] Liu D, Xia X, Chen J, Li S. Integrating building information model and augmented reality for drone-based building inspection. Journal of Computing in Civil Engineering. 2021;**35**(2):1-13. DOI: 10.1061/(ASCE)CP.1943-5487.0000958

[80] Khodeir LM, Aly D, Tarek S. Integrating HBIM (Heritage Building Information Modeling) tools in the application of sustainable retrofitting of heritage buildings in Egypt. Procedia Environmental Sciences. 2016;**34**:258-270. DOI: 10.1016/j.proenv.2016.04.024

[81] Lucchi E, Agliata R. HBIM-based workflow for the integration of advanced photovoltaic systems in historical buildings. Journal of Cultural Heritage. 2023;**64**:301-314. DOI: 10.1016/j.culher.2023.10.015

[82] Plizzari C, Goletto G, Furnari A, Bansal S, Ragusa F, Farinella GM, et al. An outlook into the future of egocentric vision. International Journal of Computer Vision. 2024;**132**(11):1-57. DOI: 10.1007/s11263-024-02095-7

[83] Penjor T, Banihashemi S, Hajirasouli A, Golzad H. Heritage building information modeling (HBIM) for heritage conservation: Framework of challenges, gaps, and existing limitations of HBIM. Digital Applications in Archaeology and Cultural Heritage. 2024;**35**:e00366. DOI: 10.1016/j.daach.2024.e00366

[84] Khalil A, Stravoravdis S, Backes D. Categorisation of building data in the digital documentation of heritage buildings. Applied Geomatics. 2021;**13**:29-54. DOI: 10.1007/s12518-020-00322-7

[85] Barazzetti L, Banfi F. Historic BIM for mobile VR/AR applications. In: Ioannides M, Magnenat-Thalmann N, Papagiannakis G, editors. Mixed Reality and Gamification for Cultural Heritage. Springer; 2017. pp. 271-290. DOI: 10.1007/978-3-319-49607-8_10

[86] Murphy M, Fai S, Chow L, Meegan E, Scandurra S, Pavia S, et al. Virtual historic centers: Digital representation of archaeological heritage. In: Handbook of Cultural Heritage Analysis. Cham: Springer; 2022. pp. 1497-1528. DOI: 10.1007/978-3-030-60016-7_51

[87] Kolivand H, El Rhalibi A, Sunar MS, Saba T. ReVitAge: Realistic virtual heritage taking shadows and sky illumination into account. Journal of Cultural Heritage. 2018;**32**:166-175. DOI: 10.1016/j.culher.2018.01.020

[88] Morita MM, Loaiza Carvajal DA, Bilmes GM. New photogrammetric systems for easy low-cost 3D digitization of cultural heritage. In: Handbook of Cultural Heritage Analysis. Cham: Springer; 2022. pp. 1439-1464. DOI: 10.1007/978-3-030-60016-7_49

[89] Verykokou S, Ioannidis C, Kontogianni G. 3D visualization via augmented reality: The case of the middle stoa in the ancient agora of athens. In: Digital Heritage Progress in Cultural Heritage: Documentation, Preservation, and Protection: 5th International Conference, EuroMed 2014, Limassol, Cyprus, November 3-8, 2014 Proc 5. Cham: Springer; 2014. DOI: 10.1007/978-3-319-13695-0_27

[90] Garcia-Gago J, Sánchez-Aparicio LJ, Soilán M, González-Aguilera D. HBIM for supporting the diagnosis of historical buildings: case study of the Master Gate of San Francisco in Portugal. Automation in Construction. 2022;**141**:104453. DOI: 10.1016/j.autcon.2022.104453

[91] Banfi F, Roascio S, Paolillo FR, Previtali M, Roncoroni F, Stanga C. Diachronic and synchronic analysis for knowledge creation: Architectural representation geared to XR building archaeology (Claudius-Anio Novus Aqueduct in Tor Fiscale, the Appia Antica Archaeological Park). Energies. 2022;**15**(13):4598. DOI: 10.3390/en15134598

[92] Lo Turco M, Bono J, Tomalini A. Parameters, modeling and taxonomy for an HBIM baroque facade. Nexus Network Journal. 2024;**26**:609-630. DOI: 10.1007/s00004-024-00786-9

[93] Partarakis N, Grammenos D, Margetis G, Zidianakis E, Drossis G, Leonidis A, et al. Digital cultural heritage experience in ambient intelligence. In: Ioannides M, Magnenat-Thalmann N, Papagiannakis G, editors. Mixed Reality and Gamification for Cultural Heritage. Springer; 2017. pp. 473-505. DOI: 10.1007/978-3-319-49607-8_19

[94] Maietti F, Di Giulio R, Balzani M, Piaia E, Medici M, Ferrari F. Digital memory and integrated data capturing: Innovations for an inclusive cultural heritage in Europe through 3D semantic modelling. In: Ioannides M, Magnenat-Thalmann N, Papagiannakis G, editors. Mixed Reality and Gamification for Cultural Heritage. 2017. pp. 225-244. DOI: 10.1007/978-3-319-49607-8_8

[95] Law AM, Chen X. 'Absent–present' heritage: The cultural heritage of dwelling on the Changjian (Yangtze) river. In: Adaptive Strategies for Water Heritage: Past, Present and Future. 2020. pp. 272-289. DOI: 10.1007/978-3-030-00268-8_14

[96] Katz BF, Cros C, Peichert S, De Muynke J. The past has ears at Notre-Dame: Acoustic digital twins for research and narration. Digital Applications in Archaeology and Cultural Heritage. 2024;**34**:e00369. DOI: 10.1016/j.daach.2024.e00369

[97] Liu F, Jonsson T, Seipel S. Evaluation of augmented reality-based building diagnostics using third person perspective. ISPRS International Journal of Geo-Information. 2020;**9**(1):53. DOI: 10.3390/ijgi9010053

[98] Mustapha G, Hoemsen R, Spewak R, Knight K. Application and visualization techniques for advanced sensor networks. In: SHMII 2017-8th International Conference on Structural Health Monitoring of Intelligent Infrastructure. Australia: Curran Associates, Inc; 2017

[99] Golparvar-Fard M, Ham Y. Automated diagnostics and visualization of potential energy performance problems in existing buildings using energy performance augmented reality models. Journal of Computing in Civil Engineering.

2014;**28**(1):17-29. DOI: 10.1061/(ASCE)CP.1943-5487.0000311

[100] Jia H, Yang B, Song C, Shen Y. 41.4: Real Time Environment Monitor with Augmented Reality Device based on Android System. SID Symposium Digest of Technical Papers. USA: Wiley Online Library; 2018. DOI: 10.1002/sdtp.12751

[101] You L. Optimization of building thermal environment and VR industrial heritage landscape design enhanced by computer vision algorithms. Thermal Science and Engineering Progress. 2024;**55**:102926. DOI: 10.1016/j.tsep.2024.102926

[102] Battisti A, Baiani S. The ethics of fox and hedgehog to endorse technologies for innovative heritage. In: ETHICS: Endorse Technologies for Heritage Innovation: Cross-disciplinary Strategies. Cham: Springer; 2024. pp. 1-6. DOI: 10.1007/978-3-031-50121-0_1

[103] Yabuki N, Miyashita K, Fukuda T. An invisible height evaluation system for building height regulation to preserve good landscapes using augmented reality. Automation in Construction. 2011;**20**(3):228-235. DOI: 10.1016/j.autcon.2010.08.003

[104] Brumana R, Stanga C, Banfi F. Models and scales for quality control: Toward the definition of specifications (GOA-LOG) for the generation and re-use of HBIM object libraries in a common data environment. Applied Geomatics. 2022:1-29. DOI: 10.1007/s12518-020-00351-2

[105] Adán A, Ramón A, Vivancos J, Vilar A, Aparicio-Fernández C. Automatic generation of as-is BEM models of buildings. Journal of Building Engineering. 2023;**73**:106865. DOI: 10.1016/j.jobe.2023.106865

[106] Alazmi A, Seo H. Thermal displacement mapping for detecting thermal expansion of heritage building during heatwave using 3D laser scanning. Developments in the Built Environment. 2023;**16**:100226. DOI: 10.1016/j.dibe.2023.100226

[107] Alva P, Mosteiro-Romero M, Miller C, Stouffs R. Mitigating operational greenhouse gas emissions in ageing residential buildings using an Urban Digital Twin dashboard. Energy and Buildings. 2024;**322**:114681. DOI: 10.1016/j.enbuild.2024.114681

[108] Osello A, Acquaviva A, Pellegrino A, Candelari E, Chiesa G, Dalmasso D, et al., editors. Multidisciplinary Team Activity Using BIM and Interoperability. A PhD course experience at Politecnico di Torino. Proceedings of the International UNESCO Forum Univ Heritage Le Vie Dei Mercanti. Aversa-Capri: Unesco; 2013

[109] Antonelli C, Cassioli D, Franchi F, Graziosi F, Marotta A, Pratesi M, et al. The city of L'Aquila as a living lab: The INCIPICT project and the 5G trial. In: 2018 IEEE 5G World Forum (5GWF). USA: IEEE; 2018. DOI: 10.1109/5GWF.2018.8517089

[110] Shamalinia S. Virtual and augmented reality applications in building industry. In: Smart City Networks: Through the Internet of Things. 2017. pp. 11-24. DOI: 10.1007/978-3-319-61313-0_2

Chapter 10

Augmented Reality for Lighting Adjustment in a Virtual Studio

Maja Michaelis and Jens Herder

Abstract

An interactive virtual studio is used for live broadcasts with live interaction in front of the recording system. Advances in Augmented Reality (AR) using video see-through Head-Mounted Displays (HMDs) also make it possible to improve the production process itself. Lighting can be improved and adjusted using AR while seeing live effects. An Augmented Reality Lighting Adjustment System (ARLAS) for a virtual studio has been developed and evaluated. The traditional process for controlling lighting in a virtual studio is complicated and time-consuming. It often requires several people to control many different components at different locations. Using AR, this process is simplified by integrating relevant programs and video streams into a single application on an HMD, allowing direct control at lighting locations. Changes to settings are immediately visible on the real fixtures. Real lights can be replicated virtually to maintain consistent lighting conditions in virtual scenes, ensuring that virtual objects are lit as they would be in a real studio. The prototype demonstrated the benefits of AR for complex virtual studio setups and was evaluated by 18 participants.

Keywords: interactive virtual studio, lighting adjustment, set design, previsualization, production control, augmented reality, augmented virtuality

1. Introduction

In video productions, virtual studios enable the blending of people and objects with virtual elements and environments, allowing real-time interaction with these virtual elements. Virtual studios consist of various hardware and software components that enable three subsystems: tracking, rendering, and compositing [1]. The adjustment of lighting is very important in a virtual studio and strongly influences production outcome. Therefore, it is essential to adjust the lighting effectively. **Figure 1** shows the conventional method for adjusting studio lights. A light bar is used to adjust studio lights, especially those positioned at inaccessible heights. It allows vertical and horizontal alignment, focus adjustments (if available), and precise positioning of the barn doors, which can be opened or closed to shape the light beam. The light bar simplifies this process by enabling adjustments without lowering the lights. It is inserted into holders and operated through rotation.

Lighting settings have a significant impact on the footage and the keying result. It must be bright enough to enable high-quality footage with the cameras. For good keying results, the subject should be evenly and brightly illuminated. In addition,

Figure 1.
Studio lighting adjustment with a light bar allows vertical, horizontal, and focus alignment without lowering the lights.

lighting contributes to creating a specific mood or atmosphere and should be used accordingly. Lighting also helps to evaluate space through shadows and by creating a sense of depth. Moreover, lighting can be used to direct the viewer's gaze [2].

The traditional process of adjusting lighting in a virtual studio is typically complex and time-consuming. It involves numerous components and interdependent connections; the configuration of one element often affects others. Furthermore, the process frequently requires the coordination of multiple individuals. **Figure 2** provides an overview of the components necessary and employed for traditional lighting adjustment. It shows that operator movement between the studio and control room is unavoidable. The virtual studio comprises lights to be adjusted and several cameras to record the virtual production. The camera arm and camera robotic in the studio are tracked using mechanical encoders, ensuring reliable data independently of light conditions. The studio lights have physical settings that need adjustment directly on the studio lights and software-based settings that are managed through the control room. The control room settings include dimming and color temperature. Since an appropriate color temperature for keying is predefined in the studio setup, there is no need for further modification. To adjust properties, lighting control software (grandMA2) is used, where Digital Multiplex (DMX) channels and executor faders are assigned to the studio lights. DMX is standard for digital lighting control. There is also software for the virtual set and virtual light, which is used in the control room. Simplified in this figure, there is software for graphic design and rendering (Viz Artist) and control software (Viz Arc) as an interface. Further details are provided in **Figure 3**. Another important component is the Chromakeyer *Ultimatte 12*, which can also be controlled via software, specifically using Ultimatte Software Control. **Figure 2** highlights that relevant imagery is necessary to properly judge the lighting

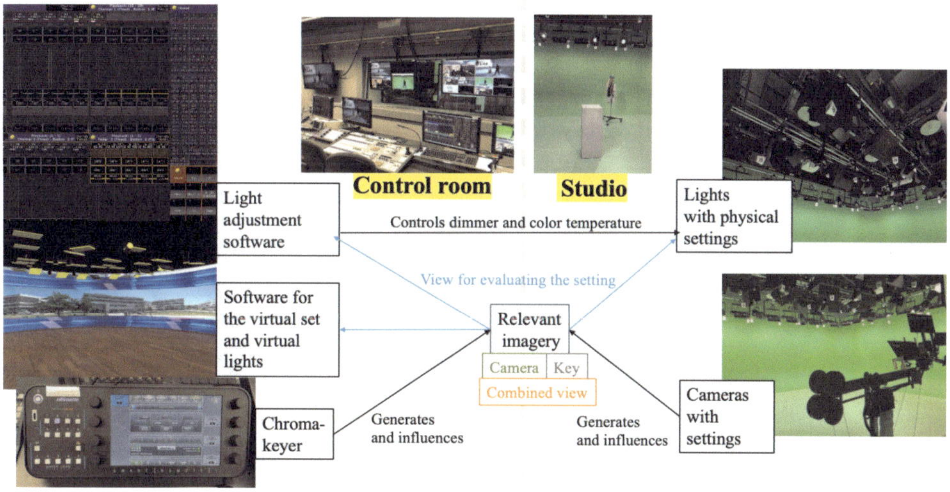

Figure 2.
Overview of the components involved in traditional lighting adjustment. The overview is divided into components that are located in the studio, in the control room or in both locations. There are dependencies between the components. Relevant imagery is available and visible in both locations and serves as the central focus, as it is used to evaluate the setting of all components. The imagery must be available as video streams within the ARLAS.

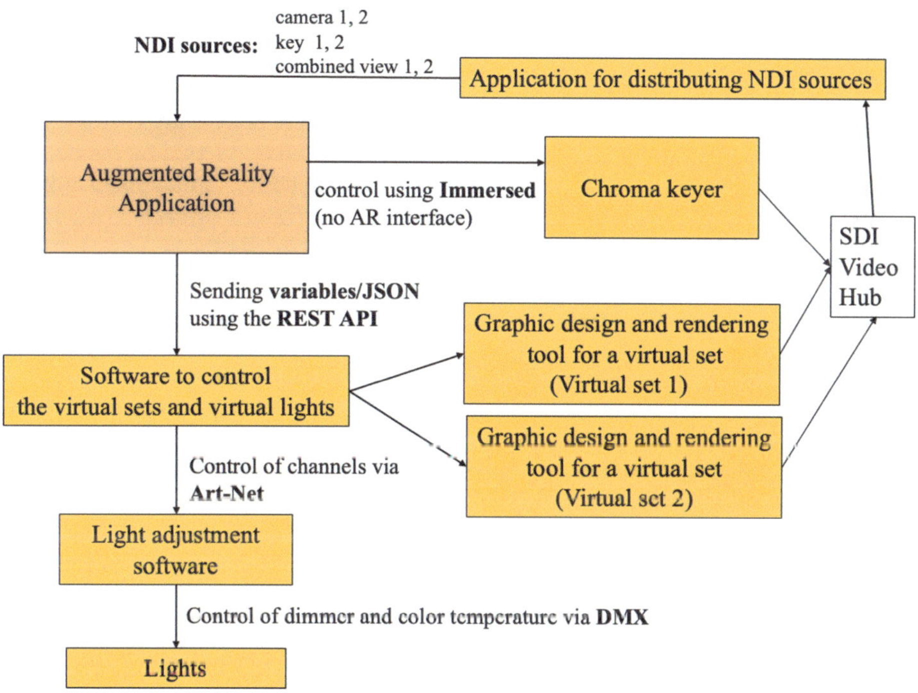

Figure 3.
Overall structure of the ARLAS. The connections of the system are shown with the relevant interfaces. (Serial Digital Interface (SDI) is a standardized interface for transmitting digital video and audio signals, used in professional video and broadcast production).

setup. These must be available as video streams within the ARLAS, as it is impossible to adjust the lighting effectively without visual feedback. In typical workflows, screens are used for this purpose. Moreover, in virtual productions, virtual light is added to complement the real light on set. Therefore, both real and virtual lighting must be taken into account. The goal is to simplify and optimize this complex process using AR. When using AR, virtual elements are added to the real world, allowing real-time interaction with these virtual elements. There are several advantages to using AR for lighting adjustment. First, control from a single location (in the studio, with no need for a control room) is possible. Second, all components are controllable within a single system. In addition, the system can be operated by a single operator who receives direct visual feedback on changes. In comparison, the traditional process often requires several operators. Our ARLAS facilitates real-time control and seamless synchronization between physical and virtual elements within the studio environment. By providing users with immediate visual feedback, it enables intuitive and efficient interaction with the system. This direct responsiveness allows precise modifications for lighting adjustment. This represents a significant benefit of employing AR, as it bridges the gap between the digital interface and the physical setup.

A video capture of the AR light control prototype is available online.[1]

2. Related research and projects

2.1 Mixed reality stage

Broll et al. describe a Mixed Reality (MR) system, called the "Mixed Reality Stage", for planning stage performances [3]. The system supports the creative planning process for stage events by allowing planners to test stage setups and choreographies using real and virtual elements. The "Mixed Reality Stage" is controlled using an HMD and a view pointer, voice commands to activate menus, and Tangible Units, which are physical objects used to manipulate virtual elements. Both the Mixed Reality Stage and the ARLAS enable real-time control and synchronization of real and virtual elements, with users receiving direct visual feedback to make changes to the environment.

2.2 Intuitive virtual production tools for set and light editing

The aim of the paper "Intuitive Virtual Production Tools for Set and Light Editing" was to develop a system that facilitates light and set editing in virtual production environments [4]. This paper presents a tablet application and AR/VR-based solutions for real-time editing on set. These are aimed at users without advanced 3D software skills. A key part of this approach involves the use of simple, intuitive interaction methods, such as gesture controls and a clean, minimalist interface. A key feature of our ARLAS is that users can move directly within the production scene to control lighting and set elements. AR is used to offer real-time control with immediate feedback, using an HMD and hand gestures for interaction. This approach eliminates the need for mastering complex 3D software, significantly simplifying object adjustments. These advantages are equally essential in our ARLAS, which employs an HMD and enables direct control at the production location.

[1] https://vsvr.medien.hs-duesseldorf.de/publications/intechopen-2025-ar-lighting/

2.3 ARStudio

"ARStudio" is a low-cost virtual studio system that also uses AR [5]. It is used to integrate virtual elements into the real scene so that the production team and actors can see them. Markers placed in the environment display virtual objects as soon as they are detected. The virtual scene is therefore captured by cameras that recognize the markers and determine the position and orientation of the virtual objects. These markers serve as an interface for moving, rotating, and interacting with the virtual objects. Because the virtual objects are directly visible in the production process, the production team can catch errors early and make changes before post-production begins, saving time and money. In contrast to "ARStudio", our ARLAS displays virtual elements directly to the user through the Meta Quest Pro. The Meta Quest Pro is a premium Virtual Reality (VR) and AR headset released by Meta in 2022.

2.4 Dreamspace

The EU-funded project Dreamspace uses AR to combine and visualize real and virtual elements in real-time during the production phase [6]. Virtual content can be viewed and adjusted during production, rather than in post-production. AR is also used to control lighting in real-time and synchronize virtual lights with real light sources, creating a consistent and realistic representation of the entire scene.

In the later development of the Dreamspace project, the Virtual Production Editing Tool (VPET) was developed [7]. Instead of an AR-based approach, a user-friendly and more efficient tablet-based control system is used. Previous prototypes based on AR and gesture control proved to be too complex and unintuitive, especially for untrained users. Difficulties in performing basic tasks made AR and gesture control impractical for light customization in this case. In our ARLAS, we try to control the application mainly through virtual menus, rather than through gestures. In addition, the user is given hints on how to control the ARLAS, as the interactive components have info texts or icons.

2.5 Homerise (HomeKit)

It is possible to control real lights with the help of AR. The Homerise[2] application leverages HomeKit to enable control of Apple HomeKit-compatible smart home devices, including lights, using AR. The surroundings are captured with the camera of an iPhone, iPad, or the Apple Vision Pro. Virtual content is then placed and anchored to the real devices. These spatial widgets enable direct control of the devices and always appear in the same place as soon as the environment is recognized in AR mode. Various settings, such as power on/off, brightness, RGB colors, and color temperature, can be changed. The new version enables immersive interaction through Apple Vision Pro. Wrist control allows users to operate smart home functions with intuitive gestures. As users move between rooms, the application automatically reconfigures interface elements using room awareness. Spatial widgets maintain persistent placement, integrate visually through wall snapping, and dynamically hide or minimize based on user proximity and line of sight.

[2] https://apps.apple.com/de/app/homerise/id1439944386?platform=vision

2.6 XRchitecture

There is also the project "XRchitecture - Remote Control of Virtual DMX/Art-Net for a Real Light-Console", which makes it possible to control real lights from a virtual application [8]. As in our project, virtual representatives are used and controlled for the real lights. The aim of this project is to enable hybrid events that can be attended both in person and virtually at the same time. An event could be visited virtually using VR, where the entire scene is recreated. The positions of the virtual lights must match the positions of the real lights for it to look the same. In addition to the virtual solution, the lighting can still be controlled by a real existing lighting console, which is also possible in our ARLAS. The project uses Art-Net for lighting control in Unity, as in our ARLAS. Art-Net is a network protocol developed by Artistic License [9], used to transmit DMX data over IP networks. It is based on TCP/IP. It is similar to Architecture for Control Networks (ACN) but easier to use. It does not require complicated configuration [10].

2.7 Coupling real and virtual light control in AR-based studio systems

A related method for integrating virtual lighting into mixed reality environments was introduced by Davin and Herder [11]. Their system enables real-time relighting of 2D video streams by estimating depth and generating simplified 3D geometry from the input image. This allows virtual light sources to interact naturally with video content, resulting in realistic shadows and highlights. Instead of modifying the video, this system allows lighting adjustment in the physical space via AR. At the virtual studio of Hochschule Düsseldorf, Lighthouse-based tracking with SteamVR and Vive Trackers was used to move virtual objects in real time within mixed or fully virtual environments for virtual productions [12]. The system also enables dynamic occlusion handling using tracked hand controllers. In contrast, the ARLAS focuses on light control, in which virtual lights are coupled with their physical counterparts. Virtual lights act as interfaces to control the real studio lights in real time.

3. Implementation

3.1 Assignment and visualization of lights

To control a real light in the ARLAS, a virtual representative must be available for each real light. This approach follows the concept of a Digital Twin (DT). A DT is a continuously updated virtual representation of a physical system. In this context, the virtual light serves as the digital counterpart to the physical fixture, enabling synchronized control and accurate replication [13]. The virtual representatives are used for assignments and are the virtual objects accessible to the user in the ARLAS. They serve as interactive elements that the user can select within the ARLAS to control the corresponding real-world light, as shown in **Figure 4**.

Another important aspect is that the real light must be recreated virtually, so that the real and virtual light in the virtual set match to achieve the same visual representation. For this reason, detailed information on each light's settings is essential and will be used at a later stage.

The virtual objects of the lights are modeled based on the original lights. As there are different types of lights in virtual studios, different 3D representations were created for each. **Figure 5** displays the various virtual lights positioned according to

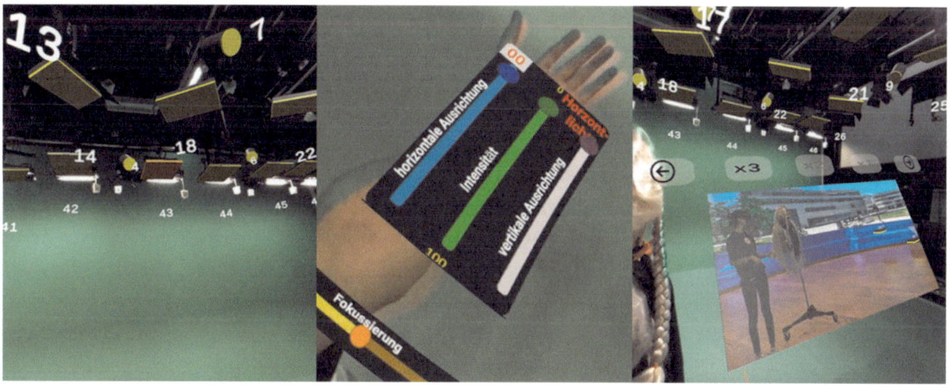

Figure 4.
Lighting Adjustment in a Virtual TV Studio with an AR HMD: (Left) Lights with AR Proxies; (Middle) AR Menu on Arm for Adjusting Light Parameters; (Right) NDI Monitor for all Video Sources.

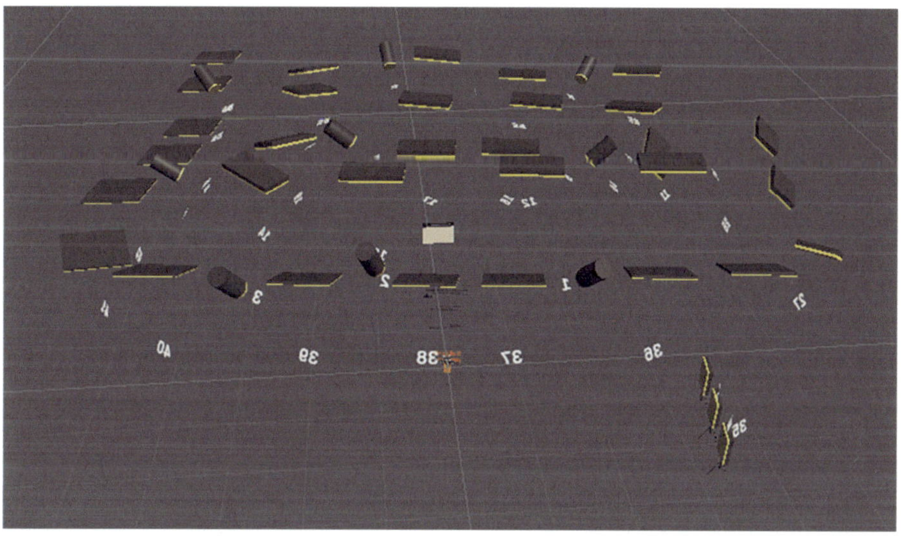

Figure 5.
Virtual scene based on the lighting setup of the virtual studio, showing different types of lights as visible to the user in AR. Highlight lights are shown as cylinders, area lights as cubes. Floor-mounted area lights include a visible frame. Numbering is displayed to enable correct mapping to real lights.

their arrangement in the virtual studio. Generally, there are highlight lights and area lights. While both support adjustments in position, rotation, intensity, and color temperature, highlight lights offer an additional option to set the focus. Within this ARLAS, highlights are modeled as cylindrical objects, while area lights are depicted as cubes. Some area lights are placed on the floor and are movable. Their 3D representations feature a frame to improve visual clarity and distinction.

The virtual lights are numbered to ensure correct mapping to the real lights. As **Figure 4** shows, the lights in the virtual studio are each assigned a numbered label, which is also used for assignment in the lighting adjustment software. There is always a yellow side on the 3D models that represents the illuminated side so that the positioning and rotation match. This is important for transferring properties of each light to ensure accurate virtual replication.

3.2 Transferring the setting of virtual lights to the real lights

After selecting a light and adjusting settings, the corresponding real light should reflect the changes. This is a key characteristic of a DT, where virtual adjustments immediately influence the physical counterpart. Although it is technically possible to send commands directly from the Unity-based ARLAS application to the lighting software via Art-Net, this approach is not practical in this use case.

As previously mentioned, we aim to recreate the virtual lighting within the virtual scene of the virtual set. Therefore, information about each light's settings must also be available within the virtual set application. To avoid sending data separately to both the lighting console and the virtual set design and rendering tool, the virtual set control software is used as the central interface. The central interface also improves maintainability, as changes can be implemented more easily within the ARLAS.

We send the information about a light to the main interface in JavaScript Object Notation (JSON) format using the Representational State Transfer (REST) Application Programming Interface (API). There, the JSON data is processed so that the correct virtual fixture is selected based on the fixture's ID and setting information. The described process is shown on the left side of **Figure 3**.

Lighting control is provided by lighting control software (GrandMA 2 on PC), which can also be available as a lighting console. DMX should be sent to the lighting control software, which then controls the fixtures. The Art-Net and Streaming Architecture for Control Networks (sACN) protocols can be used to receive DMX for the used software. The DMX standard allows the control of 512 DMX channels in a DMX universe. So a DMX universe consists of 512 control channels, and if one universe is not sufficient for all devices, an additional universe must be used. A channel in a universe can be controlled with values between 0 and 255 (8 bits). **Figure 6** shows visualization of the channels in the studio for the existing lights. A channel controls the dimming level or the color temperature. To control colored lights, multiple DMX channels are typically assigned: one for red, one for green, and one for blue.

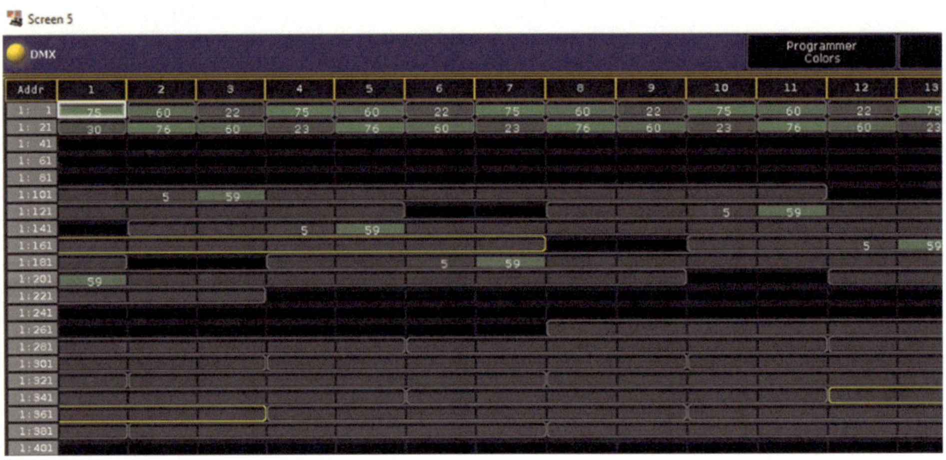

Figure 6.
Representation of the DMX channel allocation for studio lights in a single universe, which enables their control and configuration.

3.3 Transfer of relevant video imagery using network device Interface (NDI)

To evaluate the lighting setup, the user needs access to relevant camera imagery within the ARLAS. For this purpose, there is a virtual screen that receives and displays video sources. The KlakNDI plug-in, which is based on Network Device Interface (NDI), was used for implementation [14]. **Figure 3** shows the integration of NDI usage. For our purposes, the six most relevant NDI video sources were chosen to support lighting adjustments.

NDI was developed by the company NewTek and stands for Network Device Interface. It is an open protocol that enables the transmission of video and audio in real-time *via* a Local Area Network (LAN) using video-compatible products. NDI enables video systems within a network to automatically identify and establish communication with one another. A distinction is made between sending and receiving applications [15]. In this project, the ARLAS made in Unity receives the video sources using the KlakNDI plug-in's receiver script. These video sources are available in the NDI Connect application on PCs through the use of a crossbar and are sent from there. It is required that the PCs and the ARLAS operate within the same network environment.

Due to the performance limitations of the Meta Quest Pro, only one video source can be viewed at a time. **Figure 7** shows the virtual cube in Unity on which an NDI source is rendered. Arrow buttons can be used to change the video source by switching the receiver script to a different video source. The user can also use the buttons to scale the virtual screen. The screen can be placed anywhere in the scene using hand tracking.

3.4 Connecting applications for chroma keyer control

The chroma keyer is used to create a key that serves to separate a target object from its single-color background. This makes it possible to generate a new image composition by integrating the target object into a different setting, such as a virtual set. The Ultimatte, a color difference keyer, uses differences between color channels in the background to form a key [16]. A final composited result is shown in **Figure 4**. In this case, green is the reference color, and the person and the dummy are the target objects inserted in a virtual set. It is required that the chroma keyer can be controlled

Figure 7.
Virtual screens on which important relevant video imagery can be displayed. These are necessary for assessing the current light setting. The virtual screen is portable, scalable, and switchable.

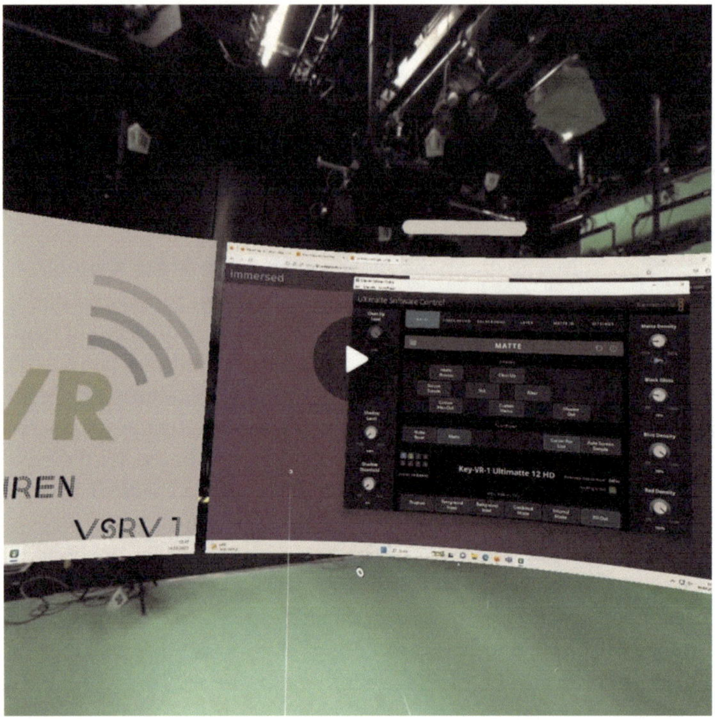

Figure 8.
Use of the Immersed software to operate the chroma keyer. Any software on a connected PC can be operated in this way.

in the ARLAS. However, since no suitable AR interface exists for the chroma keyer, an alternative solution had to be chosen.

Immersed was used in the implementation of the prototype. Immersed is an application that provides the ability to work on virtual monitors in VR and AR. The PC is connected to the app, and the screen is transmitted so that up to five virtual monitors can be used without additional hardware. Monitors can be scaled up and customized.[3] **Figure 8** shows an example of Immersed being used to control the chroma keyer. Because Immersed is not integrated into the target ARLAS and is a different application, it is necessary to switch between the two applications. Currently, one application must be closed completely before switching to the other. This is impractical and requires the last state of the ARLAS application to be saved so that the previous state can be used when the application is restarted.

3.5 Reproduction of the virtual light in rendering engine (Viz artist)

The lighting needs to be recreated virtually. The positions, rotations, and scalings of the fixtures in the studio are known and are sent to the virtual set's rendering engine when changed by the ARLAS. Accordingly, the scene with fixtures can be recreated in the virtual set, as shown in **Figure 9**. Next, the lights should be recreated virtually. To achieve realistic lighting of virtual objects with virtually recreated light, it is essential to distinguish between different types of lights:

[3] https://immersed.com/

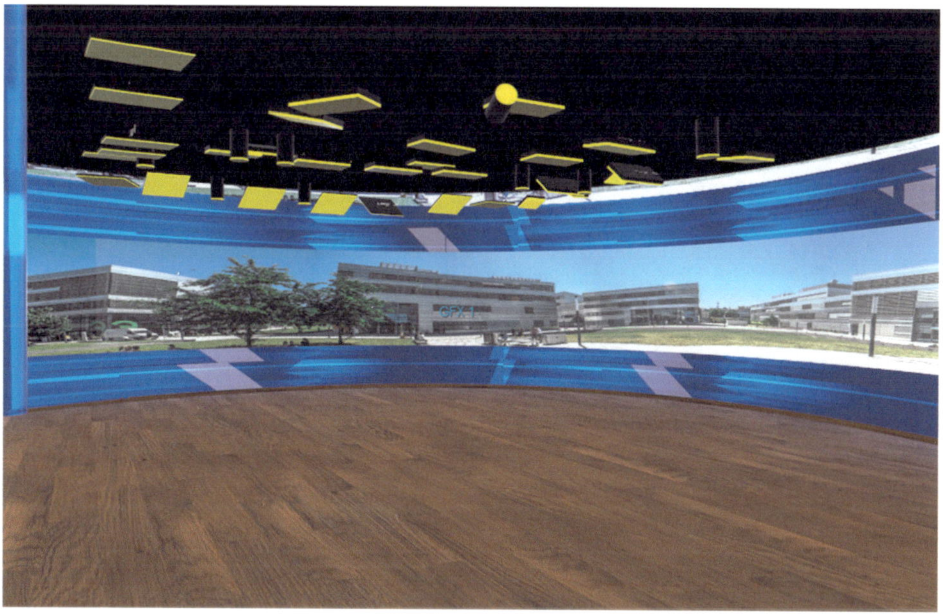

Figure 9.
Virtual lights in the virtual set (rendered in Viz Artist), based on the position and orientation of real lights. Alignment is derived from the AR setup.

- *Purely real light:* This light is only relevant in the real world and does not impact virtual objects. It can be ignored for virtual lighting purposes, such as background lighting that brightens the studio but not the performance area.

- *Purely virtual light:* This light exists solely in the virtual environment and illuminates the surroundings without affecting real objects. No special coupling is needed as it is already virtual.

- *Coupled real and virtual light:* This real light influences virtual objects and must be accurately recreated in the virtual environment. Proper coupling is essential to ensure realistic illumination of virtual objects.

The ambient lighting defined in the software should ideally match the actual background lighting conditions of the studio to ensure consistent illumination. Real-world lighting environments can be captured and stored in an HDR environment map. Although creating such a map is technically demanding, it simplifies configuration of the virtual scene and improves visual quality [17]. **Figure 10** shows the replication of a highlight. A precise implementation in the rendering engine for all lights was not pursued further, as the environment of the virtual scene must also match the real room.

3.6 Interactions for using the ARLAS

3.6.1 Determining light location and orientation (six DoF)

To correctly replicate the lighting setup, the full six Degrees of Freedom (DOF), comprising both location (three DoF) and orientation (three DoF), must be determined

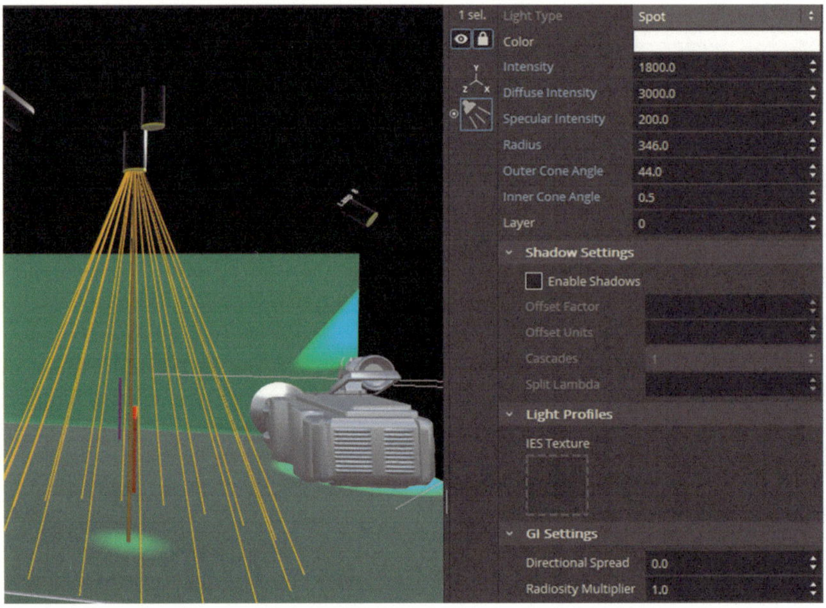

Figure 10.
Visual replication of a real highlight used as a virtual light within the rendering engine of the virtual set.

for each light. Since spatial anchors did not provide reliable results, an alternative system was implemented to fix virtual content at specific locations and orientations within the scene. For this purpose, a specific point within the studio was identified and used as a reference point. At the beginning of the ARLAS application's execution, this reference point must be recalibrated. To achieve this, three points must be correctly positioned and rotated so that the floor level and the reference point align precisely.

Due to the limited precision of the Meta Quest Pro's hand tracking, controllers are required for the accurate placement and orientation of virtual lights during the initial setup process. This decision is supported by previous observations with the Meta Quest 2, which showed that using controllers is both faster and more precise than relying on hand gestures such as pinch and grab movements for selecting and manipulating objects [18].

While the ARLAS application is intended to function entirely without controllers, their use is currently necessary for the initial placement of lights. Accurate positioning and orientation cannot be reliably achieved using hand tracking alone. However, controllers are not ideal in this context, as adjusting lights *via* the lighting bar requires both hands, and the controllers interfere with this process. Once the virtual lights have been placed correctly, the controllers can be set aside, and interaction can proceed using hand tracking.

To move the virtual lights, ray-based interaction is used. Rays, visualized as straight lines extending from the controllers, allow users to select and manipulate lights in 3D space. When grip buttons on the controller are pressed, the selected light follows the movement of the controller in both location (three DoF) and orientation (three DoF), enabling full six degrees of freedom manipulation.

3.6.2 Using the setting of a light

The user's hand menu is the control element that offers a variety of functions to efficiently control lighting in a studio. The menu contains sliders for adjusting the rotation, dimming, and focusing of the lights. The focus adjustment slider is functional only for those lights that feature a variable focus setting. The sliders in the virtual hand menu are designed skeuomorphically to resemble physical faders commonly found on lighting consoles. Skeuomorphism refers to a design approach in which digital interface elements replicate the appearance or functionality of their real-world counterparts [19]. It is used to enhance user familiarity and to improve ease of use. The center image in **Figure 4** shows the hand menu in use. Another important feature of the hand menu is the display of the number of selected lights, which is shown at the top left of the menu as a hint. This allows the user to keep track of the currently selected lights at all times. In addition, a red indicator is activated at the top right of the menu when the user tries to adjust the horizontal light. This light should not be changed, as it is already optimally configured to illuminate the green background. As the horizontal light cannot be adjusted, the corresponding sliders are deactivated to avoid user errors. Recognizable feedback is very important, as it confirms to users that their actions have been carried out successfully. Audible feedback is essential for actions performed, which is why sounds are played when a button is pressed [20]. The hand menu is anchored firmly to the user's hand. This means that the menu is always available, regardless of where the user is in the studio. This is practical, as the user can move freely in the room while the menu remains easily accessible at all times. The menu can be used directly at any light's location. Another advantage of attaching the menu to the user's hand is that both the menu and the light remain visible simultaneously within the user's field of view. This simplifies operation significantly, as the user no longer needs to constantly shift their gaze between the menu and the light. However, there is also a disadvantage: depending on the position of the user's hand, the menu can be obstructed by the user's own arm. This limitation can be mitigated by allowing users to reposition their hands, thereby adjusting the menu's placement as needed.

3.6.3 Selection of a light

To adjust a virtual light, it must first be selected, which can be done using the Meta Quest Pro's eye-tracking. A known problem here is the so-called Midas Touch Problem, where unwanted actions are triggered by constant eye movements, e.g., by a short gaze on the wrong button. A common solution is the use of dwell time, which requires the user to maintain visual focus on an interface element for a certain duration before it is selected. While this helps prevent accidental inputs, it can slow down interaction and may become fatiguing over time. Another solution involves gaze gestures, such as a quick blink. Multimodal interactions that combine eye-tracking with another modality are also effective as they are more expressive and faster than pure hand gestures [21]. An intuitive combination of gestures is important [22]. Voice control is excluded, as it tends to be distracting in a studio environment with multiple people present. Eye-tracking combined with hand gestures is less physically demanding than the use of controllers [23]. In the left image of **Figure 4**, a light is selected via eye-tracking and confirmed using the pinch hand gesture. In addition, the user receives visual feedback through the color change of the light as well as sound based feedback.

4. Evaluation

The ARLAS was evaluated with 18 subjects. Most subjects had experience with the virtual studio, but were not experts or long-time users. After a demonstration of the functionality, they were given a specific task and had to use the ARLAS by themselves. After finishing the task, they received a questionnaire including space for open-ended feedback.

Each participant was able to place the lights with the controls at least sufficiently. The best-rated interaction was the selection of the lights with eye-tracking and a pinch gesture.

Two settings could be adjusted using the sliders: light rotation and dimming. The rotation control was problematic, as it occasionally caused axis values to reset, either during adjustment or after reselecting a light. This made precise control difficult and reduced usability.

The chroma keyer control received ratings of no less than satisfactory. However, every person used the controllers to control it. These were necessary in order to access the main menu and launch the Immersed application, through which the chroma keyer's user interface was accessed. This means that controllers are necessary to adjust the light. The feedback clearly indicates that an NDI monitor with the video sources was missing on the HMD while using Immersed in order to evaluate the control of the chroma keyer.

Three participants were unable to read the real numbers displayed on the physical lights, indicating that the passthrough quality of the Meta Quest Pro is limited in certain scenarios. However, it is sufficient for assigning virtual lights to the corresponding physical lights. Only one participant reported experiencing discomfort or motion sickness after using the ARLAS. It should be noted that newer AR-capable HMDs, such as the Meta Quest 3 and newer devices, offer significantly improved passthrough quality. Devices from other manufacturers may also be suitable, which means that this limitation can be resolved by using more recent hardware.

Each participant was able to see the virtual lights from the ARLAS correctly positioned and oriented in Viz Artist, confirming consistent spatial alignment across components. This shows that the DT worked as intended and that virtual and real elements remained consistent.

The NDI preview screen was rated as helpful for controlling the ARLAS. Each participant was able to move it around the studio with them. One participant was unable to scale to adjust the light. Based on the free responses of the subjects, it can be said that the movement of the screen should be restricted.

Every participant reported that the lighting adjustment could be carried out independently and that it was not necessary to enter the control room.

A comparison of the lighting adjustment speed between the AR-based and conventional processes is not possible, since the participants' task was limited to testing the ARLAS and providing an overall evaluation. Detailed timing measurements were not part of the study.

5. Conclusions

We demonstrated that AR can effectively be used to control and configure both real and virtual lighting in a virtual studio. The ARLAS works like a DT, with the virtual lights mirroring the real ones in real time. The lights in the studio can be manually positioned and changed in orientation. While a previous setup can be loaded into ARLAS, physical changes require manual adjustments within ARLAS. If only automated lights like moving heads[4] would be used or an automatic tracking of the lights were

[4] https://vsvr.medien.hs-duesseldorf.de/tech/captury/

available, the concept of DT would be better implemented. The main advantage is that all adjustments can be made within the studio using a single application. Some issues may be resolved with improved HMDs and the Software Development Kit (SDK). Some subjects could not read the identification number of the real lights or experienced motion sickness from the distortion and delay of the real images. Hands-free interaction through eye-tracking was a major advantage, allowing users to interact with the studio physically without putting controllers away. The software development of ARLAS becomes easier because persistent spatial anchors are available, and the environment can be scanned and detected. In this work, the user still had to manually set up the HMD to the coordinate system of the studio. It is also important to design AR applications that can adapt dynamically to changes in their environment. Regarding the studio, some lights can be moved or changed, but the stored proxies are out of date and have to be manually adjusted. Having access to all video sources of the studio and controlling major components is a big benefit. In principle, an AR system becomes a universal, portable Keyboard Video Mouse (KVM) with better interaction and screen space.

Acknowledgements

Vizrt Austria GmbH supported this project by providing the software Tracking Hub, Viz Artist and Viz Arc. Thanks to A. Müller for keeping the studio equipment running and elaborating the light setup. Funded by the central publication fund of Hochschule Düsseldorf University of Applied Sciences.

Conflict of interest

The authors declare no conflict of interest.

List of abbreviations

ACN	architecture for control networks
API	application programming interface
AR	augmented reality
ARLAS	augmented reality lighting adjustment system
DMX	digital multiplex
DOF	degrees of freedom
DT	digital twin
HMD	head-mounted display
JSON	JavaScript Object Notation
KVM	keyboard video mouse
LAN	local area network
MR	mixed reality
NDI	network device interface
REST	representational state transfer
sACN	streaming architecture for control networks
SDI	serial digital interface
SDK	software development kit
VR	virtual reality

Author details

Maja Michaelis† and Jens Herder*†
Hochschule Düsseldorf - University of Applied Sciences, Düsseldorf, Germany

*Address all correspondence to: jens.herder@hs-duesseldorf.de

† These authors contributed equally.

References

[1] Gibbs S, Arapis C, Christian B, Lalioti V, Mostafawy S, Speier J. Virtual studios: An overview. IEEE Multimedia. 1998;**5** (1):18-35. DOI: 10.1109/93.664740

[2] Owens J. Television Production. 16th ed. Waltham, Massachusetts, USA: Focal Press; 2015. DOI: 10.4324/9781315732022

[3] Broll W, Grünvogel S, Herbst I, Lindt I, Maercker M, Ohlenburg J, et al. Interactive props and choreography planning with the mixed reality stage. In: Entertainment Computing – ICEC 2004. Vol. 3166. Berlin Heidelberg: Springer; 2004. pp. 185-192. DOI: 10.1007/978-3-540-28643-1_25. ISBN: 978-3-540-22947-6

[4] Trottnow J, Götz K, Seibert S, Spielmann S, Helzle V, Einabadi F, et al. Intuitive virtual production tools for set and light editing. In: Proc. of the 12th European Conf. On Visual Media Production, CVMP'15. New York, USA: ACM; 2015. DOI: 10.1145/2824840.2824851

[5] Aguilar IA, Sementille AC, Sanches SRR. ARStudio: A low-cost virtual studio based on Augmented Reality for video production. Multimedia Tools and Applications. 2019;**78**:33899-33920. DOI: 10.1007/s11042-019-08064-4

[6] Yang B, Dong W, Ma L, Hu W, Liu X, Cui Z, et al. Dreamspace: Dreaming your room space with text-driven panoramic texture propagation. In: Proceedings of the 2024 IEEE Conference on Virtual Reality and 3D User Interfaces (VR). New York, NY, USA: IEEE; 2024. pp. 650-660. DOI: 10.1109/VR58804.2024.00085

[7] Spielmann S, Schuster A, Götz K, Helzle V. VPET: A toolset for collaborative virtual filmmaking. In: SIGGRAPH ASIA Technical Briefs. New York, USA: ACM; 2016. DOI: 10.1145/3005358.3005370

[8] Milter T, von der Heide A, Runge L, Riffel L, Lobmann L, Grebenstein C. XRchitecture – Remote control of virtual DMX/art-net for a real light-console. In: Lux junior 2021: 15. Internationales Forum für den lichttechnischen Nachwuchs, Ilmenau: Tagungsband. Ilmenau: Technische Universität Ilmenau/Digitale Bibliothek Thüringen; 2021. pp. 153-161. DOI: 10.22032/dbt.49324

[9] Artistic Licence Engineering Ltd. Art-Net Specification. London, UK: Artistic Licence Engineering Ltd.; 2024. Available from: https://art-net.org.uk/art-net-specification/ [Accessed: Sept 08, 2025]

[10] Tian L, Du H, Gao C, Tang L, Xu Y. The development condition of lighting control system on stage. In: Sixth Int. Symp. On Computational Intelligence and Design. Vol. 1. New York, NY, USA: IEEE; 2013. pp. 233-236. DOI: 10.1109/ISCID.2013.65

[11] Davin T, Herder J. Real-time relighting of video streams for augmented Virtuality scenes. In: Workshop Proc. Tagungsband: Virtuelle und Erweiterte Realität - 18. Workshop der GI-Fachgruppe VR/AR. Bonn: Gesellschaft für Informatik; 2021. DOI: 10.18420/vrar2021_6

[12] Vermeegen K, Herder J. A lighthouse-based camera tracking system for professional virtual studios. In: GI-VRAR, Workshop Proc. Tagungsband: Virtuelle und Erweiterte Realität – 15. Workshop der GI-Fachgruppe VR/AR. Herzogenrath: Shaker Verlag; 2018. DOI: 10.2370/9783844062151. ISBN: 978-3-8440-6215-1

[13] Emmert-Streib F. Defining a digital twin: A data science-based unification. Machine Learning and Knowledge Extraction. 2023;**5**(3):1036-1054

[14] Takahashi K. KlakNDI. O. J. Available from: https://github.com/keijiro/KlakNDI [Accessed: Sept 08, 2025]

[15] Paredes-Páliz DF, Herrera LCA. Technical proposal of a digital television studio for educational environments. In: IEEE World Eng. Educ. Conf. (EDUNINE). New York, NY, USA: IEEE; 2018. pp. 1-5. DOI: 10.1109/EDUNINE.2018.8450944

[16] Wright S. Digital Compositing for Film and Video: Production Workflows and Techniques. 4th ed. New York: Routledge, Taylor & Francis Group; 2018. ISBN: 978-1-138-24037-7

[17] Herder J, Neider C, Kinuwaki S. HDR-based lighting estimation for virtual studio (TV) environments. In: 10th Int. Conf. On Human and Computer. Düsseldorf, Germany, Aizu-Wakamatsu, Japan; 2007. pp. 111-117. DOI: 10.20385/opus4-1666

[18] Schäfer A, Reis G, Stricker D. Comparing controller with the hand gestures pinch and grab for picking up and placing virtual objects. In: 2022 IEEE Conference on Virtual Reality and 3D User Interfaces Abstracts and Workshops (VRW). New York, NY, USA: IEEE; 2022. pp. 738-739. DOI: 10.1109/VRW55335.2022.00220

[19] Spiliotopoulos K, Rigou M, Sirmakessis S. A comparative study of skeuomorphic and flat design from a UX perspective. Multimodal Technologies and Interaction. 2018;**2**(2):31. DOI: 10.3390/mti2020031

[20] Dörner R, Broll W, Grimm P, Jung B. Virtual and Augmented Reality (VR/AR) Foundations and Methods of Extended Realities (XR). Cham: Springer; 2022. DOI: 10.1007/978-3-030-79062-2

[21] Plopski A, Hirzle T, Norouzi N, Qian L, Bruder G, Langlotz T. The eye in extended reality: A survey on gaze interaction and eye tracking in head-worn extended reality. ACM Computing Surveys. 2022;**55**(3):1-39. DOI: 10.1145/3491207

[22] Bai H, Lee G, Billinghurst M. Using 3D hand gestures and touch input for wearable AR interaction. In: CHI Ext. Abstr. Hum. Factors Comput. Syst. New York, USA: Association for Computing Machinery; 2014. pp. 1321-1326. DOI: 10.1145/2559206.2581371. ISBN: 9781450324748

[23] Sasikumar P, Gao L, Bai H, Billinghurst M. Wearable RemoteFusion: A mixed reality remote collaboration system with local eye gaze and remote hand gesture sharing. In: IEEE Int. Symp. On Mixed and Augmented Reality Adjunct (ISMAR-Adjunct). New York, NY, USA: IEEE; 2019. pp. 393-394. DOI: 10.1109/ISMAR-Adjunct.2019.000-3

Section 4

Critical and Societal Perspectives: Ethics and Futures

Chapter 11

AI-Powered Augmented Reality as a Threat Vector for Human Manipulation

Louis Rosenberg

Abstract

Augmented Reality (AR) is a powerful perceptual technology that can alter what users see, hear, feel, and experience throughout their daily lives. When combined with the speed and flexibility of context-aware generative AI, the power is greatly expanded, allowing individual users to be targeted with custom-generated AR experiences that are instantly tailored to who they are, where they are, and what they are doing. This can transform the physical world into a magical place, but only if the augmentation of a user's environment is provided for their personal benefit and best interests. Instead, if AI-powered AR systems are controlled by unregulated third parties, such as large corporations or state actors, individually adaptive AR experiences could be deployed as a dangerous form of targeted influence. In fact, if the industry adopts an advertising business model for AI-powered AR devices, context-aware *generative influence* could become a widely used manipulative path for the promotion of products and services in the physical world. Worse, similar techniques could be used for political influence, propaganda, and disinformation. This chapter reviews the power and flexibility of AI-generated augmented reality, explores the risks that emerge when used for persuasion, manipulation, or influence, and proposes policy directions to mitigate these risks.

Keywords: artificial intelligence, mixed reality, augmented reality, targeted influence, distal attribution, AI manipulation problem, large language models (LLMs), true augmented reality, generative influence, regulation, ethical AI

1. Introduction

Augmented Reality (AR) is a powerful technology that merges realistic virtual elements into a user's experience of the real physical world [1, 2]. It is often confused with simpler technologies such as smart glasses and head-up displays that annotate or embellish a user's field of view, but do not actually alter the user's mental model of reality. True AR (also often referred to as mixed reality) is a transformative cognitive experience in which the virtual content is so naturally and seamlessly integrated into a user's perception of a real physical space that their brain builds *a single mental model* of their ambient environment that includes both real and virtual elements perceived collectively as a single unified reality [3–6].

The distinction between annotating a user's view and augmenting their reality is important because true AR is a highly impactful experience in which the user can easily confuse what is real and what is computer-generated. This has the potential to unleash amazing applications across a wide range of fields from entertainment and education to medicine, commerce, science, and engineering. It also has the potential to be an extremely dangerous vector for targeted influence, especially when third parties such as corporations or state actors can selectively alter a user's perception of their physical surroundings as they navigate their daily lives [7].

Because the difference between smart glasses and true augmented reality has a profound impact on the benefits and risks of the experiences delivered, it is helpful to identify the cognitive process that governs whether an interface augments a user's reality (i.e., the virtual content is authentically integrated into their mental model of reality) or simply annotates their field of view. To make this rigorous, we must introduce the psychophysical concept of Distal Attribution [8]. It refers to our brain's ability to receive a piece of perceptual content (e.g., sight, sound, touch, smell, heat, etc.) and "externalize it" such that we experience the perceptual content as an authentic aspect or element of the real world around us [5, 10].

This process is so fundamental to our sense of reality that we rarely think about its unique importance. To explore, consider this simple thought experiment—you are holding a walking stick as you climb a trail in a woody forest. You place the stick down and it hits a soft patch of mud just one step ahead of you. Your brain quickly updates its mental model of your surroundings and adjusts your gait for the soft ground your foot is about to land on. You proceed smoothly without a stutter in your step, all thanks to your rapidly updated model of reality.

This all seems obvious until you realize that the sensation your brain received was not imparted by the soft, muddy ground—it was imparted by the walking stick in your hand. From your brain's perspective, nerves fired in your muscles as a result of the walking stick impacting your body through your hand. Your brain could have interpreted these signals as the walking stick suddenly going soft, suggesting it cannot support your weight anymore. But that is not what happened—your brain *distally attributed* the perceptual information to the ground on the other end of the stick. In other words, your brain correctly projected the sensory information into an external spatial model of the world. That model is what you perceive as reality (**Figure 1**).

This example highlights the fact that the reality we experience is not a direct representation of the sensory information reaching our brains but the result of a complex process in which sensory content is incorporated into an internal mental model we experience as reality. It is not deterministic, meaning perceptual content can either (a) be correctly added to our mental model of reality, (b) be incorrectly added to our mental model of reality, or (c) simply fail to integrate with our mental model at all. If you project a standard movie on a wall, it could depict people in an adjacent room, but you are unlikely to believe the scene extends into the wall. That is because it does not get integrated into your mental model of reality. It is perceived as an annotation on top of reality and is analogous to the experiences provided by early head-up displays [9] and today's smart glasses and weak AR devices.

Distal Attribution rarely fails in daily life because what we see, hear, feel, and experience are usually highly coherent, both spatially and temporally [11–13]. In fact, the only breakdown of distal attribution that I regularly experience in the real world is when I get my car washed. Despite knowing that my car is parked and that large

Figure 1.
Distal attribution turns perceptions into our mental model of reality.

furry rollers are moving outside my windows, my brain often builds a mental model in which I actually feel my car moving. This error is caused by a mismatch between my vestibular and visual senses. My brain is forced to choose between a model of reality where either my car is moving forward or the scene outside my windows is moving backward. This choice is called a *Perceptual Hypothesis* and is influenced by my senses in combination with my memories of prior experiences driving in cars. My memories win out, and my brain makes the wrong hypothesis (**Figure 2**).

Because Distal Attribution is the process by which our brain integrates content into our mental model of reality, achieving it is central to enabling true augmented

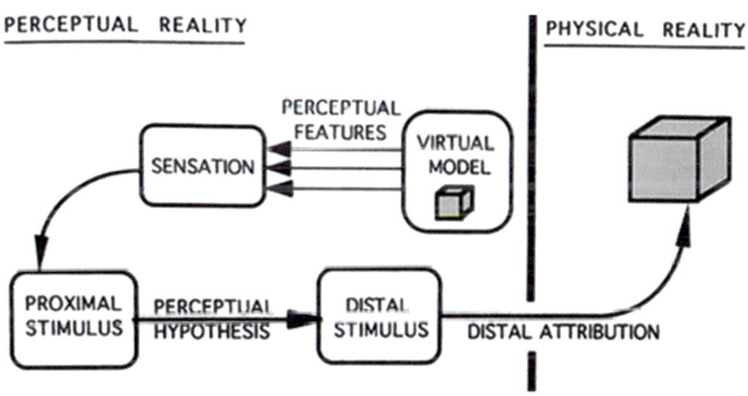

Figure 2.
Diagram of distal attribution in augmented reality [5].

reality experiences [5, 10–13]. The first AR system to foster distal attribution and thereby enable users to experience a single *unified reality* of real and virtual objects was the Virtual Fixtures Platform developed at the Air Force Research Laboratory (1991–1994) [3, 5, 14]. That early research uncovered guidelines for interactive virtual objects to be perceived as believable additions to a user's "ambient reality." These requirements for generating an authentic mixed reality experience include: (a) real and virtual objects must be spatially registered in 3D within the limits of human perception, (b) the user must be able to interact naturally with both real and virtual objects, (c) real and virtual objects must interact with each other in authentic ways, and (d) the sensory modes of sight, sound, touch, and proprioception must be synchronized in time within human perceptual limits. For example, it was found during the Virtual Fixture studies that a relative time delay as low as 70 ms among sight, sound, and touch could hinder distal attribution and make interactive virtual objects not be accepted as authentic elements of a real environment [16].

In addition, this research found that "a natural and predictable relation" must exist between *efference* (i.e., a user's active engagement with an environment) and *afference* (i.e., that user's changing perception of the environment) [5]. This might sound obvious, but it drives one of the most common failure modes that hinders distal attribution in AR and breaks suspension of disbelief. Consider a user placing a virtual book on a real desk. If the virtual book sinks into the real desk, afference and efference do not match, and the book may not be integrated into the user's mental model of reality. If the solution is to restrict penetration of the virtual book into the real desk as a visual illusion, the book might appear on the desk, but the user's hand will likely have penetrated below the desk (as perceived proprioceptively), which also creates a perceptual mismatch that hinders AR by breaking distal attribution.

To address such a mismatch, a variety of techniques have been developed. For example, haptic "impulse" sensations that mimic the instant of contact between the virtual book and the physical desk have been found to mask proprioceptive conflict and sustain distal attribution [17]. Other techniques that help ensure virtual objects are perceived as authentic elements in real environments include the casting of virtual shadows on real surfaces and the simulation of real-world lighting conditions on virtual objects [18, 40, 62]. Such cues have been found to increase realism, foster distal attribution, and enhance depth perception [19]. Also, sound field matching in the audio domain can ensure that virtual sounds match the acoustics of real environments [41]. In addition, auditory cues that emulate interactions between virtual and real objects can significantly enhance realism and performance [20, 49, 61]. Finally, pinning virtual objects to physical artifacts for tangible manipulation can support realism by aligning visual, haptic, and proprioceptive senses [21].

What all of these examples have in common is that enabling users to form a unified mental model of reality that integrates both real and virtual content requires achieving sufficient levels of *perceptual consistency* (i.e., spatial registration, temporal synchronization, and predictable relations between efference and afference among real and virtual objects). What is *not* required is perfect visual, audio, or haptic fidelity. That is because our brains require consistent percepts, not high-fidelity percepts, in order to accept elements into our reality. For example, if you walk into a dark room where you can barely see the furniture, that room is just as real to you as it is under bright lights. However, if you bump into a table when crossing that dark room and your leg passes through it, realism is instantly lost.

1.1 True augmented reality is finally here

As described above, it is challenging to create perceptual experiences in which the real and virtual are genuinely perceived as authentic elements of a single unified reality. This can be referred to as *true augmented reality* or Mixed Reality [15, 37, 38, 45, 47]. For decades, this has only been possible in research labs and highly controlled product demos, but recently two high-profile devices, the Apple Vision Pro and Meta Quest 3, were released that finally cross the "uncanny valley" of augmented reality at consumer scale. The Apple Vision Pro achieves this by accurately registering virtual content to the physical environment using LiDAR, depth sensors, inertial sensors, and high-resolution cameras that work together to map the user's surroundings and identify real surfaces as spatial anchors. It then uses a combination of precision head-tracking, pass-through video, and AI processing to maintain the registration and stability of virtual objects in 3D space. Powered by Apple's custom M2 and R1 chips, the system achieves AR with very low latency, ensuring that sights, sounds, and motions maintain spatial congruence and temporal synchrony. The result is a transformative experience for many users [22].

Similarly, the Meta Quest 3 also employs sophisticated depth sensors and high-resolution cameras to map and recognize real-world surfaces, objects, and spatial layouts in real-time. Inside-out tracking enables alignment and stability of virtual elements as the user moves, while hand-tracking enables natural interaction. Powered by the Snapdragon XR2 Gen 2 chip, the system renders content with very low latency, maintaining coherence and fostering distal attribution. In addition, the Meta Quest 3 provides improved haptic feedback compared to their prior systems, enabling more subtle sensations as real and virtual elements interact.

While the Vision Pro and Meta Quest 3 represent major strides in the production of high-quality headsets, even bigger advancements were made on the software side in 2024 that may finally make AR devices an essential aspect of our digital lives, potentially replacing the mobile phone as our primary interface within the next 5 years. The core advancement was the widespread deployment of next-generation AI systems called Multimodal Large Language Models (MLLMs), which enable foundational AI systems to receive as input, not just text, but real-time streams of video and audio. This means that AI assistants and other onboard AI systems have "eyes and ears" that allow them to react to the context of real-world environments.

When MLLMs are integrated into augmented reality eyewear that contains onboard cameras and microphones, AI assistants and other generative models powering the experience can now see and hear everything the user sees and hears in real-time. The addition of context-aware AI agents to AR systems means that every user will be able to navigate their world with an AI assistant *hovering by their shoulder*, scanning their surroundings in real-time, alerting them to things of interest, informing them of factual information, reminding them of nearby tasks, and providing them with custom-generated AR content in any place at any time. This, more than any other advancement in the evolution of AR, has the potential to mass-produce AR experiences for consumers that feel like superpowers [23, 25].

These context-aware AI agents will provide real-time information via eyewear through text and imagery, but even more importantly, they will assist users through natural dialog delivered through earbuds. This means that in the near future, we may all find ourselves with an AI whispering in our ears as we walk down the street, browse store shelves, hike mountain paths, attend classes, or perform jobs. This immersive "whisperverse" will feel like a mental superpower—a voice in our heads that continually informs us, reminds us, guides us, and even entertains us [24].

In some embodiments, these AI assistants will be deployed as *"Electronic Life Facilitators"* (or *ELFs*) that appear visually to us in augmented worlds as embodied characters. As shown in **Figure 3**, I believe these AI-powered entities will likely be rendered in AR as cute creatures that earn our trust, hovering around us as they give guidance or flying ahead to point out elements in our world [25, 26]. Whether deployed as disembodied voices or personified characters, the addition of context-aware AI assistants to our augmented future will be so impactful to our daily lives, I refer to this capability as *Augmented Mentality* and predict it will drive mass adoption [27]. After all, anyone not wearing AI-powered AR eyewear will be at a cognitive disadvantage.

The possibility of mass-produced AI-powered AR glasses may have seemed out of reach only a few years ago, but over the last 6 months, Meta and Google have both unveiled high-profile devices that bring these capabilities to consumers. Meta has already deployed MMLLMs for use in Meta Ray-Ban Smart Glasses and Meta Quest 3 headsets [39]. In late 2024, Google unveiled their Project Moohan aimed at deploying AI-powered glasses and headsets in partnership with Samsung, driven by a spatial operating system called Android XR. In 2025, they partnered with Warby Parker for stylish frames [59]. In other words, Meta, Google, and Apple are in a race to market, at scale, the superpowers that AI-enabled AR eyewear will provide [60].

In addition to adding powerful assistive features, context-aware AI has the potential to make AR experiences increasingly realistic. As described above, the cognitive process of *distal attribution* occurs when AR content is so naturally integrated into our perceived surroundings, it gets incorporated into our mental model of reality. Context-aware AI will enable AR content to instantly adapt to changing conditions of our surroundings. This will reduce perceptual inconsistencies between the real and virtual, fostering distal attribution. In addition, when AI assistants are added to AR

Figure 3.
Our augmented future may include "ELFs" whispering in our ears [25].

worlds that can see and hear everything that we are experiencing in real-time, these simulated entities will be significantly more likely to be accepted as authentic participants in our reality. Even if these agents are not truly intelligent, they are more likely to be perceived as "conscious beings" if they are responsive to our shared environment. This cognitive process is often called "Anthropomorphic Attribution" [28] and is likely to make context-aware AI assistants in AR seem far more real to us than those on flat screens [29].

2. AI-powered augmented reality will be magical but dangerous

With large corporations such as Meta, Apple, Google, and Samsung racing to deploy AI-powered eyewear that can provide convincing mixed reality experiences, our daily lives may soon be filled with immersive digital content that we engage with all around us. This will enable magical applications for consumers and professionals. It will also unleash new forms of targeted influence ranging from immersive ads to new tactics for fraud, manipulation, and deception [14, 29, 30, 48]. Specifically, two emerging forms of targeted content are expected to gain traction: Virtual Product Placements (VPPs) and Virtual Spokespersons (VSPs), detailed below.

Virtual Product Placements (VPPs) are promotional objects or experiences that are incorporated naturally into a user's ambient reality (virtual or augmented) on behalf of a paying sponsor. VPPs can be presented simultaneously to large groups of users, but with the advent of generative AI, such experiences are likely to be personalized at an individual level. In other words, VPPs will be custom-crafted for specific people at specific times and places to achieve specific influence goals. For example, if a user is profiled as a sports fan of a particular age, gender, and income, they might have a real-world experience in which they see someone walking past them on the street wearing a jersey for their favorite team that advertises a sports bar a few blocks ahead. Because this is a *targeted VPP*, other people around them might not see the same content, instead being targeted with very different customized promotional experiences [29].

With AR technology rapidly advancing, VPPs could soon be integrated into our surroundings so seamlessly that users could easily mistake them for authentic objects, activities, or even people in their proximity. If consumers cannot distinguish between true experiences and targeted content, marketing could become highly predatory. This means that as digital marketing shifts from flat ads and videos to *promotionally altered environments and experiences,* consumers need new protections [30]. A simple but powerful protection would be to require that all VPPs look *visually distinct* from their corresponding real-world artifacts. For example, if a digital product is placed into natural surroundings as promotional content, that virtual product could glow, shimmer, or be highlighted in some other visually noticeable way so it cannot be confused with authentic elements.

Virtual Spokespersons (VSPs) are simulated humans or other characters that are introduced into immersive environments to verbally convey targeted content by engaging a user in interactive promotional conversation [29, 30]. As AR technology becomes commonplace, it is likely that physical establishments such as retail stores and restaurants will be serviced by AI-powered virtual salespeople, virtual servers, and other virtual representatives that supplement the human staff. Similarly, when users exercise, they will likely be supported by a VSP virtual trainer giving them guidance and encouragement. While this seemed like pure science fiction just a few years ago, LLMs and generative avatars have made VSPs not just viable, but likely to be deployed widely in immersive platforms, motivated by cost savings associated with replacing human employees with interactive AI agents [14].

As shown in **Figure 4** below, the use of AI and AR in retail establishments was depicted in the award-winning 2023 short film "Privacy Lost" that aimed to educate policymakers and regulators on the unique manipulative dangers of AI-powered augmented reality glasses. In the film, a family sits in a restaurant wearing fictional AI glasses called "carbons" that enable them to be serviced by VSP servers. What is potentially most interesting about the film is that members of the family—husband, wife, and son—each see a different-looking server, optimized for their perspective. And the server, by reading their facial expressions and other emotional cues, is able to upsell each family member with AI-powered manipulative skill (video link, https://www.youtube.com/watch?v=IsE_Pas2OQU).

Another instructive short film is "Hyper-Reality" (2014) that depicts the daily life of a headset wearer in the first person as she navigates a busy city. What is most memorable about the depiction is how visually overwhelming promotional content can become if advertising is unrestrained via smart glasses or AR (video link, https://www.youtube.com/watch?v = YJg02ivYzSs). With the addition of AI agents that target users through interactive dialog, it is likely that promotional content deployed through AR systems will become less of a visual competition for our eyes and more of a cognitive competition for our attention. As every salesperson knows, the best way to persuade a customer is not to hand them a brochure or have them watch a video, it is to engage them in an interactive dialog that earns their trust, discovers their reservations, and works to sway their intent [29].

While using AI agents to optimally upsell customers is not a societal threat, these same AI-powered tactics could be used to deploy optimized and customized propaganda, misinformation, and disinformation at scale [33]. For these reasons, new regulations should be considered to protect consumers from predatory AI tactics that employ targeted conversational advertising [30, 32]. At a minimum, regulators should consider requiring VSPs in virtual and augmented worlds to have a *distinct appearance* from authentic human representatives, and they should be required to explicitly

Figure 4.
Image from short film "Privacy Lost" about AI manipulation dangers [31].

announce when they are expressing targeted promotional content and indicate who the sponsor is for that content [29, 33].

Such protections are important because these AI-driven conversational agents could easily have access to detailed profile data about the targeted user they have been assigned to engage through interactive dialog. This data is likely to include their preferences, interests, political leanings, hobbies, and a historical record of their reactions in prior promotional conversations. This could enable such agents to charm users in friendly small talk, customized to their interests and leanings, thus drawing them into misplaced feelings of trust and familiarity. In addition, without strict regulation, these AI agents are likely to also have access to real-time emotional data captured from the user's facial expressions, vocal inflection, eye motion, pupil dilation, and even vital signs [14, 29, 30, 43, 52]. This will enable the AI agent to adjust its conversational tactics in real-time to optimize persuasive impact.

Intellimorphic Avatars are adaptive AI agents that intelligently adjust their appearance, behavior, and tactics in response to individual human users in order to maximize that user's receptiveness to persuasive messaging. If not regulated, such avatars could adapt their gender, hair color, eye color, clothing style, voice, accent, speech patterns, and mannerisms to maximize influence on a targeted user based on that user's previous interactions and behaviors in combination with their real-time reactions. Even more insidiously, advertisers could deploy Intellimorphic Avatars that capture a user's facial features in real-time and incorporate hints of those features into their own facial rendering. Research has shown that incorporating a small fraction of a person's own features into an AI-generated face can significantly increase a user's feelings of trust [14]. This tendency is likely due to our implicit trust of family members who share genetic resemblance. This "familial mirroring" tactic, as well as incorporating vocal features and gestural mannerisms copied from the target user (or from a family member), could be greatly abused when VSPs are deployed for marketing, propaganda, or disinformation purposes and should be strictly outlawed [30].

Additionally, research on human behavior shows that subconscious mirroring of the verbal and non-verbal behaviors of a conversational counterpart—such as emulating their speech rhythm, gestures, intonation, and breathing patterns—can build rapport and foster feelings of connection [42]. Although using such techniques could achieve similar benefits for AI-powered agents serving as personal assistants, tutors, or other supportive roles, the potential for such "behavioral mirroring" to be abused or even weaponized is significant and should be highly regulated.

Intellimorphic Environments—Similar to how avatars can be deployed that intelligently adapt their appearance, voice, behaviors, and mannerisms to optimize impact on target users, environments can also be intelligently adaptive to individuals in real-time. For example, when a user wearing AI-powered eyewear enters a retail store, car dealership, or other commercial setting, the environment itself could be subtly adjusted to subconsciously guide a user in a certain direction or increase the probability that the targeted user notices a particular product or service. For example, a system that is aware of a user's tastes, interests, background, or economic status could coax that user down particular aisles, maybe offering more expensive products, by subtly increasing the perceived lighting in that area or by projecting simulated spotlights or other visual accents on specific physical products. Similarly, virtual blinders or occluding barriers could be added to an environment to ensure a user does not go in that direction or does not notice things the system wants to steer them away from. In an extreme example, users walking down streets could see simulated construction fences or other barriers instead of homeless encampments or other real-world events or artifacts that an organization or municipality might want to conceal [34, 46]. Such "reality-masking" techniques, which harken back to tales of fake "Potemkin Villages" in eighteenth-century Russia, could easily be abused as individually targeted distortions, and should be highly regulated.

3. The unique danger of AI-powered conversational agents

When a user is engaged in real-time dialog with an AI-powered conversational agent such as a VSP that represents a third party, or a dedicated personal assistant such as an Electronic Life Facilitator (ELF) that follows the user through their daily life, the power balance has the potential to be highly skewed, with the human at a significant disadvantage [33]. The potential sources of power asymmetry between humans and AI agents are summarized as follows:

Familiarity Asymmetry: As described above, it is likely that AI agents will have access to personal data about target users, ranging from age, interests, education, and political views to their favorite sports teams, movies, books, and music artists. This will empower the AI to optimize the receptibility and persuasiveness of dialog for individual targets. In contrast, the human will know nothing about the artificial entity they are conversing with. If the AI agent is assigned a visual or vocal persona that represents a particular age, gender, style, or background, it is merely a façade, and yet the user will subconsciously make assumptions about the AI entity and its intentions, values, or trustworthiness based on its appearance. This represents a deeply asymmetric relationship that has no equivalence when engaging with human salespeople or other representatives.

Emotional Asymmetry: As described above, it is likely that VSPs and other AI agents will be capable of evaluating a user's emotional state during conversations from the user's expressed dialog, vocal inflections, and facial expressions. Already Open AI's latest o4 model with multimodal video processing can assess a user's emotional state from facial expression [36]. The human, on the other hand, will be unable to "read" their digital counterpart. That is because any emotions or vocal inflections conveyed in language, voice, or face of the simulated avatar are entirely fabricated, potentially chosen to maximize impact, and do not reflect an intrinsic emotional state of the AI representative. This is a highly asymmetric relationship [33].

Continuity Asymmetry: It is likely that platforms deploying conversational agents will keep track of each user's reactions to targeted influence and will learn what types of persuasive tactics are most effective. The human in the loop, on the other hand, will learn nothing about the digital representatives they engage throughout their day, for they could be *digital shapeshifter*s that can assume any style, tactics, or persona. In other words, the platform generating the VSP or other conversational avatar can "get familiar" with the target human over time, learning what tactics work best, while the human may believe they are engaging a variety of different entities. This too is a deeply asymmetric scenario that has no equivalent with human-human interactions.

Information Asymmetry: Unlike human influencers who can make arguments and counterarguments based on human-level knowledge and experience, AI agents will be able to instantly craft a compelling conversational response that draws on a nearly infinite information pool and could easily cherry-pick points that the human could not possibly validate in real-time. In fact, an AI agent in a virtual or augmented environment could create the illusion of expertise by conversationally referencing an overwhelming barrage of factual information as a deliberate form of persuasion. This is a deeply asymmetric situation that has no direct equivalent in human-human interactions.

Strategic Asymmetry: Unless restricted by new policy protections, it is very likely that VSPs and other conversational agents will be trained in sales tactics, negotiation tactics, human psychology, cognitive biases, game theory, and other persuasive strategies that make them extremely effective instruments of influence, manipulation, or even deception. For example, in 2022, DeepMind developed a strategic AI system called DeepNash that learned to bluff human players in the game of Stratego and sacrifice gaming pieces for the sake of long-term victory [37]. While humans are often trained in sales tactics, it is likely that AI agents will harness a far deeper, broader, and more nuanced range of persuasive strategies than any human could master, creating a highly asymmetric power imbalance.

Intelligence Asymmetry: The range of cognitive tasks in which AI agents can match or exceed human performance is expanding at an astonishing pace. Between 2012 and 2020, AI systems have surpassed human abilities on critical benchmarks for image recognition, speech recognition, reading comprehension, and resolving language ambiguities. Since 2021, AI systems have exceeded average human abilities on benchmarks for text summarization, software coding, medical diagnosis, and mathematical problem solving, and can produce written documents that are perceived as indistinguishable from human-generated content.

Looking forward, many researchers expect AI systems to surpass humans in benchmarks for logical reasoning and multi-step planning within the next few years. As we consider the impact of AI agents that are designed to assist us throughout our daily lives via augmented reality eyewear, we must assume they will soon be able to outreason us, out-plan us, and out-strategize us as they pursue conversational objectives. This asymmetry greatly increases the manipulative risk if AI agents are allowed to impart targeted influence without regulatory oversight.

Authority Asymmetry: We must consider the psychological impact on human users when it is clearly established that the AI agents whispering in our ears and guiding us through our days are significantly smarter than us on nearly every front and are likely to find better solutions to our daily problems than we could come up with ourselves and do so almost instantly. I refer to this looming intellectual power imbalance as AI systems achieving "Cognitive Supremacy" and worry it will cause many individuals to blindly defer to their AI assistants rather than using their own critical thinking. Whether caused by "authority bias" or "expert bias," it is well-established that humans often defer to perceived experts, greatly increasing the potential for influence and manipulation [53, 54]. This will likely result in excessive deference to AI agents that are perceived to possess super-human intellect.

Clearly, conversational agents pose unique interactive risks that have not been faced in traditional forms of targeted media. To help the public, regulators, and policymakers appreciate the new dangers posed by interactive and adaptive forms of "generative influence," it is useful to characterize the risks using a formalization referred to as the AI Manipulation Problem, elaborated on in the next section.

4. Generative influence and the AI manipulation problem

As described above, AI-powered mobile devices have the potential to accurately track where users go, who they are with, what they are doing, what they are looking at, what they hear around them, and even their real-time emotional reactions based on facial expressions, body posture, and physiological reactions. At the same time, AI-powered immersive display has the potential to use this information to modify what the user sees, hears, and experiences in their surroundings. When combined, these two capabilities have the potential to be an extremely powerful form of digital manipulation that could become a significant risk to human agency [32, 35, 44]. To help policymakers better appreciate how this new threat compares to prior media technologies, it is helpful to formalize the risk using some basic concepts from the engineering discipline of Control Theory (CT).

Across many engineering fields, control theory is a widely used paradigm for automatically optimizing the behavior of a target system. The target system could be the inside of a home, and a thermostat is a simple mechanism that utilizes control theory to optimize the behavior (i.e., temperature) of that home. A homeowner sets a target temperature, and if the house falls below the target, the heater turns on. When the heater is on, if the house rises above the target, the heater turns off. When the system is operating as expected, the thermostat keeps the house within a narrow temperature range around the target value. This is the basic concept of a *control system,* as shown in **Figure 5** below.

When the schematic above is applied to a home heating unit, the block labeled *"System"* represents the house whose temperature is being controlled. The box labeled *"Sensor"* is the thermometer that detects the indoor temperature, and the box labeled *"Controller"* is the thermostat that modulates the heating unit. This creates a *feedback loop* that continually detects behaviors (e.g., temperature) and imparts influence (e.g., adjusts the heater), to guide the system toward the goal.

To appreciate the manipulation risk of AI-powered eyewear, we need to consider the case where the *System* being controlled is a human user. As shown in **Figure 6** below, the input could be an Influence Objective from a paid sponsor, for example, a request to encourage the target user to enter a particular store and buy a particular product. From an engineering perspective, this is very similar to setting the temperature on a thermostat, but in this case, it could be a complex promotional or manipulative goal with respect to the target user.

To optimally achieve its Influence Objective, the controller must access real-time sensors, which are the various onboard components that track the location and behavior of the targeted user within his or her environment. These sensors can include cameras, microphones, GPS sensors, LiDAR sensors, and other modules that monitor a user's location, orientation, actions, and dialog. These sensors could also include heart rate monitors, eye trackers, and other more invasive elements such as skin galvanometers and EEGs. The sensor data can be processed by multimodal large language models to instantly generate a real-time assessment of that user's behaviors, intentions, and emotions with respect to their surroundings.

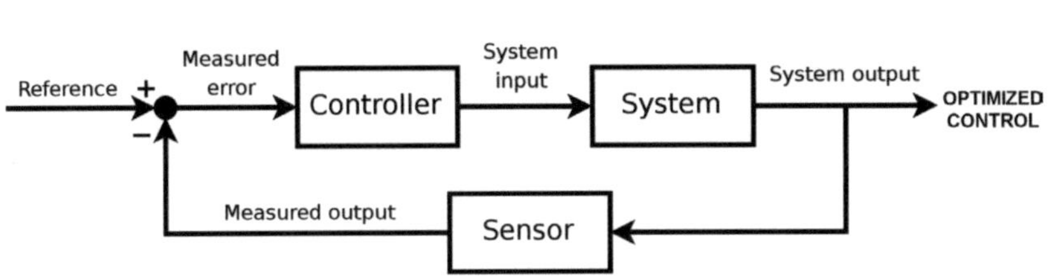

Figure 5.
Classic control system diagram [35].

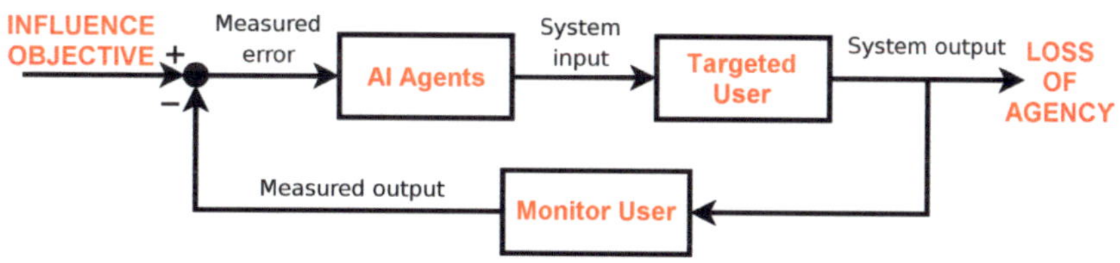

Figure 6.
Control theory representation of the AI manipulation problem [35].

The system also needs a Controller that, like a thermostat, continually adjusts its tactics to guide the system toward the desired goal. In this case, the controller is a powerful Generative AI system that deploys AI agents to modulate the sights and sounds experienced by a user as they navigate their world, including targeted conversational dialog from AI-controlled avatars. Like a thermostat modulating the temperature of a home, this can be deployed as a feedback loop that continually monitors the state of the user and adjusts tactics to achieve the influence objective.

For example, imagine a user in a coffeehouse wearing AI-powered AR glasses. The target user may not notice that a simulated couple has been added to the local environment, since the controller (which has access to gaze direction of users) could easily make the couple appear at the nearby table at an instant when the user is glancing in a different direction. The couple could be rendered photorealistically and therefore perceived as authentic customers by the target user. Once the couple is created, the controller could begin imparting targeted content in a subtle way: by having the simulated couple strike up an audible conversation between themselves, their dialog being spoken within earshot of the target user. The conversation could begin as a casual dialog and gradually shift to an influence objective. The controller would then monitor the user's reactions during the casual dialog to determine if and when the target user begins paying attention to the nearby couple.

Assessing attention could be as simple as detecting changes in the user's gaze or biometrics in correlation with real-time comments made by the simulated couple. For example, the user might form a slight smile when the couple says something funny, or the user's pupils might contract slightly when the couple says something provocative. Regardless of the cues, the controller could easily detect engagement, determining that the target user has begun paying attention to the overheard dialog. The controller could then drive the virtual couple to shift their conversation toward the influence objectives.

For example, the target user may be in the market for a new car. A sponsor might have purchased the right to target this user from the AR platform provider via an advertising-based business model. Without regulation, the platform provider would have no obligation to inform the user that the virtual couple are VSPs that were added to that environment for promotional purposes. Therefore, when the virtual couple begins discussing how happy they are with a recent purchase of a particular vehicle, the targeted user may believe he is overhearing the authentic dialog among customers in a coffeehouse and not a targeted influence campaign.

As the overheard conversation proceeds, the controller could monitor the target user, assessing facial expressions, body language, pupil dilation, posture, eye motion, respiration rate, and blood pressure to detect emotional reactions and adjust conversational tactics to optimize persuasive impact. For example, if the user shows increased focus when the couple begins talking about the car's engine, the controller could adapt its tactics, shifting the conversation toward vehicle performance. On the other hand, if the user's attention fades when the couple talks about the sound system of the car, the controller could adjust, shifting off that line of influence. Meanwhile, the user could be unaware that the conversation is not authentic and may have no idea that it is reacting to his facial or biometric reactions.

In other words, the target user could easily become an unwilling participant in the overheard conversation, interacting through subconscious physical reactions. This may sound dystopian, but this type of feedback loop is feasible in virtual and augmented environments powered by generative AI systems. Taking this one step further, an AI-generated spokesperson could directly engage a user in interactive conversation, and using the adaptive power of AI, gradually talk them into accepting a targeted influence objective, whether it be buying a specific product or service, embracing a marketing message or propaganda, falling for a scam, or believing disinformation. In all such cases, it is the interactive and adaptive nature of generative influence that creates the unique risk. This is especially true when a real-time control system is established around the user, creating a feedback loop that can optimize persuasive tactics in real-time.

Thus, *The AI Manipulation Problem* refers to the unique manipulative risk to human agency when an AI-powered system establishes a feedback loop around a target user and performs the following steps:

i. Impart targeted influence on an individual user,

ii. Detect that user's reaction to the imparted influence,

iii. Adjust influence tactics in response to the user's detected reaction,

iv. Repeat steps i, ii, and iii to optimally achieve influence objective.

These are simple steps, much like a thermostat controlling the temperature in a house, and yet it could result in the most effective form of targeted manipulation ever developed. The danger is significantly amplified when the generative AI systems are placed onboard devices such as AI eyewear that can track a target user's location, behavior, and emotions, while maintaining a context-aware model of that user's environment. Unless regulated, this unique convergence of context-aware generative AI, mobile computing, and augmented reality could compromise human agency at scale by enabling individually customized targeted manipulation and persuasion with unprecedented levels of effectiveness [35, 51].

5. Regulatory protections

As it becomes increasingly likely that AI-powered augmented reality will be central to our digital lives, we must consider the need for regulatory protections and potentially even "immersive rights" [29, 55–57]. With respect to the AI manipulation problem described above, the most direct regulatory approach would be to ban the use of *real-time feedback loops* around human users in which AI agents work to optimize their persuasive impact [33, 35]. In addition, we must consider the risks of behavioral tracking, emotional profiling, and virtual product placements:

Behavioral Tracking: To enable real-time AR experiences through AI-powered eyewear, platforms must be able to monitor user location, orientation, interactions, and behaviors, but they do not need to retain this data over time and should not be allowed to. Limiting persistent data storage would prevent invasive behavioral profiling of user activities [7, 29]. In addition, new AI-based techniques are being explored to mask personally identifiable motion data within virtual and augmented environments [58].

Emotional Profiling: Already, many immersive devices enable real-time tracking of facial expressions, eye motion, posture, and vital signs to determine a user's real-time emotional and physiological states. Without regulation, emotional profiling could be performed to optimize the emotional impact of targeted AR content and the manipulative effectiveness of AI agents. Limits should be placed on the tracking and usage of emotional data, and users should be clearly informed whenever their emotional or physiological reactions are monitored [7].

Virtual Product Placements: As augmented reality becomes commonplace, advertising will include promotional products and services seamlessly integrated into our daily lives, potentially becoming indistinguishable from real experiences. This can easily be used to impart subconscious influence, affecting consumer sentiments and even political views. Regulations should mandate clear visual indicators for virtual product placements in a user's environment [29].

6. Conclusions

Technologies for augmenting or annotating our reality have been in development for decades, from the early head-up displays of the 1950s, to the early immersive systems of the 1990s, to the highly realistic systems of today [3, 9, 50]. During most of that period, little concern has been given to the manipulative risks of targeted AR content. In recent years, however, the convergence of augmented reality, generative AI, and conversational AI agents has created significant new threat vectors for immersive influence and targeted manipulation [29–33]. This is especially significant for "true AR systems" that foster distal attribution and thus reduce the mental distinctions between what is real and what is digital [3–6, 14].

As described above, we must consider regulatory protections, such as banning the use of *feedback loops* that enable AI agents to optimize their influence during real-time interactions [33, 35]. In addition, regulators should ban the appropriation of a user's own facial features, vocal qualities, gestural mannerisms, and speech patterns in the depiction of conversational agents. Also, regulators should require all promotional alterations to a user's environment be clearly distinguishable from authentic elements [7, 14, 29]. Finally, regulators must be aware that the manipulative risks posed by AI agents could increase dramatically as AI systems achieve real or perceived *cognitive supremacy* with respect to human users.

Author details

Louis Rosenberg
Unanimous AI, Pismo Beach, CA, USA

*Address all correspondence to: louis@unanimous.ai

References

[1] Extended Reality Technologies. GAO-22-105541. Available from: https://www.gao.gov/products/gao-22-105541

[2] Cipresso P, Giglioli IAC, Raya MA, Riva G. The past, present, and future of virtual and augmented reality research: A network and cluster analysis of the literature. Frontiers in Psychology. 2018;**9**:2086. DOI: 10.3389/fpsyg.2018.02086

[3] Rosenberg LB. Augmented reality: Reflections at thirty years. In: Arai K, editor. Proceedings of the Future Technologies Conference (FTC) 2021, Lecture Notes in Networks and Systems. Vol. 1, 358. Cham: Springer; 2022. DOI: 10.1007/978-3-030-89906-6_1

[4] Turner C. Augmented reality, augmented epistemology, and the real-world web. Philosophy and Technology. 2022;**35**:19. DOI: 10.1007/s13347-022-00496-5

[5] Rosenberg LB. Virtual fixtures: perceptual overlays enhance operator performance [thesis]. Stanford, CA: Stanford University, Center for Design Research; 1994. Available from: https://search.worldcat.org/title/123253939v

[6] Sandor C, Fuchs M, Cassinelli A, Li H, Newcombe R, Yamamoto G, et al. Breaking the barriers to true augmented reality. arXiv. 2015

[7] Rosenberg L. Regulation of the Metaverse: A roadmap: The risks and regulatory solutions for largescale consumer platforms. In: Proceedings of the 6th International Conference On Virtual and Augmented Reality Simulations. ACM; 2022. pp. 21-26. DOI: 10.1145/3546607.3546611

[8] Loomis JM. Presence and distal attribution: Phenomenology, determinants, and assessment. In: Human Vision, Visual Processing, and Digital Display III. Vol. 1666. SPIE; 1992. DOI: 10.1117/12.136005

[9] Windshield TV screen to aid blind flying. Popular Mechanics. Jan 1954:101

[10] Auvray M et al. There is something out there: Distal attribution in sensory substitution, twenty years later. Journal of of Integrative Neuroscience. 2005;**4**(4):505-521. DOI: 10.1142/S0219635205001002

[11] Wirth W, Hartmann T, Böcking S, Vorderer P, Klimmt C, Schramm H, et al. A process model of the formation of spatial presence experiences. Media Psychology. 2007;**9**(3):493-525. DOI: 10.1080/15213260701283079

[12] Loomis JM. Distal attribution and presence. Presence: Teleoperators and Virtual Environments. 1992;**1**(1):113-119. DOI: 10.1162/pres.1992.1.1.113

[13] Epstein W, Hughes B, Schneider S, Bach-Y-Rita P. Is there anything out there?: A study of distal attribution in response to vibrotactile stimulation. Perception. 1986;**15**(3):275-284. DOI: 10.1068/p150275

[14] Graylin AW, Rosenberg L. Our Next Reality: How the AI-Powered Metaverse Will Reshape the World. Nicholas Brealey; 2024

[15] Sandor C et al. Breaking the barriers to true augmented reality. arXiv. 2015. DOI: 10.48550/arXiv.1512.05471

[16] Rosenberg L. Design of a virtual rigid surface: Haptic/audio registration.

In: CHI '94: Conf. Companion on Human Factors in Computing Systems. CHI; 1994. pp. 257-258. DOI: 10.1145/259963.260473

[17] Rosenberg L. Perceptual Design of a Virtual Rigid Surface Contact. Center for Design Research, Stanford University, Air Force Material Command. USAF; 1993. pp. 1-41. Report AL/CF-TR-1995-0029

[18] Sugano N, Kato H, Tachibana K. The effects of shadow representation of virtual objects in augmented reality. In: The Second IEEE and ACM International Symposium On Mixed and Augmented Reality, 2003. Proc. IEEE; 2003. pp. 76-83. DOI: 10.1109/ISMAR.2003.1240690

[19] Lim C, Ji YG. The effects of physical coherence factors on presence in extended reality (XR). International Journal of Human-Computer Studies. 2023;**172**:102994. DOI: 10.1016/j.ijhcs.2022.102994

[20] Zahariev MA, MacKenzie CL. Auditory, graphical and haptic contact cues for a reach, grasp, and place task in an augmented environment. In: Proceedings of the 5th International Conference On Multimodal Interfaces, November 5-7. ACM; 2003. pp. 273-276

[21] Billinghurst M, Kato H, Poupyrev I. Tangible augmented reality. ACM Siggraph Asia. 2008;7(2):1

[22] Egger J, Gsaxner C, Luijten G, Chen J, Chen X, Bian J, et al. Is the apple vision pro the ultimate display? JMIR Serious Games. 2024;**12**(1):e52785

[23] Rosenberg L. Augmented Reality Will Give us Superpowers. Big Think; 2022. Available from: https://bigthink.com/the-future/ar-will-make-us-superhumans/

[24] Arena F, Collotta M, Pau G, Termine F. An overview of augmented reality. Computers. 2022;**11**(2):28. DOI: 10.3390/computers11020028

[25] Rosenberg L. Carbon Dating. In: Spring Into Sci-fi 2021. Suring, WI: Cloaked Press; 2021

[26] Rosenberg L. The Metaverse Will be Filled with Elves. TechCrunch; 2022. Available from: https://techcrunch.com/2022/01/12/the-metaverse-will-be-filled-with-elves

[27] Rosenberg L. Why 2024 Will be the Year of Augmented Mentality. Venture Beat; 2024. Available from: https://venturebeat.com/ai/2024-will-be-the-year-of-augmented-mentality/

[28] Airenti G. The development of anthropomorphism in interaction: Intersubjectivity, imagination, and theory of mind. Frontiers in Psychology. 2018;**1**:7-19. DOI: 10.3389/fpsyg.2018.02136

[29] Rosenberg L. Marketing in the Metaverse and the need for consumer protections. In: 2022 IEEE 13th Annual Ubiquitous Computing, Electronics & Mobile Communication Conference (UEMCON), New York, NY, USA: IEEE; 2022. pp. 35-39. DOI: 10.1109/UEMCON54665.2022.9965661

[30] Rosenberg L. The Metaverse and conversational AI as a threat vector for targeted influence. In: 2023 IEEE 13th Annual Computing and Communication Workshop and Conference (CCWC), Las Vegas, NV, USA: IEEE; 2023. pp. 504-510. DOI: 10.1109/CCWC57344.2023.10099167

[31] Privacy Lost, Short Film. 2023. Available from: https://www.imdb.com/title/tt27802969/

[32] U.S. Patent Application US20060282317A1. Methods and

Apparatus for Conversational Advertising. U.S. Patent Application US20060282317A1; 2005

[33] Rosenberg L. Generative AI as a dangerous new form of media. In: Proceedings of the 17th International Multi-Conference on Society, Cybernetics and Informatics (IMSCI 2023). IMSCI; 2023. DOI: 10.54808/IMSCI2023.01.165

[34] Big Think. Augmented Reality Pioneer Warns it Could be Far Worse than Social Media. Big Think; 2022. Available from: https://bigthink.com/the-future/metaverse-augmented-reality-danger/

[35] Rosenberg L. The manipulation problem: Conversational AI as a threat to epistemic agency. In: 2023 CHI Workshop on Generative AI and HCI (GenAICHI). Hamburg Germany: ACM; 2023

[36] Edwards B, Orland K. Major ChatGPT-4o update allows audio-video talks with an "emotional" AI chatbot. Ars Technica. 2024;**2024**

[37] Perolat J, De Vylder B, Hennes D, Tarassov E, Strub F, de Boer V, et al. Mastering the game of stratego with model-free multiagent reinforcement learning. Science. 2022;**378**(6623):990-996. DOI: 10.1126/science.add4679

[38] Sandor C. Keynote address - 2: Breaking the barriers to true augmented reality. In: 23rd International Display Workshops in Conjunction with Asia Display (IDW/AD'16). Society for Information Display; 2016. pp. 4-7. (International Display Workshops in conjunction with Asia Display, IDW/AD)

[39] Bosworth A. Accelerating the future: AI, mixed reality and the metaverse. Meta. 2024;**2024**. Available from: https://about.fb.com/news/2024/12/accelerating-the-future-ai-mixed-reality-and-the-metaverse/

[40] Madsen CB, Jensen T, Andersen MS. Real-time image-based lighting for outdoor augmented reality under dynamically changing illumination conditions. In: Proceedings: International Conference On Graphics Theory and Applications, Setúbal, Portugal. SciTePress; 2006. pp. 364-371. DOI: 10.5220/0001353703640371

[41] Neidhardt A, Schneiderwind C, Klein F. Perceptual matching of room acoustics for auditory augmented reality in small rooms - literature review. Trends in Hearing. 2022;**26**. DOI: 10.1177/23312165221092919

[42] Reed BS. Reconceptualizing mirroring: Sound imitation and rapport in naturally occurring interaction. Journal of Pragmatics. 2020;**167**:131-151. DOI: 10.1016/j.pragma.2020.05.010

[43] Ramirez-Saffy GN et al. Visceral interfaces for privacy awareness of eye tracking in VR. In: 2024 IEEE International Symposium On Mixed and Augmented Reality (ISMAR), Bellevue, WA, USA: IEEE; 2024. pp. 396-405. DOI: 10.1109/ISMAR62088.2024.00054

[44] Qayyum A et al. Secure and trustworthy artificial intelligence-extended reality (AI-XR) for metaverses. ACM Computing Surveys. 2024;**56**(7):170. DOI: 10.1145/3614426

[45] Narayanan S et al. Current trends, challenges, and future prospects for augmented reality and virtual reality. In: Tyagi AK, editor. Multimedia and Sensory Input for Augmented, Mixed, and Virtual Reality. Hershey, PA: IGI Global; 2021. pp. 275-281. DOI: 10.4018/978-1-7998-4703-8.ch015

[46] Nijholt A. Toward an ever-present extended reality: Distinguishing

between real and virtual. In: Adjunct Proceedings of ACM International Joint Conference On Pervasive and Ubiquitous Computing, ACM International Symposium On Wearable Computing. New York, NY, USA: ACM; 2023. pp. 396-399. DOI: 10.1145/3594739.3610726

[47] Milgram P, Takemura H, Utsumi A, Kishino F. Augmented reality: A class of displays on the reality-virtuality continuum. In: Telemanipulator and Telepresence Technologies. Vol. 2351. SPIE; 1995. pp. 282-292

[48] Heller B, Bar-Zeev A. The problems with immersive advertising: in AR/VR, nobody knows you are an ad. Journal of Online Trust and Safety. 2021;**1**(1). DOI: 10.54501/jots.v1i1.21

[49] Dam A, Siddiqui A, Leclercq C, Jeon M. Taxonomy and definition of audio augmented reality (AAR): A grounded theory study. International Journal of Human-Computer Studies. 2024;**182**:103179. DOI: 10.1016/j.ijhcs.2023.103179

[50] Infographic. History of Augmented Reality. Available from: https://www.blippar.com/blog/2018/06/08/history-augmented-reality

[51] Wallace C et al. “Metaverse and Standards” White Paper for Australian Government on XR Safety. Melbourne, Australia: Standards Australia; 2023. Available from: https://www.standards.org.au/documents/h2-3061-metaverse-report

[52] Crum P. Hearables: Here come the: Technology tucked inside your ears will augment your daily life. IEEE Spectrum. 2019;**56**(5):38-43. DOI: 10.1109/MSPEC.2019.8701198

[53] Grundmann T. Deferring to experts and thinking for oneself. Social Epistemology. 2025:1-10. DOI: 10.1080/02691728.2025.2449605

[54] Worsnip A. Deference to experts. In: Sylvan K, Sosa E, Dancy J, Steup M, editors. The Blackwell Companion to Epistemology, 3rd Edition. New Jersey: Wiley Blackwell;

[55] Rosenberg L. Marketing in the metaverse: Emerging risks. In: Future of Information and Communication Conference. Cham: Springer Nature Switzerland; 2023. pp. 41-51. DOI: 10.1007/978-3-031-28076-4_5

[56] O’Hagan J, Gugenheimer J, Bonner J, Mathis F, McGill M. Augmenting people, places & media: The societal harms posed by everyday augmented reality, and the case for perceptual human rights. In: Proceedings of the 22nd International Conference on Mobile and Ubiquitous Multimedia. ACM; 2023. pp. 225-235

[57] Ruocco M, Saeghe P, Kerber F, Gugenheimer J, McGill M, Khamis M. From redirected navigation to forced attention: Uncovering manipulative and deceptive designs in augmented reality through retail shopping. In: 2024 IEEE International Symposium on Mixed and Augmented Reality (ISMAR), Bellevue, WA, USA: IEEE; 2024. pp. 720-729. DOI: 10.1109/ISMAR62088.2024.00087

[58] Nair V, Guo W, O'Brien JF, Rosenberg L, Song D. Deep motion masking for secure, usable, and scalable real-time anonymization of ecological virtual reality motion data. In: 2024 IEEE Conference on Virtual Reality and 3D User Interfaces Abstracts and Workshops (VRW). IEEE; 2024. pp. 493-500. DOI: 10.1109/VRW62533.2024.00096

[59] Stein S. Exclusive: Google Sees Smart Glasses as the ‘Next Frontier’ for AI and it’s Not Working Alone. CNET; 2025

[60] TOI Tech Desk. Apple's AI Smart Glasses Could Come by Late 2026 to Take on Meta Ray-Ban's and Google's Android XR Smart Glasses. The Times of India; 2025

[61] Cummings JJ, Bailenson JN. How immersive is enough? A meta-analysis of the effect of immersive technology on user presence. Media Psychology. 2016;**19**(2):272-309

[62] Bailenson JN, DeVeaux C, Han E, Markowitz DM, Santoso M, Wang P. Five canonical findings from 30 years of psychological experimentation in virtual reality. Nature Human Behaviour. 2025:1-1